Richard T. Van Wyck, a week before his enlistment. *Collection of the East Fishkill Historical Society.*

A WAR TO PETRIFY THE HEART

The Civil War Letters of
A Dutchess County, N.Y. Volunteer

Richard T. Van Wyck

Edited by Virginia Hughes Kaminsky

Chapter Introductions by John C. Quinn

BLACK·DOME

Published by Black Dome Press
RR1, Box 422
Hensonville, New York 12439
(518) 734-6357 fax (518) 734-5802

First Edition 1997

Library of Congress Cataloging-in-Publication Data

Van Wyck, Richard T., b. 1838.
    A war to petrify the heart: the Civil War letters of a Dutchess
County, N.Y. volunteer/Richard T. Van Wyck; edited by Virginia H.
Kaminsky; chapter introductions by John C. Quinn.
      p. cm.
    Includes bibiographic references and indexes.
    ISBN 1-883789-12-5 (hardcover) −ISBN 1-883789-11-7 (pbk.)
    1. Van Wyck, Richard T., b. 1838−Correspondence. 2. United
States. Army. New York Infantry Regiment, 150th. Company K
(1862-1865) 3. Soldiers−New York (State)−Dutchess County−
Correspondence. 4. United States−History−Civil War, 1861-1865
Personal narratives. 5. New York (State)−History−Civil War, 1861-
1865−Personal narratives. 6. Dutchess County (N.Y.)−Biography. I.
Kaminsky, Virginia H. II. Title.
E523.5 150th.V36   1997
973.7'447−DC21   97-3120
                                              CIP

Design by Carol Clement, Artemisia, Inc.
Cover photo by Lee Ferris
Printed in USA

This book is respectfully dedicated to the memory
of Edith A. Van Wyck, daughter of Richard T. Van Wyck,
Harriet Van Wyck Osborn and Margaret Van Wyck
Memmott, granddaughters, who lovingly preserved these
letters and gave them to the East Fishkill Historical Society.

The title of the book is from Richard T. Van Wyck's
letter to his cousin, Sarah E. Van Vechten,
dated December 4, 1862, in which he writes,
"The effect of war is to petrify the heart."

A War to Petrify the Heart

Table of Contents

Acknowledgments

Richard T. Van Wyck's Civil War letters, carefully preserved by his mother, and later by his wife, Sarah, were presented to the East Fishkill Historical Society by his daughter, Edith A. Van Wyck, through her nieces, Harriet V. W. Osborn and Margaret V. W. Memmott, daughters of his son, James R. Van Wyck. To these go the first tribute of appreciation, as well as to Mrs. Memmott's family and grandson, Justin.

We also owe a debt of thanks to the late Charlotte Cunningham Finkel, prime founder of the East Fishkill Historical Society. It was her friendship with Edith Van Wyck, and her understanding of the deep pride Miss Van Wyck took in her father's war service, which kindled Miss Van Wyck's interest in the East Fishkill Historical Society and led to her decision to present her father's treasured letters and artifacts to the Society for publication and preservation.

To Lawrence J. Majewski, current president, and to Dr. Kenneth W. Walpuck, long-time past president of the Society, we are beholden for their unflagging enthusiasm and their commitment to the publication of the letters. We thank Charlotte Cunningham for beginning the work of transcribing the letters. An enormous debt of thanks is due Virginia Hughes Kaminsky for her meticulous transcription of the bulk of the letters, and for interweaving into the text, by means of Editor's Notes and footnotes, relevant Civil War events and family history. To John C. Quinn goes our gratitude for researching and writing the chapter introductions, and for helping us locate and select illustrations, and to Deborah Allen of Black Dome Press for agreeing to take on this monumental task.

In most community endeavors, there is one person whose guiding spirit sets a pace and character essential to success. Dewey Owens has been tireless in pursuit of the preparation of the manuscript and the coordination of its publication, and we are truly in his debt.

We are grateful to Matina Billias, Patricia H. Davis, James Velez and Steve Hoare for proofreading the manuscript.

Furthermore, we extend our thanks and appreciation to the following individuals and organizations for their help in researching photographs, plowing through library newspaper files, locating photographs, suggesting illustrations and maps, and recommending ideas for the book: Mr. Benedict R. Maryniak; Vicki Weiss, President, Friends of the NYS Newspaper Project; Michael J. Winey and Randy W. Hackenburg, Department of the Army, U.S. Army Military History Institute; Mr. Kenneth Burk, The Museum of Rhinebeck History; Sharon K. Quinn; Ann Calhoun, Assistant Archivist, Baltimore and Ohio Railroad Museum; NYS Library Reference staff; Mr. Robert W. Schoeberlein, Maryland Historical Society; Hudson River Maritime Center; Anne C. House, Archivist, University of Baltimore, Steamship Historical Society of America; Eileen Haden, Executive Director, Dutchess County Historical Society; Erica Bloomenfeld, Curator, Dutchess County Historical Society; and Noah Dennen, Medford Historical Society.

CONTRIBUTORS

In addition to the major contribution to this publication made by Margaret V. W. Memmott, other contributors include Elton Van Vlack Bailey, Jr., Todd Brinkerhoff, David & Jan Bushey, Richard Campbell, Mr. & Mrs. Edwin Davis, First Hudson Valley, Vincent Frisina, Lucille W. Hahn, Margaret M. Hamilton, Mrs. Frederick W. Heaney, Alice Hoecker, Anita Hoecker, Rita & Roy Jorgensen, John B. Laing, Marie Lesher, Lawrence J. Majewski, Patricia McGurk, John M. Osborne, Dewey Owens, Edward R. Painter, Ray Pool, Edith J. Rosen, Mr. & Mrs. R. Thomas Scannell, Jr., Patricia A. & Frank L. Simone, Tom Tierney, Hilda M. Vinall, Barbro & Ernest Visconti, and Kenneth Walpuck.

The East Fishkill Historical Society Board of Directors

PREFACE

Richard T. Van Wyck had just turned twenty-four when he enlisted in the Union Army in October of 1862.*

This chronicle of a young Yankee farmer takes us through the vicissitudes of war, from the wrenching adjustment to army life to the monotony of guarding the nation's capital, through the crucible of Gettysburg to the audacity of General Sherman's expeditions into the rebellious Southland. All the while, the burning issues of this most sorrowful of wars were hotly debated over campfires and in letters, as well as fought out in mortal combat on the fields of slaughter.

At the same time, these letters introduce us to the daily round of country life in the Hudson Valley in the mid-nineteenth century through the depiction of an unfolding family saga that reads like a novel. In short, this is a story of war and peace–a true story.

Of sturdy Dutch-English stock, Richard Van Wyck's forebears had fought in the Revolutionary War and in the War of 1812; it was his turn, he felt, to help defend the young Republic.

The warmth of the family bond sets a steadying counterpoint to the rigors of war, and the letters reveal the influences which shaped his character and helped keep him on course throughout these dangerous times. His odd syntax reflects his Dutch heritage, but he is well-educated, with a discerning mind and a sharp eye, and his acerbic comments on friend and foe alike add spice to his letters. Wherever he traveled, he took the measure of the soil and locale. "Write to me of farm matters," he tells his father. "I think of the farm all the time."

He was equally concerned with the doings of his young friends back home, but he was shy and diffident with the ladies. In the latent romance with Sarah Van Vechten he conceals his own feelings from himself behind a jocular teasing and an occasional fraternal scolding.

A cheerful outlook and a sense of fun helped alleviate the hardships of life in the field for him and his two friends from home,

---

* The average age of the Union soldier was 25-26.

George Burroughs (aged twenty) and Jacob G. Montross (aged twenty-eight). "This life is fast making bachelors of us, for as to cooking, baking, washing and mending the [*local*] females bear no comparison to our skills." He also observes, "A man that can't wring a chicken's neck or skin a hog can't be a soldier." Later, deep in enemy territory, living off the land became a necessity for survival.

After his safe return from the war, Richard T. Van Wyck became the farmer he had planned to be. He married and settled down on the old family farm in a land where, in Daniel Webster's words, "Liberty and Union, now and forever, one and inseparable," once again prevailed, bought at an untold cost in lives, fortunes and prospects by Richard Van Wyck's generation.

V.H.K

In this vast collection of nearly two hundred letters over a period of three years, some were deemed not sufficiently pertinent to be maintained in the body of the book. For example, from October 1862 until June 1863 he was in Baltimore, where one day flowed very much the same into the next, and many of the letters are rather repetitive. Any deletions will be found at the end of the collection.

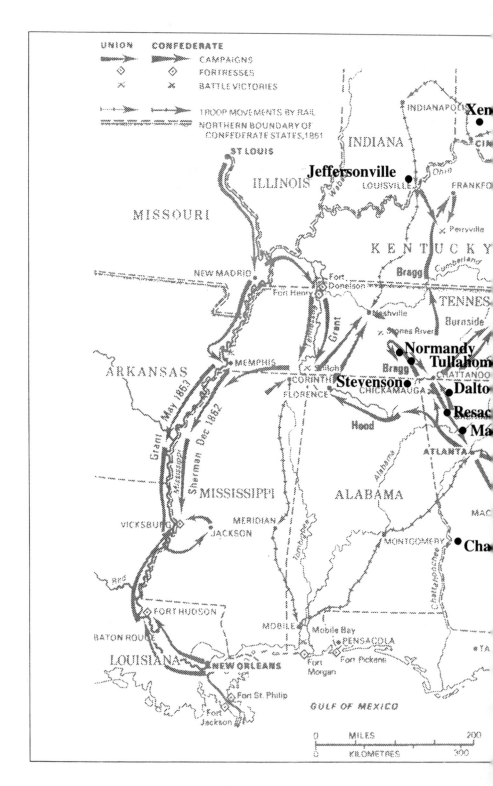

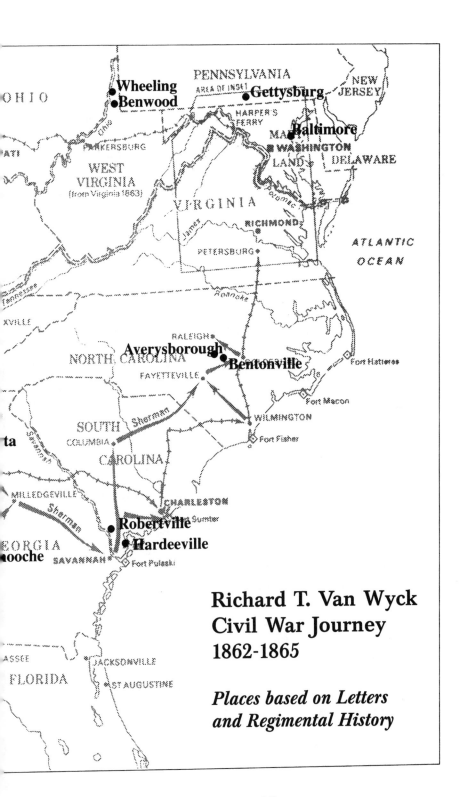

Richard T. Van Wyck
Civil War Journey
1862-1865

*Places based on Letters
and Regimental History*

INTRODUCTION

The Civil War was America's bloodiest conflict, leaving nearly as many dead as all of our other wars combined. The military aspects of the war have long been the focus of attention while, until recently, the lives of the common soldier and citizen have been largely ignored. This collection of letters by Richard T. Van Wyck does much to redress that. It offers the reader a truer understanding of a soldier's experience in the war, and depicts how the war created a greater sense of community throughout the North.

The course of Van Wyck's Civil War journey is remarkable. After enlisting in the 150th New York Volunteer Infantry and spending nine months encamped in Baltimore, the author was engaged in the following battles: Gettysburg, Resaca, New Hope Church, Kulp's Farm, Peachtree Creek, the Siege of Atlanta, Sherman's Campaigns of Georgia and the Carolinas, Savannah, Averasboro and Bentonville. The one-hundred-and-ninety-seven letters which span the period October 10, 1862, through December 7, 1865, are part autobiographical, part confessional, part report, part journal and part conversation, an amazing collection in all.

Richard T. Van Wyck was one of thousands of New York State volunteers who believed in the defense and preservation of the Union. During the summer and early fall of 1862, patriotism had been kindled throughout the villages, towns and cities of Dutchess County. Enthusiastic gatherings proliferated at which posted broadsides offered inducements to recruits for joining the "Dutchess County Regiment" with the theme "come in out of the draft." A popular song of the period, "The Rising of the People," expressed the sentiments that pervaded much of the North in the early years of the war:

> They come, they come with patriot zeal,
> From work-shop, store and farm;
> Resolv'd to save their Country's Flag,
> And traitor foes disarm!
> Like ocean's roar their voices swell
> From plain to mountain crag;
> Union and Liberty they cry:
> One Country and One Flag!

Like many of his contemporaries, Van Wyck left his home and the comforts of civilian life to enlist for his "grand adventure." As his letters reveal, Van Wyck hastened to the defense of his country with a deeply felt understanding of the true nature of the cause for which he was to suffer fatigue, exposure, hunger, thirst and the perils of battle. It took the war itself, however, for Van Wyck to refine and sharpen his convictions in his many letters home.

Van Wyck lived in a letter-writing culture. The thousands upon thousands of letters written by soldiers and civilians which have come to light in recent decades offer us a broader and more balanced perspective than ever before on this pivotal moment in history. But Van Wyck's letters are unique. They reflect the views of the volunteer soldiers–the farmers, the skilled and unskilled workers who did most of the fighting.

Over the course of his enlistment Van Wyck averaged two letters home per week, sharing many observations of the devastation and economic impact of the war throughout Tennessee, Georgia and the Carolinas, including the suffering that "total war" imposed on the civilians of the region. He complained about the quality of the food, especially hardtack and Uncle Sam's beef, which claimed several of his teeth. The letters, rich with the values and attitudes of mid-nineteenth-century Americans, reflect his strong family ties and his growing affection for Sarah E. Van Vechten, whom he would marry in 1867.

Combat, military discipline, moral conviction, the ebb and flow of unit morale, the difficulties of leadership and command, respect for the spirit and determination of the Confederate soldier, and recognition of the contributions of the Regiment's chaplains–all are important themes in this story. Fortunately for us, Van Wyck, unlike many soldiers, recognized the significance of the military campaigns in which he participated. He was reluctant to accept anecdotal information and rumor as fact. Instead, he sought out newspaper accounts and news from home to shed light on battlefield and other war-related events he encountered. On March 11, 1863, in continuation of a previous letter to his mother he writes:

> I was interrupted and obliged to finish this morning. The news–Heavy marching orders–it stands one in need to keep <u>cool</u>, for it is probably only a

ruse. It requires one being in service six months or more to sift truth out of so much deception. Camp stories are fairy tales.

Richard T. Van Wyck's spirit was renewed each time he took up his pen to write home. The letters forestalled a soldier's alienation, maintaining instead his connection with his family and community, holding his place at the family table. On January 14, 1863, he noted:

> I am rarely homesick except when my letters are not speedily answered, and often feel I am talking to you when seated upon the railing of my bunk, having the box sent me from home serving me for a table, and deaf to the noise of the men around me, while giving you by the means of pen and paper the state of my health, the pleasure of which is next to be with you in person.

Letters home kept soldiers in touch with those they had left behind, but they also revealed the growing distance between the disparate worlds of civilians and combatants. The letters which comprise *A War to Petrify the Heart* take the reader on an incredible journey that places us at the heart of events that changed the nation.

John C .Quinn

The Regiment Departs

Our whole course is shrouded in mystery, or what little is designed by our Generals for us to know, much more what is in store for us by the Wise Dispenser of the Universe who is guiding our course through life, as best suits His infinite wisdom in the great wheel of National revolution. The sure indication of an old soldier is his indifference as to where he goes or when he goes or how he goes.

–R.T. Van Wyck

On October 4, 1862, at East Fishkill, Richard T. Van Wyck enlisted for three years as a corporal in Company K* of the One Hundred and Fiftieth New York Volunteer Infantry. The regiment was mustered into service at Camp Dutchess, Poughkeepsie, New York, on October 11, 1862. The next day, the regiment sailed down the Hudson to Jersey City on the steamer *Oregon,* and from there proceeded by rail to Philadelphia and Baltimore. The jubilant scene of the 150th marching off from Dutchess was reported in the October 13, 1862, *Poughkeepsie Eagle* Daily Log:

The camp was the most impressive we have ever seen, but not withstanding there was quite a large number to take a last farewell of their friends. Each one seemed to cling to their friends till the very last moment. As the troops moved through the streets, citizens and ladies from all parts of the city and county lined the streets so that it was difficult to pass on the

---

* The company was the basic unit of the Union Army. Van Wyck's Company K, recruited from Fishkill, East Fishkill, Rhinebeck, and Poughkeepsie, contained 127 officers and men and was commanded by Captain John S. Scofield. Company K was mustered into United States Service for three years on Saturday, October 11, 1862. The 150th was comprised of ten companies. The companies were not all recruited to the maximum, there being 875 men present for muster. The regiment was commanded by Colonel John H. Ketcham.

walks, every house was open and the windows filled with women waving handkerchiefs, while upon every side cheer after cheer went up. On arriving at the river the escort opened line and the regiment passed through on board the boat. Thousands were gathered on the wharves and Kaal Rock and as the *Oregon* cast off salutes of artillery gave the last goodbye. They are the pride and honor of old Dutchess.

Those must have been heady times for the young men and their families. The local volunteers were held in high esteem because they represented the embodiment of the noblest of community values–self-sacrifice. They were patriotic defenders of home, family and Union. Looking northwest from the departure point, the grand old Catskill Mountains rise from the floor of the Hudson River Valley. It was the last glimpse of home the citizen soldiers of the 150th had on their way to war.

MARYLAND
1862—1863

The despot's heel is on thy shore, Maryland!
His torch is at thy temple door, Maryland!
Avenge the patriotic gore
That flecked the streets of Baltimore,
And be the battle-queen of yore, Maryland,
my Maryland!

Maryland! My Maryland*

Van Wyck and the 150th New York Volunteer Infantry arrived at Baltimore on the afternoon of October 13, 1862. They would be detained there for thirty-seven weeks. During that period, while

---

* A week after the riot in Baltimore in 1861, James Randall, a twenty-two-year-old English professor, published his poem, "Maryland My Maryland" in a Louisiana newspaper. Randall hoped that his stirring words would help tip Maryland into the Confederacy. The poem was very well received, and when set to the German melody "Tannenbaum," it achieved the heights of popularity in the South. This rallying song was first published by Blackmar & Co., New Orleans, in 1862.

waiting impatiently for his turn at battle, Van Wyck found comfort in his faith, gained acceptance among his campmates and learned to be skeptical of rumors.

Throughout his stay in Baltimore, Van Wyck was keenly aware that the city's residents were divided in their loyalties. With farms and plantations dotting the northern part of the city and its surrounds, Baltimore was Confederate-leaning, but Union occupied. A year and a half earlier, on April 19, 1861, civilians had savagely attacked the 6th Massachusetts Volunteer Infantry on Pratt Street in the heart of Baltimore. Four soldiers and eight civilians had died, and scores had been seriously wounded.

Over the course of his long tour of duty in Baltimore, Van Wyck's initial critical assessment of the city became much modified. Of the charitable actions of the female Baltimorean Unionists, he wrote:

> If you and many others could only know what the benevolent people of Baltimore does to brighten the homeward march of the soldier, discharged, enfeebled by sickness and often wounded in battle, without the means of helping himself; for him to receive the volunteer assistance of good nursing, tenderly carried from the cars to the bed and back again, is a noble act for any city, and to think this city has been so stygmatized by citizens of other cities, whose benevolence has fed not one-quarter of the soldiers or given the necessary assistance to the needy— needs someone to give her justice, which if the facts were everywhere known, would be readily acknowledged.

Following several months under tents, the regiment was housed in wooden barracks for the remainder of its stay. During their long sojourn at Camp Belger, the members of the regiment developed greater proficiency in use of arms, marching and drilling in battlefield tactics, and became better adjusted to the boredom, distractions and daily unplanned challenges of camp life.

Late in December, there was a welcome break in routine when Company K proceeded in freight cars to Adamstown, near Monocacy Junction, to protect the Baltimore & Ohio rail lines from a possible raid by Confederate cavalry. Twelve miles from Harper's Ferry, Van Wyck stated:

> The rebels were reported to have crossed and we were ordered out, together with the Sixth N.Y. Artillery of four pieces to intercept their progress. In conversing with the people [*we heard that the Rebels*] were poorly clothed but well armed. They were shoeless and hatless, but as fast as they came upon a supply, they would cast off their old articles of clothing, and the effect upon the roadside was a string of rags the whole distance.

No enemy could be found, however, and the expedition–his first campaign–was an uneventful one.

On June 24, 1863, intense excitement and alarm spread throughout the city in anticipation of Lee's northward invasion. Measures were taken to strengthen the defenses of the city against attack, and the regiment hurriedly packed in readiness to move out to join General George G. Meade's Army of the Potomac. On June 25, 1863, with full ranks thoroughly drilled and disciplined, in bright uniforms, with colors spotless and untarnished, to the strains of martial music, the Dutchess County Regiment marched out of Camp Belger and turned its face toward the enemy. On the same day Van Wyck informed his father, "We are off again, our destination unknown. I have no doubt the service will be very active, as the Rebels will make us so, or we will succumb to their victorious armies, which I hope the latter will be averted. Their marches are rapid and ours must be doubly so."

His destination was Gettysburg.

J.C.Q.

Richard T. Van Wyck
Civil War Journey
1862 - 1863

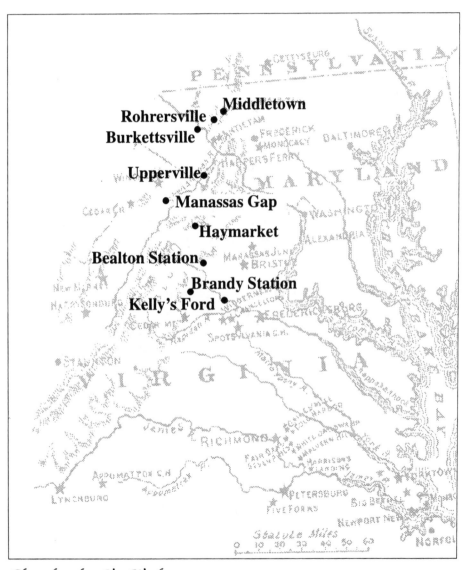

Places based on Van Wyck
Letters and Regimental History

To Mrs. James Van Wyck, Fishkill, New York

Baltimore   Oct. 13, 1862

Dear Mother

When I saw [*you*] at home I supposed I soon would see you again, but I am debarred that pleasure by the prompt dispatch of our regement [*sic*] to the seat of war. I left home on Wednesday and reported myself to camp,* whereby satisfactory arrangements could not be made, so I took my quarters at the Gregory House till Friday evening [*when*] we were called upon, J. G. Montross and myself, to proceed to headquarters immediately, intending to have been mustered into United States [*Army*] by the officer appointed for the purpose. As our company were the last company formed, our turn did not take place till Saturday.

My first experience in Camp life commenced on Friday Evening the 10th. I made myself comfortable in the quartermaster department [*at Camp Dutchess*] with the Army blankets but next day rather rough, not having been given any rations, nor the means of getting them ourselves. I satisfied myself about 10 o'clock in the evening by a sandwitch [*sic*]. During the confusion that ensued [*en route to N.Y.C. headquarters*] I knew no state rooms or berth could be procured, but unfortunately I got asleep on a couple of chairs and slept till early in the morning, when my opportunity of getting a chance was gone; however, I was very well satisfied at that time as it was very refreshing. Our rations the 12th were in the form of a loaf of bread, a piece of cheese, onions, and beef cooked in the shape of a chowder. I took the first and hoped the future would make amends for the shape the food was put in, by a powerful appetite. And I hope the want of delicacy of handling the food will be overcome.

I was there** writing on Sunday when father unexpectedly came upon me, knapsack in hand. I would have been over to Brooklyn, but I would have to bid you goodbye again and I believe I had done so. Take my word for the deed. I hope for the time when there will be no separation, and when all these trials of leaving for motives of Gov't. and great personal hazard will be passed. I assure you it were

---

* Camp Dutchess, north of Poughkeepsie.
** The 150th was mustered into service for three years on Saturday, October 11, 1863, and that night left for New York City army headquarters, and thence on Sunday evening left by train for Baltimore.

not from any but great uncontainable feeling that I did not come and bid you [*goodbye*], but how can I forget my friends–<u>impossible.</u>

I left Jersey City in the cars to Philadelphia and there we were treated to a sumptuous repast, the first we had had for two days, but it was made up by being transported by the cattle cars of the Phil. & Bal. railroad. Arriving at Baltimore after marching for some time there were inconveniences. We were encamped in the railroad depot of Baltimore and passed quite a comfortable night. Arrived during the night six carloads of Reb prisoners. The first I have seen.

I would like to write you more in detail about the arrangements so far. It being something as I bargained for, a life of great deprivations calling for all the strength of character and phisical [*sic*] ability to come out, provided we get in no engagements. I will write you soon again. In the meanwhile I would be glad to hear from home. Address my letters Camp Millington, Company K, 150th N. Y. Regt., Baltimore, MD. [*See Editor's note*]

I enjoy excellent health and never were in better spirits to go south. It is (our camp) on the Baltimore and Ohio RailRoad. We will be detailed to guard the track. I will address you at Fishkill, presuming you will be there.

Your afft son

R. T. Van Wyck

EDITOR'S NOTE:

On August 22, 1862, the district war committee empowered the county board of supervisors to raise a Dutchess County Regiment of volunteers so that the county's full quota of troops could be raised without a draft. John H. Ketcham, a business man of Dover, N.Y., was selected as Colonel of the regiment, designated as the 150th. Each company of 80 men received its alphabetical designation, commencing with A, as soon as it was fully recruited. Co. K was the tenth and last company to be raised for the 150th N.Y. Vol.s.

Over a thousand men from Dutchess County had already answered President Lincoln's first call for troops in April 1861. The prospect of an early peace in the spring of 1862 put a halt to the formation of new regiments, but by July the severe losses of the Union armies led the President to issue a call for an additional 300,000 men to serve for three years, or for the duration of the war. The 150th N.Y. Vols. was part of New York State's response to this call to arms. *The History of Dutchess County, New York,* ed. by Frank Hasbrouck, Poughkeepsie, N.Y., 1909, pp. 194-5.

Camp Millington Baltimore
Co. K. 150th Reg. N. Y.
Saturday [*Oct.*] 18th 1862

Dr Parents

I was glad to receive a letter from you yesterday. I admit I was a little blue, the reception of it was a rich treat. Since I last wrote you at Balt. we have occupied this post after a fatiguing march of four miles. My clothing of which I had become overstocked, had become a burden. I was necessitated to express them home (that is, my light suit). The exposure the first day and till yesterday had given me a little cold but am now much better, as well as ever, although we slept in muslin tents 5 ft. square, open at both ends and often times without rations. The camp is located in the vicinity of Gen. Stuart of C.F. Battery, a beautiful location and very popular as we are surrounded by Mass. Nat'l Guard Regt., forming with our own a brigade. The regements [*sic*] are without proper discipline to make them available troops. The destination is unknown.

Maryland is known by the marks of war demonstration along its railroads, which are used for the transportation [*of troops*], and guarded by sentrys upon bridges or in a hostile community. The feeling in this state will follow the popular party or the strongest. And they are very few who will advocate secession principles openly. I saw an old man in Balt. yesterday who was bold enough to denounce us as Yankees. The discipline in camp has not become stringent as yet, but I hope it will become so soon because it will tend to decrease the license given to all kinds of vices.* They are as bad as I ever thought they were. As I am now writing the drums are beating a death march. A private of a neighboring Regt., Mass., broke his neck on the cars and found dead. God knows who of us will be the next.

You ask me to forgive you for your intimation on the subject of religion. I thank you from the bottom of my heart, and everyone whose zeal induces them to become solicitous in the welfare of

---

* No facilities were provided for recreation for soldiers at camp in the Civil War since such activities were considered extraneous. With camp discipline so poor, the men in general whiled away their time in gambling, drinking, swearing, thievery, and prostitution. With profanity "universal and prevalent" and card playing at that time looked upon as sinful, vice was indeed prevalent. *The Common Soldier in the Civil War*, by Bell Irvin Wiley, Indiana, 1943.

others. I have much thought on the subject of religion and it has been my great misfortune not to have had the boldness to openly profess them. This great sin I have prayed might be forgiven me, and receive strength to resist the evil influences of camp life. I do hope if it is so, we here who we love so much shall meet in heaven above, where all this separation shall end. This most blissful thought has been my only solace through many a weary day, and may God give me courage to the end. Bless them all who think of me in their prayers. I do hope I may never like this life so well, where wicked-ness rules over piety, but rather after this end is accomplished, to relinquish that which is hazardous to my future life to pursue. If not, if it should please Him [*to take me*], may I be prepared. It will be a short time compared with the great Eternity that we shall be sepa-rated.

I think it a Providential accident that I have no office to occupy my time, to monopolize my whole attention, [*otherwise*] these serious reflections would not have given me safety and comfort. In looking back upon all my friends, some of whom I scarcely know familiarly have expressed the strongest friendship, [*and*] have endeavored to use their influence in getting a position for me. That of itself will prompt me to do the best in my power not to disappoint them.

Those officers who were ignorant of their duty have experienced rather hard times. Discipline in camp is rather relax and the officers will soon attempt to make up the deficiency. It is the most irregular Regt. about, owing perhaps to its being commanded by inexperi-enced officers. It makes a great thing in having men over us who are acquainted with camp life. Father thought of sending that Brandy. He need not take any trouble about it as perhaps if I need it, it can be made up in the medical stores.

I wrote to Robt. Johnston.* I thought I omitted to give him the directions. You will be kind enough to do so if you see him. We see little of outside of the camp. The privates are restricted. Often the officers the same. Give my love to all, and write soon.

Your truly afft Son,
R. T. Van Wyck

---

* A neighbor at home.

To his cousin, Miss Sarah E. Van Vechten, Fishkill, Dutchess County, New York

Camp Millington
Oct. 22, 1862

Dear Cousin [*Sarah*]

I have been here now just a week. I often think of you and of all my friends at home, more so at first than now, perhaps because I have become more reconciled with my position and occupation. I was exceedingly blue at first, I admit. It may give you merriment to know that soldiering did take the back track at first. But you were wrong in supposing hardships would bring discouragements or have the effect of blasting my hopes of future comforts, pleasures, etc.. No, I was well aware that war brings no substantial comforts and what I am now enjoying in the regularity of meals, the labor not arduous, and abundant time for reflection, is owing to our stationary camp life. But when we have marching orders, we must be prepared for roughing it in earnest.

The time in camp is divided for the morning. At half-past five, the drums beat for us to get up. Between that hour and nine o'clock, breakfast, and leasure [*sic*]; between nine and eleven, drill. With the exception of two hours between three and five, drill, we have leasure. Leasure is meant meal time or anything we choose to do. Nine o'clock is to commence to sleep if you can. The latter command I have obeyed implicitly lately, but at first it was under great difficulty I was able to do so. However, my health is no way endangered by it. I only hope I may still have my present good health during the remainder of the campaign.

But [*we are*] unfitted for active life or to take the offensive or defensive. Still, a month's discipline might possibly make us. Our greenness becomes very conspicuous on grand maneuvers, as a brigade drill. This consists of six regiments, in all about six thousand men. Discipline is everything to officers as well as men. I have great reason to congratulate myself on my inability to get a command,* when now I see the incessant nervousness and labor in being able to hold their command, when privates are acknowledged fitter to take command, particularly those who have seen service, than their officers. In our own company the officers all have seen service,

---

* Upon enlisting R.T.V.W. had, with the encouragement of friends and relatives, tried to obtain a commission.

and our instruction did not come from a theorist, much to my liking.*

I received a present from Ritie, T. J. V. W.'s little girl, of writing materials, consisting of pen, ink, paper and all the little necessities of correspondence, also some papers containing our exodus from Po'keepsie, etc. I surely am obliged and appreciate the kindness, and will when opportunity offers transmit the same on paper. Although she said her mother would like to hear from me, I do not like second parties.

The demoralizing influence of Camp life is as bad as ever I thought it was. I pray its evil influences may never cast a blur over the sweet pleasures of friendly intercourse which it has been my privilege to experience. However, in deserving the confidence my friends have bestowed upon me, I hope I may not prove a wreck of virtue, here. There is a Higher Power than that of men or will, which can shape, reform, counteract, and may that Power that has given me friends, has raised me in their esteem, has surrounded me by all good influences which has prompted me to defend the institutions that have given so much happiness to the many, now not desert me, [n]or I desert asking for that protection and guidance.

Dear Cousin, you know my thoughts of religion have been very inconsistent and contrarywise. But I continually pray for a faith which will elevate me above the troubles, cares, and disappointments of this life, looking forward to the time when there will be no separating, when friends will have cultivated intercourse with friends, and that Love of Christ here, which is so lukewarm and is dependent on our feelings of spirit and disposition, is <u>there</u> of that ardent, impetuous zeal which knows no adulteration. Many thanks for your solicitude on my behalf, and His spirit be with me to the end, is the earnest prayer of

Your afft. Cousin
R. T. Van Wyck

---

* Most Civil War recruits entered the army in volunteer regiments, like Richard T. Van Wyck's, organized by the states for mustering into Federal service. These volunteer companies were usually raised by prominent citizens who were then commissioned as officers by the state governor. Since these officers in most cases were inexperienced in military training, the post drillmaster usually ended up in the hands of veterans in the ranks. Poorly written and out-dated manuals were another handicap to turning out well-trained units. *The Common Soldier in the Civil War, op.cit.*

Envelope addressed to his father.

Camp Millington
Oct. 24, 1862

[*Dear Mother*]

I received your letter yesterday. I could not treat a correspondent shabbily in neglecting to answer immediately, when I have abundant time to do so. It sure brightens the monotony of camp life, and makes me recall many pleasant recollections of home on their reception. The Left. Col. says our present situation is the "pie of camp life." The "salt junk"* and rough life is yet to come. I surely do not dislike it now. The duties are not too arduous or tiresome, and but for some companions whom I had known at home, it would be pleasant indeed. Although I am forming some acquaintances here. One particularly from New Paltz Landing, a member of Comp. A. A fine fellow and also a private. Our regement [*sic*] is much behindhand in drill, and at the review the other day before the Gen. who has command of this department, it showed itself very discreditably.** So much so that a report was current in Camp that many of its officers were to be dismissed. This is merely a caution for more instruction of its officers. They are scolded at, and talked to pretty hard sometimes, by the Left. Col.

I think Capt. Scofield is not as proficient as he should be, and but for the First and Second Lefts. our Company would not be very progressive. My friends at home have said I should have a Commission. If they could only see the embarrassment of persons who at home were regarded smart, they would think it a business, if they were here, that required more practice than theory.

Yes, our First Left. I underrated at Po'keepsie, but here he has shown more fitness for the office than any of the others. He is an Irishman of seven years' experience, has been in service since the war began, has all the good points attendant upon a commander, and all the evil attendant upon Camp life. For my own part, I think it of

---

* Salted, dried meat.

** Drilling involved more than parade-ground marching. The Civil War soldier had to master a series of intricate maneuvers aimed at getting him from marching columns into battle formation, learning how to spread out from the columns into the countryside in a long line, two ranks deep, at precisely the right moment and without getting hopelessly tangled. *Bruce Catton's Civil War*, N.Y., 1984, p. 116.

a serious nature in the evil influences in a command. And much more than being a private, for the reason that you are obliged to associate and look up to those of a higher standing, while privates can form their own associates, and out of duty be their own masters. Of course in the discharge of your duty, the very slime of Creation is before and mingling with you. Just so the officers. As a class they are not a bit better than their privates. But so long as they can instruct me, I am satisfied and hope I shall always be so.

Someone has sent me the "Christian [*Endeavor?*]" I suspect it is Sarah V.V. It looks like her writing. It looks homelike and [*it gave me*] much pleasure to receive it. I received a visit from T. J. Van Wyck on his return from Washington. I was very glad to see him. It was a mark of kindness he has shown me in taking the trouble to see me. My privileges for seeing my friends are very slight.

The Colonel [*Ketcham*] has lost his Child. He went home and returned. I have endeavored to follow your instructions implicitly, and I hope my love of religious things may be sensibly increased and more faith [*given me*]. This has been my great misfortune heretofore. Give my love to all inquiring friends. From your son,

R. T. Van Wyck

P. S. I have addressed this letter to Mother. But it is all the same I hope.

*To his cousin, Van Wyck Van Vechten**

Camp Millington
Monday Oct. 27, 1862

Dear Van,

The reception of your letter on Saturday was unexpected and pleasant. I sit, or rather recline, in attempting to answer it. It is true I labor under great difficulty to do so, but if my ideas were as fluent as the elements that surround me (mud and water) I could give you a semi-description of Camp. We have been stationary so far, since I have been in Maryland, that is, sleeping in tents by night, drilling by day. The first was necessary, and the latter very essential to make good soldiers. Thus far, we have been on the defensive till Saturday night, when we were attacked by a rainstorm; which is now showering down a liquid torrent, completely saturating those who remain

---

* A. Van Wyck Van Vechten, Sarah's married brother.

out, and those remaining within the slight covering are forced to exercise considerable ingenuity in escaping the element by sitting near the center as much as possible, the rain coming in from the outside near the surface. By the by, I should say we have only to move our position but a few feet, and we are upon the other side. The tent is only seven ft. sq. and meant to contain five persons. My position in the company insures me from guard duty* altogether.

I went down to the cook house this morning, to see what we were to expect in the way of substantials. I found the cook had deserted his post. The rain had put the fire out and we were obliged to make the most of the store of bread we had laid in the day before. But by the kindness of one of our company we were furnished some molasses.** This will suffice till the elements will allow us to make another foraging expedition. In returning to my tent I thought if I could keep dry I would write you.

To the question you would put, how I like this side of the picture? I can say it is very inconvenient and unpleasant and were it not I had suffered from want of comforts before, I would think it very hard. Still, if we call this hard, what will it be in the future, on a march? To be sure, there are pleasant matters connected with this affair, if one likes it, and that is, the responsibility. This does not pleasantly entertain itself to my mind because, if I thought I were fitted by experience for a command, I should like to have one. So much now for my position here.

My reason for coming, you all know. It certainly was not the novelty of this situation attendant with all its hardships, deprived of friends and luxurious comforts of home. And now when I think of quiet and comfortable homes, lucretive [sic] business arrangements, and every means devised to ensure pleasure and happiness to the many, the protection of which, the hardships, deprivation and even death itself consequent on this course of life does not induce me to retract or in any way make me feel blue or discouraged. The kindly reflections of yours upon the Great Reunion in Heaven, is to me a blissful subject of thought and has brightened many a weary hour,

---

* He was made corporal.
** Civil War soldiers, especially out in the field, often had to provide their own food, and even with a camp chow line, individual soldiers formed messes with their friends with whom they shared in the preparation of meals.

surrounded here by the vilest of mankind. I need all the comforts of the Gospel and the Power of His Spirit to keep me from falling into temptation. I hope you will remember me also <u>There</u>. Give my love to all. I will answer if you write and glad to do so. From your Cousin,

R. T. Van Wyck

P. S. Before I mailed this I saw a chance to go down to Baltimore, and you better believe I appreciated one good dinner. This to us is an item, so I mention it.

To Mr. James Van Wyck, Fishkill, New York

Camp Millington
Oct. 30, 1862

Dear Father

Yesterday considerable excitement in Camp, arising from a riot in Baltimore, or properly from the arrest of some influential men, who were operating against Gen. Wool.* They were said to be Union. This made considerable stir, and all the Regiments in the surroundings were ordered to leave at a moment's notice. As usual among new troops there was great fever, particularly upon giving out the ammunition. Also upon the order to sleep on our arms during the night. Of course, no one supposed there would be an engagement, but hoping their [*sic*] would be one. Such doings are systematically practiced to keep the Camp from a state of blueness or spiritless activity. And also to accustom the men to be always ready for anything to turn up. There is always a feeling of restlessness after a few weeks, and the men do not care where they go if it is only a change. I could not help imbibing the same feelings. Although I know I cannot expect better quarters except that if we should go farther south it would be warmer for tent sleeping. That seems the only disagreeable thing just now.

T. J. Van Wyck gave me a call a week ago. He was returning from Washington. He was acquainted with many of the men in the 128th Regt.** He staid [*sic*] an hour or two and took the next train for N. Y. I was surprised to hear of Mr. Lane's*** misfortune. I did not

---

* Gen. John E. Wool commanded Fort Monroe, VA, for the Union.
** On Sept. 4, 1862, a sister regiment, the 128th N.Y. Vols., had already been raised and mustered into service, comprised of men from both Dutchess and Columbia counties. *The History of Dutchess County, op.cit.*
*** Robert Lane, an uncle by marriage, who suffered some business losses.

think his embarrassment with Van Zandt was of such serious nature. Will he come up to Grand Father's to live? It was said it snowed with you. It was very cold. We stood it well, however, in our tent.

The sale of my horse you can do just as you please. I think he is worth $250. I had much rather you would keep him if you cannot get that amount. I certainly think he is worth that amount. He certainly is worth it to you.

Give my love to all, and still address me at Baltimore. We possibly will leave here soon, and I will notify you on the change.

From your afft Son
R. T. Van Wyck

Camp Millington
Nov. 3, 1862
Dear Parents

I received Mother's letter on Saturday. It seems perhaps I have nothing else to do but to write letters, or to answer them. But I am sure it never seemed half so pleasant to me before. And as to time, why, I had abundant leasure [sic] to do so formerly. Now one half of the Regiment have left to guard the national property at Baltimore.

There is scarcely 200 men in Camp, too few for dress parade, a formal ceremony at which the colors are always present[ed]. But when less than five companys are only on hand, this is dispensed with. So you see, that as to leasure the future looks very encouraging. It seems from this that I should be more particular and should not write in pencil, but the accomodations [sic] which I had used were taken down to Baltimore......Now I am situated on some bales of straw, fronting the Sutlers* on the west and within view of our cook arrangements. As I am seated there has arrived a cartload of beef, or as some of the boys I hear cry out, there comes the "Dead Cavalry." We are fed or feasted on this ration two or three times a week, usually boiled. Commonly we have salt meat and the stereotype vegetables: beans, rice and potatoes. And coffee twice a day and oftener. Our bread rations: one loaf to each man each day. This is the bill of fare.

To make variety, I have for the last week or two taken breakfast with a Secess. family near the mill–the place the boys are allowed to

---

* A camp follower who peddled provisions to the soldiers.

go and wash every morning, which liberty I abuse and take a meal. This is allowable.....It certainly is [*allowable*] in my mind and it includes many in the Regiment who think likewise, including our company officers.

Jacob G. Montross arrived on Saturday, he said I look better than when at home, a conclusion indicative that I take well to the fare. But J. G. came here very sanguine to make the most of the rations and the primitive style of living. He has availed himself of his citizen's clothes and taken his lodging down in Baltimore Saturday and Sunday, a good indication that he is sick of it just now. But he will think better of it when he gets used to it.

The spirit of the camp is very good. The regiments here, six in all, have received orders to leave within the next ten days. Our regiment, or the officers of it, were trying very hard to have this one included, but so far, we are destined to remain here during the winter. I hope not, however. To go down to New Orleans or Texas would be very agreeable to me and to all.

Last Sunday, or Sundays generally, there is Sunday inspection in the morning, occupying most of the forenoon. The afternoon is spent in listening to a sermon from the Chaplain. Which, by the by, is a smart able man of Methodist persuasion. It was delightful to hear him, for it has been now three weeks since Sunday has been spent as it should be. Mr. Vassar is a man much engaged in his calling and a very good man. I have been pleased to see so many professed Christians among the soldiers. It requires great force of character to make a confession of Christ here, as well as to keep from falling into temptation.

Since writing the above I have learned that our regiment will be detached to guard duty in Baltimore and the railroads in the surroundings. I am sorry that it is the case, as I expected to see some active duty down south. The impression at home will be, I fear, that we choose to remain here than go to a more active, exposed situation. I am sure the officers in command tried hard to effect it. By being near home I will hear from home oftener and should anything turn up, I might get a furlough, but that is next to an impossibility to do. I should like very much a blanket, but I will write you when it is definitely settled about our staying. The more baggage one has here the more trouble it gives.

To add still further to my now very extensive sheet, I received a letter from Robt. Johnston. You have no idea what pleasure it gives me to hear from home and know what is going on. He tells me of the draft. The poor distressed set you all are in East Fishkill in avoiding it. Also the raising of the barn and sundry other news.

I am afraid too much talk is made of my promotion [*to corporal*]. I have asked for nothing, but was detailed as one of the Color Corporals, one being taken from each Company. The Sargeants [*sic*] of the guard, there being two, are <u>bearers</u> of the Colors and the duties are arduous in the extreme. I do not wish the position. The pay is $5 more a month. I do [*not*] know how you hear such for it is only the last week I had taken the position. Do not think positions or promotions are of speedy occurrances [*sic*]. When I get fully acquainted with this business, I will speculate upon it a little. I am ashamed to send a letter in pencil, if you will excuse it and remember me as your afft son

R. T. Van Wyck

Camp Millington Nov. 11 '62

Dr Parents

Received your letter today together with Father's and Sarah's. They were truly welcome. I might possibly have given you some anxiety on acct of the severe snow storm which we all experienced on the 7th. And from the short letter I wrote you or to Father for the needful will not alarm you, I hope. As I then wrote you, I had just returned from the guard duty of the conscripts. And being cold and tired I thought it would not be disagreeable to substitute straw for our boards, making a <u>nest</u> of comfortable appearance. We had omitted doing so before, for the reason of a strong resemblance to the state of some of our domestic animals, when we call them well littered. Now pride took a fall before cold bleak winter and glad enough were we when morning came with its snow, to find us refreshed and comfortable. The day was spent dreary enough without stoves or fires, without the cold, sleet and snow. And when comfortable, were congratulating ourselves upon being relieved from guard duty at Baltimore. The night following we followed the same thing, that is, a bunch of straw and roll up in our blankets for our substitutes for domestic bedding. The morning following, the snow was banked up against our tent door and sides. It was soon cleared away, however, and Mother Earth in a dry state made its appearance before night. I have not removed the straw, however.

The state of the weather is soft and I had returned from a trip to Baltimore in no way inconvenienced from a cold or otherwise unwell. However, the health in camp is not as good as it might be, but cases of ill health are the result of very dissipated habits attendant upon the exposure to this camp life. If a person is of temperate habits he soon recovers from sickness. The opposite is the way of life here. I forgot to mention that we invariably go to <u>bed</u> with our <u>overcoat</u> on. And appear the remainder of the day without it.

The camp is anxious upon the situation of winter quarters. The expected removal to Texas has fallen through. All the neighboring regiments have been removed. Most men in camp are very indifferent as to their destination (and well they may be), all they want is a <u>change</u>. Possibly our duty will be guarding Baltimore during the winter unless something unexpected turns up. The men are mostly Democratic and were highly pleased at the recent elections in the North, and much displeased at the removal of Gn. McClellan from command* upon the eve of decisive loss or gain in this great question of the day. What does GrandFather say about the times? In our Company the only bold Champion for Republicanism is Robt. Jones from Matteawan, formerly a slater** and seen much of the <u>world</u>. He is invariably on the alert to get up a discussion. If it were not for his conceitedness he would be quite a smart fellow.

A Rhinebeck Editor is also with us. He does guard duty and does not grumble. We see his editorial correspondence and it is first-rate, somewhat humorous. Our Chaplain we have not seen much in his official capacity. Last Sunday so very unpleasant and not sufficient accomodations [sic] under canvas [so] his sermon was omitted. I hope when we get settled down such interruptions will

---

* General George B. McClellan had been appointed General-in-Chief of the Union Army in Nov. 1861, but instead of taking action he spent the winter training and equipping his army. In March 1862 he was removed from supreme command and put in charge of the Army of the Potomac. In April 1862 he began the Peninsular Campaign which collapsed after the bloody Seven-Days Battle (June 26-July 2) because of his overcaution. On Sept. 12 he defeated Lee at South Mountain, and in the Antietam Campaign he checked Lee's first invasion of the North, but he allowed Lee to escape across the Potomac and was again charged with overcaution. On Nov. 7, 1862, Lincoln had him removed from his command despite his great popularity with the troops. *The Civil War: A Narrative,* by Shelby Foote, N.Y., 1958-74.

** A roofer.

not happen. I promised Mr. Woodhull I would write him when I got down here. I intend doing so. I have many reasons to thank him for his kind solicitude for me. I certainly could not neglect him. I told you perhaps before of the want of moral character of the officers as well as the men. One of my tent fellows is an exception, and I greatly prize him. Geo. Burroughs* is down at the Continental Hotel, now a hospital. He is <u>corporal</u> of the guard. He has a nice warm room heated by steam and mattresses to sleep on. He cannot find fault.

How can you believe [*home*] news can be any other than agreeable? My great fear is that such hasty dispatches are but a poor equivalent for such kindness. You were away from home when I left. You possibly heard what a desperate <u>flirtation</u> seemingly that was to go and see <u>Marietta</u>. Going at 3 o'clock and waiting till 6 o'clock for her to come home. I think they must have thought I was frantic. What foolishness! The evening would have been ill spent if it were not for the accident of going in at Mr. Brink's. I was more than paid for the previous tediousness of the evening.

I wish the correspondence were more agreeable to you, but I hope as we change about there will be some news and incidents to narrate. Give my love to all.

Your son
R. T. Van Wyck

Baltimore Nov. 12, 1862

Dear Cousin [*Sarah*]

Eight o'clock a. m. we begin moving. Not the moving of heavy, well-plenished wardrobes or dusty carpets. Nor meet the curiously anxious countenances of matronly housekeepers; but the bustle, joy and cheerfulness of boys, looking for something to turn up. The order being given at half-past five, to be ready to move at 7 o'clock. Knapsacks are first packed with the blanket. The tents are drawn on the pins that secure them to the ground. Our downy pillows or pallet of straw is burnt up, and the removal of it being unnecessary, there being nothing therefore to mark the place of our former habitation but blackened ruins. I never thought the obsolete command would be so accurately carried out in practice as now, "Take up your bed and walk."

---

* George Burroughs is one of his neighbors from home.

We remove to Camp Belcher [*Belger*], the same distance from Baltimore to the north. The same address, 150th Regt., Balt., will be sufficient. We have been here only a month and expect to go in winter quarters there. You seemed disposed not to answer my letter, at least I expected an answer, not supposing you would be so formal. I am glad it was overruled.

There is the same gossip at Church Sundays and at the Sewing Meetings as usual. I really miss them, and my scribbling letters to home is a sure indication what pleasure it affords me. It is the next to being with you, except the pauses are sometimes long and far between. Did you ask the question or did you propose it? Wether [*sic*] I had written or should do so to Miss Hasbrouck. I have written to her father thanking him for some papers sent me. I certainly would not mind corresponding with her. Miss Ritie has answered my letter and I reproach myself of not being more prompt in correspondence, not wishing to give any cause for a discontinuance of such kind favors. Also the appreciation of Frank Kip's letter which I truly value. I know the reluctance to write when at home, but here it is the only connecting link with civilization and you see it is improved. The last Evening at home is much remembered. What do you hear from our friends at HopeWell? [*sic*]. I regret making such a fool of myself at John Adriance's. They thought I must be getting desperate. Write me about it. I suppose your visit to New York was marred by the unfortunate state of Mr. Lane's finances. I am glad it is so well terminated.

It again occurs to me that the Draft will create some uneasiness in Hopewell. It will be a pity if some of the young men are not drafted. If they only could see the pain the carrying out of this draft occasioned, they would have readily volunteered, those that could. I have been guarding the drafted men from the County of Balt. They were a sorry spectacle. I feel so rejoiced I took the position I did, and was at liberty to make a choice in the matter. I have omitted thanking you for those papers, which afforded reading matter to a few of our Company. They generally have arrived upon Sunday, till the past week. .....

I had completed this letter so far, when an interruption has ensued, and I am now commencing it at Camp Belcher [*sic*]. I am very much pleased with the change. It is a grove. We are now under canvas, but will soon have substantial quarters. Everything is going on swimmingly. Within view of the reservoir supplying the city, and connected by a fountain. A beautiful scene. I will not omit speaking of the cooking arrangement, which were somewhat new and hard. I have taken to it "as to the manor born" and it is surprising what an <u>appetite</u>. Our reporter for the Rhinebeck paper compares it to a "Chatham Junk shop stewed up in <u>Whale Oil</u>," a far-fetched but an apropriate [sic] representation, and is as near it as the culinary process of such constituants [sic] would make. You can imagine the rest. You need not feel alarmed that your correspondence will not be answered, for I have abundant leasure [sic] to do so. Give my love to all and remember me as your afft. Cousin

R. T. Van Wyck

Excuse this substitute for a letter as my advantages for penman-ship is limited and the material rather windy.

Camp Belger Nov 18th

Dear Mother

I find upon reflection that commencing this letter, I can't promise you much in new incidents. The future has the appearance of monot-ony, not tiresome, laborious, or unpleasant; but the rigid law of mil-itary discipline is become what it should be, to divide the time into periods of drill, and to prepare the men [for] what is expected of them. The men that were recruited upon the usual intrigueing* [sic] system, are a discontented, troublesome, and good-for-nothing set, have no love of country at heart, and as far as honor is concerned consider it no dishonor to do whatever ignominy they may be sub-ject to, satisfied to get the large bounty and their rations. Whatever motives influence men to go, soon reveals itself here. The officers as well as privates.

Of the officers there is a Mr. Sleight, a Left. in a Company from Po'keepsie,..a person you perhaps remember seeing at Mr. Alfred Van Wyck's at a strawberry visit. He is a Nephew of Mrs. Edmund Van Wyck, a fine fellow. I omitted thoughtlessly mentioning Geo. Burroughs in my previous letters. We were tent fellows together till his being detailed for guard duties downtown. But he said the society

---

* Some men would enlist to receive the bounty offered (usually around $300) and then they would desert in order to re-enlist in another company to receive another bounty, etc. *The Civil War*, by Shelby Foote.

was so very unpleasant that he prevailed upon the Capt. to have him removed and substitute another in his place. He prefers the rough tent sleeping to the luxurious beds of the hospital, our social tent (for I am inclined to think it is) to the foreign companions there. He possesses more decision of character than I ever gave him credit for and I am glad he is with us again. The Barracks are in the course of erection, and the prospects indicate a speedy removal.

Montross is not tenting with us at present, not disposed yet to forsake his former habits. He finds companions in the officers of the Company and the orderly sergeant, who will for a time (as long as his money lasts) excuse him from duty. It is shirks like these who find the most fault with the restrictions of this despotic rule. What fit material these are for officers!

The finest body of men and officers are the 151st N. Y. Regt. encamped here. They are from Western New York, have left lucrative businesses and made great sacrifices; men whose appearance denote and practice showed them to be gentlemen, for they omitted none of the ordinary courtesies of life so common in officers and altogether forgotten in a private. During their company on guard a week ago, they gave many a silent reproof to this regiment. I hope [we] will profit by it. I do not write this because I am tired; but that some might think and [not] take the 150th Regt. as a pattern. I learned that the Militia Company from the [Fishkill] Landing, called the Denning Guards, are ordered to Texas.

I became acquainted with the Chaplain under novel circumstances. He happened to be surveying the ground for an outside prayer meeting and I accidentally being present, when a conversation took place, whereupon I told him my name. He, after inquiring with the Col. and Major, called upon me and invited me to his tent and we had a very social talk. He is zealous in his efforts to do the soldiers good and I hope he may succeed. I have received a letter from Aunt Mary.* Tell Caroline that I thank her for her intention in wishing to send that cauliflower...Anything eatable comes here in poor condition. Remember me to all enquiring friends

From your son
R. T. Van Wyck

---

* His mother's sister in Brooklyn.

Camp Belger
Nov. 23, 1862

Dear Cousin [*Sarah*]

I have been thinking sitting in my tent this afternoon, whether it were possible for me to write a letter. The query is (putting aside the inconsistency, for it is Sunday afternoon) how is it impossible? To you who are at present seated by the furnace register, such a question would be absurd undoubtedly, but in my tent this afternoon I thought I would try how well I could use the pen, though much inconvenienced by cold.

This morning the sermon preached at Eleven o'clock instead of two in the afternoon. The sermon, "The deceitfulness of sin," was truly appropriate. He said it were not those who bold and daring made themselves noted, but those commonly known as gentlemen containing all the address and polish of this world and all the wickedness of it. How poisonous their influence we all know. I was very sorry to see so few out to hear it.

Saturday I went down to Baltimore, and there visited the Union Christian Association Reading Rooms. It was a beautiful sight to see the enjoyment the poor soldiers from the hospitals, those who were convalescent, could obtain. There were papers and books, Dailys and weeklys from all the states.* As well as the many individuals hailing from all parts of the Union. I had a great mind to get transferred to some duty downtown to avail myself of the advantage of the rooms to engage my leisure hours. But upon consideration, I thought I would keep myself identified with the Regt. to improve myself in drill and military discipline. Next winter if possible during the inclement season, such a change I will endeavor to effect.

The last week has been a very unpleasant one, dark and rainy. I am told the winters are similar in Virginia, and sleet and snow of the North is substituted here [*by*] rain. I hope it may remain pleasant during the week and then I will bid goodbye to tents for this Fall.

From what you tell me of our Hopewell friends, they are preparing for a grand party at the Horton's. I am sorry you are not invited. Don't you feel <u>cut</u>? I suppose the Villagers are getting up something for the winter. Isaac Kip will see the deceitfulness of human nature

---

* In the Union armies it was noted that the men showed a vast appetite for newspapers and books. *The Life of Billy Yank*, by Bell Irvin Wiley, Indianapolis, 1952.

in the position he intends taking, to a greater extent more than ever before. It would not surprise me if after a few months spent in the army he should become dissatisfied, especially after he sees what a farce this patriotism is. Still, he might take another view of it and feel perfectly contented. I have been trying to get a <u>Rebel</u> paper to send GrandFather, one printed on the brown cinnamon paper. If I do I will send it. Your letters give me great pleasure I assure you.

from R. T. Van Wyck

P. S. I sent <u>Diana</u> an apology. I wish I could hear from it.

P. P. S. Grandmother wishes that in sending me the <u>good</u> things I will remember <u>Thanksgiven</u> [sic] in my bright vision, try to keep it as at home, but then it is: where is the <u>turkey</u>? Old junk* is a poor substitute for it. But I hope the Quartermaster substitutes something else. We have four ladies now in camp—the wife of the Colonel and three Capt.'s wives.

To General Abraham Van Wyck

Camp Belger, Baltimore
Nov. 27th, '62

Dear GrandFather,

I have neglected to address you personally heretofore presuming you have been informed of my doings from my many letters home. I am now in Camp, as you know, and the time is constantly occupied in drill and constant exercise. I occasionally go to Balt. and take a look at the city, but have seen little of the country which surrounds it. The important sight of which visitors are curious to see is the Washington Monument and take a ride around and see the various other minor ones of which Baltimore is styled the monumental city. The city is well laid out and affords excellent facilities for commerce and many excellent depots for business. The many marble-front houses in the upper part of the city denotes that business has been lucrative heretofore, but at present is not as prosperous, except certain kinds which receive the patronage of Government. The city is intersected by horse Rail Roads [*trolley cars*] from all points.

The Bay is defended by Ft. McHenry on the water and Ft. Federal Hill to the Northeast, through which means Baltimore could be reduced or defended at a moment's notice. It is a great shipping

---

* See page 28 footnote.

point to all the Army South. To Ft. Monroe. It is surprising what amount is sufficient to furnish the Army with the necessary articles. While at Millington near the Washington R.R. it seemed that there were trains leaving constantly loaded with hay, provisions, grain and other Army stores, besides the many carloads of heavy ordnance, cannons, gun carriages, Army wagons, etcetera. Even the rails upon the tracks are splintered and worn to an alarming degree.

The Turnpike to Frederick runs in an Westerly direction, a superb road and in other times than these, would show to some extent the character of the back country. As it is, you see wagons drawn by four and six mules. Cumbersome and heavy, the width of the [*wheel*] rim is commonly eight to ten inches wide and would ride three or four tons with all ease. Light wagons, as in use with us, is not of frequent occurance [*sic*], except at our present encampment, where we see some fancy driving ocassionally [*sic*].

The soil, as I have seen it in the country, is of a light loam of redish [*sic*] color, often very sticky in wet weather. The surface of the country is undulating, often very many fine prospects as well as fine mansions, which at present look to us on the decay.

The Union feeling in the city, I was told by Mr. Pudney, that "The Union feeling with the wealthy was very strong; with the class of questionable character, who fan any excitement that they hope may turn up in their favor, they are consequently Secession where it is profitable." The negroes are not as abundant as I supposed.

Our future is much discussed among the boys, but no reliance can be placed upon Camp stories. They are noted as not being very authentic.

I have thought of you all today, Thanksgiven [*sic*]. I wish very much to be with you, and had hoped there would be some special cause for Thanksgiven in our success of arms in Virginia. Much love to you all, I remain your Grandson

R. T. Van Wyck

Camp Belger
Dec. 4, 1862

Dear Cousin [*Sarah*]

It seemed I was more favored than common to be the recipient of your [*letter*] and three others on Sunday. They gave me a good hour in their perusal and speculation upon home affairs. How rich in gossip your sewing society meetings are, I can readily grasp: what Miss-such-a-one wore, and how Miss-another was dressed; besides the repetition from one week to another of all the marriages or proposals finds open ears and unclosed mouths, to herald the news at home and abroad to which your humble correspondent is both privileged to hear as well as glad to receive.

I must not forget to mention the weather, a vital question to my comfort; but a hackneyed subject of conversation in parlor circles; which you will pardon me in a letter when I say it is exceedingly pleasant and delightful, although last evening it froze water to the depth of an inch or more, still not very uncomfortable in our tent. However, the sun is so hot here that you almost forget without it, it can make one so miserable. I remember at East Hampton I have skated many times on Thanksgiven [*sic*]. I didn't dream at that time to be here writing it down in Maryland at this season of the year.

Your kindness in thinking of my quarters in your bleak climate need not give you great anxiety, for in "this genial climate of the South," winter is not near as bad as represented, or as you read about. There might be on the margin of <u>Secessia</u> a blast of cold air from the frigid Yankee States, but when we get down in Dixie (which I hope we may) they say the weather is no longer a matter of consideration.

I mustn't forget to remind you that the officers of the 150th Regt. are very desirous of making it "A No. 1." They spare no pains in disciplining the men, and what do you think? This week the men must polish his trappings and put on a pair of white gloves and be march[*ed*] downtown, for the admiration of the officers and some of their <u>tender</u> attachments in the city. I thought my chances of putting on this ornament, reminding me of better days, was not to be repeated. But I presume the officers thought it the most expeditious way of making us of uniform appearance.

I might cite cases "which like the story in Wisconsin" of a man submitting himself to a good scrubbing down in the river for a short time [*which*] revealed to his astonishment an article of clothing he had missed for the last two years! Now if you should hear of the neatness of the 150th Regt. <u>coming</u> <u>from</u> <u>Bal.</u> you need not say anything but forget not to extol the officers for their artful exhibition.

We are paid off. This is, all the privates have received their pay up to the first of Nov. If it were gold instead of Treasury Notes, I should certainly put a hole in it, and treasure it as the first reward of merit Uncle Sam has bestowed upon me. Many a cheer is given around the social group for the success of the Union cause and the repetition of the Pay Master, or from the Prison of Ft. McHenry, and the various gin shops of Bal. to this regimental Guard House. All this comes from the peculiar merits of the Green Backs* [sic].

You speak of Sarah Kip's enthusiastic wishes to become a nurse in hospital for the sick Soldiers. It is bad enough for rugged constitutions to submit themselves to exposure, for the sake of conscientious duty or a life of fame or change. But to one of her feeble health it is madness to undergo the exposure, or to be the observer of the shameful disregard of this business by officers appointed by government for this purpose, and under whose authority they are. It would be far better for her at home to possess those tender feelings of sympathy for their distresses (which God knows they deserve) than to be the witness of this without the power to do anything and see the abuses from which this department, like the rest, are not exempt. I hope she will not see or experience the disappointment which will inevitably result from such a step.

I have seen a little in Balt., enough to convince me that the Government does as well as it can under the circumstances by procuring nurses from among the convalescent soldiers, those who are not capable for active duty but are used to and hardened to all the casualties of war, and are thus able to witness the suffering of their patients, which ladies couldn't undergo. The effect of war is to petrify the heart. Mr. Vassar has given me some incidents from his experience while visiting the hospitals around Balt. Excuse [me] for writing so much. You need not tell Sarah what I say. She will find out soon enough through Isaac if she is jesting or serious. But the same will apply to any lady taken from the common walks of life.

The death of Delia was so long anticipated, I did not feel surprised. She has been a great sufferer. She is now where there is no pain and where the weary are at rest. Give my love to all,

from your Cousin,
R. T. Van Wyck

---

* Greenbacks were first issued during the Civil War.

Camp Belger, Bal.
Dec. 5th, 1862

Dear Mother

I do not know but what I am tiring my correspondents by answering letters so immediate, and causing them to suppose a like return, however inconvenient, is expected. But your assurances to the contrary is an exception in my home correspondence and we will consider it as mutual pleasure. It is this, together with the perusal of the Baltimore *Clipper* and a few books, that occupy my leisure hours. You have received the specimens that I sent you and have seen the political character of the paper. Although it gives the news for a small consideration, in advance of the N. Y. papers, it shows a great submission to the wishes of Government tutching [*sic*] the war question, something unlooked for to one who is accustomed to the defying and fearless discussion of the N. Y. *Tribune.* For old companion's sake I occasionally take a look at it.

The President's message finds many ardent supporters and an explanation of our inactivity and ill success in not subjugating the Rebels. Also the report of Gen. Halleck upon the McClellan Mistery [*sic*].

Among the great champions of good Republican principles is one R. L. Jones of Fishkill Landing. His profession is a slater, little known except there and in Orange County. He is a Welshman of great shrewd argumentative talents, and conversational ones, invariably "blowing," as they term it here. He does not fail to proclaim his principles to advantage in the face of shoulder straps.* He gives them many a cut, to my gratification. Last week after reveille (6 o'clock a. m.) while the men were washing down to the spring, by some accident his tent took fire and burned up. But among the few things that were saved was a small memorandum book of his. In viewing the scene from a distance, his principal anxiety was for the safety of this book, although his whole stock of clothing were destroyed. But upon finding his treasure, he was seen giving an Irishman his views of the New York elections, which he was discussing with more seriousness than he felt for the destruction of his property.

Such are some of the cases one meets with here. A good place to study human nature, a delightful one in this case, but more often a subject of much pain.

---

* i.e., officers.

We have Regimental excursions or marches, downtown and in the country. We visited today the Druid Hill Park, an extent of from two to four hundred acres of wild land, beautifully ornamented with carriage roads in many directions and at one situation commanding a view of a small town in the suburbs of the city. The view and country reminding me of old Dutchess. I must close now, nearly 8 o'clock and with the termination of a day, after a week of such beautiful weather of hail, snow and rain storms.

I received a letter from Uncle Anthony from Davenport. I am much pleased he resumes his law and seems known at <u>large</u>. Remember me to all

from R. T. Van Wyck

Camp Belger   Dec. 12th

Dear Parents

I received your letter today. I had been expecting one for the week, and had got out of the way of writing quite as often as usual. The cold weather of Saturday, Sunday, and Monday last was hard for the boys, I assure you, but we came out of it as well as usual. Last Saturday I went downtown and had ascertained where some straw could be obtained. Accordingly, before night a party of us went after it. We have been without it while we have been at this Camp. In view of such luxurious sleeping quarters, we were in good spirits. Nor were disappointed in the morning to find how cold a night we spent in such blissful repose. The thermometer indicated 10 degrees and ice is now being housed from a small pond in view.

We are looking anxiously at our Barracks but I fear our seclusion will not be as perfect as now in our tent. Still, our general comfort will be better.

There is nothing new in Camp, except lately great interest is felt for the safety of the army of Gen. Burnside in Virginia.* What effect it will have on our situation is thought to be very apparent: should he succeed we will remain here, but if not our departure is sure. Our Regiment has diminished considerably since we have left Po'keepsie.

---

* On December 11-12, 1862, the Union Army under Gen. Burnside was crossing the Rappahannock River at Fredericksburg preparatory to attacking Gen. Robert E. Lee's forces on the impregnable heights above the river. His attack on Lee was a fiasco, with Union losses more than twice the Confederate—over 12,000. The defeat caused profound depression in the North. *The Civil War*, by Shelby Foote, *op.cit.*

Many have gone into the Regular army, and many deserted. The remainder is the best part of the men, and [*it has*] been a great blessing to be rid of such companions.

Aunt Mary has invited me to come and meet you at Brooklyn to spend Christmas. I would certainly accept the invitation if I was at liberty. But if Commissioned officers cannot obtain passes or furloughs to go home, surely it is impossible for privates, but still I am thankful for the invitation.

I had completed this letter so far when interrupted [*sid*] by "dress parade." I resume it again after "Supper," and a great one, too. Just imagine yourself a board running lengthwise one of our tents, serving for a table. The writer, carving from a bake pan two chickens purchased from a negro vendor, standing to the far end of the tent. My tent-fellow wearing spectacles, opposite, and the other one sitting next to me, and to the door of the tent is George Burroughs and opposite him is an invited guest. I cannot say so, for we consider him one of the <u>family</u>. Well, after assisting each of them to the chicken upon tin <u>platters</u>, I was helped in turn from the contents of a box received from New York by one of them, consisting of <u>Tobacco</u> (of course I was excused) but to the Preserves, Cake, Butter, Concentrated milk, etc., I did justice to. The former is the first I have seen since leaving home. Upon or at the time of this entertainment, the personal satisfaction of each individual would be better seen than described. But you can easily imagine.

Now then, for Christmas something of this kind would not be <u>amiss</u>. Remember that the <u>richest</u> articles take less room, and better pay the freight upon them, than of more <u>bulky</u> ones. However, there being nothing [*lacking*] for my comfort which I know of, these you may class as <u>luxuries</u>. I was glad to hear of Robert Johnston's doings, perhaps his attraction in another direction accounts for his [*discontinued*] correspondence. I wouldn't care about it <u>at</u> <u>all</u> if he only succeeds in effecting his object. Remember me to all.

From your Son   R. T. Van Wyck

My direction for Box the same as for letters, with any of the express Companies:

R. T. Van Wyck
150 Reg. N. Y. S. V. Co. K
Baltimore   Maryland

My stockings (Woolen) would be very acceptable.

Camp Belger Sat, Dec. 13, '62

Dear Mother,

This morning we gave the 151st a specimen of our battalion movements. What they thought of our commander's orders I can readily guess. However, it was by no means disagreeable to me, for a march in early morning is true enjoyment to prisoners such as we are here. The time in the afternoon is given to cleaning up of streets, muskets, side arms of soldiers, and if water is available, the use of it for individual purposes is particularly recommended.

The weather today is exceedingly fine for this season of the year. And the Camp fire at night, how social, how novel, and how comfortable, yet no one but a soldier can appreciate it. For some time past it has been built in the center of our street, around which the company cluster. Sometimes if present, our friend Jones, (nicknamed Squire) who is a monomaniac upon argument and public speaking, he takes the lead upon all questions, reproving the boys for their intemperate language, but oftener on the engrossing subject of the day politically. While upon the other side of the fire, and sometimes by his side, his friend <u>Clarky</u> the Rhinebeck editor, or William Smith, one of the Smith family, makes a song much to the merriment of the crowd, when Jones takes up the intermission with a speech. Thus you see how the time is spent around the camp fire generally, when these persons are present. The fires will shortly be at an end, and we will be crowded into the buildings, the agreeableness of which is extremely difficult to tell, but time will show.

Sunday, Dec. 14, is at hand. Noticable [sic] by the inspection of knapsacks, etc., which I wrote you before. How different from a Sunday at home, where the great preparation for Church and where the solemn and steady strokes of the bell fall pleasantly upon the ear. Or oftener, where the compulsory command of arms does not clash upon the ear, the better to remind us of the sinful and fallen state of humanity, for with a previous due regard to the Sabbath, we would not have been called hither. And yet how much there is in this life of change and interruption to draw our minds from our duties here below, to tire us and make us better prepared for that inheritance above.

As I am now sitting after tent inspection, I hear the work upon the Barracks progressing as upon an ordinary weekday. Although the day is fine, no reliance can be placed upon fair appearances, and prosecution of the work is evident necessity.

I met Capt. Wicks of Po'keepsie today. I have not spoken before of those whose fortunes has placed them upon the ladder of Military fame. It is the first overture he has directly made to me since leaving Po'keepsie. I have not availed myself of the previous knowledge of such persons here, those I do not directly meet in my present duties, believing that politeness is usually showed from one whose position is acknowledged to be superior, [*that he*] should be the advancing party. I do not admit such superiority to be other than in a military point of view. It shall always be my endeavor to keep my position, notwithstanding the palaver of others, to such as he. I feel as consequential as a private in the 150th Reg. as he does as Capt., and shall endeavor to do my whole duty as such. If he is condescending to notice a private, he is at liberty to do the other thing and no love lost. But if he has just come to his sences [*sic*], I will give him the benefit of it and call upon him as he invited me to do.

The death upon Friday night of O'Neil[*l*], a private in Co. F who, I fear, has gone without the comforting assurances of a Heavenly home. It should be the duty of everyone, but more so of a soldier, whose profession is the champion for the right, and if it need be, to march into the jaws of death, but how few realize their situation and become perfectly hardened in sin and iniquity.

The sermon today in the new building, from the 64th Chapt. of Isaiah, sixth verse: "And we all do fade as a leaf." Appropriate to the first death in the Regt. and a beautiful illustration of our transitory condition, which he beautifully applied to the members of the Regt. I have written this [*letter*] soon following my last,

From your son   R. T. Van Wyck

Camp Belger   Dec. 17, 1862

Dear Cousin [*Sarah*]

You have, and are still enjoying, your visit at the village. And I would have answered your letter before if I had not supposed you would not be home to receive them. I hope, however, that answering my letters does not enjoin a duty disagreeable to you. But supposing the pleasure derived from the company you were entertaining has likely given you some unpleasant reflections in having such a dull correspondent, in comparison to the social, intelligent, lively young lady whose society you have been enjoying. She indeed is an inestimable lady and it is a marvel to me she is so long in the eyes of unmarried gentlemen.

I accepted Mr. John Pudney's invitation, and called upon him, accompanied by Mr. Vassar. I saw the elder Miss Pudney and I should have been exceedingly taken with her hadn't she been too much admiring of the shoulder strappers, (the Left. and Capt.). As it was, her cultivation in music is praiseworthy, which is far in advance of her conversation powers. We spent a very pleasant evening, going at six and returning about nine. The effort for us privates, of the firing up of our appearance, is slight, consisting merely of the use of brush and comb. The choice of outfit doesn't require much skill.

The debating society which I attended last Monday evening, the leading disputants were not very interesting, except James Wicks from Po'keepsie. He is considered the best educated person in the Regt. having been a graduate from Williams and pursued a course (scientific) at Harvard College. He ranks as orderly sergeant. The younger brother is Captain [*Edward Wickes*].

An interesting person in Company K, called Sq.[*uire*] Jones for his proneness for dispute, has made himself unpopular with the officers. Being present at the meeting, he objected to having a staff of commissioned officers to decide upon the merits of the question, without they were commissioned by a Higher Power with more brains than they usually possessed, we having been showing up Judge Emmet of Pok. I hope no more of that feather will give us a visit, for a march of six or eight miles is not a pleasant duty. I hear tonight our Captain and the quartermaster goes tomorrow to survey a location upon the Baltimore and Ohio Railroad, for our location, preparitory [*sic*] for repairing it. But however, it all may be conjecture. We are looking forward to a [*move*] into the Barracks; perhaps tomorrow. We shall be more comfortable but not as pleasantly situated. The war in Virginia looks dark, we cannot tell how things will shape. Remember me to all

From your afft Cousin
R. T. Van Wyck

Wednesday, Dec. 24th, '62

Dear Father

I have been expecting that box since Sunday, but it may come all right yet. If I knew by what express line you sent it I would make suitable inquiry. I don't imagine any trouble, but I thought you would like to hear from it as soon as possible.

I suppose you are enjoying yourself down in Brooklyn and I will direct this there. Nothing new in camp or in prospect that is exciting. Give my love to all,

From your Son, R. T. Van Wyck

This Christmas eve I thought I would add a postscript and send you a representation of myself in my general costume of a soldier. Having been down to Baltimore, it occurred to me there it would be the only return (if acceptable) I could make for that box (which I expect to receive). But do not make any display of it home. That is the reason I make it an ambrotype* instead of photograph and [it] cannot be made an album member.

One is writing opposite to me having a tallow-dip stationed into a loaf of bread, for a candlestick, to light him. This substitute is quite common.

Homesick So-gers Lament
By Old Hoss

Verse the first
I wish that I was home again
Near tranquil Hudson's shore,
Three hundred miles, or there abouts,
Just North of Baltimore

Verse the seccund
'Tis there that I would like to dwell
In peace for evermore
There I'd have butter on my bread
And pancakes by the score.
To be continued

---

* An early type of photograph made on glass by backing a thin negative with a black surface.

51

The above was taken from a Rhinebeck paper written by the editor of our Company. Don't think I endorse it – the spirit of it.

Camp Belger   Balt. Dec. 27th

Dear Mother

I have received that anxiously looked-for <u>box</u> of good things. I don't know which of the many was particularly enjoyed. But justice was done to many and to all. The famous boiled saucage [*sic*] of Caroline and pie of Belinda we proved their goodness by experiment to be fine and have much enjoyed. The <u>preserves</u> and the bottles came in good order except the jar of current [*sic*], which was broken. But the material had not flown and was brought to use forthwith.

Mrs. Kip's Rasbbery [*sic*] and tomato came safe, I was glad they came so, for I am much indebted to her for such a testimonial of her kindness. With the surfeit of good things, if we were children, and indeed we were not far from it in the ecstasy with which we received them; you might have added as a caution, "don't make yourself sick;" but presuming that we knew enough to be a little considerate, though I assure you our judgment is much taxed.

I could not help observing the packing, which was admirable. Nor were we alone in the recipient of like gifts from home. Last evening the express was laden to overflowing with Christmas boxes to the boys, but were detained till the day following.

Christmas was a very dull day with me. I was not a little pleased to be called out in the afternoon for drill, which duty oftentimes is not very pleasant. I have not missed a drill or other requirements demanded of me by sickness, or by playing sharp, as the boys term it here, except getting a pass of going downtown once in two weeks or less. I have reason to be thankful that my health has been so excellent so far. The ambrotype fully justifies what I say, in my rough and ready costume.

There is very little of news in camp that is worth mentioning. An incident that occurred last evening will show how difficult a matter to get furlough to go home is. A member of a company from Brooklyn, received a telegraphic dispatch, informing him that his wife was dieing [*sic*]. He proceeded forthwith to get a furlough in an honorable manner; but was denied by the Gen. commanding this department, though approved by the Col. and Capt. He has taken the responsibility and gone as a deserter, to return.

This week we took up our quarters in the Barracks and retire to bed in the usual manner, between our blankets: the first change from our everyday clothes, which we have worn constantly night and day for nearly three months. We think this a luxury, but what must it be if we should again get between sheets and a mattress underneath. I will add, we have the virtue of a bath if we choose to get it, by going downtown, which privilege I have enjoyed since leaving home.

You have possibly heard of my call upon John Pudney. I have since seen himself and family at camp. I don't admire his address and manner, though I should feel myself much privileged with his acquaintance, by his presumption and great pertinacity to become acquainted with the great men, "The Shoulder Strappers." This is not unlike the Sherwoods. This may be a good thing, "but I don't see it." There is not half of the Commissioned officers that I care to become acquainted with. Capt. Wicks, his brother, and the Adjutant Thompson, their sisters, are keeping house a short distance from Camp. They attend to their requisite duties and are surrounded with home.

You intend spending New Year's in Brooklyn, and will receive this there. Remember me to all,

From your aft Son   R. T. Van Wyck

Note: the letter is addressed to 27 Smith St., Brooklyn, N. Y. C.C.F.

Camp Belger   Bal. Dec. 27

Dear Cousin [*Sarah*]

This Saturday afternoon I thought I would answer your letter received yesterday. Also thanking you, as well as making you a medium of giving to the contributors of that box sent me, my warmest thanks for this testimonial of their kindness.

Can I perceive in that most excellent gift of Mrs. Kip's the tender solicitation of Sarah [*Kip*]? For, from the aromatic and spicy liquid condiment of the gift, I observe a good similitude to the general character of the would wished-to-be-giver, Miss Sarah. She need not palm off such consistency for the genuine gift she could make me. But as I was scrutinizing the raspberry, I noticed the palm of a delicate kid glove was used for a leakage preventitive [*sic*]. Could it be that such a disposal of it did or would bring to my mind the happy associations connected with that bottle, if not with the glove in its early days? Having tried the vinegar, I found it a highly valuable <u>fluid</u> for giving a delightful delicacy to salt beef, commonly called

Salt Horse. I find no difference to the raspberry labelled [sic] syrup. This latter we diluted with water, drank up and did not find our mistake till we tried Mrs. Kip's, but I suppose it is all right. Do not fail to express my thanks to Mrs. Kip.

The stockings of Grand Mother are just the thing and are likely to last longer than the rest of the things. The daily marches is hard upon stockings. The cake of Uris and Genet and other gifts were well appreciated. We shall very likely give part of the preserves to some sick boys in the hospital as our present quarters is not suited for them. Many, many thanks for this kindness and should I ever return, it will be one of long rememberence [sic].

There is nothing new in Camp, just at present. The boys are so much engaged with their boxes that little time is given to war rumors. I have sent Mother my ambrotype giving her my appearance as a soldier. You have not told me if at the dispersal of my *cartes visite* you obtained an equivalent in one. If there is not enough to go around to the many fair circle of my acquaintances, I will have some taken after the manner in the ambrotype. A striking difference you will observe immediately, no doubt.

I am writing this letter in the Captain's tent and much interrupted, so you will excuse mistakes. Much love to all from

R. T. Van Wyck

Adam'stown, MD.
New Year's Eve

Dear Parents

Arrived here this morning after a night's ride in the cars. Yesterday after a march for diversion downtown we unexpectedly received orders to be ready to march, in about fifteen minutes. Knapsacks were packed, in double quick time, and we had the misfortune to leave a good share of the good things received from home behind us, for the length of time we were required to be away, or if totally away we do not know at present. This town is near the Potomac ford where there is soon to be made or expected a rebel raid under [*Gen. Jeb*] Stuart, near the famous battle grounds of Antietam and Sharpsburg. In fact, the whole country is rich in incident of the last summer engagement with the rebels.

We are the distance of four miles from Point of Rocks and twelve miles from Harpers Ferry. The rebels were reported to have crossed and we were ordered out, together with the Sixth N. Y. Artillery of four pieces to intercept their progress. We have not seen them or heard from them yet and have picquits [sic] out in all directions. We are a few miles nearer the Potomac to where the whole Rebel Army passed into Frederick, pursued by the Union forces. In conversing with the people the appearance and doings [of the Rebel exodus] were ludicrous in the extreme. They [the Rebels] were said to be composed mostly of young men and appeared to be in excellent spirits. They were poorly clothed but well armed. They were shoeless and hatless, but as fast as they came upon a supply, they would cast off their old articles of clothing, and the effect upon the roadside was a string of rags the whole distance.

This is a beautiful country. To the north of us is a mountain called Rattlesnake, and between that and the Blue Ridge there is another mountain, the memorable South mountain in the news last summer. And now we are looking for them again. The light or flying artilery [sic] is stationed on a little elevation near us, their horses all harnessed and ready to start at a moment's notice. The horses have a hard time of tonight, as it is getting cold.

The different companies are quartered in various old buildings unoccupied, in town. We have the kitchen of an old Southern house, and a stove, and are doing first rate. The people are Union of course, just now. They say that heavy firing was heard at Harpers Ferry yesterday. But nothing has been heard from it, yet. We might be here for some time to come, or we may go along tomorrow.

R. T. V. W.

Camp Belger
Jan 7th 1863

Dear Cousin [Sarah]

I received your letter upon my return from a New Year's expedition towards Harpers Ferry. I have also been on a tour to Washington, returning last evening. The first was a call for troops to defend the border against a raid of Stuart's cavalry, and as we were unoccupied and ready for duty, were sent. However, the object for which we were sent was unnecessary as Stuart was checked in Virginia, but we were extremely thankful for this opportunity to get a view of Antietam and witness some of the remains of rebel spoilation [sic]. I enclose a leaf of a plant medicinal, the only one of green

55

character I could find to mark the place upon which I visited where I obtained a view of this beautiful country, ravaged by war. My companion and myself called this place Point Desolation. We returned greatly disappointed in not getting a glimpse of a rebel in arms, still we saw some of their homes, who were strongly so, but we returned greatly pleased with this adventure.

After remaining here a few days I was fortunate in being selected, together with four others, to guard some convalescent soldiers to Washington. Many of which were some of the finest men I have seen as soldiers, but whose health has given out, and who are not willing to take a discharge from the service. We took them, and delivered them to the officers in charge to return to their regiments. Our first excursion was the scene of joyful excitement, but in the later [ones] we saw the miseries which this war engenders.

Now, at Washington, the streets are thronged with discharged, disabled soldiers, the hotels with Band Box officers, the main thoroughfare trodden by cavalry and artilery [sic] and transportation wagons. The Halls of Congress by their quietness to what it was formerly, seemed the solemn meditation of surrounding suffering.

In my last, I spoke of an ambrotype instead of a photograph I had taken and sent to Brooklyn to Father, showing my appearance at the present time. I don't expect to have any photographs taken, nor am I desirous that any should be forced upon those who are unwilling to make an exchange. Although I am complimented in getting a position in their album [sic], but "I don't see the point." It is a poor rule that won't work both ways.

I noticed puffs* upon the 150th, etc. also on Isaac Kip. I wrote to Frank [Kip] an acct. of my travels down towards the Potomac upon the receipt of a letter on my return. He enclosed one of Isaac K's *carte visite*.

I have been out to tea again, the guest of the Adjutant W. Thompson. Were present his sister and Miss Wicks and the Col., a very pleasant evening. I was the only representative of my rank.

I received a letter from Father today informing me of the funeral of Adriance Van Brunt, who died Monday. It was sudden, indeed! The comments in the papers upon the 150th are only a blind.

    Remember me to all Your Cousin R. T. Van Wyck

---

* Newspaper articles.

Camp Belger   Jan 10, 1863

Dear Mother

I received your letter today by way of Adamstown. Father has told you of a "change of base" to this place, by this time. Many thanks for your sincere anxiety for my welfare. Indeed I felt quite blue and did not know what should have prevented an answer to my letters. But was partially solved by Father's note, informing me of Uncle Adriance's death.

Father has given you all the information up to my leaving to Washington the first of last week. We took our departure from Camp (Major Smith and five others including myself) and were ordered to guard some convalescent soldiers from the Baltimore depot to Wash. Our business was not an arduous one but it seemed hard to guard old soldiers, who had seen the strife of war more than ourselves, back to where the government will order them. Many desired to go to their Regt. while others would get their discharge after a while. It is needful to say that we tried to make ourselves as pleasant as possible, and finally bid them adieu in Washington, to their quarters assigned them, and wended our way towards Willard's [*Hotel*], the chief resort of the No. 1's. The Major found our Congressman, Stephen Baker, and introduced him to all of us. He invited us, should we visit the Capitol (which we did) he would show us about. The hotel was so crowded by officers from the army and others, we were recommended to the Hayward House, a short distance below, for a night's lodgings. Would you believe it that my rest was very unsatisfactory between white sheets, but such was the case.

I apprehended a fit of sickness upon retiring, having a great aching of my bones and some fever, but in the morning all was over. Whether to attribute it to the diseased soldiers or otherwise, I thought the latter till my companions complained of the same symptoms of sickness as myself, and one of whom not feeling the effects then, has been and is now very ill. But what a change Wash. presents to the time I last visited it. Now you realize the miseries of war. The streets are thronged with disabled discharged soldiers, or the hotels with Band Box officers and the main thoroughfare trodden by transportation wagons, cavalry, and artilery [*sic*]. After visiting the Patent Office, Navy and Treasury buildings, and also the White House, we went to the Capitol and called upon S. Baker. He gave us a Page who took us all about, and showed us the prominent men in both houses.

The most noticable [*sic*] characteristic now is the unusual quietness that reigns in the absence of that representation, from that malicious portion of our country. We were very well pleased, and met Major, who had been visiting his brother, at the depot, ready to come home where we arrived in due season. I may call this a special favor shown me, in giving me this opportunity to see Wash.

Just one week from today after my return from Adamstown and previous to my visit to Wash. as I was writing an account of my Adamstown excursion to Frank Kip, I was called upon by the Adjutant W. Thompson to invite me to tea at his house. As I wrote you before, this Miss Wick[*e*]s and Miss Thompson are keeping house for the boys in a small house adjoining the camp. I was introduced to the Col.'s wife, at about the same time. Accordingly I went over. They thought it not expedient to get very extensive housekeeping utensils, and [*we*] were served with oysters from an iron skillet, the Col. doing and desiring to do the honors of the table. Our next course was Ham and eggs and finally closed with cake and coffee. I was the only representative of my rank present. My first appearance among the Shoulder Strappers since being in the regiment now three months.

I don't know where we shall move again. Our past has been a pleasure excursion. Give my love to all in Brooklyn,

From your aff Son   R. T. Van Wyck

P. S. It seems that looking over this letter, there seems little in it for the one from you, giving me such pleasure. It would go dull, indeed, without the comforting assurance of a final reunion hereafter in Heaven and the helps thitherward, which your letters give me. When at Washington and observed the suffering of the soldiery, of those who were inmates of hospitals, could they feel that life is a delusion, and when here is nothing real, permanent, they would hail the end with joy, instead of painful indifference so common to meet with.

Camp Belger Jan 14th '63

Dear Cousin [*Sarah*]

I received your letter today and hasten to answer it, under the following replies to your queries. First, the <u>leaf</u> from Rattle Snake mountain. Second, my frame of mind under the existing circumstances of camp life. Third, the name of your horse. Fourth, the pleasure of my acquaintance with Miss <u>Lotte</u> <u>Wickes</u>. Fifth, when

Nature bestowed upon me my great personal beauty and military attraction in the growth of my wiskers [sic]. Sixth, my promotion to some more exalted station in the defense of the liberties of those at home but not our own here. Seventh, whether I will favor you with a visit this year or in the short period of time, three weeks.

I feel in doing justice to myself in answering these previous questions, that I will be unable to go into detail and give you the where and wherefore, but having been very unfortunate in being deprived of my regular sleep the past evening, and feel much the want of this luxury, the reason why I have divided your questions, so I should not omit them, will I hope be a sufficient excuse for my conciseness. You have received the memento of the battlefield from Antietam by this time. My carelessness in not sending it in the first, has received its due notice at your hands. I will be careful it may not occur in the future. My pleasure in the fleeting moments or dull hours of a soldier's life has not been more irksome than anticipated when I enlisted, nor has the moments passed by swiftly in its gayities [sic] and delicious pleasures. I am rarely homesick except when my letters are not speedily answered, and often feel I am talking to you when seated upon the railing of my bunk, having the box sent me from home serving me for a table, and deaf to the noise of the men around me, while giving you by the means of pen and paper the state of my health, etc., the pleasure of which is next to be with you in person.

My bunk companion, the spectacled one from Rhinebeck, is a good chess player and I have availed myself of his proficiency to learn the game and find occupation for the spare moments in its deep thinking. I think it suits me first rate. Besides this, the debating society of which I am an attendant but not a participant, now as I am writing this, I hear the noise of approbation from the halls below, drawn from some of the many would-be political orators, upon [the] great question of the day, "The expediency of arming the black."* This has so much absorbed the minds of all, both officers and privates, that the question has been adjourned three evenings. In questioning the reason of the cheering that I was just hearing, I find our friend Jones of Co. K, whose pertinacity for debate I have given you or Mother in my previous letters, so characteristic on all questions of

---

* The Emancipation Proclamation had been issued on January 3, 1863.

a political nature and particularly this one, upon an attack by Capt. Wick[e]s who was opposed to so doing, "but thought it expedient the men in exalted position in our country should be the persons who should decide the expediency of which, without the popular sentiment of the people." Jones, in answer to which brought the house down in his pointed sarcasm upon the shoulder strappers, he firmly believing the privates the backbone of the country and the hope of it, and the necessity of its preservation. His views are agreeable to mine, but with my friendship to the Capt. I cannot endorse his sentiments, and if he does not wish himself attacked he must not make himself <u>liable</u>.

With these news from downstairs comes the message for us to leave to guard some Baltimore <u>hospital</u>. However, I will finish this letter, not knowing how soon I can address you again. It quite surprised me of the new event of the purchase of a new horse. He may be deserving of a military name like Volunteer, Union, not probably, Secession.

Again I will interrupt you and inform you that I am joyfully thinking of the visit I have just received from Allard Anthony.* I expect to see him again on his return from Washington. He says he would not know me, if the Col. had not sent purposly [sic] for me to see him. How glad I was to see him. I don't know how soon it may be my pleasure to see another from home.

The pleasure of my acquaintance with Miss Wick[e]s was so casual, and of such short duration, that I have not thought much about it. I certainly could not have been very prepossessing in my appearance, if I take it from your <u>observation</u> of my ambrotype. The only difference was that the pants were outside my boots. The strong or marked feature that time makes to those who use the razor in a limited way, is the only noticable [sic] change in our appearance from leaving home.

I have been offered a Sergeancy in our company, the place of one who deserted. I have flattering accounts of my capabilities and sentiments entitling me to a commissioned officer commencing from the first men in the Regt. This question of my acceptance of such will decide when the opportunity offers. This is very pleasant to hear but must be listened to with discretion.

---

* A relative from Dutchess County.

And lastly, whether I shall come home on a French furlough and desert, or do the other thing, stay where I am. Pardon me for saying it, but I choose to decide for myself and will come home in an honorable way, when offered, but should not follow the way constantly going on of those going home when they feel like and returning again.

Many thanks for your kind letters heretofore and you will please excuse in my own, a critical way, if any, which I have not <u>meant</u>. I have sat down tonight determined to apologize, knowing the effort after a night's watching in the hospital, having the care of eight patients. You will take this as the fag end of a day of some fatigue, and I will finish this some other time.

Give my love to all. I should like to get a <u>measure</u> of patriotism from someone, for I fear my own is getting low under the existing state of the country. Tell Mother I have answered her letter directed to Smith St. If not received she need not hesitate to write again.

R. T. Van Wyck

P. S. Excuse my envelopes of buff instead of white. I take the hint and use it. I received a letter from Mr. Woodhull.

Baltimore Jan. 15th, 1863

Dear Mother

You have heard from Sarah by this time of my absence from Camp Belger and our destination down to Baltimore. Having arrived here though voluntary on my own part, for I suppose I could have remained at our previous camp, but I much prefer being here, if the duty is not hard, to my being at total leisure elsewhere and confined to the strictures of military duty or rule in camp.

In taking a view of things about, I find we have total possession of an old house upon a street surrounded by hospitals, which we are to guard. That is, if any of the veterans of Antietam, Bulls [sic] Run and of the Peninsula campaign, should have the opportunity of passing the <u>guard</u>, they would feel so inclined to skadaddle [sic] and get slightly inebriated. To prevent such procedure we are sent.

As I said, it is an old house containing rooms enough for our whole company, consisting of a room for the first relief, of which I am acting <u>corporal</u>, and also three others, making our turn coming off every two hours of duty, and six hours of leisure. We also have the privilege of going over to the Reading rooms, which will compensate us a little for our filthy quarters.

Yes, they are shockingly so and I availed myself of writing this in the officer's room above, which is a trifle better than mine downstairs, surrounded by the men who have not the remotest idea of cleanliness, and seem desirous of having it look as bad as possible, notwithstanding our remonstrance.

You were aware that I saw Allard last evening, and I saw him this morning in marching to our duty here. He saw me with my knapsack on and he undoubtedly would not have known me had he not seen me the previous evening. I was very glad to see him and will have a good opportunity next Saturday of getting his views of the state of the country, or what the Dutchess Co. people think of it. I must say that the patriotism of mine that has induced me to make such incongruous companions and expose myself in every way and manner, without the pleasure that many derive in so doing, I feel is slightly giving way from my various observations of the High moral principle of those high in command and our ill success attributable to their inscrupulous [sic] demands upon the country for men and treasure, without a higher motive than personal ambition or sensual pleasure. Can the people at home and in the field ever be as slaves to this intriguing usurpation of the liberties of the people, and yet be always zealous for the blessed institutions formerly enjoyed? For if corrupt men supersede honest ones and instead of the just fruit of right motives and patriotic hearts we have the miseries of the whole country instead, we would rightly infer that all was not well, and if the country is irrecoverably lost, desire a new order.

However, it may be that our disappointment in not receiving our pay upon the expiration of the usual time, two months [*has set me off*], yes, and much more, for it thereby shows who and for what motives influences their devotion to their country. But money is certainly desirable to us privates who go for $13—I mean, only receive this when they can do better at home—and but for the officers with whom I feel on an equallity [sic] and who are more zealously looking after the "loaves and fishes" than the right, I would deprive myself willingly of our Green backs and not think as the multitude, that Uncle Sam is worth fighting for only when he pays well.

The full amount of cash on hand on inspection is just $1.05 and this is the balance from last pay day. It is questionable whether this will suffice till next March, the time government is supposed to visit us with the pay master, if at all, as the limited amount of cash on hand and the uncertainty of getting more is a question.

I certainly feel <u>blue</u> over the final destiny of the country, and could have previously given you a little of my short experience of false motives that influenced the masses to go into this thing, and particularly the officers. Why, our Left. Col. is reported in Balt. as the <u>best</u> gambler in it, and has been seen at camp late at night playing for a pile of <u>Green backs</u>. And my only hope of our success is the honesty of the privates and officers backed by the people, as has been in the <u>West</u>, but we have been <u>cursed</u> by the regular army since the commencement, and I fear we always will be. Let not this make you think I am dissatisfied here. No, for my observation, should my life be spared, will be abundantly equivalent to all this, and the pryings into human nature will not be forgotten.

You are at Fishkill* again so Sarah writes me, and I will enclose a spicy <u>secession editorial</u>. I have not heard from Fred** this winter. How does he do?

Give my love to all   from your Son
R. T. Van Wyck

Baltimore   Jan 24th, '63

Dear Mother

I sit down this Saturday afternoon to give you a more satisfactory letter than my last. I was seated in the midst of excitment [*sic*] and could scarcely collect my thoughts together, as you have perceived. I do not know whether this will be an improvement. But enough of this.

I am still at the National Hospital and not removed to camp as I thought of. By the way, I gave camp a visit and it did look so lonesome, that I thought I would defer going for the present.

This is my first experience in City life, which I enjoy in taking a walk in the business part of the city, in <u>noticing</u> in a very diverting kind of a way, the ways of things here. The reading rooms is my daily resort in the afternoon, and find excellent matter to improve the leisure hours. It is fortunate for me that such is the case.

I suppose my appearance does give some questioning, and my costume looks not very familiar in your eyes. But what subjects to habits and tastes we mortals are. I have become so accustomed to

---

* His mother and aunts and cousins were often away from home on long visits to relatives in Brooklyn and New York City.
** Fred Van Brunt, a relative on his mother's side.

military suits, and dark shirts, that the citizen dress looks odd, and as for white linen and all those things, I fear my taste is irrecoverably lost. How we will look if we should return from the war and wear the government shirt of a grey color, with the collar turned down, in lieu of one of snowy whiteness! And as to cooking I have not tried my hand in that yet, but have been cultivating my taste for government rations, as given to us, cooked.

I met with an unfortunate accident which gives you some idea of the state of Uncle <u>Sam's</u> beef (commonly called Mule) that sent me to the <u>dentist</u> in double quick time, having endeavored to masticate a small portion for my dinner. Our meat is generally <u>boiled</u>, the universal practice with all meats, and it shows the superior judgment of our cooking, for however tenacious consistency our food is, it finally arrives at just such a state upon being submitted to this process. The juice that remains answers a good purpose in assisting in friing [*sic*] our bread into, which, by the by, is not a bad way in helping us to make things <u>palatable</u>. This to you might be questionable.

I received a letter from Sarah giving me an account of the Sewing Society meetings which might be very interesting. I infer from her letter that they* go into society very much. Have formed the acquaintance of the Conklins–La Dues, etc. How does Aunt <u>Louise</u>** like this? Does it meet with the ambitious desires of her daughters? They were so particular soon after they returned from boarding school into what society they should enter. They have bought a horse. Have they disposed of their old one? If not, I don't suppose Father likes this <u>much</u>. I often get thinking about <u>farming</u> in observing the way they do those things <u>here</u> and often wonder what change has taken place since my absence.

The political affairs of the country have not taken any noticable [*sic*] change since I last wrote you. The sentiment it seems is going stronger against the administration and in favor of an early termination of the war. How this is to be brought about I cannot see. Col. Van Wyck has resigned his commission, I understand. The feeling hostile to him is no doubt owing to his views on the "peculiar institution" [*slavery*]. Give my love to all at home. From your afft son

Richard T. Van Wyck

---

* Sarah and her sister Anna.
** Louisa Van Vechten, Sarah's mother.

Baltimore Jan 26th, '63

Dear Cousin [*Sarah*]

I was happy to receive your letter giving me an account of the doings at home. I have changed my quarters <u>again</u>—a much more comfortable and desirable situation than my previous one, but how long it will last I do not know.

Geo. Burroughs and four men were detailed to duty at the Union Relief quarters, for giving the soldiers as they are passing through the city, meals and sleeping quarters, he becoming sick with a cold, I have gone over to relieve him. I hope I can make it a permanent thing. I certainly do not want to build up my good fortune upon the misfortune of others, but this is decidedly as near like comfort that I need expect since I have been in the army. A good table to sit by, I could have a bed but I <u>prefer</u> sleeping on the floor instead, for certain <u>reasons</u>. My business this morning was to go down to the Fortress Monroe boat and solicit the wounded and discharged soldiers to come up to the Relief rooms and get refreshments and prevent the swindler and other <u>raskals</u> [*sic*] from defrauding these men returning to their homes. This is not a very disagreeable task for me, I assure you.

I received a letter from Mr. Lane* yesterday. I was <u>fearful</u> that Aunt Susan had forgotten me in not noticing my letters. I presume he holds his house in the city yet. He has not lost his acute sense of economy yet. As for us here, <u>that</u> gives us little trouble, except when our money is nearly exhausted, to husband a little for next Pay day.

You asked after Noah Wixon for Genet or Margaret. He has been sick at one period since being out, but now is perfectly recovered and enjoys himself for aught I know, very well. I see very little of him.

Sunday we had a visit from the Col. who said that we would not remain long on this duty down in the city. So if you hear of our change again, you need not feel surprised. A soldier's life is one of pack up and march, no questions asked, but a sort of a don't-care sort of way of thinking of all things pertaining to themselves. He is really a machine, and he is not long in thinking so himself. One gets selfish soon here. He must look out for himself for nobody will look out for him. Give my love to all at home.

From your cousin   R. T. Van Wyck

---

* Robert Lane is the husband of his Aunt Susan (his father's sister).

Union Relief Rooms, Balt.
Jan. 31st, '63

Dear Mother

I received your letter yesterday and joyfully endeavor to answer it. For these reasons. First, because we have received our Pay, Second, our quarters seem now more like living than at any time since leaving home. Previously we have merely stayed.

We had been long in anticipation of a call from His Excellency, the Pay Master, and were gratified yesterday by his presence with the Green Backs. The consequence of such effusion of money among the men of the 150th Regt. will be a slight inebriation, perhaps enough to send them to Ft. McHenry. And again those that are so disposed, of which there are said to be many, to take a French leave home, not intending to return. These are the evils attending the use of this fortunate act of Uncle Sam. The blessings which it sheds upon the soldier, maintaining his family at home, and furnishing him with tobacco, keeps many a one from leaving the army.

As I am not of either class, I presume you think my presumption in asking assistance from home, and the thirteen Dollars a month, would give me abundance. It does. And gives me some of the trifling purchases that stares you in the face in a city like Balt. for the extras of the culinary department.

I am happy to inform you I am getting more than my share as a soldier. I relieved Geo. Burroughs at this place on acct. of sickness, which is not at all dangerous, and in this position, we sit down to a well-furnished table at all meal hours, and generally have sleeping on mattresses. To cap the <u>whole</u> of this delightful situation, our employers (the association)* at whose services we are placed, is so far better to the arbitrary, exacting control of military rule by men whose manners is so highly repugnant to sensitive natures; where here the association of minds and natures imbued with tastes, feelings and sympathies like our own; and have no ambitious passions to gratify, or hampered by superior officers to debar a friendly act—this contrast is more sensibly felt than expressed.

If you and many others could only know what the benevolent people of Balt. does to brighten the homeward march of the soldier, discharged, enfeebled by sickness and often wounded in battle,

* Union Christian Relief Association.

without the means of helping himself; for him to receive the volunteer assistance of good nursing, tenderly carried from the cars to his bed and back again, to have men to settle his accounts with government and get his pay—all this without compensation, is a noble act for any city, and to think that this city has been so stygmatized [sic] by citizens of other cities, whose benevolence has fed not one-quarter of the soldiers or given the necessary assistance to the needy – need someone to give her justice, which if the facts were everywhere known, would be readily acknowledged.

I saw <u>80</u> <u>Rebels</u>, gurillas [sic], some of <u>Morgan's</u>* men, captured last summer, going over to Ft. McHenry. They were a good specimen of the South. They were confident of a final success of their cause, and heard much more about peace since coming north than while at home. If our whole army were possessed with the spirit and determination of both officers and men that is possessed by the <u>South</u>, we would have succeeded <u>long ago</u>. Much love to all. The papers I sent you, I endorse the <u>editorials</u> which you have seen.

From your afft. Son   R. T. Van Wyck

Baltimore Feb. 6th, 1863

Dear Mother

You must excuse me for so immediately answering your letter. I had been looking for one during the week past; but the accounts of home matters abundantly warrent [sic] the delay. Besides, they do not need the apology you give them; but far from it. They refresh my mind with what is going on at home far beyond what my letters can give you, I know.

Yes, I am enjoying myself in my present position much better than at any time since leaving home, and every day some new incident occurs, by meeting someone from the battle field, whose narritive [sic] of his adventures finds me a very eager listener.

One person whose acquaintance I made in my line of duty to conduct the discharged from the Ft. Monroe boat, and who possessed a greater share of intelligence than most of those whom I usually conduct to the Relief Rooms, gives me almost the first instance of this class where talent and profession have been <u>swayed</u> by patriotic feeling.

---

* Brig. Gen. John Hunt Morgan of Confederate cavalry, famous for his raids behind Union lines.

He enlisted as a private in the ranks at the first call to arms. He was a native of Pittsburg[h], Penn., educated for a profession which he was intending to pursue as a <u>Dr</u>.; but his love for the adventurous found him out in Missouri teaching school at the breaking out of the rebellion. He described to me his first settlement in the country, and his success in getting friends, which appeared to me with his vivid description of it, more like a romance than real. He told me his trouble in getting out of the country[*side*], and his final joining with some of his schoolmates in Pittsburg[h] for the war. His war experience was almost exclusively upon the Peninsula where his health broke down, and effecting his discharge he was taken as ward master to one of the Hospitals in Ft. Monroe. His previous knowledge of medicine and his experience of it in the Hospital has given him a good position in Phila. He says he is agoing to return to Missouri, come what will, be they Rebel or Union. His accounts of <u>war</u> affairs quite gave me a favorable impression toward him. Every day something of this nature turns up.

The desertions in the Regt. is very alarming. Some of the Comp's [*companies*] have lost as high as thirteen since pay day. Our own have only lost six. Thus you see what has actuated the mass to come <u>hither</u>. The First Left. has been discharged from the service for drunkenness and we, the privates, are speculating whom the Col. will appoint in his place. The position was held up to me before I enlisted, but what disposition they will make I do not know, and as long as I am comfortable I don't <u>care</u>. It gives me no thought at all. I suppose if I should bring myself more into notice of the <u>officers</u> in this particular it would be better for me, but I prefer <u>not</u>. If they forfeit their word it is no more than I expected. If I should stay <u>three</u> years, my judgment upon human nature will be very <u>critical</u>.

I suppose I will hear from Sarah when the Kips leave. And hear the whole <u>gossip</u> that has turned up. The new <u>game</u>, I should like to know what it is. I will not soon have the opportunity of hearing it in person. Is it matrimony? I never knew this was a game, but perhaps it is. Much love,

R. T. Van Wyck

P. S. I feel thankful for that <u>genuine</u> remembrance and regard that you spoke of in your letter (I mean, out of our family), but you know <u>Chesterfield's</u> politeness consisted in making every one feel satisfied with himself.

Union Relief Rooms Baltimore
Feb. 14th, '63

Dear Mother

I received your letter, also the papers. The latter gave some of the employees of the Rooms a fund for amusement. It is my idea of their character exactly. It must have been very interesting to listen to. The Baltimore people say it is unfair to subject them to Marshal [sic] [martial] law when such treasonable proceeding and views are constantly eminating [sic] from the North as expounded on by Van Buren. And I think myself we would be better off, for I am extremely doubtful as to their efficacy in the field, when privates are so disaffected upon this slavery question.

I saw a Sergeant of the 22nd N. Jersey on his return home to Englewood on furlough. Said V. B., he says, is taking the position he formerly occupied previous to his promotion as Quarter Master Sergeant of Brigade, consequent upon taking marching orders. He (the sergeant) is the class of men whom the latter Regt.'s class as their superior officers (an Irish man). His early experience judging from some of our own Company, Non-Commissioned officers, he might have taken French leave of absence from some of the early Regt.'s in the field. I don't wonder of his dissatisfaction of the war. From the No. of men returning home of about 1,000 to 1,500 a day discharged, furlowed [sic], etc., I think the army is weakening all the time, or is getting rid of the "dead Beats," as they are called, and hospital invalids. They say the desertion in the whole army amounts to 100,000, decreased by sickness a greater No. So there must be a draft to retain the active strength of the army. The people at home will not feel very well satisfied with the result of this conflict so far, should they resort to draft which is inevitable. There is only one way: to succumb to the Rebels or fight it out.

Your suggestion is a good one not to scan too closely the motives that govern the actions and feelings of individuals, for we find to our sorry [sic] much that will make life miserable. I don't think I am so critical of human nature, not too much so, for I am fearful lest I should fail to appreciate good society when thrown in my way. I call your attention to my present situation, which is more of a contact now with citizens than with soldiers.

I wish you would ask Father to see Green when he goes down to the Landing about that Coat and vest. I am fearful he will send it and I will not know when to receive it.

It must set the <u>girls</u> in the Village all in a fever about Mr. Lee's marriage. A good demonstration of the old truism, "Still water runs deep."

The letter of Lossing in the *Eagle* is as the Reg't would wish to be reported to the people of Dutchess Co., and is far different than it really is. It won't bear scanning too closely. The Assembly meetings are a source of pleasure to the officers in the <u>City</u>. You would much better be pleased to hear of this only cause of <u>regret</u> (should it be one) than the great corruption just brought to light in this city by the Quarter Master Col. James Belger, an active participant of those <u>Union</u> Meetings so happily expressed by Lossing. I don't believe <u>merit</u> shines always in Newspapers or can efface the stain, by attending meetings called Union (undoubtedly by rebel) by the correspondent.

Give my love to all   from Your Son   R. T. Van Wyck
Your letter came <u>unsealed</u>. It revealed nothing of importance.

Union Relief Rooms, Balt.
Feb. 17th, 1863

Dear Cousin [*Sarah*]

I have delayed answering your letter on acct. of press of business. This seems strange to you to think I should have my hands so full that I cannot find an half hour to give you, particularly upon this duty upon which I am placed. But by the passage through to Ft. Monroe of the 168th Regt. from Newburgh and also by other ones, have given me some duty in keeping order while stopping at the rooms for refreshments, and when something unusual turns up I am not in a fit state to soberly write you.

I am glad you had such a nice time when the <u>Kips</u> were staying at your house, and although I was not particularly fond of society, I have much thought of wishing to have been at home when they were staying in the Hook*. It has surprised me much that Miss Mary has not joined the State of Matrimony: undoubtedly she has enlisted and only waiting the requisition upon the Clothing and subsistence department from <u>her</u> <u>Van</u>. From all appearances he appears to be abundantly able to furnish the <u>said</u> requirement.

The brilliant affair of Mr. Lee's has given many a shock to the speculative old maids and some of the ambitious mothers of Fishkill Village.

---

* Fishkill Hook, a farming area, including the hamlet of Johnsville (now Wiccopee), where the Van Wycks and the Van Vechtens resided.

The young ladies, <u>of</u> <u>course</u>, never cared at all about him. You must look [out] for still people in future, they are dangerous characters in this business. I need not exclude the ladies, for I expect to hear, and prepared for it, of some expeditious and unceremonious transaction, even including my Cousins, whose quiet manners have been long established.

I can readily grasp or conceive of how the neighborhood gossip flies about, and the amusement it furnishes. By it, the seasons pass away quickly and pleasantly, and almost too soon the Winter has passed away unperceptably [sic] with you in anticipation of next summer's pastime in garden employment and perhaps horseback riding, now that you have one to ride.

It is now snowing very hard, something like a New York Northwester. I might perhaps see a sleigh. If I do it will be the first one.

Army operations you know almost as much about as I do myself. With the 168th Regt. and others to the seat of war, might indicate a desire to use the men in action before their term of service expires. Our whole course is shrouded in mistery [sic], or what little is designed by our Generals for us to know, much more what is in store for us by the Wise Dispenser of the Universe who is guiding our course through life, as best suits His infinite wisdom in the great <u>wheel</u> of National revolution. The sure indication of an old soldier is his indifference as to where he goes or when he goes or how he goes, and I begin to feel the same thing myself, although I have been stationary the last six months but always looking for something to turn up and talking about it.

Hasbrouck DuBois has returned much pleased with his tour but not so much benefited by it. An active soldier's life would fully establish his health if he should be fortunate enough to escape the malignant diseases. The Newburgh Regt. 168th has now 18 men in the <u>hospital</u> here, if not more, <u>by</u> <u>the</u> <u>way</u>, taken down with typhoid fever and measeals [sic]. My health is as good as usual. It surprises you that I have succeeded so well soldiering, undoubtedly. I do hope it will ever remain so, as well as you all at home, for the sake of your

Afft. Cousin   R. T. Van Wyck

Union Relief Rooms   Baltimore
Feb. 28th, 1863

Dear Mother,

By some strange coincident [sic], I have at different times received your letters accompanied with Aunt Mary's welcomed letters. To receive such a good budget of news is not by no means disagreeable, especially after so long an intermission of home correspondence. I have very little news to give you except to inform you that Mr. Hasbrouck gave us a call yesterday. He happily found the Fishkill men in Capt. Scofield's room, at his quarters, and after he gave them the news at home, I took him over to my quarters at this place and showed him about. After which I went with him to Mr. John Pudney's store, and then saw his wife. After that, I walked with them down to the Philadelphia depot. Had a long talk with them about everything at home—very particularly asked after Miss Hasbrook [*sic*] and would have ventured to send her my *carte visite* if I had one, not as I am now, but how I <u>might</u> look in appearance. Hem! How this sounds to talk thus, down in Baltimore! No fear of expressing my deep regret just at present, in <u>person</u>, and consequently did my best to feel inexpressibly flattered by the request. You have only to take my hat off, cover my whiskers, change my pants to a blue and outside of my boots, and you have the clothing and appearance of the writer as best I can make it, just at present.

Don't think I am getting more particular than is consistant [*sic*] with a soldier, but I have wore a paper collar only twice, on certain occasions. I don't believe in putting on "airs." My reason for getting a coat from Green was because the regulation will give the boys all a coat with a skirt, and from my peculiar difficulty in getting a fit,* I thought it would be better to order one.

From all accounts we are destined to remain near Baltimore for some time to come. We return to our Barracks Monday and leave these quarters, perhaps never more to return. I have enjoyed this duty better than has been enjoyned [*sic*] on me since coming in the service, and the opportunity of seeing much that will be useful to me in after life, will not pass by unheeded. Besides, I have made friends at the Relief, and as long as we remain here in the city will be a good thing in the way of subsistence, etc.

I failed to notice in your last letter the loss of Abram's little boy. He must feel the loss very keenly, from the misfortune of his eldest son. George will come in as a soldier now if the bill in Congress passes,

---

* He was over six feet two inches in height.

which it will, in probability.*   It will take every available man or all those who are phisically [sic] requisite. I think this does not exempt him.

We are having or have had, the same snow storm you have experienced at Fishkill, and have seen but little sleighing here in the city, but plenty of slush and mud. I thought I would have no better opportunity to answer your letter in view of the moving up to camp Monday, and accept this from your Afft. Son,

R. T. Van Wyck

Union Relief Rooms
Sunday March 1st, 1863

Dear Cousin [Sarah]

I am forgetful whether I had answered your letter before. At any rate, in not hearing from you, I had supposed I was your debtor. Mother writes me of the sewing society's meetings and the glad anticipation of an discontinuance of them. They have been very pleasant for you in passing the winter months in meeting the gay society of the Hook, which till winter you have not had the pleasure of meeting.

The new horse has given you many a sleigh ride, and does perfectly realize all your fond hopes of what you like in one. I sometimes think of home, of all these things, of the pleasures of such home fixtures, but alas, upon second thoughts, they seem far in the distance and seem doubtful of ever being realized again.

I saw Mr. Hasbrook [sic] Friday on his return from Washington. Was glad to see him and showed him around with pleasure and for the sake of the "Miss" at home.

It might not be proper today [Sunday] to write you, and seemingly to you I might much more profitably use it in a better observance of it.** But of all days it gives me more of a longing to be home than of all days spent on duty, which even this [day] does not exempt me [from].

I sometimes see a Chaplain, who tell me of their difficulty in getting a hearing in the soldiery. One particularly, of Irish nativity and

---

* On March 3, 1863, the first National Conscription Act was passed, making all men from 20 to 45 years of age liable to the draft, but military service could be avoided by payment of $300 or by procuring a substitute to enlist for three years.
** Sarah Van Vechten's father was a minister, and no doubt the family kept Sunday rather strictly.

of Methodist persuasion, whose labors since his capture by the rebels and his exchange has been spent at Camp <u>Parole</u> (where the parole soldiers are taken and kept till they are exchanged) gave me a not very sanguine account of his doings there, but more satisfactory than any chaplain I have met. He has been a laborer among the Indians and he is thereby better qualified than most men to come down to the rough usages of this life and mingle with the boys and "show by their lives and conversation the holy gospel they profess." By so doing the fruits are immediate as his statement of it was. He acted for officer in conducting the men and furnishing them with food, enabling and assisting them in the same way as a commissioned officer while they, as they usually do, follow their own sensual pleasures, leaving their men to get along as best they can.

It wants a man who can sacrifice comfort, submit to all rough usages of war, do acts which no one will appreciate and are expected of him, to do all this without the proper courtesy from those we are obliged to look up to and acknowledge as superiors, to do this requires more inate [sic] goodness than is common in human nature, and which very few possess.

How our friend Isaac Kip will succeed it is very difficult to tell.* I know he will be often disheartened, and should he come out of it, [it] will be of vast benefit to him. So far everything goes on smoothly and pleasantly and I hope it ever may go on so, and it would ill become me to throw anything in the way to mar his Christian enterprise, and I hope he may receive such an inspiration of the only true source of strength to support him and avoid the shoals that make many shipwreck. Not only he, but all that persevere to live a consistent life in camp.

It seems the course of events which is now leading the country, and in which in the past two years (next April) we have been involved and which even now is more dark and uncertain than then, is conclusive proof of the inability of individuals and the people to receive the blessings of peace without the smiles of the Great Governor of Nations. Is there a soul so corrupt, so dead to all the great blessings of this life, whose soul does not <u>throb</u> with the great convulsions now going on in the country, even should he not bear a hand, but not give us his well wishes for our success, [he] forever

---

* Isaac Kip was a young minister. He was probably a chaplain.

should be spurned from the community and [*deemed*] unworthy of a <u>man</u>.

    I must close this long letter, supposing you are tired of reading it.
        With love to all   From your Cousin   R. T. Van Wyck

                                       March 11th

[*Dear Mother,*]
    I was interrupted last evening and obliged to finish this morning. The news–Heavy marching orders–it stands one in need to keep cool, for it is probably only a <u>ruse</u>. It requires one being in the service six months or more to sift truth out of so much deception. Camp stories are fairy tales. The Col. says he is doing all in his power to remain <u>here</u>, and is opposed to going in the field just at present. There is nothing going on or interesting, with this exception. I think Robt. should not now regret having embraced the opportunity and come down when <u>Allard</u> came. I should think he is old enough to assume the responsibility and come down without an <u>escort</u>.

    An amusing case came under my view last week. A friend having been detailed as clerk in Col. Belger's Quarter Master Gen. and required to dress in citizen's clothes, suddenly disappeared one morning for home, remained there about a week and returned, reported he had been "just about here." In the meanwhile, the Col. B was under court marshal [*sic*] and no one knew of his absence but his Capt. Yesterday he told me about it. He said he was prepared to go to Ft. McHenry.* But it is a good game well <u>played</u>.

    The excitement has died away and a battalion drill is the order of exercises. This is an exciting life, I assure you. Geo. Burroughs has been suffering from a slight attack of the lungs–cold, etc., but is now better. The general health of the Regt. is good, and every one is in good spirits.

    My clothes have not arrived, if they are not completed when Father goes to the Landing; he may let them remain on his hands. I am under no great <u>stress</u> for them, and could get along without them altogether. Much love to all and expect to hear from you soon from
            Your affectionate Son   R. T. Van Wyck
I have received a letter from Uncle Anthony. He says he has been delivering a course of five lectures upon his travels for the benefit of Soldiers, and hoping that ultimately they will make him known

---

* Military prison.

as a writer and lecturer and thereby make it pay. I hope he may succeed.

To Mr. Robt Johnston

Belger Barracks, Balt.
March 10th, 1863

Dear Friend

Your letter was truly welcomed. Since I first wrote you, soon after my arrival and my last to you, from Camp Bradford, guarding some drafted men, it has been on my mind several times to write you, upon the signs of the times. But fearful my letter would not meet with a response, so meager of interesting matter. Indeed! You have only to look at the direction of the paper I sent you, to perceive how bungling I execute such matters, although it does revive old associations to get one from you.

In the meanwhile the political and national horizon has been portentious [*sic*] of great things. The defeat of [*Gen.*] Burnside* and the November election at home. Of the latter, your construction is the true one to be taken of it, but the army would have it otherwise, as it has been so widely circulated by the Democratic party, with the ever to be hoped for, and never obtained, glad tidings of <u>Peace</u>. But where or in what respect, can such a conclusion be drawn, with the Union Army defeated or a strong enemy in front constantly threatening us, is more than I could conceive. Then comes the Negro question and the Proclamation with almost the whole soldiery opposed, including some of the officers. This however is merely a pretext for the homesick, though they are willing to fight for the Constitution, but not for the Negro now (as they term it). I should say if you could see them handle a negro, you would suspect <u>that</u> was their mission here in arms—to forever extinct [*sic*] the race and settle the question politically.

Again the corruption of the army is got to be so self-evident and proverbial a fact that even a private does not stand in fear of reproof, in stating in the presence of officers that they (the officers) came because it paid well. Also implying they were good Union when it paid well—and the contrary the reverse. This also is the sentiment

---

* After Gen. Burnside's overwhelming defeat at Fredericksburg on December 13, he was replaced on January 15, 1863, by Gen. Joseph Hooker.

of the rank and file, the $13 a month and $150 bounty. The regular army, the first to get the positions in the army on the commencement of the rebellion and being steeped in corruption, gave their influence to those of the like as themselves; consequently a person having the venery [sic] of a knave or the spice of a rascal his promotion is sure, and never in no instance except they are great outlaws, meet with a reduction or dismissal. This principle is in operation here to some extent.

Many thanks for your kindness in effecting my promotion through the Col.'s friends at home. No, I still believe the intention of the Col. is honest, but is so besieged with a lot of "thumb suckers" whose cry constantly is "position, position." But he will never find me a worshiper at his <u>shrine</u>. The Capt. demonstrates great friendship, and said he tried and endeavored to get me the Left., but the commission was given to the Sergeant Major, a gentleman and one whom, of all others, I much prefer. The Col. is good for a Brig. Gen. When that time arrives there will be a chance for a commission. We are brigaded–and commanded by Gen. Briggs.

Jacob G. Montross is now promoted to <u>Corporal</u> (the same as myself) he says "that had he stayed away from Camp oftener and been put in the guard house a few more times" he would have assumed that position before.

Geo. Burroughs (say nothing of this) is as sick of it as he was sanguine before enlistment. His health has not been good lately. The Regulation so positively affirms that black is black and white is white, which is construed black for white, etc.–so much like the Jewish construction of the moral law.

But you are tired of this. An engagement often separates the chaff from the genuine. What effect it will make in this case remains to be seen. How much you told me is so true, relating to the management of things, and I look back on my verdancy last fall as quite ridiculous.

Lossing's* superficial estimation of the officers while they were away upon guard duty in the city is sufficient of itself to condemn him. Still more the desertions that followed pay-day, was still another proof of his ignorance. I might be fortunate to be sent officially to Dutchess Co. The chance is good for me if anything turns up but I wish my friends at home would know nothing of it. A furlough is an

---

* See page 70.

impossibility. You quite revived my horse fever again. I wish I could drive that sorrel colt a few times this summer. He goes so honest. Anything that combines that virtue in their composition, looks very large in my eye, <u>now</u>.

Remember me to your Mother and all at home. Something will turn up soon, I firmly believe, from your afft friend,

R. T. Van Wyck

Belger Barracks, Balt.
March 16th, 1863

Dear Cousin [*Sarah*]

Today has been the termination of one of the March snow storms. Of course the snow makes it unpleasant for drilling; and the day has been somewhat tedious and has given me somewhat of a homesick feeling. This is nothing new for me, however, as you can bear witness from some of my past letters of a prevalence of the <u>peculiar</u> feeling. The antidote is usually a letter home.

I do not agree with you wholly in the interpretation of that hackneyed and much abused word, patriotism. Indeed, it seems one should give now, a special investigation of this subject should he intend to <u>soldier</u>; the many conflicting opinions as regard the object in view and the selfish, corrupt motives of the inducement offered, would make it of questionable character, and should finally rest in the truth and character of the person. I do not know whether it is a commendable act to volunteer, and should receive the compliments of such disinterested public feeling with considerable feeling of scrutiny. So you think, I suppose. I intend getting Mr. Lane's opinions on war matters, by which means some conclusion of the home feeling I can thereby draw. Do not think I am desponding upon my position.

Again the Pay Master has visited us with the Green Backs. We might style ourselves the paying Regt., so punctual has our dues been allowed to us. The thirteen dollars is a trivial sum, hardly giving us the extras of rations, and requires considerable frugality in its expenditure; but still sufficient. As long as it comes punctual as it has done I am satisfied.

You are enjoying yourself down in the city, visiting, shopping, etc. My particular friend, whom I mentioned in Anna's* letter, you

---

* Sarah's sister.

will condole with her in her bereavement, on my account. My inability to do so in person rests in a higher power than my own will or inclination, for Uncle <u>Sam</u> seldom allows us to leave his protecting arm, as long as we are serviceable to him. Consequently without an detached duty, my absence this Summer will be one of necessity.

I have not much new to write you except to acknowledge the receipt of the news from home. It seems a one-sided affair, and could I make the information, upon matters of interest here more compensation to you, my failure to give to letters what I could give verbally, is my only excuse.

At present there is no indication of a change in our arrangements here. It wouldn't grieve me much if we should remain here till the season is settled and then the field would not be objectionable. My letter to Anna comprises all this. Give my love to Aunt Susan, etc. I remain your afft. cousin

R. T. Van Wyck

To Van Wyck Van Vechten

Belger Barracks, Balt.
March 24th, 1863

Dear Cousin,

It may be I am in your debt for a letter, or it might be the other way, I have quite forgotten which. At any rate, it is a matter of little consequence knowing you are usually very busy, while my uniform leisure should make up the difference in correspondence.

We are much about the same here, and nothing new in the regular routine of duty, etc. In looking at the papers that is the case all over: "All noise and no wool." Since Sunday the Ninth Army Corps were passing through Baltimore in rought [*route*] for Rosecrans* in the west. They showed much roughness in exterior but were very humorous, jovial. The Cavalry and Artillery horses were rough and poor beyond description. The boys upon them say "they are iron-plated, gotten up purposely for the rebels." It might be something of this sort, poor subjects of military skill like ourselves, that they are trying to discipline to perfection, to live upon air. The specimens of

---

* Gen. William Rosecrans's Army of the Cumberland, which had defeated the Confederate Braxton Bragg's Army of Tennessee at Murfreesboro in December 1862, was now trying to oust Bragg from Chattanooga.

that race down South are much better, for they subsist upon Hope and consequently have more spirit. So you see, we will fear no Stuart's Cavalry after our horses arrive upon that ingredient.

Well, the Conscripts Act will soon have to be tested. Will it be put in force in the city? The Democratic influence will operate against it. I wish, should there be a call, I had some Democratic friend in N. Y. City, who would recommend me to Gov. Seymour for an appointment in the Drafted men, as Commissioned officer. I feel myself sufficiently qualified to take that position and could bring excellent proof, etc., from the Colonel at any time.

My Republican influence at home would not help my cause in that quarter. Do you hear of any commissions for sale or anything in that way? If so, I wish you would write me about it. If this war is going to last forever, I don't see but what it would be better for <u>me</u> to look out for No. 1. And, if I have appeared to have too much of a tendency that way, I have inhaled some of the spirit from the "Patriotic" army, whose honesty everyone <u>knows</u>.

I hope we will blunder through the troubles of war and war itself after a while. If not, the "wipt [*whipped*] spaniel" instead of the "Bald Eagle" should be our standard, and [*we*] deserve to be swept from the face of the Earth ... for instead of men we are "chickens."

Give my love to all, and write soon about the signs of the times so that I may have my "platter up."

From your Aft. Cousin
R. T. Van Wyck

Belger Barracks, Balt.
March 28, 1863

Dear Mother,

I received your letter today. I do not know whether I can suitably apologize for my blueness [*which*] I manifested so strongly in my last letter. But ... everything has blown over, a boil which has made me half sick has relieved me from suffering [*and*] I am happy to say I am in better spirits now.

I know my friends you mentioned comment upon my station here from the best of interests, and it was the unhappy reflection over how I could better myself and whether my friends I had counted upon here were true to me: all this set me thinking, and if you will allow me to take back my last resolve I will tell you what I have done.

I saw the Adjutant to [*find out*] what could be done in getting a commission among the drafted men. [*I saw*] the Colonel, who first treated me with very cool civility which set me thinking over my past action to further his interest while recruiting at home. [*He was*] then very friendly and demonstrative, but now since he has me securely in his grasp he just treated me with great disdain. I left him and went to my bunk, feeling keenly the unmasked friendship now so apparent for the first time.

Were I not constrained to go to that Friend whose friendship is never warped by interest, and who has taught us to come to Him when all others forsake us, I might have made some rash resolve of satisfaction, but the morning came and with it a call to go to the Col.[*onel*]'s. He then wished me to state what I wanted, which was an inquiry as to the expedience of an effort in getting an appointment among the drafted men. He was upon the eve of starting home, and also to Albany. He gave me to understand he would do what he could there for me, and said my friends at home could do more to get the appointment than he could.

Accordingly I wrote to Allard at ten-thirty, and also to Van Wyck V. Vechten in N. Y. The latter I received a letter from today giving me great encouragement of succeeding in finding among his friends an opening for a bonus or an appointment in the conscripts. The Col.'s manner is unaccountable to me, but as long as he came around it's all right again. Again since then, there is to be an examination of the officers of the Regt. as to their competency. This is making quite a talk amongst them. I could suggest a remedy for these difficulties and quarrels – more active service and [*moving*] further away from Baltimore. I don't feel so very sanguine as to my ultimate success – but then it might be a step in the right direction, and as to the Sergeantcy [*sic*], I would be doing more of the officers' dirty work, which reasons I gave you in my last [*letter*].

The box of J. Montross came to hand last Monday. Jacob said they must send a box of pills the next one, as he thought so much of it he was obliged to call in the Doctor. I was obliged for the things you sent me. We made out after a while what that prepared article was, especially after a trial. We found it fine.

You have obtained some [*news*] of Aunt Margaret's Western experience. I hope her health is not impaired by it. If she is still at Fishkill give my love to her and [*the*] children–and accept this as an apology for my last letter, written in a blue state of mind. Hoping never to have a recurrence of the same, and if you will please to remain quiet upon what I have written, much love to all

From your aff't Son
R. T. Van Wyck

To Sarah E. Van Vechten
    care of Mr. Rob't Lane
    215 E. 10th Street
    New York, N.Y.

Belger Barracks, Balt.
March 31st, 1863

Dear Cousin,

I regret not having answered your letter before. This does not appear to be an eventful Spring to us, as a Regt., so far. But I hope as Summer approaches I can have the pleasure of giving you something interesting. Our everyday life you have heard repeatedly in my many letters home. Some rumour of going to Fort Monroe or Western Virginia or somewhere else puts one in a fever. But I have learned to take things quietly and it must be an extraordinary report that moves me and which has more confirmation than the fiction takes in Camp.

When we glance at our position thus far, we have reason to feel fortunate in our comfortable quarters and near to mail and city privileges, and too far distant from danger to sicken the faint-hearted, and hav[ing] the bright side of soldiering constantly in view, not to make us sick of and disgusted with it.

I might suppose you are enjoying in the city "tea drinks," first in one place and then in another, visiting Central Park to see style and beauties of artificial scenery, and finally limiting yourself to a walk down Broadway daily to see the fashions and dress – that last [an] all-absorbing topic with you ladies.

I must admit my own incompetency to give you a report of the like or dislike of the Spring styles in Baltimore. But you may decide yet upon New York as the center of this particular interest to you, for as long as there is an Army and gold in Wall Street to back it, we can yet conclude that it is the end of all things on this Continent.

By the by, that word dress has a very significant thought of that never-ceasing "Dress Parade," at which time we are exhibited by the officers. They dress in broadcloth and epaulets – to an admiring throng of the fair sex. This "tomfoolery" has so disgusted me so much, in dress which any "flunky" can don himself, that were the truth told the officers are better pleased to excel the rebels in dressing than in fighting.

Well, we have plain sailing now in our National affairs and we hope to press the rebels to the wall before anything else turns up. Much love to all in the city, I remain,

Your Afft. cousin,
R. T. Van Wyck

Write soon.

Belger Barracks, Balt.
April 4th, 1863

Dear Mother,

Your letter was received today and was gladly welcomed. I can say I feel much better than formerly, in every particular. And wonder I could be so sensitive to the "cold shoulder" of the world. Well – it is all past, and with it, I hope some experience [gained]. Like the days of yesterday and the preceding [if] one forgets the past winter or the soft summerlike pleasantness of yesterday, one is ill-prepared for the unseasonable cold bleakness of the day. So in life, starting with buoyant spirits, scouting the idea of despondency one moment, almost ready to succumb to gloom the next, is enough to learn us that "one Summer day does not make the Summer," and were we not stung occasionally by hollow friendship we would not know how to appreciate the genuine.

I did not ask Col. Ketcham to give me a Commission in this Regt. in my interview with him, or with an inducement of money offered. But was trying to avail myself of his unusual political sagacity to enable me to proceed to work to get one (for I know there will be many opportunities) and more particularly to test his interest for me, should he know of an appointment [for which] to voluntarily recommend me. This is the gist of the matter; all I am confident he will do, and all I expect to obtain from him: to recommend me for an appointment in the Conscriptions or elsewhere, when I can find a vacancy. But I have heard nothing further in the matter than what I last wrote you. I have little hope to do anything in Dutchess Co. through Allard Anthony, but Van Wyck in New York has given me some hope to succeed. All this the future will determine.

Just at present I am enjoying myself here famously. The Regt. is now detached upon guard duty in the city and elsewhere. Our Company is on the RailRoad a few miles from camp. I go down to see the boys, to take [*them*] their letters, they are in squadrons of eight men each, at four small manufacturing villages, a mile or more apart, making 32 men in all. They are quartered in vacated houses and are much pleased. I remain in camp and do about as I please.

Today, went down to the fishing ground out in the bay, to see what the prospects for fishing were, and found the season did not commence till next month. So if we are here I will go down quite often. Returning, stopped in the market and caught, not with silver hook, but [*with*] "Papier Machier" as they term it here, some fine Pike which I gave to the cook for tomorrow's breakfast.

I can imagine the pleasure the visit of Aunt Margaret gave you. I am sorry that it had so sudden a termination. She returns to seclude herself from the world again; if to Kenosha not quite as bad as the farm.

If you have [*an*] opportunity to send me four woolen shirts, two of fine white thin woven texture for undershirts: the other two of flannel plaid of light color, not <u>red</u> if avoidable, and that will not fade. Either made to order or of very large size if ready-made. This will constitute my summer arrangement, if it does not give you any trouble to send to me by express, enclosed in strong wrapping paper.

You must write me, and <u>perhaps</u> I will do as well as I can here. I would like very much indeed to spend if only a few hours to talk about matters which I cannot express upon paper. How soon that happy day arrives no one knows. How had Daniel been this winter? When I go out in the country it always reminds me of the old farm and [*I wonder*] how they all are. Give my love to all at the other house* and at home. I remain your affectionate Son,

R. T. Van Wyck

Belger Barracks, Balt.
Apr. 13th, 1863

Dear Mother,

Your letter came yesterday. I was pleased to hear of the transfixing events you gave me in your letter. Also was sorry to hear that

---

* The "other house" is the Van Vechten homestead, situated near his own father's house.

Father has the symptoms of his former complaint. The unpleasant Spring is very inductive of the disease which has prevailed quite extensively in Camp. Our Second Left. (the one promoted) has not been out of his room in four weeks, part of which time he has required very careful nursing; all owing to night exposure returning from a <u>Ball</u> down in the City—taking cold settled in his limbs and rendered him helpless.

I received a letter from Uncle Van Vechten* a few days ago saying, "You probably have heard that I have been something of an invalid since early in January. My bronchial difficulty is very much affected by colds." I infer from this that the "Other House" is as usual turned into a Hospital or has not altered from being the home of sympathetic invalids.

Van Wyck writes me to know if Cavalry would be agreeable to me, saying that openings would offer more readily in that than any other branch of the service. This encouraging information was very unexpected to me; although my schooling has been in infantry, my habits, taste, etc., have been the other way, and I am sanguine of being competent to fill a Lieutenancy in some newly organized Cavalry Regt.

Robt. Johnston writes me [*asking*] what I anticipate doing, getting out of the 150th Regt. if practicable. I have written him what Van Wyck has informed me, and I await his opinion about it. I don't think it is my duty to stay here if I can do better elsewhere. Don't you think so? I believe you have answered that question before in your wonderment at my refusing the sergeantcy [*sic*] in Co. K, which is called a promotion.

I hope something will turn up favorable. My course so far has been a good deal like the Grape Vine (speaking egotistically) for it is never allowed to get much top till the roots are able to maintain the fruit and wood properly. And it might be just so again in this instance [*that*] my failure to obtain this appointment or get a commission will only stimulate me the more not to stay put and be sandwiched with beer-drinking Dutchmen and etc., while their crafty cunning will teach me many important lessons in Human Nature, very essential in the position I have in view.

---

* Rev. Samuel Van Vechten, Sarah's father.

The news from Charleston* is the same old song, "a failure." The only way now left for us is to build a wall around them and starve them out. We have now a fence of bayonets and our only hope [*is that*] it will have the desired effect after a while. Gen. Butler's speech is the best thing that has happened. He is not a half-dead-and-alive man.

I will write to Rachel. Give my love to all from your Afft. Son

R. T. Van Wyck

Belger Barracks, Balt.
Apr. 17th, 1863

Dear Mother,

I received your letter today upon my return from visiting the boys upon the Railroad. Do not put yourself to much trouble about those shirts. The large ones will not be too large, as they are of wool and will shrink – and as they are they will be more comfortable than if they were a close fit. I had more regard to length than to breadth, as my previous ones were somewhat curtailed. The undershirts you can do as you see fit about, either one kind or the other, I am not very particular.

You might also send a doz. paper collars of No. 15 1/2 and a necktie. I have said that as long as we eat upon tin I will bid adieu to white linen. I have carried this out with two exceptions since leaving home. But during the Summer months it will protect my neck from the sun and will make amends for my appearance when my coat is off, etc.

I have nothing new to write you. My last letter, which you have not received, will give you the idea I have in mind of getting out of the 150th Regt. and getting into the Cavalry as a Lft. – that is, if the prospects are anything like what Van Wyck writes me. I am looking for a letter from him every day about it. If this thing can be consummated I will have the pleasure of seeing him once more, at any rate, and will ameliorate my situation considerably. I can do nothing more than hope, trusting my friends will embrace any opportunity to assist me or as I can suggest to them.

---

* In 1863 the Union began naval attacks on Fort Sumter in Charleston harbor and kept the city under continual siege for the next two years, but failed to capture it until February 1865, when Gen. Sherman forced the city's evacuation.

Remember me to Aunt Mary, whose letter I will answer when any material offers to make a letter interesting; and also to GrandMother. – with much love I remain your Affectionate Son

R. T. Van Wyck

Belger Barracks, Balt..
April 20th, 1863

Dear Father,

It has been a long time since I have addressed you personally, but presuming you have appropriated my letters home to yourself as [*well as*] the person to whom written.

From Mother I learn you have been spending a few days in New York. And you have heard from Van Wyck something in regard to my making an effort to get out of the enlisted ranks and strive to get Left., either in the drafted men's or in some volunteer Regt., Cavalry or infantry. I didn't wish you to feel that I have become unhappily circumstanced; or that the novelty "to go as a soldier" has worn off and unmasked the state of affairs, as I sometimes have given you illustrations. No, I think I quite anticipated the personal sacrifices before coming and now, by time, have become insensible to the unpleasantness and found out how to enjoy myself and make myself contented.

The idea that my <u>practical</u> experience would capacitate me to take a position now, which my timidity and inexperience refrained me from while at home, has prompted me to make an attempt in this direction. In writing to Van Wyck (as he has told you) I spoke of a <u>bonus</u> or a sum of money given to one entitled by the No. of men enlisted, to a Commission; which often such people sell for the expenses of recruiting, and who are not competent for like trust.

The sum of money which Robt. Johnston said could be afforded to be paid for said commission, and which he said he would advance if I would let him, was $500, and which is cleared from the monthly pay in less than six months. The expenses, including the purchase of said Commission and necessary expenses, would certainly amount to this sum, if not exceed it. And should my life be spared that length of time, or the war does not terminate within that time, would make the cash account balance–perhaps. The monthly pay is equivalent to $105 a month.

I know you have some trouble in your own pecuniary affairs to manage and arrange without giving yourself mine to manage. And I do not feel disposed to accept Robert's proposition to loan me that sum without the consent of my friends. What are GrandFather's ideas? Or could he be induced to do this for me?

I wish you would write me about it, and you may mention it to him if you think best. I wrote to Van Wyck to do this for me and should I be unsuccessful in getting the money I will countermand the instructions I gave him. If the draft does not take effect I do not hope to succeed without the "needful."

In the meanwhile I remain your Afft. Son

R. T. Van Wyck

P. S. If I hear from Van Wyck I will write you. And if he should find an opening for me, will let you know.

Belger Barracks, Balt.
April 25th 1863

Dear Father,

I received your letter today. I feel thankful to you for so readily granting my request. I have communicated to Van Wyck the necessary instructions, hoping it will result in the object in view. By no means do I think it will make my path the smoother or [that] I will thereby avoid the rough places of this life; but besides my personal health, which will be less sacrificed, the new change of life will throw me into a different sphere of society now impossible to enter [and] will thereby improve my general information, which now is very limited.

The young horse, if running out, perhaps does not look much like [in] selling order, but to those who know him is a matter of little consequence. The man at Five Corners (S. Hemel) [?] has an exalted opinion about that stock, [thinking] their worth to be some five or six hundred dollars. But I think him to be worth at least three hundred, because the necessary exhaustion of this property by the army will eventually make it high and you are not forced to sell him; in the meanwhile he is improving. Why not sell the bay horse?

I hope to get home sometime in May on furlough and then we can talk more about it. I notice the great upward tendency of beef. I hope you have a good stock on hand that you have wintered: if you have, you are very fortunate. I suppose Mr. Briggs* is on the farm

---

* His father's tenant farmer.

yet. He must be somewhat troubled about his son Charles being liable to military duty.

If I should be so fortunate as to get a furlough <u>before</u> the middle of May I will be in need of perhaps ten dollars travelling expenses. After that, I can refund it to you, as our payday takes place just about the 15th. Hoping to hear from you soon I remain your afft.

Son
R. T. Van Wyck

Belger Barracks, Balt.
May 13th 1863

Dear Mother,

I arrived here this morning. I have been more successful thus far in the city than I expected. I have secured a position as second Lieutenant in Col. Henry F. Liebenan's Regt., called the First Seymour Light Infantry, Headquarters, 491 Broadway. The Regt. is not [yet] full and consequently my commission will be necessarily delayed some months, but I am endeavoring by getting the influence of certain parties, including Col. Ketcham, to effect my muster out [so] that I can give my personal attention to it. And [it] will give me an opportunity to take a vacation before going into service again. I am not so sanguine of immediately getting released from duty, for matters of this kind take a long time to have the matter go through the necessary form, even if all were right.

I had the pleasure of seeing Fred last Monday night and [he] was with me till I went off in the cars last night [for return by train to Camp Belger].

The foliage is more farther advanced than at Fishkill and the sun and heat so penetrating [that] to get in the shade of the trees [is] a great luxury.

Nothing new in Camp has turned up since my absence except the visit from the Pay Master with the Green Backs. Hoping to hear from you soon I remain your Afft. Son

R. T. Van Wyck

Belger Barracks, Balt.
May 20th 1863

Dear Mother,

I received yours yesterday. My placid, smooth course of life was disturbed by a new order from "H" Quarters to regulate the drill, duties, etc. We have <u>reveille</u> at 4 o'clock in the morning, breakfast at half-past five, drill at six for an <u>hour</u>, after which, till four o'clock in the afternoon we can spend as best suits us. And we retire from eight to nine. This is easy enough but [it] is somewhat troublesome to get up so early in the morning.

Did you receive that pamphlet of the Army of the Potomac? It seems to be a fair statement of the possible result of that move, and a successful one, if the plans had not been altered by the War Department. But such are his views from a McClellan side of the war. Otherwise he describes everything so beautifully without going into detail, which always makes these accounts tiresome and uninteresting. What food for the future historian in all forms, from the small pamphlet to large volumes. But the trouble is, not one of the present generation will ever appreciate them, as the newspapers are as sure to depict our blunders as our successes and it leaves no pleasant emotion in the mind.

You have possibly seen that editorial in the Richmond *Inquirer*, copied into the daily New York papers. This shows to some extent the seeming policy of the North, and to them by no means flattering.

I don't know how that matter in New York will result. I have secured a promise of this Commission, and were I there in person to attend to it, [it] would be well enough. And so far as the influence of the Col. of the Regt. at the present condition of the Regt. itself, my chances are as good as anyone's into it: none of them have received their commissions yet. But the Regiment may fall through and all go to smash. But I hope for the influence of certain parties to free myself from the <u>ranks</u>, after which I can decide and arrange that matter to better advantage. I can also receive a commission while here, which will liberate me from this duty also. However, it will turn out for the best which[ever] way it assumes. And now I almost wish I had spent my time at home rather than in New York. But I haven't heard of the matter since I left. Perhaps it will come out right after all.

With much love I remain   Your afft. Son   R. T. Van Wyck

Belger Barracks, Balt.
May 25th 1863

Dear Mother,

I am uncertain whether your last letter has been answered. At any rate, it is a matter of little consequence to be so formal, inasmuch as it is a good improvement of <u>my</u> time to write two for one, so much do I appreciate and value your letters.

We have learned from experience not to trust or anticipate our successes, gleaned from the papers, but this morning the Capture of Vicksburg seems too undoubted not to credit this great achievement.* By it, the West is released to open through the Mississippi river the only outlet for its products, and by it the Rebels are cut asunder and deprived from the source of their supplies in the Southwest.

Still Bragg confronts Rosecrans, but <u>he</u>, finding nothing to contend for and being harrassed[*sic*] in [*the*] <u>rear</u> by Grant, will be obliged to retire into the interior. If we could be so successful as the Western Army, we would be safe to conclude that the great struggle is ended, but alas! – our repeated failure in this quarter gives us the only hope by the march of the victorious army towards the seaboard, to finish the war, which we all hope and pray <u>may be.</u>

My affairs in New York, Van Wyck writes me, are progressing finely. The only obstacle in the way now is to assure the Governor that the company to which I am to be attached already contains forty men; that is to satisfy the authorities [*that*] the organization is commencing in good faith. To this, I am in the dark, but which I think Van Wyck can arrange with the Colonel and which can be easily adjusted.

The weather has been hot and sultry, to which we have become highly sensitive, particularly in exercising in the middle of the day, but as I wrote you last, our division of time obviates this difficulty.

Dear Mother, for me to "be ready to give an answer to every man that asketh you a <u>reason</u> of the hope that is in you with meekness and fear," to do this with an influence beneficial to those around and associated with me, is of all things what I most earnestly pray for. And yet how futile any endeavor of my own, if I am not imbued with Power from on High, that the spiritual graces so beautifully delineated in 1st Peter 1 Ch., may be delightfully entertained in my mind and grounded by faith in my heart and purpose. Were I not assured and encouraged by all the promises and helps granted us in the Gospel to live a truly Christian life: my own insufficiency to express in my conversation these so soul-absorbing truths is so very apparent, I would

---

* It wasn't until July 4th, nearly six weeks later, that Vicksburg finally fell before Gen. Grant and his converging Union armies.

despair, but no one knows but those who have "tasted that the Lord is gracious," can value the serene, calm, contented mind which is consequent upon His truth, mercy, and grace granted to all who call upon Him.

And when I observe the poor, distressed, and depraved men about me who know nothing of this <u>Peace</u> but whose ideas of contentment is the phisical [sic] stupor of liquor; could they but know of this other Peace to make them fitted for this life, and the one to come; to keep them in the path of virtue, and upon <u>Whom</u> they will find a Friend to <u>lean</u> upon amidst all the trials and dangers of life; to such, then, how unspeakably dear the religion of our Saviour is to them, if they would accept it. Such might have been my course had I not been constrained by His love. Our Chaplain narrated of a Missionary society, whose motto is: Expect great things for Christ and expect great things <u>from</u> Him. This is the hope of the <u>army</u>. And in all such success in <u>life</u>, we must aim high and never despair of success, and never cease our exertions.

Excuse this long letter–hoping to hear from you soon, I am your

Afft. Son

R. T. Van Wyck

P. S.   I think that commission appears somewhat definite and if you do not think it too presumptuous I would like to order a suit of clothes costing about forty ($40) dollars in Baltimore.

R. T. V. W.

Belger Barracks, Balt.
May 27th 1863

Dear Cousin [Sarah]

Do not apologize for your letters, I beg of you, for it gives me very gloomy appreciation of my own.

Letters are a good substitute for personal attention: but for the love of it, and to say I prefer this method of transmitting ideas, you are much mistaken to think I am, except in that <u>particular</u> case mentioned in my last letter, which I don't think I would be so apt to extend the boundary of propriety in that case by this way as by any other.

What thinks you about it?

My laboring under a dearth of ideas, as you see, makes this appear ridiculous, but I cannot write anything new in the way of incidents here–our situation is so very monotonous.

There is one thing, however, I intend doing and that is: to have some photographs taken and have you to exchange the one distributed about the country.

Don't think I show some vanity about it, but as long as I am insisted to be made a member of a photographic album they might as well have one that makes me out a great deal better than the original, as one that is already truthful.

I will be home during the summer, I hope, but how soon I do not know. But I am always glad to hear what is going on. Love to all, I remain

Your Afft. Cousin
R. T. Van Wyck

P. S. You have taken many rides on the new horse, I suppose. The ladies down here ride a great deal and look splendidly upon horseback.

Belger Barracks, Balt.
June 3rd 1863

Dear Mother

I received your letter today. I answered it so immediately because nothing else to do. The situation of Suydam Van Wyck's property is in a much worse state than I anticipated when heard from it while home. His children will not suffer from this misfortune, I presume, but will tend to reduce their pride, perhaps. T. V. W. Brinckerhoff will look more serious than usual when talked to about Western enterprises now, since this has happened. What thinks you? Think it an assignment for a <u>purpose</u> or one of necessity?* You know he was never known to make a blunder.

I wish I could make an assignment with as little conscientious scruples as some people, to clear me of my indebtedness to U. S. A. I mean a temporary one. But in view of such contingency, it leaves a forfeiture of honor, principle, but little chance of success.

But why should I talk thus when the 150th is destined to spend the pleasant summer months in, and in the vicinity of, this great metropolis; whose band discoursed its melodious strains to throngs of visitors in the Park amid the plaudit of the enthusiastic Baltimoreans, while the echo comes to us in ten thousand different

---

* The transfer of Suydam Van Wyck's property title to someone else.

ways and shapes, that our Regiment is a good "institution," a "Big thing," a "fortunate location by our Col.," "out of harm's way" also of the Rebels, and finally ending in the query "who wouldn't go for a soldier?"

Admitted that circumstances have greatly tempered our warlike intentions and have quite favorably changed our course of thought, but then why not have remained at home? But no, we are patriotic, but the heroism of Malvern Hill, of Fredericksburg, of Antietam, is too much of a Pill for our nerves, and we take it diluted, with the pleasurable reminiscences of Baltimore.

My expression, [*that*] I can also receive a commission while here, was intended to say that this commission in view, or any other, could transfer me from this without the intervention of the War department, which a favorable influence of the Governor would authorize. But without this, a Commission in hand is the next step. I could not obtain one <u>here</u>. The Regt. has not a sufficient number of men now to fill vacancies should they occur provided everything else would be favorable. As to my prospects in New York I know nothing except what Van Wyck writes respecting which: "I hasten to say that everything seems to be in that train which I think approaches success. <u>It seems a question of time</u>.* If this fails I have another matter in view, just discovered this morning. Be assured I will watch for your interests in this matter until accomplished, unless a direct Providential indication precludes all further effort."

Love to all, I remain
Your Son
R. T. Van Wyck

*Not like the taking of Richmond, I hope.

Belger Barracks, Balt.
June 4th 1863

Dear Cousin [*Sarah*]

I received your letter yesterday. You are very likely counting upon the approaching nuptials in the village. Events of this kind are of such pleasing rarity; if not usually heralded by the many for months and years [*they*] would take the marriageable men with a depressed feeling, and even surprise the many envious ladies, of which Fishkill has a few; whereas by the Providential procrastination of this long looked-for pleasure and happiness by the interested parties, outsiders have dismissed the subject from their thoughts, and but for attention by way of example and a reminder to be present at the ceremony, we all thought it settled long ago. How lucky for me to be here in Baltimore out of the web and maze of attendant gayeties [*sic*] which this event will inaugurate, which I have always thought useless and trivial, causing much "noise and no wool" and resulting in no new marriages.

It would be well to suggest and enforce this prerogative, that no more celebrations be allowed, if not resulting in the beneficial influence above stated.

I quite like the summary way of managing this <u>delicate</u> matter, as they do it here. They have all the amusement previous to it, whereupon the <u>bride</u> is brought in camp as a new recruit, a willing subject to military discipline, feeling perfectly at home, and some taking to it as to the manor born. Like that Lieut. Col.'s matrimonial arrangement, who did it quite as methodically as if laid down in Army Regulations. No furloughs or leaf [*sic*] of absence granted to the newly married, and their traveling must be confined to within one mile of camp.

I must mention a little gossip of a certain private commonly called Lieut. <u>Low,</u> a nephew of Gil Deen of Po'keepsie, who had made himself very acceptable as the adorer of a certain young lady living near the camp in a fine mansion, said to be worth considerable property. He has a good thing of it in this way: he is detailed as hospital attendant, which [*hospital*] just now is vacant, but if occupied he is the recipient of dinners of choice luxuries, including champagne, wines, etc., or if unoccupied they go out riding, driven by a negro in livery in great style. Of late he spends most of his time at the house, and Madam Rumor says they will shortly be married. But how true this may be, he is said to be on the same terms of intimacy with several <u>ladies</u> at home. Do you know him?

The inference from this long letter is that you may have a nice time at the village, that you will not let this opportunity go misimproved [*sic*], that expecting but not having received a formal invitation to be present, yet I volunteer my heartfelt congratulations upon this important event to them, then and throughout life, and also congratulate myself on my absence from Fishkill.

With much love, I remain your

Afft. Cousin

R. T. Van Wyck

P. S. Strawberries are abundant. We have had them a couple of weeks. They cost us eight cents a quart, and will be much less soon.

To Mrs. James Van Wyck
Politeness of Geo. Burroughs

Belger Barracks, Balt.
June 10th 1863

Dear Mother:

So far the week is spent without bringing me your usual letter. I am fearing you may have taken exception to my frivolous apology to support the vanity I suggested. But hoping you have both destroyed the letter and discarded it from your mind, and in future rest assured I will give you no uneasiness on that point.

I might recapitulate the often said truth [*that*] we are safe here; as yet no disposition is made favorable to expose us, but the very reverse. By management again our Col. has had no thrust from the Brigade, which has been ordered to Western Va. or Western Md. This Regt. is detached as heretofore for this duty in the city. With this exception everything is quiet.

The strawberry season is creating some commotion in culinary circles and government rations are taken with great reluctance after this delicious condiment. A visit to the South of Baltimore across the Patapsco River one gets a view of the fruit and vegetable gardens of the city, said to be very handsome and promising great crops of <u>peaches</u>, cherries, and etc. We begin to look forward to these things as they no longer put in "if we are ordered away," but say with positive assurance such will not be the case, while those who can are working at their trades and surrounded by their families.

The marriage in the village is all the talk this week with you, I suppose, as well as in all that circle of acquaintance. It will be a hard matter to find a couple that has furnished as much talking matter for gossip as these individuals.

My return is not so immediate as I expected when home; there is this satisfaction, that the war is shortening to its close, and living in hope this summer will decide the result. I hope the Government will not relax its energy to enforce the draft and thereby put the army on a good footing. We are bound to <u>Win</u>. "I can feel it in my bones," despite the croaking of copperheadism at home.

Hoping to hear from you soon, I remain your afft.

Son

R. T. Van Wyck

Belger Barracks, Baltimore
June 13th 1863

Dear Cousin [*Sarah*]:

Your letter of yesterday giving me the particulars of the wedding was welcomed. I have received a box of cake from somebody, I think from Mother, which contents were, I regret, more rapidly appropriated to the phisical [*sic*] than what is usually expected of such symbols to effect; that is, to stimulate the imagination to give a vivid outline of future prosperity and happiness; which I long ago thought was decreed to them. And I suppose upon such previous philosophical conclusion, I slept so soundly that the drum failed to rouse me in the morning at half-past four, and had it not been for my unusual promptitude heretofore in such matters I should have been censured. Well, it marks an epoch in summer pleasures and gayeties for you and will make a happy point of reference in all tea drinks, meetings, etc. Who comes next on the carpet?

We were greeted this morning with the news of another raid of the <u>Rebs</u> into Maryland. I am sorry our situation is such that possibly we will not be ordered to leave for Western Va.. A little variety just at present would be a fine thing, perhaps not so fine after we get out there and [*are*] deprived of our special privileges here. But I am willing to see some rough life now after such a season of apathy and indolence. Two years and three months passed as the previous nine would be anything but agreeable and besides, quite as injurious to future active life as the risk of phisical [*sic*] debility would be in the field. I don't believe I will have the pleasure of mentioning by letter our departure from here this summer.

So Chatham Sherwood is somewhat conspicuous in the celebration at the village. [*Of*] whose society is he the satellite? The younger Miss Talhemus? [*Polhemus?*] If so, write me; his uncle down in the city must know it. Like the rest of the family he needs no confidence to worm himself into anything that's going on, perhaps his professional calling will assume that for him. Has he improved much in his sermons? My short visit has just whet my curiosity upon what is going on, which letters give me in part, but not so good as one's personal presence.

Much love. Your afft. Cousin   R. T. Van Wyck

Belger Barracks, Balt.
June 16th 1863

Dear Mother,

I received your letter today. You have heard of the great cause of excitement in Maryland and Penna:* Our detachment of sixteen men at Westminster reported to have been taken prisoners. It's about 28 miles from here. So you see we are likely to have something to do with the Rebels before long. I have packed up and will be off before long, probably tonight. It's cavalry that is over here that's committing these depredations. We have some point in view, which I know nothing of, to defend.

You will hear from me as soon as I can do so. And if we remain here several days longer I will write again. With much love I remain your afft. Son

R. T. Van Wyck

Belger Barracks, Balt.
June 20th 1863

Dear Mother,

I was about commencing this letter with the evacuation of Belger Bcks., but from the heading you will perceive that we have reoccupied it again. The night of the 16th we were ordered away, but after marching downtown the order was countermanded. I must say I don't like such fooling. But then as the city was threatened by the Rebels, the streets were a perfect ovation who cheered us on the march. In returning [we] were taken for the seventh N. Y. M[ilitia] while to the credulous [we] represented ourselves as the 7th Georgia, who were looking for the 150th N. Y. V.: by so doing we tried to make the most of it.

But finally on the afternoon of the 17th we were ordered to pack up all our things and occupy Fort Marshall in the suburbs of the city. We found this to be no pleasant affair, as the sun was hot and roads dusty, although the march was only five miles. We took up our quarters

---

* The advance signs of General Lee's movement to invade the North.

in the "Hotel de terra firma," having only two hard tack for supper. The morning of the 18th found us encamped on the north side of a sand pit (it being dark when we arrived the previous evening). I slept well during the night and managed to get some coffee during the morning. About nine o'clock we occupied the outer works, and while we were making preparation to put up tents, which were in a fair way of completion, [we] were ordered back again to Belger Barracks to be relieved by the 7th N. Y. M., they having just arrived in Baltimore.

The day passed in looking for them to arrive [*at our camp*], but in this we were disappointed. The report says "they were looking with quite envious glances at Belger Bcks.," but by an active interference of our Colonel the order was not revoked. They occupied the Continental Hotel for the night preparatory to taking our place. The quarters at Ft. Marshall are filthy and the situation for camping by no means inviting. J. G. Montross and myself rigged up a tent and slept on the ground while the rest of the boys took possession of the mess room. I rested well, though it rained hard during the night.

At 11 o'clock, the 19th, in taking survey of matters and things from rumors, etc., I find the Colonel of the 7th is quite as good a man to further his own interests as Col. Ketcham. It is reported [*his men*] are smoking segars [*sic*] on Baltimore Street and not hasty in settling themselves, saying that if quarters are not to their liking they will go home. Our quarters at Belger Barracks strike them favorably. But as to coming here and being under the command of Col. Graham of the Ft. is to them as much to be dreaded as [*it*] is troublesome and annoying to our own officers.

It amuses me a little to see this "diamond cut diamond" policy. The 7th are no soldiers as they have been so famed, or they would have obeyed orders immediately; but I am amused at this clashing of interests: a contemptible way to operate with political influence and to effect things more suited to a picknick [*sic*] excursion than the emergency of times like the present demands. Such were the feelings in Camp up to this hour, when orders came to put everything right.

The 8th N.Y. Artillery evacuated Ft. Federal Hill in favor of the N.Y. M[*ilitia*], while they (the 8th N.Y. Artil.) were coming to Ft. Marshall, and we were going back to camp (at B. Bcks). This was not consummated till late in the evening, and having got somewhat accustomed to marching I found no ill effects from it. The cake you sent with Geo. Burroughs with coffee came very acceptable, I assure you.

The news you know as much of as ourselves from the papers. The times portend stirring events soon. It may be on this side of the Potomac in Md. or in Va., or more directly against this city and Washington. And while writing I am fearful my letter now indicates haste [and] that before its termination we will be off again. We can't stay here long, that is certain. With the exception of a paper sent me by Van Wyck to present to Gen. Schenck, which the anxiety of matters connected with his department forbids me to present now, I wouldn't care how soon we moved.

By the by, Geo. Burroughs brings no later advices [sic] from home. He says "everything is dull and he was glad to get back again." I only hope times here would assume that dullness that would bring us back again. Much love I remain,

Your Afft. Son
R. T. Van Wyck

P. S. The letter I speak of is one from Col. Tompkins of Cavalry to Gen. Schenck wishing him to release me from service here by promotion in his organization. It wouldn't do to present it now. I think Col. Ketcham will give me his influence in the matter.

Belger Barracks, Balt.
June 24th 1863

Dear Sarah,

Your letter I received while at Ft. Marshall, our stay being only a couple of days there, since which time we have reoccupied this camp. Military affairs are taking a more active form than heretofore. Forts are being erected, rifle pits, breastworks, barricades, and everything that can be done to strengthen the defenses of the city against an attack. The work is done by impressment of the negro population in Baltimore by the military force, of which the writer has had little to do with. By this management we have been relieved from this arduous duty and of course are very happy at this substitution.

You can faintly imagine the excitement this raid of the Rebs has given the people of Baltimore. By this morning's paper we learn of the possible collision of the two armies upon the old battleground of Maryland. The result no one knows, but [it] will be solved in a few days. And I hope, as we have said for the six times before, that it is the "last kick of the C.S.A."* It will be in reality.

My prospects in New York for a Commission are not now very flattering. A consolidation of the various regiments now in the course of formation was ordered a few days ago and [they] have been mustered into United States service, including the Regt. I had the prospect of joining. By being unable to attend to the matter in person I am thrown out. I am sorry I have given Van Wyck so much trouble in the matter, which has come to <u>naught</u>. I wouldn't say anything about it, however.

What induced Miss Sarah Kip to think or infer that any matrimonial connection in its incipient state were at all entertained by me is certainly preposterous. If those whom I had considered my friends found it difficult to pierce my rough exterior, what must those [feel] with whom my appearance alone must recommend me. Well, it makes fun for the hour and amuses me when with my blanket over my shoulder marching out to do Picket duty, expecting to make wakeful slumbers in that spacious enclosure common alike to man and beast, 'tis then my fitness for to do such honors as would befall me who had such an unlimited abode to bestow upon the object of his affections puts the matter in a very ridiculous light. I hope to hear from you soon — with much love I remain your afft. Cousin,

R. T. Van Wyck

EDITOR'S NOTE:

These events set in motion in June were to culminate at Gettysburg on July 1 - 3,–considered the three most critical days in American history– in the greatest battle of the war.

On the strength of his victory at Chancellorsville, Va., General Robert E. Lee laid plans for his second invasion of the North. His Army of Northern Virginia crossed the Potomac on June 17th via the Shenandoah Valley, which his advance troops under General Ewell had swept clear of Union forces.

As Federal outposts fell in the Shenandoah Valley, hordes of civilian refugees took to the roads, thus alerting the North to invasion. The government

---

* Confederate States of America, comprising South Carolina, Mississippi, Florida, Alabama, Georgia, Louisiana, Texas, Virginia, Arkansas, North Carolina, and Tennessee, listed in the order of their secession from the Union--eleven states in all. The border states of Maryland, Kentucky, and Missouri remained in the Union, although they had many Rebel sympathizers.

sent out a call for volunteers, to which militia regiments from Maryland, Pennsylvania, Ohio, and New York responded. At the same time some of the garrison forces guarding the capital were dispatched to fill out regiments depleted at Chancellorsville. Among these garrison troops liberated from guard duty was the 150th New York Volunteers, which was sent to join General Slocum's 12th Army Corps hurrying northward on Lee's trail.

Belger Barracks
June 25th 1863

Dear Father,

I expressed to Fishkill some extra clothing for myself and Jacob G. Montross. The articles are not worth much, but some things, including my shaving apparatus, I thought best to send home than throw away here, as I cannot take them with me. The freight will be <u>one</u> <u>dollar</u>. Jacob sent one blanket at the bottom and the <u>brown</u> linen coat.

We are off again, our destination is unknown. My affairs in New York I take as a failure. The consolidation of the various regts. in the City, including the ones I thought of entering, and then being mustered into the U. S. service, precludes the possibility of a position with them. I have not written to Van Wyck, but he is aware of the difficulty. I have presented the paper to Headquarters but have no hope of its success.

I will try to write as soon as possible, as soon as the plans of the Regt. are known.

I have no doubt the service will be very active, as the Rebels will make us so, or we will have to succumb to their victorious armies, which I hope the latter will be averted. Their marches are rapid and ours must be doubly so.* I will write in a few days again, if I remain here.

With much love I remain your afft. Son

R. T. Van Wyck

---

* Both Union and Confederate armies made forced marches northward, the Union army in hot pursuit of Lee, and when they intersected at Gettysburg, their troops were tired, hungry, and footsore.

PENNSYLVANIA—VIRGINIA
1863

We were present at Gettysburg the 2nd and 3rd and there first experienced my first battle. I cannot say my feelings were of the most pleasurable kind under the wizzing of missiles of all kinds. The music was very fine but sometimes it was pitched in too low a key.

—R.T. Van Wyck

Union victories had been few during the past two years. The Emancipation Proclamation had been announced on January 1st, and President Lincoln had called for an additional 300,000 volunteers. Early in May, the Army of the Potomac had been defeated by the Army of Northern Virginia at the Battle of Chancellorsville and had retreated north across the Potomac River. On June 15th, Robert E. Lee followed up his victory by taking the war north. He crossed the Potomac River with his triumphant rebel army to attack the Union on its own territory.

On the night of June 30th, after a forced march north, the 150th NYV Infantry was encamped twelve miles from Gettysburg. On the morning of July 1st, the Confederates, looking for shoes, reached Gettysburg, Pennsylvania, and were met by Union cavalry. Both sides rushed reinforcements to the crossroads town to engage in what was to become one of the most important battles ever fought.

After another forced march of two hours from the small hamlet of Two Taverns, covering eight miles, the 150th was placed on the extension of the 12th Corps' line south from Culp's Hill, one of the rocky hills near Gettysburg. On the afternoon of July 2nd, the 150th was hurriedly moved to the left to reinforce General Sickles. The following day, July 3rd, they were called upon to repel the furious Confederate onslaught launched by General Ewell. Ewell's attack was repulsed, the Federals successfully recovered their old lines on Culp's Hill, and the Union "fishhook" line was re-established.

Lee's original battle plan collapsed, causing him to re-think his strategy. The 150th was ordered to Cemetery Hill to reinforce the lines upon which the rebel General Pickett and about 15,000 brave Confederate soldiers made their desperate and famous "Grand Assault" to cut the Union Army in half. Pickett's Charge failed, and on July 4th, in heavy rain, both sides rested.

Lee started his retreat south on the 5th. Out of 75,054 men, he had lost 28,049. Meade began the battle with 83,289 men, and lost 23,049. On July 4th, Vicksburg surrendered to General Grant, thus removing another 30,000 Confederate soldiers from the strategic chessboard. The news of the fall of Vicksburg and the defeat at Gettysburg reached the Confederate capital in Richmond at about the same time. One coming fast upon the heels of the other, they were devastating blows to the Confederacy's hopes of winning independence by force of arms. The end had begun.

By August 1st, the Army of Northern Virginia had successfully evaded pursuit by Meade's Army and escaped back into Virginia. On September 15th, there was another forward movement of the Army of the Potomac, and the regiment again crossed the Rappahannock. Van Wyck's Company K was assigned to picket duty until September 24th. On the 25th, they marched north to Brandy Station where, for the first time since leaving Baltimore, they were paid.

While the 150th NYV Infantry was on picket duty along the Rapidan, some of Grant's troops were defeated at the Battle of Chickamauga, in the lower part of eastern Tennessee. Sherman was hurried forward from Vicksburg towards Chattanooga with reinforcements. The Western Theater of the War was beginning to heat up. The 11th and 12th Corps from the Army of the Potomac were important elements in the reinforcement plan.

Van Wyck's final letter from Virginia came from Brandy Station on September 25th. On the next day, the "Dutchess County Regiment" traveled to Bealton Station to make ready for transport by freight train for the journey west as part of the Army of the Cumberland.

J.C.Q.

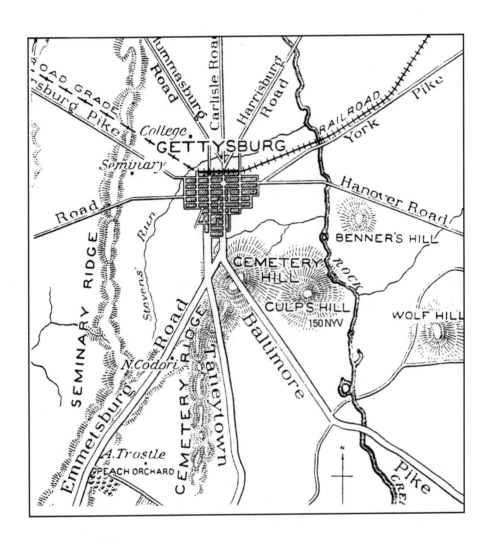

Battlefield of Gettysburg, by George Gross, Philadelphia, 1866.

On the March
July 6th 1863

Dear Father,

I enclose a small note to inform you that I came out of the battle of the 2nd and 3rd [*Battle of Gettysburg*] without any injury. I cannot give you the particulars and the many hard marches since I last wrote you the 25th of June, as I am momentarily expecting notice to leave. But from that time we have been exposed to the elements in every shape, and strange to say I am all right as yet, although have suffered considerable from hunger. The government allowance has been extremely limited and by the passage of such a large army [*through the countryside*] I have found it a hard matter to get anything to eat. I am surprised to find how little it takes to keep the machinery amoving.

We are on a forced march to intercept Lee before he reaches the Potomac. He received the first signal defeat he has ever received, and the number of his dead and wounded was very great. I never was on a battlefield before and the Lord preserve me from such a sight again. Some were wounded in our company and but few killed in the Regt. This was owing to the protection of breastworks behind which we did terrible execution, literally piling the Rebs up in masses. In front of our Regt. alone in one place where the enemy were agoing to charge, at least five hundred were killed and some 1700 stocks of arms captured. And their line extended in a circumference of six or seven miles; you may imagine the losses which of the enemy, were three to our one. It is a desperate affair with the Rebs. Many were taken prisoners, say ten thousand. If we can [*only*] prevent him from crossing; besides, his waggon [*sic*] and pontoon train has been destroyed and I hope and pray his army may be so demoralized that he will never attempt it again.

I wish I could give you my impressions of the scene, which was awful beyond description. The cannonading [*was*] more terrific than that of Chancellorsville and the shells and iron missiles of every description fill the air with their whizzing noises.

This success may be owing to the first entry of the 150th into active service. They did behave excellent and were highly commended by the General. The boys are anxious for another brush, but I hope it will not be so bloody but will be as effective. Write me soon. Address me: 150th Regt., N. Y. Vol., Lockwood Brigade, 1st Div., <u>12th</u> <u>Army</u> <u>Corps,</u> <u>Army</u> <u>of</u> <u>the</u> <u>Potomac.</u>

R. T. Van Wyck

EDITOR'S NOTE:

"Two markers on the fields at Gettysburg commemorate the 150th Regiment, New York Volunteers. One is a large monument on Slocum Avenue, North Culp's Hill, where it was engaged in action. The other is a smaller marker indicating that the 150th Regiment, New York Volunteers was one of the New York units in the engagement.

"The 150th arrived on the field of Gettysburg between 4 and 5 o'clock in the morning of July 2nd, 1863, and was assigned to the 2nd brigade, first division, of the 12th corps. It was held in reserve until the afternoon of that day when, with the first division of its corps, it was marched to the support of General Sickles, who had injudiciously posted his forces in an untenable position and was forced back with the loss of half his troops to the position originally designed for him by General Meade.

"The 150th returned during the night to the position of the 12th corps, on the extreme right of the National line, at the barb of the hook formed by Cemetery Ridge, on the crest of which from Culp's Hill to Round Top, Meade's army was posted. While the contest for the possession of Little Round Top was in progress, Ewell, who had discovered that Culp's Hill was weakly defended from the withdrawal of troops from Slocum's command to the left of the line, made a vigorous attack late in the afternoon and succeeded in getting a foothold within the exterior entrenchment, but was dislodged at the point of the bayonet early the next morning. This was the first actual fighting in which the 150th regiment engaged. Its casualties were 8 killed* and 23 wounded. Some 200 of the rebels surrendered to it."

From: *The History of Dutchess County, op. cit.* p. 196.

On the March
July 10th 1863

Dear Mother,

We have now arrived within four miles of the Potomac and are awaiting another battle with <u>Lee</u> who, I understand, is surrounded by Couch on the river, the right of the circumference of the circle, the Potomac Army the center, including ourselves, who are more to the left, and finally fresh troops fill up the gap between this and the

---

* Barnard C. Burnett, Henry Barnes, Charles Howsgate, Judd Murphy, Levi Rust, John Van Alstyne, John P. Wing, and Tallmadge Wood. *Ibid,* pp. 196-7.

Potomac. So then Lee is entirely surrounded with the river in front, 12 feet above fording. This is at Williamsport, or more properly, where the old battle took place last summer.*

The future will decide the contest. If successful, a forward movement on Richmond will be the order of the day. We have a fighting General [*Meade*].** You will observe that the 12th Corps was especially mentioned in the papers.

Since the battle I have stood the journey well, except one day I was under the weather and rode in the ambulance – much better than I had any idea of, considering the exposure, and the small amount of baggage I can carry on my back, consisting only of a rubber blanket and shelter tent with a change of clothing (two shirts). In tenting for the night we make the discovery of a wheat field, and we appropriate a sheaf of wheat if hay cannot be procured. This, with the blanket over us, answers well.

The cooking has got to be an individual affair, one has either to "fish or cut bait," or he starves. I boil the coffee and Geo. Burroughs cooks bacon, pork, or very rarely, fresh beef. Accordingly, we carry a small tin kettle and fry pan. Sometimes (for experience has taught us to be on the alert) we get a loaf of bread and butter, pie, milk from the farmers. Here [*in Maryland*] we are better accommodated than in Pennsylvania.

Today I was on a foraging excursion, I went into a farm house and the lady gave me a slice of bread and butter without compensation and regretted not having more on hand for the boys. She is a blessed woman. Don't talk no more about Picknick [*sic*] excursions – if this don't go ahead of anything I ever experienced, then I ain't a soldier. Then for beautiful scenery and fertile country you Dutchess County people know nothing about it. Just imagine how abundant [*it is*] when soldiers sleep on sheafs [*sic*] of wheat and forage on houses by the main roads, given bread and butter when wanted, perhaps you get some idea of the situation of affairs on the march.

The battle will come off soon. Some skirmishing was heard on the right. Everyone feels confident of success. I hope we may have it. What a Glorious Fourth, with news of Vicksburg and Gettysburg,

---

* Antietam.
** On June 28 President Lincoln had replaced Gen. Hooker with General George G. Meade as commander of the Army of the Potomac.

two important and decisive victories. Our losses in the battle of Gettysburg I think is over-estimated, the Rebel not so.* I judge from my own observation. In the last day's fight we had 120 pieces of cannon playing upon the Rebels at one time. You may judge of the desperate contest. They said (the Rebs) that the musketry was more deadly.

I will write as soon as possible again. Perhaps you will receive this after the battle.

With much love I remain your afft. Son.

R. T. Van Wyck

Harpers Ferry [*W. Va.*]
July 17, 1863

Dear Mother,

I received your letter last Sunday, giving me the news to July 2nd. You could not imagine my joy at thus receiving a package of letters from home. We were then in line of battle at the time, and [*received them*] through the kindness of Mr. Gaylord, our old Quartermaster, who had them forwarded from Balt.

As you have learned before this of the escape of Lee from Williamsport, even after we had surrounded him with breastworks, etc., expecting to take his army entire, but you see he out-Generaled us. If we (that is, the Potomac Army) had given him battle on Saturday we would have cut his army to pieces. But his army was overestimated by our General and the precious opportunity was not improved. The mortification of the army knew no bounds for they saw in future a long protracted war, and a march more injurious and deathly than balls.**

Well, soon after the discovery of Lee's crossing, we were ordered to march to Harpers Ferry where we were [*given*] a slight prospect of a rest. Since we left Balt. [*it*] has been incessant marching from 15 to 30 miles a day. And today we have a respite of one day. We go onward to Richmond if we do not intercept the enemy at Bull Run.

---

* Union: 3,155 killed, 20,000 wounded or missing. Confederate: 3,903 killed, 24,000 wounded or missing. *Encyclopedia of American History*, Rev. ed. 1965, N.Y., p. 241.
** After Gettysburg Lee withdrew west of Hagerstown, MD, where the flooded Potomac blocked his retreat. Lincoln ordered Gen. Meade to attack but rains stalled his reconnaissance. In the meantime the river subsided and Lee escaped into Virginia.

I have stood marching very well till near the Ferry when I was forced to give out from exhaustion with nearly half our Regt., but this rest will reinstate me again, I hope. Today, although it rains in torrents, will very much recruit the Army and prepare them for the advance.

The country on our march has been exceedingly beautiful. My observation of last winter's visit to Adamstown was but a faint expression of this supreme farming region. But the devastation of this Army and the Rebs has turned this into a waste [*land*] and our last day's journey was [*through*] the old battleground of last Summer [*Antietam*]. You have my directions and will give me a letter once in a while.

No doubt you would like to hear from me oftener, but it is only now and then that I am fit to write a letter, being tired when we halt for the night, and hardly can give a satisfactory expression of my thoughts. But when opportunity permits will give you the position of our whereabouts.

I wish I could realize this summer's battles would end the war, which now seems exceedingly doubtful. It rests on a Higher Power whose directing power controls all transpiring events.

Give my love to all. Although I cannot answer letters promptly you will not think it amiss.

With much love to all from

Your Afft. Son.
R. T. Van Wyck

To: Mr. Robt. Johnston
Johnsville
Dutchess Co., New York

Brickers Gap, Va.
Tuesday, July 21st '63

Dr. Friend,

We left Balt. the 25th of June; in the meanwhile were present at Gettysburg the 2nd and 3rd and there first experienced my first battle. I cannot say my feelings were of the most pleasurable kind under the wizzing [*sic*] of missiles of all kinds. The music was very fine but sometimes it was pitched in too low a <u>key</u>. Our position there was of a most favorable kind, more so than ever I expect again, behind breastworks [*we*] were little exposed, and did terrible execution upon the Rebs. We have made ourselves quite a laughing stock for the old soldiers when we remark it was a terrible fight and say we only lost eight or ten men and as many wounded. They have diminished their Regts. by half or two thirds by dead and wounded, alone by hunger and exposure.

I assure you that active service is a hard thing, let alone a battle now and then. Our first march from Baltimore to Monocacy River, a distance of 45 miles, looked very short to us before we undertook it. Our first afternoon's march of nine miles gave us a night's sleep through a drenching rain without anything over us, so tired were we. We completed the march in ten days and then rested a day before we joined the Potomac Army. Many came in without shoes, footsore and weary.

Since that time [we] have got quite used to it, we have diminished our clothing to a shelter tent and rubber blanket, and a few kitchen tools, consisting of tin cup and a fry pan, knife and fork, besides from one to three day's rations of uncooked food, crackers, bacon, pork, coffee and sugar, and every rest or camp we speedily make a cup of coffee.* It took some time to systematize this branch of the business (for it's all in a soldier's life).

I have repeatedly been so nearly exhausted as scarcely to be able to navigate, but a little rest and some nutritious food soon put me on my pins again. From Frederick to Gettysburg a distance of forty miles we retraveled again after the battle, and made the journey to Williamsport some forty miles further to escort Lee to the Potomac and see him safely on the other side. After which we followed the river down to Harpers Ferry, crossed into Va., and am now watching this hole in the mountain range that separates us from him. This place is 20 miles from the Ferry. Va. looks different than Maryland as being the battleground of the contending forces so long.

Our company were sent out on a picket at Williamsport and some sheep happened to get within range of our guns, a certain fatality attended two of them, and handsomer mutton I never saw or tasted. A man that can't wring a chicken's neck or skin a hog can't be a soldier. Here in Va. the country is used up and foraging is unsuccessful.

---

* Coffee was issued to the army in the whole bean to prevent adulteration by crooked suppliers. It took the men just a few minutes to pound it down with a stone and boil it in a tin can over a little fire of twigs. *Bruce Catton's Civil War*, p. 108.

Sometimes we have been on short allowance, and this is sheer necessity.

You are looking after the hay and grain just at present. The quantity uncut, wasted, destroyed by the armies [*here*] might be estimated as millions. And better grain I never saw grow. Maryland is worth a trip to see this excellent section of country.

The draft is creating some excitement in New York. The people in the country might take the alarm. I think the war will soon be ended if we can get more reinforcements.

Don't be discouraged; if you can see the enormous outlay of all things to meet the enemy, we need not despair. With much love I am

your afft. friend
R. T. Van Wyck

Address: R. T. Van Wyck
    Co. K 150th Regt. N. Y. Vols.
    1st Div., 3rd Brig, 12th Corps
    Army of the Potomac

Brickers Gap, Va.
July 22nd 1863

Dear Mother,

I last wrote you at Harpers Ferry. We crossed into Va. Sunday, the 19th, and rested here yesterday and will [*leave*] quite likely today. We are now about 24 miles from the Potomac and guarding this mountain pass from the passage of Lee's army, who are to the right of us.

I was unwell when I last wrote you, but now have perfectly recovered and as well as ever. I have not received any letters from home since the 2nd of July and I hope these letters written on the march have reached you. They are not prepaid in consequence of the scarcity of stamps and likewise to a dearth of the pecuniary. I have been looking for the distribution of the Greenbacks, our last dues. But as we are constantly on the move it affords a good excuse for not paying us, which would be very acceptable.

I have previously made an extension of our rations of fresh beef by purchasing of the Quartermaster, and while in Maryland by getting food of the farmers. This has limited me now, and for fear of getting entirely bankrupt I would like very much about 10 dollars, hoping by that time the paymaster will pay us. My address is now 150th N. Y. Vol., Ist Div., 3rd Brig, 12th Army Corps, Army of the Potomac, Washington.

I suppose Father is now busy haying and will be much engaged for several weeks. This gives very little trouble here as the people have all deserted the country, and rich farming land is looking desolate indeed. There seems to be a certain fatality of all things here in Va., irrespective of political opinions, [*especially*] those that can be converted into food for man and beast.

Our Brigade confiscated 30 or 40 head of cattle; they being difficult to drive we thought it best to convert them to use, and accordingly the last day the boys were doing something like we read about the Indian tribes when they get into a Buffalo hunt, boiling, wasting,* and eating the meat in all possible ways and shape, everyone on his own hook. The mountains abound in berries and snakes; one is not avoided for the other, and consequently we have abundance. They are worth the risk to get them for a change, even without sugar.

I do not get the papers regularly enough to advance an opinion but I will venture to say and confidently expect a termination of the war during this summer campaign in consequence of the brilliant success in all the Union armies, and victories will attend the army throughout.

With much love I remain your afft.   Son

R. T. Van Wyck

July 28th 1863
Washington Junction, Va.

Dear Mother,

I received last night a package of letters from home. They were truly welcomed, I assure you. I have sent on the letter in which I wanted some money, which while at Harpers came very acceptable in sutlers' stores, and thinking I might again meet with like good fortune if I was in possession of the needful. Since leaving Harpers Ferry in passing down Loudon Valley we had abundance of good water but latterly the country has become sterile and the water slightly sulfurous and otherwise impure. The White Sulphur Springs are only a few miles from here, as also the battlefield of Bull Run.

---

* i.e., cleaning and discarding the viscera.

At Manassas Gap at which our forces had a slight skirmish with the Rebs, our own Corps was held in reserve. We arrived there in time by traveling all one day and nearly all night, likewise repeated the next day and night, to hold this present possession. I have stood it quite well considering the heat, etc., and the rest at this point will wholly recruit me.

Yes, I am very fortunate to have been so preserved thus far amidst the dangers of battle and the fatiguing marches from which numbers fall out, and suffer from neglect and necessary privations. And my gratitude to God for his preservation of me cannot be too freely acknowledged or be at first expressed. I wonder at our signal successes when the immorality of the army is so conspicuous, besides the action against the war in N.Y. City.* The matter gave us little moment upon consideration, for the men of influence in the City have educated the populace for this outbreak as also have they incited the Rebs to their present position.

We here are encouraged with the reflection that this Autumn will settle this trouble for the reason that while Grant advances from the Southwest and West, our forces will press Lee either into Richmond or into the Mountains on the Rappahannock towards Gordons [Mill?], leaving him without supplies, and preventing the possibility of any reaching him. Their hopes are now based upon the success of their arms in the West and the feint to again invade Penna. When this is an impossibility with them, they will come to terms. Probably there will be many outlaws, etc.,** but the great army will be scattered as they now are demoralized. This we all hope for and earnestly desire.

Our advance upon Williamsport was interpreted by the illustration of the initials "U. S." That is, the Rebs were in the horseshoe with our forces all around; while we described the "S" in getting there through the mud, they crossed over. We describe very few of those curves on our marches. We take a direct line through the country, passing deserted villages and meeting few inhabitants. No one can justly realize the comforts of <u>home</u>, but those that have been on just such marches as the ones the army have been engaged in. I hear

---

* The draft riots of July 12-16, which left at least 105 people dead, and resulted in much destruction and looting.
** i.e., guerrilla warfare.

we intend resting here three or four weeks. If so, I hope to write and hear from home often.

With much love I remain your afft.

Son
R. T. Van Wyck

Address: Co. K 150th Regt. N. Y. Vols.
1st Div, 3rd Brig., 12th Army Corps
Army of the Potomac

July 28th 1863
Washington Junction, Va.

Dear Sarah,

I received your letter last night and [it] was truly welcomed. Since my last letter from Baltimore you will know full well the reason for my inability to write. Besides, I was assured that you could hear from Mother as to my whereabouts. Being tired and weary at our halts, it seemed almost impossible to write and only the prospect of getting one off and making you feel I was <u>well</u> induces me to do it.

The usual Birthday festival [*Sarah's*] has been kept and passed. It seemed like old times while reading your letter to imagine myself there as of old. But my position at that time and my previous occupation of that day was somewhat different. I think I could do better justice to the eatables than ever before. This has come to a fine point. Our individual cooking of the army stores of Beef, Pork, Bacon and boiling of coffee is changed by some deviation of frying, boiling, wasting, and stewing to suit the tastes which unfortunately we have. But I don't know as to that either, for the desperate necessity of nutriment has overruled that most whimsical sense of taste.

The battle of Gettysburg was a desperate engagement but fortunately we were well posted and acted upon the defensive, consequently the Rebs got the worst and we were little exposed. We all here are sanguine of success and I hope there will be no disappointment as to the speedy result of the disposition of our armies in Va.

How has the Picnick [*sic*] season been pleasurably spent with you? <u>You</u>, of Picnick renown little know how truly rustic this soldier's life, diverted now and then by a skirmish, battle, etc., is. You must excuse the pencil as my ink is exhausted as well as <u>stamps</u>, and yours came very acceptable, as you would eventually have to pay for it if worth taking out of the envelope. This writing material I have kept with me while my other goods have gone the way of all wearysome [sic] goods.

Write soon. Remember me to GrandFather. I hope the old Gentleman's life will be spared till this war is settled and the Union is reconstructed, which I think will shortly come to pass.

I left Jacob Montross in Gettysburg and he afterwards went to Frederick where he is recruiting his health in the Hospital. Geo. Burroughs, like all the rest of us, is sometimes almost overcome with heat and fatigue. But unconsciously we get well upon short notice and march along with the army.

With much love I remain your afft. Cousin

R. T. Van Wyck

Washington Junction
July 29th 1863

Dear Mother,

I received another letter from you today, dated July 25th. And it seems I am more fortunate than most of my comrades, receiving three out of four for our Company, thanks to your kindness.

We remain here I do not know how long. Some say three weeks till the conscripts come on, but quite likely till the pontoon bridge is lain across the Rappahannock some dozen or more miles in advance. Lee is said to have crossed the river and is making speedy progress towards Richmond.

The position of the armies will be precisely the same as before this excursion into Penna. Except perhaps we may make an effort to hold our position at Chancellorsville or Fredericksburg. No doubt the Rebs are much worn out and require much rest to take the offensive to hold some ill-chosen position. What the coming three weeks will reveal no one knows. The Government intends to be active to follow the Rebs up. And the hopes of the officers in command, those whose experience has been valuable to the Government, feel sanguine of the close of the war this Fall. Without some great misfortune on our part I think myself that it is certain.

The bad hay weather for Father has been a fine thing for marching, and the hot days so very suffocating that for a cup of our well water or an hour's rest under that apple tree with a cool breeze could not be estimated by money. Today the weather changes and what is bad for you sends refreshment to the army.

I forgot to acknowledge the receipt of some papers from Anna or Sarah, but they are just the thing. We get a daily paper here but [it] is soon read and anything of that order comes very acceptable. More so here than in Baltimore, for there we could patronize the Book stores.

The bribing [?] system among our officers commenced on our first march. Some have given out by fatigue while the most conclude. War is not so pleasant now as at Belger Barracks. For myself I can take fatigue in good part with the satisfaction that they [the Rebs] begin to realize their position.

With many thanks for your kind letters, I remain your afft. Son
R. T. Van Wyck
150th Regt. N. Y. Vols.
1st Div. 3rd Brig, 12th Army Corps
Army of the Potomac

To A. V. W. Van Vechten

Washington Junction
July 30th 1863

Dear Cousin,

I left Baltimore the 25th of June, have marched to Gettysburg and returned, crossed the Potomac at Harpers Ferry and have proceeded thus far on my way to Richmond. I am attached to the 12th Corps which did good service in battle. Thanks to a merciful Providence who has preserved me this far I have escaped unharmed. The fatigue is great indeed in marching through the hot sun.

The matter in reference to that letter to Gen. Schenck I have not heard from since sent. At that time he was much engaged in his department to protect the city from invasion. [As to] The letter of your bearing, dated the 13th of July, by this time opportunities have passed for positions in Regt. now filling up by the conscripts. I deeply regret your past trouble for my welfare has amounted to so little, but the change in Public Affairs gives one no definite course to pursue.

Excuse pencil. Your letter I received last night. Address me:
150th Regt. N. Y. Vols
1st Div., 3rd Brig., 12th Army Corps
Army of the Potomac
Washington

and I will get it immediately. With much love I remain your afft.
Cousin.

R. T. Van Wyck

Kelleys [*sic*] Ford, Va.
Aug. 3rd 1863

Dear Mother,

Presuming you have received some of my letters in pencil I
will not apologize now for so doing; knowing you will understand
that my ink is exhausted and almost the balance of my writing
material.

In yesterday's letter I acknowledged the receipt of the money,
but if no sutler arrives here it does me little good. I hope he will
be here in a few days. And in the course of two weeks you may
remit the balance.

I think I have answered most of your letters, but so much time
elapses before I can get them off [*that it*] seems very disconnected.
Yesterday was the first Sunday we have spent as such since we left
Baltimore, that is, we were quiet and were resting on our arms all
day till about six o'clock when we recrossed the Rappahannock
and have encamped in a fine location where we can get plenty of
good drinking water.

You have wondered how the clothes washing process is conducted in the army. It is, like all such movements in military
affairs, a <u>great</u> question of <u>expediency.</u> On coming to any large
stream of water it is soon swarming with life and activity. First the
whole person is washed, and then comes the whole clothing, not
excepting coat and pants. They are put on immediately and soon
dry in the sun. With me I have a change of shirts, so it frees me
from such hasty cleanliness and has given me sufficient time to put
my underclothing in good order. (Those woolen shirts wash well),
that is, they smell and look clean, much better than the appearance
of the water they are washed in, which has a muddy red appearance. But this morning, embracing the opportunity of the probability of remaining here, I washed my whole wardrobe, and it's
drying in the sun in the rear of my tent. So much for this branch
of the trade.

As to cooking, I have previously enlightened you into some of
the mysteries of the act. I would suggest, however, if you have a

118

receipt [*recipe*] to make a palatable compound of flour and water, or water and Indian meal, or soaked <u>hard</u> <u>tack</u>* and water, or anything that does not require eggs, butter, milk, lard, raising powders, yeast, etc., if you have such, do give it to me, for it will be a Godsend. We make a batter of the aforesaid articles and fry them in the grease of Pork, bacon, beef, etc. (that is played out). It takes some consideration of life and patriotic duty to make them slip down. I am much reduced in flesh, but I feel about as well as usual, rather better now than at any previous time on the march.

In looking back I am surprised to find God has so preserved me in such good health. I have much to praise and thank Him while many apparently stronger have succumbed to disease and exhaustion. I would not recommend a soldier's life to recruit one's health, but just the reverse. However, we are prospecting a little upon next winter when we will get full rations from the Government, and with a box now and then from home we can mess among ourselves quite comfortably, I hope. Then, with the sanguine hopes of the country to put the war down by that time buoying up our spirits, we will get along till that time very comfortably.

We do not apprehend much more marching till September. This weather is fine for Father in the hayfield. I suppose Mr. Briggs has a heavy crop of wheat to husband. Va. is stripped of everything that can be converted into food for man. Our pickets captured 40 head of cattle and a hundred sheep. What few inhabitants remain are robbed of everything whenever an army passes by. Yesterday our brigades stripped a flour mill and the adjoining houses, going into their cellars, garrets, etc. It is difficult to prevent such atrocities. It is equally as safe for one to hold to Rebel as Union proclivities, it does little good. Va. is destined to pillage and destruction. The hopes of the people are gloomy in the extreme as to the success of their cause. Some of our boys have been obliged to fall out from sickness and have been treated well at their hands and furnished with all they had on hand to give them.

With the exception of some 20 or 30 miles of Loudoun Valley east of the Blue Ridge I would give the balance for any 400 acres in Dutchess Co. That is, what we have passed over.

---

* Hard tack, the main staple of the Civil War soldier, was a solid, nourishing slab of unleavened bread about 3 inches square and half an inch thick. Nine or ten of these made a day's ration. *Bruce Catton's Civil War*, p. 109.

Aben* writes me that he has been sick during the winter and that he has now a better position than formerly, which I am glad to hear. Who is dead in the Montross family? Jacob received a letter indicating some death in the family, which I forwarded to him to Annapolis Hospital.

With much love I remain

Your afft. Son
R. T. Van Wyck

P. S. The money you sent me is not current here. If you will please exchange it and send me the <u>greenbacks</u> instead, they give me no trouble. Please remember this.

Kelleys Ford, Va.
Aug. 12th 1863

Dear Sarah,

I received your letter last night. Lest I should give you unpleasant reflections upon my style of living I must apologize for my indiscretion. And accordingly I must take objections to the supposition that I should have the sympathies of all my friends instead of the general gossip and [news] of home affairs, as they come to brighten and relieve the mind from the monotony of camp life, which all letters give me. It has been said "one half of the world don't know how the other half lives," and my previous letters are intended to give you an insight from observation and experience.

As to sympathy and condolence I had long ago depended upon that, so that need not cloud your mind when either amid the gay society of Hopewell or the Village, or in giving me the account of it in a letter. Again, if I should choose to make myself miserable it would be selfish in me to expect others should partake [with] me in my suffering.

And now, seated upon my corduroy bedstead, coat off, sleeves rolled up, as if expecting an attack, I can just imagine your indignation at this thrusting aside of your tender sympathies, but permit me to say I have lately enjoyed this life first rate and therefore all controversy is unnecessary.

I have repeatedly heard of your doings in picnics, etc., with the Hopewell people. I suppose they improve upon acquaintance. They

---

* His brother.

are said to be good-hearted people, if they don't have their hearts into their pockets. Of course, you will exercise a vigilance over Miss Adriance, but I fear our friendship will very soon wither under existing circumstances. I was agoing to give you a long letter, but my domestic arrangement forbids it and the mail will soon leave. I remain your afft. Cousin

R. T. Van Wyck

Kelleys Ford, Va.
Aug. 18th 1863

Dear Mother,

I received your letter yesterday. I suppose you have received the letter acknowledging the receipt of the money you sent me, also the one enclosing the <u>check</u>. I had supposed you were down in the city and therefore addressed them to Father.

We have had it very warm but I suppose we are so getting used to the effects of the sun and also remaining inactive that we scarcely believe it to be as hot as before the 1st of August while we were marching. So far this present week is cool, rather too cool during the night toward morning for sleeping.

However, there is going on a change in the army and we are likely to move any moment. Several old Regts. in our Brigade have left us, destination unknown, conjectured Charleston. We being encamped on the East Bank of the River with pickets thrown out to the bank; the Rebs likewise, and conversation between the parties [is] quite common. Their cavalry and our artillery water their horses in the same stream, not much larger than the big <u>creek</u> at the White Bridge. No one seems to be alarmed and all the different duties of camp life are performed the same as if no enemy was nearer than five hundred miles.

Have heard the adjutant had resigned and also the Chaplain. There are several officers whose resignation will be accepted. Our Capt. looks bad and should he not recover before another campaign he will be forced to leave us. There are many cases of the same kind among the officers who have suffered as much as the <u>privates</u>. There have been seventy or eighty sent to hospitals since being here, to say nothing of the No. left on the battlefield, along roadsides, etc., lessening the Regt. full two hundred and fifty men.

Jacob writes me he will join us in a week or two. There is nothing serious the matter with him. I hope when the reinforcements of conscripts come in we will be into movements that will finish the thing up, for to be out longer than next Spring will disappoint me very much. I should say they are coming in largely from other States than N. Y.

Now there being no trouble connected with the hay harvest, it will be no rest [*until*] after it is through and you will quite miss it. Tell Father I should like him to write me a <u>farming</u> letter once in a while, for occasionally my mind rests upon the subject and would give me great pleasure to know how everything is going on.

With much love I remain your afft. Son

R. T. Van Wyck

Kelleys Ford, Va.
Aug. 29th 1863

Dear Cousin [*Sarah*],

You will excuse this pencil letter in reply to your kind letter of the gay and festive sports of Fishkill. But just one hour ago we had orders to break camp and remove to a more salubrious situation one mile or more from here, accordingly my tent fellow and myself had stood and made ready to carry our worldly goods in our knapsacks and provisions in our haversacks and are trying to console ourselves upon leaving since we had recently reorganized our <u>cedar</u> bed and spent no little pains to make ourselves comfortable, but just then in view of the weather the order was countermanded and having finished putting up our quarters again I have sat down to speculate on passing events around Fishkill.

Such speculations I doubly assure you are exceedingly interesting and afford me great pleasure, for I cannot help the direct inference adduced from your letter that there might be some fascination about those picnics, sociables, etc., to make them appear so uncontrollably delightful to you. For till the present moment I couldn't account for this relapse into such scenes of dissipation, since they were always noted for their sobriety at the Hook, but it seems that when a Parson is to be settled it does require a vigilance committee among the ladies, so great is the fuss they kick up.

Let me congratulate you upon your anticipated prospects at Bloom [?] and when you give me reason to believe anything definite I will write you some experienced advice upon household economy – very valuable to know for you will become somewhat of a migratory set as ourselves.

I have been dreaming that something pleasant was agoing to turn up and often would seize the paper to know whether Charleston had surrendered, but happily I have at last got some idea of what is passing on at home.

Should an admission of what I have written be contraband to write me, by no means [do it], but let your silence assent to what I have written.

Love to all. With much love, I remain your afft. Cousin,

R. T. Van Wyck

Kelleys Ford
Aug. 31st 1863

Dear Mother,

I received your letter on Saturday and would have answered it before, but a "change of base" of our Regt. to a more healthy locality a few miles distant prevented me.

Father's letter gave me some idea of what is going on on the farm and quite revived my feelings of farming matters. The success of Van Wyck in New York to obtain that situation is very uncertain, so great is the call for such places by those personally acquainted with the donors of such offices that to a stranger [the chances] seem doubtful. Rest assured I will not feel disappointed if he does not succeed: besides, I couldn't treat his effort and success so rudely, as well as my own position, as to decline it.

Our own camp now overlooks a wide reach of bottom lands on the Rappahannock. The farm lands show the slovenly hand of slavery upon it. Directly in front lie the Blue Ridge Mountains enclosing alike between the Bluff on this side the two contending armies, that is, their picket lines. We have deserters coming over quite frequently. They come down and exchange [news]papers and talk about matters in general. It seems hard that by the united sentiment upon the discontinuance of the war by both sections we wait the tardy movement of legislature upon it. The fall of Charleston removes the visage of the invulnerability of the South. The speedy end is conclusive.*

---

* Union ships had again begun pounding Fort Sumter on August 17, 1863. As it was a vital port and the birthplace of the secession, the general desire was to batter the city into submission. But despite siege and blockade, Charleston did not fall until Feb. 1865, evacuated by Gen. Hardee because of the supposed proximity of Gen. Sherman's army. By that time it was pretty badly bombed.

I cannot be too thankful for your letters, and my desire to know something of farm matters induced me to write for such information. By no means think they are tiresome or otherwise, for it gives me [*much*] pleasant reflections of my own. The girls this Summer seem to have been on quite a spree and have given you no [*in*]considerable amusement to see their arrangements. I expect you to keep me posted if anything turns up in that quarter. I remain with much love, your afft.

Son
R. T. Van Wyck

Kelleys Ford, Va.
Sep. 11th 1863

Dear Mother,

In answer to your letter of yesterday, I have not much to communicate. We are dull, indeed. We get up in the morning, perform our necessary ablutions in the stream of clear water near camp, dispatch our breakfast and remain the rest of the day, except those who are detailed upon picket, in perfect idleness. The papers, magazines you sent me were certainly a great blessing and I should have acknowledged them before.

The day before yesterday we had a brigade review and inspection, yesterday a division review and inspection. As usual the Chief officers improve such occasions of display to partake largely of the "Critter" [*liquor?*] and several stories reported of a ludicrous character took place in consequence which would be contraband to write.

The "Johnny Rebs" (as they are termed by the boys) are on the best of terms with us. We exchange [*news*]papers, sometime [*they*] come down to the water's edge and halloo over to us for permission to come over and give themselves up. Of course, we don't object. The arrivals have been quite numerous of late, owing to the peculiar eloquence of Gillmore's three hundred pro quo [*?*] and [*they*] are treated with considerable respect to take thus early the conclusive opinion of the C. S. A.'s cause as impairably [*his word*] lost.

By some exertion I am posted up to yesterday and am now waiting the arrival of the news boy who has for the last few days failed to visit us. The papers and letters constitute the chief food for talk and thought.

It seems you at home have not forgotten to celebrate such glorious news as our nation's success by social meetings and gayeties [*sic*] generally. I am glad you were able to participate.

Since Anna wrote me of Fred's arrival at our house, my thoughts would occasionally linger about the old homestead and imagine how cheerful you all were. I have received a letter from Sarah in answer to mine in which she discusses at some length upon the subject gossiped about, and promises to notify me when everything is arranged. I hope to be liberated by next <u>May</u>, so if the domine is not fast in getting married I might see the performance. It excites my curiosity a little to know what "that something more to tease Sarah about" is. But I will know in good time, I suppose. Love to all, I remain, your afft. Son

R. T. Van Wyck

P. S. Please send the *Atlantic* [*Monthly*].
PPS [*In pencil*] I have received it by mail tonight. Montross has joined us from Hospital. He looks well. I wish Father would send me $10.

Near Raccoon's Ford, Va.
Sept 19th 1863

Dear Mother,

I received your letter last night. You had some intimation of our departure from Kelleys Ford in my letter to Sarah dated the 15th.

That day we crossed the Rappahannock and marched to Bladensburg and camped there for the night. Resumed our march next morning and proceeded to the Rapidan River at or near the junction of the small stream Cedar Run. If you have one of these maps <u>in</u> <u>detail</u> you can get some idea of our situation. The River is strongly guarded on the opposite side by the Rebs who will make a determined resistance should we attempt to cross. It has rained incessant since our arrival and although encamped in a dense forest I feel much better than while at the Rappahannock.

What is the policy of the Government remains to be seen. We have concentrated a large force at this point. The Rebels have the mountains directly in front, and without a flank maneuver it would seem impossible to dislodge them.

I received the $10. I was sorry to hear of the death of those inestimable ladies. To one [*lady*] undoubtedly, it was a great relief from a life of suffering to one of happiness. While to the other it was a sad warning to those who expect to enjoy permanent happiness in this world, but to her who was prepared for the change a good one.

How does Uncle Henry like his being drafted? Does GrandFather pay his $300 for him? for his exemption? I suppose patriotism is played out when it gives the party no discretionary power, either pay the money or go. Their want of it [*patriotism*] has brought this about. And it is right it is so, for our numbers should be kept full.

God be praised I have enjoyed a fair measure of health, while a couple of hundred of our Regt. are now in hospitals.* Although I am not burdened with superfluous flesh I feel much better in easy marching than in remaining stationary. The country looks more inviting as we go nearer Richmond. I hope it will be an incentive to our speedily bringing down the Reb stronghold.

With much love I remain your afft. Son

R. T. Van Wyck

Brandy Station, Va.
Sept. 25th 1863

Dear Mother,

We withdrew from the front at the Rapidan River yesterday afternoon about 3 o'clock and marched to this place about eight o'clock, a distance of eleven or twelve miles. We have an indication from the eight days' rations given us, and from being relieved by the first Corps, and also by all the teams, cattle, etc., being turned into the Quartermaster, that we were destined for another department. We certainly are bound for Alexandria by rail. From there we are in blissful ignorance.

I have seen enough of Va. and will always remember the pursuit of Lee down to the Rappahannock with thankfulness, as being able to survive the heat and exertion which has sent many to a premature grave. My general appearance and habits of life have induced many to believe I would soon succumb to this hard life, but I have earned for myself considerable hardiness thus far.

---

* Dysentery took more lives in the Civil War than bullets. For every one killed in battle, four soldiers died of sickness. *The Common Soldier in the Civil War,* *op.cit.*

Geo. Burroughs is just about used up. By negligence to a diarrhea he is much reduced in flesh and energy, besides he yields to a morbid state of mind, which without [*being*] unwell, will make his [*ill*] health doubly certain to be permanent. My spirits have been the best throughout, by them I mastered the <u>fever</u> at Washington Junction (although I did not know what it was at the time) and which subsided into a dysentery which did not impair my appetite, but had the effect to fully recruit me, to which my present health and appearance will attest.

Montross had seen little of hard life and has escaped the heat and <u>fever</u> this season. He is in good health and we are forming numerous conjectures as to our destination, but the more I see of Military affairs the more intricate they always are to foresee the future.

The climate of Va. has little to recommend it. We had a severe frost on the 22nd, which perhaps was the first indication of Fall with you [*too*]. The heat is no more intense than with you, but then the want of cool delicious water makes it unhealthy.

Sept. 26th – 2 o'clock p.m. Traveled today to this place (Bealton Station) on the road to Alexandria, starting at 5 o'clock. And are awaiting the [*railroad*] cars to finish this journey. You think it considerable of a misfortune to miss a train and be delayed a few hours when going down to the city (what think you of waiting 36 hours out in the open field and sleeping?). However, the paymaster improved the opportunity to pay us. I thought, should we go to <u>Tenn.</u>, I should certainly want the most of my money.

Sunday morning, Sept. 27th. Arrived in Washington this morning in route for the West, to go by rail to Murfreesboro and from there into the field. You will address me as usual until I write you from there.

They say we will not get our mail under ten days or more. They also say we are under the command of Joe Hooker, who has been assigned part of the eleventh and all of twelfth corps.*

Write me as soon as possible.

R. T. Van Wyck

---

* In September 1863, Gen. Hooker along with the 11th and 12th Corps of the Army of the Potomac were rushed by rail to the West to aid Gen. Rosecrans, trapped in Chattanooga by Gen. Bragg's reinforced Confederate Army following the bloody rout at Chickamauga on September 19-20. The transporting of 20,000 men over 1,233 miles within eleven days was an extraordinary feat of logistics. *Battle Cry of Freedom*, by James M. McPherson, pp. 672-75.

This is Richard T. Van Wyck's ambrotype, which
he references in letters from Camp Belger.
Collection of the East Fishkill Historical Society.

James Van Wyck House, circa 1890. Birthplace of Richard T. Van Wyck in Wiccopee, Dutchess County, New York. *Collection of the East Fishkill Historical Society.*

James Van Wyck, Richard's father. *Collection of the East Fishkill Historical Society.*

Elizabeth M. Van Wyck, Richard's mother. *Collection of the East Fishkill Historical Society.*

Van Wyck family coat of arms. *Collection of the East Fishkill Historical Society.*

Interior James Van Wyck house. *Collection of the East Fishkill Historical Society.*

Interior James Van Wyck house. *Collection of the East Fishkill Historical Society.*

Dining room, James Van Wyck house. *Collection of the East Fishkill Historical Society.*

Reverend Abraham J. Van Wyck, Richard's brother Aben, with whom he corresponded. *Collection of the East Fishkill Historical Society.*

Judge Anthony Van Wyck, Richard's uncle, with whom he corresponded. *Collection of the East Fishkill Historical Society.*

General Abraham Van Wyck, Richard's grandfather.
Collection of the East Fishkill Historical Society.

Elizabeth M. Van Wyck in her sitting room. *Collection of the East Fishkill Historical Society.*

The "other house," home of General Abraham Van Wyck, where Sarah lived. *Collection of the East Fishkill Historical Society.*

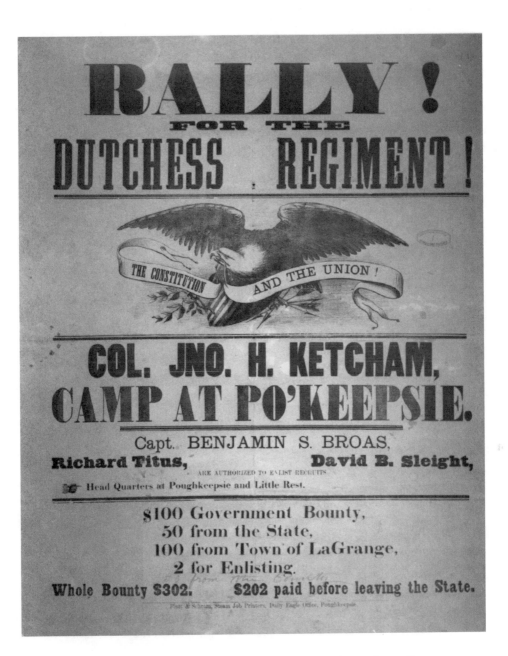

150th NYVs enlistment poster. *Courtesy of Dutchess County Historical Society.*

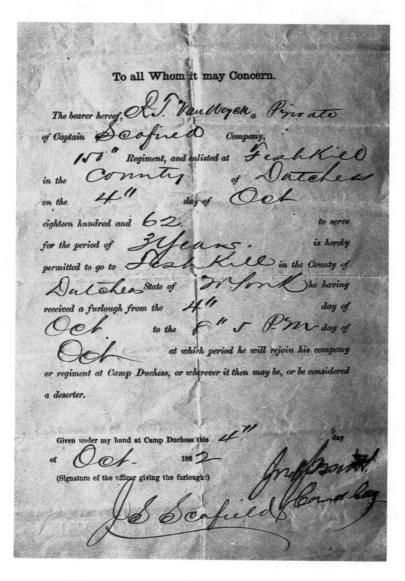

Richard T. Van Wyck's enlistment paper. *Collection of the East Fishkill Historical Society.*

The steamboat *Oregon* the 150th NYV Infantry took to Jersey
City. *Courtesy of the Steamship Historical Society Collection,
University of Baltimore Library.*

On the way to the front, the 150th was marched from the train at Philadelphia to a "Soldier's Retreat" for a free meal. *Frank Leslie's Illustrated Newspaper. Collection of John C. Quinn.*

Camden Station. On the afternoon and night of October 13, 1862, Van Wyck's regiment stayed on the platform of the Baltimore & Ohio Railroad station before taking up quarters at Camp Millington. *Courtesy of Maryland Historical Society, Baltimore.*

U.S. Army Hospital, Camden Station. The hospital buildings shown at right were the National Hotel, which Van Wyck guarded. *Courtesy of the Maryland Historical Society, Baltimore.*

Colonel John Henry Ketcham (1832-1906), chosen to head the 150th NYV Infantry. Ketcham was severely wounded on Argyle Island, in the Savannah River near Savannah, Georgia. He recovered and later served nineteen terms in the U.S. House of Representatives. *Courtesy of Dutchess County Historical Society.*

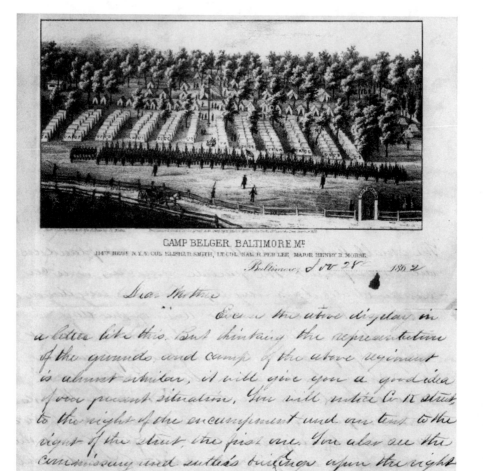

Letter from Richard T. Van Wyck on Camp Belger letterhead.
Collection of the East Fishkill Historical Society.

Camp Belger. *Courtesy of the Maryland Historical Society, Baltimore.*

Reverend Edward Otis Bartlett, Poughkeepsie, New York, Chaplain of the 150th NYV Regiment. Served from November 20, 1863, until the unit was discharged on June 8, 1865. Van Wyck wrote: "He makes no pretensions and is becoming much liked by the boys." *U.S. Army Military History Institute. Collection of John C. Quinn.*

Return of Foraging Party. "This has been a very successful attempt to supply ourselves from the country south. I saw 100 loads of corn gathered in less than two hours. How would it seem for a Dutchess Co. farmer ... upon getting up to find his fifty-acre cornfield disappeared ... I believe he would have some idea of the devastation of war."–R.T. Van Wyck. *Frank Leslie's Illustrated Newspaper. Collection of John C. Quinn.*

The breastworks on the line of Greene's brigade, Culp's Hill, Gettysburg. Van Wyck wrote of the events on July 3rd at Culp's Hill: "I never was on a battlefield before and the Lord preserve me from such a sight again. Some were wounded in our company and but few killed in the Regiment. This was owing to the protection of breastworks behind which we did terrible execution, literally piling the Rebs up in masses." *The Massachusetts Commandery Military Order of the Loyal Legion and the U.S. Army Military History Institute.*

July 21, 1864 letter from Richard to his mother. Map sketched by Richard showing his position near Atlanta. *Collection of the East Fishkill Historical Society.*

TENNESSEE—GEORGIA
1863—1864

Yet I firmly believe that the successive changes now going on in the army under the direction of the President is of great material benefit to the country; My own observation of officers commanding Brigades and Divisions convinces me that they would do anything to better themselves. Besides, the army suffers nothing from want of confidence in its generals. They fought as well under Meade as under Hooker and feel assured that the change of Grant for Rosecrans is a good one.

                                                    —R.T. Van Wyck

Scarcely a home, North or South, remained untouched by the war. The November elections declared the North's approval of the President's proclamation of freedom to the slaves, and the policy of making them soldiers. Universal freedom was now as firmly established a condition of peace as the surrender of the insurgent armies.

In the West, the Confederacy had lost two armies, considerable materiel of war and immense territory in its desperate effort to maintain control of the Mississippi River, the "Father of Waters." The central offensive line now rested upon eastern Tennessee and the northern limits of Alabama, Georgia and North Carolina.

The Army of Tennessee's Pyrrhic victory over the Federal Army at Chickamauga on September 20th, while the Dutchess County Regiment was doing picket duty on the Rapidan, failed to secure possession of Chattanooga, and the gateway to the Confederacy remained in control of the Army of the Cumberland. The cut-up Confederate forces under General Braxton Bragg seized Lookout Mountain and other heights to the west, and Missionary Ridge to the east, thereby closing off all routes to Chattanooga except for a miserable trail north of the city, which served as the only supply line for the Union Army. Hence, the Army of the Cumberland, with less than 50,000 men, was penned in at Chattanooga by rebel forces to the front and the forces of nature to the rear. It was a desperate situation. Unless a speedy rescue was organized, the threat of starvation might result in the only alternative–a disastrous retreat.

On October 16, 1863, the War Department consolidated the Departments of the Ohio, the Cumberland and the Tennessee under "The Military Division of the Mississippi," and placed it under the command of the hero of Shiloh, Fort Donelson and Vicksburg, General Ulysses S. Grant. By the same order, General Rosecrans was relieved of the command of the Army of the Cumberland, and General George H. Thomas, "The Rock of Chickamauga," took command. Grant's first executive action was to telegraph Thomas to hold Chattanooga at all "hazards." Grant also ordered General William T. Sherman to hurry forward from Vicksburg with reinforcements.

In accordance with the overall rescue plan, Fighting Joe Hooker's 11th and 12th Corps, including the 150th NYV Infantry, were detached from the Army of the Potomac and transported west by rail. The train ride across the Allegheny Mountains was breathtaking and beautiful, but also extremely uncomfortable in the box cars' limited space. The soldiers, however, engineered an ingenious way to use the only available unused space. They lashed themselves by their canteen straps and gun slings to the center plank which ran across the entire length of the freight car roof. By so doing, they were able to take advantage of a less cramped, better ventilated and more accommodating place to stretch out and sleep.

While traveling through Ohio and Indiana, the regiment was greeted by the sight of "Old Glory" waving from farmhouse porches, and lining towns and hamlets. At several places the soldiers were given receptions, and at Xenia, Ohio, a group of young ladies, arrayed in red, white and blue, sang patriotic songs. These demonstrations renewed the deep sense of purpose among the soldiers, and strengthened their belief that the cause for which they were fighting– the preservation of a great country–was the noblest of all endeavors.

By early October, the regiment had arrived where east Tennessee borders on Georgia. They settled into their winter quarters at Normandy, seven miles north of Tullahoma, in early November.

The regiment was assigned to guard the rail lines between Nashville and Chattanooga to prevent supplies from being cut off. Along with a brigade of cavalry, they went out into the countryside on several occasions to forage and to collect taxes levied on rebel citizens, which were paid as a form of reparations to the families of Union soldiers who had been ambushed and killed by local guerrillas.

During mid-November, Union troops, reinforced by Hooker, forced open a supply line called the "cracker line." On November 23rd, at Orchard Knob, Hooker's troops dashed forward and successfully swept the rebel forces from the top of Lookout Mountain. Bragg's Army retreated south to Dalton, Georgia.

In December, Lincoln offered a pardon to the rank and file of the Confederate Army—an act which would greatly influence the campaigns of the coming year and the confrontation between the Army of the Cumberland and its old enemy, the Army of Tennessee. Braxton Bragg left the western Confederate Army, and Jefferson Davis reluctantly appointed the immensely popular General Joseph E. Johnston to succeed him.

During the first several months of 1864, Union forces continued to nibble their way into the Confederacy. They were positioned from Knoxville, Tennessee, to Bridgeport, Alabama, and along the rail line from Bridgeport to Louisville, Kentucky. After the failed attempt to seize the town of Dalton, Georgia, an important railroad junction, in late February of 1864, the Union Army's posture was mainly defensive in preparation for future aggression. It was imperative to make Chattanooga a reliable base of operations to support the advance toward Atlanta, the "Gate City."

In March, Sherman was given command of the Military Division of the Mississippi. The overall situation gave encouragement to the government in Washington and strengthened the resolve of those who were determined to strike blow after blow until the South was defeated.

On April 4, 1864, by General Order No. 144, the 11th and 12th Corps, including the 150th New York Volunteers, were consolidated into the 20th Army Corps. The five-pointed star was the new corps badge, and it was placed under the command of Major-General Joseph Hooker.

On April 26, 1864, the spring advance commenced. On May 5th, Grant ordered his three armies to move forward simultaneously for their various theaters of war. Sherman's 100,000 bluecoats at Chattanooga, the Right Wing of the plan, advanced south on General "Joe" Johnston's army, whose headquarters were then at Dalton, Georgia. Sherman met Johnston head-on at Resaca on the 14th and 15th of May.

On Sunday, May 15th, the 150th, on the left of the front line, marched out on the plain of battle at Resaca. With rebel shells exploding in their midst, the regiment, still on the extreme left, made its way up a little hill where the men hastily constructed breastworks of fence rails. The rebels came out of the woods in force, formed their line of battle, and advanced on the 150th's position in the face of volley after volley of deadly musket fire. The on-rushing rebel troops were repulsed, but not before their dead lay within eighteen feet of the 150th's slender line of breastworks.

In the morning it was found that the enemy had deserted its strongly fortified position: the Battle of Resaca was over. The *Rhinebeck Gazette* published the following account of the 150th NYV's exploits at Resaca in its Tuesday edition, dated May 31st, two weeks after the engagement had ceased:

> We had a desperate battle all day yesterday, ending in the complete defeat of the Rebels who are now flying, hotly pursued by the Union Army. The 150th was in the thickest of the fight, holding a hill against a terrible charge of Rebel infantry for which they were handsomely complimented by Gens. Williams and Hooker. –Our only casualties are Adjt. Cruger, Tivoli, severely wounded in both shoulders; J. Richardson, Co. B, shoulder, severe; Corp. Stage, Co. E, face, severe: Benj. Watts, Co. E, neck severe; A.J. Mosher, Co. K, neck.

Over the next five months, Van Wyck and the other officers and enlisted men of the 150th NYVs would be in the thick of one of the most intensive military campaigns of all time–Sherman's Army was about to move against Johnston and Atlanta.

J.C.Q.

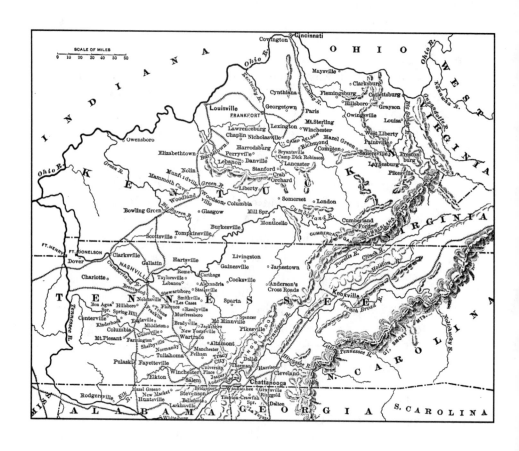

The Army of The Cumberland, by Henry M. Cist, New York, 1882.

Balt. & Ohio R.R. near 4 Md.[?]
Wheeling, [W.] Va.
Sept. 30th 1863 8 o'clock A. M.

Dear Mother,

Being drawn up in mass on the Ohio shore of the Ohio River awaiting transportation to Cincinnati I thought I would drop you a line. I have experienced all kinds of freighting and travelling by cars but this goes ahead of anything for discomfort and unpleasantness than anything I ever experienced. However, by sitting on the deck of the cars and packing myself in like a herring for the night I have got along first rate, and expecting to reach our destination in three or four days.

It seems something like old times to be moving on the cars. We have received splendid treatment so far out here, but the worst of it is, it cannot be appreciated by the mass of the soldiers, who are more like the genus <u>homo</u> than human beings. I am anticipating seeing some fine country through this, and am in hopes of getting off soon that it may not be dark.

The difference in Va. prices of living is this:

Virginia:			Ohio:		
Butter	60¢ per lb.		Butter	25¢ per lb	
Cheese	40¢ " "		Cheese	15¢ " "	
Ham	20¢ " "		Ham	12¢ " "	
Sugar	25¢ " "		Sugar	15¢ " "	

And everything else in proportion.

Jacob G. M. said from a letter received from his father that Aben was expected home and is now with you. I hope to hear from you soon and will give you my address – although for the present the same will answer. George Burroughs is at the Hospital in Washington.

We held our <u>own</u> still at Chattanooga* and by this time makes this twice doubly sure. This winter campaign will close the war, I am sure. With much love, I remain, your afft. Son

R. T. Van Wyck

---

* The Union line had at first cracked and broke on the field at nearby Chickamauga in the face of an overwhelming offensive by Confederate Gen. Longstreet. But Union Gen. Thomas, later called "the Rock of Chickamauga," repelled the Confederate advance until reserves saved the day. *Encyclopedia of American History*, ed. R.B. Morris, p. 242.

Stevenson, Alabama
Oct. 4th 1863

Dear Mother,

We arrived here last night and for the first time slept upon Terra Firma since leaving Va. We have almost finished our journey which we expect to complete by marching. Upon the whole had a nice time, for in passing through Western States were treated well by the inhabitants. From Bellaire we passed through Xenia and Columbus, Ohio, to Indianapolis, Indiana, then South to Louisville, Ky., then to Nashville, Tenn., and then to this place. Saw the country under favorable circumstances by travelling little in the night, and the weather fair in the daytime.

We find the news from [*Gen.*] Rosecrans very encouraging, he having inflicted more loss than received. Besides, everyone is sanguine of his successful generalship.* We don't expect to remain long idle as he has never been known to be guarding wooden guns.

You will hear from us before long. In the meanwhile write, and don't expect I can correspond as readily as on the Potomac. With much love I remain, your afft.

Son
R. T. Van Wyck

Oct. 11th 1863
Tullahoma, Tenn.

Dear Mother,

I received yours of the 23rd inst. last evening in answer to mine, prior to my leaving Virginia. I hope you have received mine since, at different points on the route, and also at Stevenson in Alabama. You probably wonder at this retrograde movement, for I intimated our destination was to directly reinforce Rosecrans in front. But while awaiting orders from our commanding Gen. Joe Hooker, the supplies of the army were in a fair way of being cut off by the burning of several Bridges on the RailRoad between here and Nashville by a large body of Rebel Cavalry. Accordingly [*we*] were ordered back to guard the erection again. Part of our Brigade, however, got

---

*In actual fact, General Rosecrans had faltered badly at Chickamauga. He was subsequently relieved of command and sent to the Missouri theatre of war. *Civil War Battles*, by Johnson and McLaughlin, N.Y., 1977.

into a fight with them at Shelby[*ville*]. We took 600 and one piece of artillery.

It is the design of this corps to relieve or strengthen the troops now doing duty on this road and prevent such a mishap in future, for it would be very disastrous to the army. We have therefore been much occupied during the week in being moved about and [*this*] has given me a better view in detail of the country [*here*] about. Permit me to say that finer streams of water running over solid limestone, larger forest trees of oak, chestnut, whitewood and cottonwood I never saw.

Tullahoma, you recollect, was to be the last ditch of Bragg on his retreat from Murfreesboro, and accordingly the country is much devastated by the contending armies. Directly surrounding the town are rifle pits which will shelter sixty thousand men and positions for many pieces of artillery which the Rebs had the laborious task of making, which answers of some use to us.

The country it seemed was quite unfitted for so to be made memorable by the last struggles of the heroic chivalry, for no sooner did Rosecrans appear ready to flank them on their right than they beat a hasty retreat towards Chattanooga. The town might have possessed some beauty in its day, in the center of a plain of <u>oaks</u> which Bragg had cut away, as well as destroyed most of the town by fire, as well as converted into tent fixtures all unoccupied houses including the church, which might once have been quite a comely structure. Their vandalism has given us the wherewithal to make ourselves comfortable in tent buildings.

The weather is fine and I never felt better in my life than at present. I had the misfortune to lose a tooth the other day, making the second of my doubles[*?*] gone, a sacrifice to hard tack and hot coffee. In view of [*lack of*] attention in the field we had them all fixed up in Baltimore, but rather than make myself miserable by their aching I had them taken out.

I received a letter from Sarah with yours of last evening, giving me the news up to the thirtieth, stating of Aben's arrival, but said nothing about his family, also of Fred and Aunt Mary's visit. He seems to have gone with them to Albany; if that is the [*length of*] time he stayed home, he is making a short visit. She speaks of John Sherwood's anticipated marriage and tour. I presume she is not quite as well posted in their family affairs now as she will be or will become, for if I mistake not she has a hereditary claim that way.

Robt. Johnston's first gleanings of his vineyard has indubitably put him in first-rate humour. I hope it might incite him to a line once in a while, for I have used my eyes a little that way and could tell him of a vine whose trunk was all of eight inches in diameter and reached into (without a turn or throwing out any lateral branches) a white-wood from eighty to one hundred feet high, whose base body was five feet through, and whose branches joined with a chestnut, which Capt. Scofield said would cut 150 Rails. I didn't look for the <u>grapes,</u> for I thought I would see some new wonder and would be obliged to narrate of several sumptuous meals from one berry alone, sounding too Californian to be believed.

But I drank of an adjacent spring which might have been the juices of the grape compared with our previous Virginia mud, gushing from the base of a limestone Mt. giving power to a mill of several stone, and the main tributary of a river 150 feet wide and two feet deep two miles from its source (called Duck River) and which I was under the painful necessity of fording the other day twice.

But I must close this, lest I should task your credulity too much at once, and hoping I might in the course of time get an answer.

Love to all. With much love I remain, your afft. Son

R. T. Van Wyck

Direct: 3rd Brig., 1st Div., 12 A.C., Army of Cumberland.

The following note is written on the back of this same letter:

Oct. 26th

My dear Wife,

Louisa has just told me that John Sherwood will have a reception at his Brother Isaac's, Wednesday or Thursday of next week. Mrs. Sherwood says that you and the Girls must be home to be present. I will hear before I come down, so you and the girls must be in readiness to return with me either Wednesday or Thursday.

I received this morning this letter from Richard. I will send by Mail today. I am going today down to the Village on business of the farm. Jackson's. I wish I could be relieved from it, but no help for me. All are well here and at the [*other*] house.

Yours affectionately,

(signed) James Van Wyck

Normandy, Tenn.
Nov. 1st 1863

Dear Mother,

Yours of Oct. 20th and 22nd reached me last evening. Glad to hear of the general good health of those at home. I am sorry Aben's visit was so unsatisfactory. He received some wholesome advice from the old gentleman, however disagreeable it might be to him.

We had a severe frost this morning which gave us a smacking of old Winter. When last I wrote you I expected to move towards Chattanooga from Tullahoma, but fortunately the Regt. was ordered back after crossing and recrossing the mountains that separated us, which gave them some sore feet and limbs. As luck had it, I escaped the march and after their return came with them to this point, about seven miles north of Tullahoma.

It's a picturesque little place enclosed in the hills (not like Normandy in France, noted for its wines and fruits) but might be made historic as the home of the Tenn. freemen, growing corn hardly sufficient for their consumption. Many of these come into our camp daily and give accounts of their sufferings during Bragg's rule, and their conscription and escape.

We get the papers very irregularly and consequently are little posted in the general topics. I hardly am able to say whether to feel confident of our permanent settlement here for the winter, for no sooner than we had begun to make ourselves comfortable by building houses than we were ordered to leave them.

The express on a box would be $7.25 per hundred lbs. from New York. So if you have been thinking of any such a thing, I can forgo such expensive luxuries, under such circumstances, and can appreciate your good intentions for my comfort and phisical [sic] health which, particularly the latter, would not be much benefited were they not of such solid and substantial food such as butter, dried fruits, etc., except apples, as they would be of all others most desirable. With frequent letters from home I can survive the Winter without this contribution of your kindness, hoping they will fit me by good spirits to digest Uncle Sam's compounds all the better. By the way, we manufacture flour into pancakes and biscuit which are very palatable.

With much love I remain, your afft. Son

R. T. Van Wyck

Normandy, Tenn.
Nov. 5th 1863

Dear Mother,

Today has commenced one of those spells of wet weather common in this climate. Fortunately, I am pretty well housed, now and then a drop strikes near where I am sitting, but I feel fortunate to have a dry place to sleep in, to say nothing of writing accommodations, etc.

We have at different times been deluded with the hope that we had put aside our migratory nature and were agoing to be stationary for the winter; but as often disappointed and been obliged to leave partially finished houses, sometimes to occupy shanties erected by other regiments, and as often have been obliged to take up quarters upon "Terra Firma," well ventilated. As to shanty building we have many different styles, differing with the materials used, (cut uniformly of one length, perhaps 12 ft. by six). The fireplace and door in one end, tier of bunks for four in the other. The hight [sic] of the sides not often more than four feet. If made of logs, the same every way, except some rough. In some of the fireplaces an oven is inserted which, at one encampment we occupied only a few hours, we had the satisfaction of baking delicious biscuit (so we thought in comparison with Tenn. manufacture).

The Potomac Army are decidedly the best builders of shanties. The Western [army]* are more shiftless and careless. But enough of this. Suffice it to say while we are thus occupied our mind is employed and our minds are not dwelling upon the disagreeable inconveniences of this position, shut out of mail and news facilities. You can easily grasp how my mind reverts to home when I get a letter and would wish to sit down and have a long talk upon various subjects.

I wrote you Sunday and then today. It is now the first time I can write without either substituting the top of my cap or some smooth board, but now I have got things in a little different shape and will

---

* When the Eastern 11th and 12th Corps from the Army of the Potomac were first transferred to Tennessee they were subjected to considerable ribbing by the battle-hardened veterans of the Western armies. *The March to the Sea and Beyond*, by Jos. T. Glatthaar, N.Y., 1985, pp. 30-33.

give all my correspondents a dip of my pen soon. The girls are now in New York at Mrs. Lane's. By Sarah's letter of Oct. 29th, John Sherwood's wedding party will be given at Isaac's at Johnsville [*Wiccopee*]. She also says Isaac Kip has returned from the Army, having got enough of it.

With love to all, I remain your aff't Son

R. T. Van Wyck

Normandy, Tenn.
Nov. 11th 1863

Dear Mother,

Yours of Nov. 1st and 2nd were received Nov. 9th and 10th. The latter enclosed the $10, which I was glad to receive. No change has taken place here yet and apparently the same as when I last wrote you, except the weather has turned quite wintry. Luckily we have a cook stove in our shanty which throws out abundance of heat, so it makes little difference outside as long as it is comfortable within.

I have received a letter from Uncle Anthony also informing me of his estimation by his countrymen, to be nominated for the State Senate. I differ from you in believing it is not the thing for him to accept the office, if elected. For with the exception of his health, I believe his qualifications, experience, universal popularity, and moral principles would not only place him in a position very creditable to himself, but to his constituents that had the good sense to elect him. As to the way of redeeming his indebtedness, his chances are as good in that as [*they*] would be in the present business; because his present position (if acquired) comes to him without money, why shouldn't the gains from it, besides what is strictly wanted for his family, go to that office. I only hope he has his health, should he be elected.

I am glad to hear of Fred's increased business. It is astonishing how the country is humming with activity during this gigantic war, except in parts, the center of and theater of this rebellion. We are receiving good news from Meade's Army in Vir.[*ginia*]. And the suffering and poverty comes to us oftener than ever from the South. From what I see in these parts of their situation [*in the*] South and what I learn here, it is true. This alone will finish the war if nothing else.

165

What are Aben's prospects?* The same as usual? It doesn't surprise me in the least to hear of Isaac Kip's return home. He could easy enough get up a quarrel with the Colonel to get his discharge, if that would effect one. He hasn't made much by leaving South Brooklyn.

Please excuse this hurried letter. I will write again as soon as possible. I remain with much love your afft. Son

R. T. Van Wyck

Normandy, Tenn.
Nov. 15th 1863

Dear Cousin [Sarah],

I have been repeatedly called to mind [for] my negligence of epistolary duty by receiving a letter from you. But unfortunately my time has been so occupied at various things, with scarcely time to let the folks at home know of my whereabouts, that so long a period has ensued since last heard from personally. And then again I thought during your visiting at Albany and New York my letters would not reach you in time at those places and [I] would defer my doing so till you arrived at home, as you are now.

In leaving Va. I assure you we did it with a cheer. My own feelings upon the matter was somehow very indifferent upon the subject, only we should go somewhere, and the sooner the better. The railroad trip here, through Ohio and Indiana was much enjoyed, even notwithstanding our <u>very</u> <u>commodious</u> <u>cattle</u> <u>cars</u>, inside serving as sleeping quarters for the night laid away like <u>herring</u>, while during the day sat up on top and surveyed the country. Fortunately, there always seemed some trouble with railroad transportation when it came dark, and we generally halted for the night in some village.

As a sample of Western ladies' hospitality, let me mention a case that happened at Xenia, Ohio, where they set before us upon our

---

* Aben (Abraham J. Van Wyck), Richard's older brother, was graduated from Williams College and the Poughkeepsie Law School, and began practicing law in Brooklyn, New York, but family records state that "he was converted at a noonday prayer meeting and joined the Methodist Episcopal Church. Believing he had a call to preach the Gospel he gave up the law, to the disappointment of his friends, and began his life work in Michigan." Remembered as a man of few words and of unusual strength of character, a colleague wrote of him, that, "he read the best books, thought the best thoughts, spoke the best words, and did the best things." He died at the age of fifty in 1886, leaving a wife and four children.

arrival all manner of eatables. Upon getting out of the cars, all dusty and dirty and not presenting withal a very comely appearance, I soon made myself acquainted with two ladies of fine appearance, who inquired of our Regt. and Corps, which led to some remarks of the fine country surrounding – as they expressed it, "A right smart bit of land." In pursuing the acquaintance still further, I found them informed in all army movements and [*they*] made all allowance for the many rude, drunken men in the cars. I was much pleased with this testimonial of their kindness and came to the conclusion they were "right smart" patriots. It seemed the farther we went west the better we fared, and voted Government rations a poor institution.

In your letter of Oct. 29th you mentioned the return of Isaac Kip. With no reflections upon his changeable habits, I cannot censure his course. He has "seen the Elephant"* like the rest of us and agoing to quit the concern. I will give it a year more fair trial and then you may hear what I will have to say under the heading of patriotism. As Artemus Ward expresses it, "I will be ready to shed the blood of all my wife's brothers to prosecute the war."

Address as before 150th Regt., 12th Corps, 1st Div., Army of the Cumberland. You can give me the particulars of that party at the Sherwood's. With much love, I remain

Your afft. Cousin
R. T. Van Wyck

Normandy, Tenn
Nov. 21st '63

Dear Mother,

Not having received a letter recently I thought you might not have received some of my letters to answer them. No material change has taken place here. The weather has been quite pleasant but now the rain is visiting us again.

I am comfortably situated, being with two others the occupants of a shanty, six by ten, with a cook stove. This latter <u>institution</u> gives us splendid biscuit, etc. We have lived famously the last ten days or rather a week upon a carcass of mutton, and upon looking into our larder we find nothing remains of what was once 75 lbs. of meat. The bacon and hard tack we always have [*in*] abundance, the other stores

---

* Soldiers' slang for having been in combat.

of sugar, coffee, tea, has played out. The dinner today consists of baked beans, what tomorrow will consist of may be the old one of fried bacon and tack. First a feast, then a famine, is the way here. It doesn't make any difference with my health, for I find it keeps the equilibrium very well.

Jacob Montross says there are some things coming for _me_ in his box which was shipped Nov. 13th. I don't know but the welcomed articles you sent will induce me to send for such, during the winter.

I had written so far when I was handed your letter of Nov. 12th informing me of the box, etc. The stamps came very acceptable, so will the paper and envelopes. The sugar, etc., will be truly enjoyed, so will the shirts. I had made up my mind to content myself with Govt. shirts. As I have not got them yet, those coming from home will be very acceptable.

It quite surprised me to hear of J. Sherwood's ill health. A "smart" idea, that, to get married and go to a water cure, there having the kind nursing of his wife to comfort him. She must be a very "useful" woman, and be so regarded, by her "better half." This politic arrangement of J. S. has caused some talk, has it not?

I had forgotten to ask you (in answer to your letter) wherein Mrs. A. V. W. Van Vechten* was so extremely polite in not extending to you the hospitalities of her house, if that's got to be the latest custom among housekeepers, or is there some malicious feeling still existing from associations in 10th Street? I would like to hear of Uncle Anthony's success. I hope he will be elected.

We were paid yesterday – I have acknowledged the receipt of the $10 in a previous letter. Geo. Burroughs has told you something of hard times in Virginia. And you have observed he is not over-hopeful as to the success of the Union cause. He has written me of his present situation upon David's Island and his intention of coming on to the Regt. I wish I could have his length of furlough to hear what is going on, and to tell you many things almost impossible with pen and ink to do. However, I am perhaps hoping against hope that our troubles will come to an end by next June so that I may be with you again.

From the papers you know of Sherman's reinforcing the Army of the Cumberland to the amount of 40,000 by way of the Memphis

---

* Sarah's sister-in-law.

and Charleston R.R. A conflict is inevitable, as the Rebs are likewise massing large forces the other side of Chattanooga. I think our position will be permanent here during the Winter; at any rate I hope so.* Write soon. I remain your afft. Son

R. T. Van Wyck

P. S. Enclose a fine [*toothed*] comb in your next letter.

Normandy, Tenn.
November 25th 1863

Dear Mother,

Yours of November 19th was received today. I am glad to hear RailRoad enterprise had not altogether died out in your part of the country. As to the stock paying such handsome dividends, to many it must bring to mind the Fishkill plank road while yet in its infancy, and many conclusions are now being made among the landholders as to its successful enhancement of property. I dare say this is [*the*] most [*that*] can be said of it.

Walter Anthony on his visit to his Uncle at Kenosha (so Uncle Anthony also writes me) met with little favor, as to his political principles. His views of the war are decidedly contracted and narrow, being blinded by party partiality and looking only at the shocking schemes of corruption and intrigue everywhere prevalent.

I am glad to hear of Sarah Hoyt's arrival in Fishkill after such trouble. Were it not for the refined tendencies of her excellent mother, a permanent settlement in the East would of all things be most desirable. A total isolation from an active enterprising society like their position is, is to be much deplored. Of course, their situation is not exactly similar to the inhabitants in these parts, but from specimens of the women seen here at all farm houses who are so decidedly filthy and looking as if they had been submitted to a boiling process like the sugar cane, and all their goodness extracted. On being addressed [*by them*] with the common remark, "Oh, John, give me a chew of tobacco," with this, all sympathy would certainly vanish and with it very likely all visions of sweet <u>femmes</u> to be found here.

---

* Once again, by the luck of the draw, R.T. Van Wyck's regiment was kept "out of harm's way" of the bloody Chattanooga campaign (Nov. 23-25) since the First Division of the 12th Corps under Gen. Henry Slocum had been detached from Hooker's forces to guard the vital railroad lines from Murfreesboro to Bridgeport, Alabama, during the next six months. *The Shipwreck of Their Hopes: The Battle for Chattanooga*, by Peter Cozzens, 1994.

I have often wondered how you stand it for apples, cider, and nuts. And this evening I can picture the dishes of fruit and cider set before you (usually about eight o'clock, the old custom.) Although at present living, we call it here "famously," I cannot subdue a yearning for Caroline's dishes, and with a view to familiarize ourselves to a little civilized niceties, my companion has intimated to me [*that*] a cookbook of small size, to get an idea of cooking <u>crullers,</u> etc., would be very useful. Have no fears of its practicability, for we are practical men and always obliged to eat our own cooking.

The box has not come yet. I shall be quickly informed of its arrival by my friend Jacob G., whose whole thoughts seemed absorbed in its contents, the disposition of which has a hundred times been made in his mind with evident delight. From a letter to Jacob from home, it therein states of the gradual failing of GrandFather's health. [*Of*] this I was sorry to hear, but as you wrote nothing about it I presume it is so gradual as not perceptible by the family.

The marriage of Maria Jane Van Brunt, whose engagement you mentioned in a previous letter, is to be consummated tomorrow. She has my hearty wishes for her future happiness, and may he have <u>soul</u> enough to at least pass well as her representative for a husband. And on the morrow, [*Thanksgiving Day*] the occasion for offering thankful hearts to God for national successes in battle and universal prosperity throughout the land, <u>he</u> ought to be thankful that his perception of human nature made this discovery, of so smugly reinstating himself in such a household, with the rank "Imperial."

The boarding scheme of Mr. Lane's* is a good thing if they are to pursue the economical plan, but where will the girls stay while in the city? Will the generous hospitality of 47th Street be offered? [*I*] don't believe there is any difficulty in monetary matters with its stacks of paper currency. For why shouldn't the country feel the pressures of the present times: An army a million strong to clothe and feed, taken wholly from the producing industry of the country, would certainly bring about some upward tendencies in the price of things, should the currency be gold or paper. To say nothing of this taxation for raising exorbitant bounties to volunteers in <u>patriotic</u> neighborhoods like E. Fishkill. It would be equivalent to asking more for our butter and farm products. Or to an army capitalist and contractor who

---

* His Aunt Susan's husband.

honorably discharges his duty, is advantageous to the country in preventing a want of confidence of the Govt. securities by his circulation of capital. The Govt. doesn't seek its supplies abroad, either of food and clothing. It has not nor never will have any heavy indebtedness to be met with <u>Gold</u> from imports. The <u>mines</u> of California* will meet the present demand and will certainly do so in future for all necessary importations. <u>The people</u> only have confidence this structure will not collapse yet.

And now as to "patriotism" in connection with army sacrifices, it may be at a very low ebb, and valued as so much money or the prospect of so much political influence to be gained by it. Yet I firmly believe that the successive changes now going on in the army under the direction of the President is of great material benefit to the country; to prevent (like McClellan) the popularity of the army to give him the rank of dictator and altogether subvert our government and make it a military despotism. Would McClellan have done this? Or Burnside? Or Rosecrans? My own observation of officers commanding Brigades and Divisions convinces me that they would do anything to better themselves. Besides, the army suffers nothing from want of confidence in its generals. They fought as well under Meade as under Hooker and feel assured that the change of Grant** for Rosecrans is a good one.

At present the great cry of McClellan's mistreatment is altogether died away, and at any time more of it [was] shown among the people than in the army. It comes with ill grace from those who have shielded themselves from personal danger in a war, by their pecuniary means, to think patriotism is "played out" by this expedient. But what must those who have passed through a Summer's

---

* The discovery of gold in California in 1849 was, without a doubt, a key factor in the Union's survival. During the Civil War $5 or $6 million in gold from California flowed monthly into the economy, adding up to $785 million by war's end. This influx gave a boost to business and trade and enabled the government to sell its war bonds, thus sustaining its credit and giving it the wherewithal to provision and maintain its armies. *Assembling California*, by John McPhee; Farrar, Straus & Geroux, 1993, New York.

** After the Union fiasco at Chickamauga, President Lincoln, looking for a general who would fight, appointed Gen. U.S. Grant to the supreme command of the Western armies.

Campaign feel, who perhaps may have an apology for their want of it. I am assured that God in his own good time (and that, not far distant) will bring harmony out of confusion. Excuse this long letter poorly expressed, hoping to hear from you soon again, I remain your afft.   Son

R. T. Van Wyck

P. S. I wish you would send me a paper of C[ourt]. plaster. My hands are somewhat sore.

[*Thanksgiving Day*]*
Normandy, Tenn.
Nov. 26th 1863

Dear Cousin [*Sarah*],

After the receipt of your letter of the 17th I made the attempt to answer it, but so poor an apology for a letter it seemed to me that I could not send it. Again I have put the machine in operation to see if I could devise something that would at least pass not to reflect upon my correspondent's correspondence with the army.

While you today are making the most of what Providence has set before you in the shape of Turkeys, Chickens, and the like, I am occasionally casting my eye upon a beef stew on the stove before me which, upon its completion, that, with some biscuit (that we make) Sorg[h]um molasses, butter, and coffee, will constitute our meal.

Among all the blessings I am thankful of receiving, first of all is good health, then comes the comforts of a roof to sit under, a stove to sit by, and enough to eat. If our house is of an abridged style (being no larger than the old Plank Road Gate Houses) every board and nail was made into it for a purpose. And the economy of room would put modern architecture on unexplored garrets, in the shade (for we have lots of room).

The festivities of the season now being over, you must feel somewhat dull and lonesome. That is, the inclement weather during the winter season will prevent those except such as are drawn by the force of female attraction, from visiting.

---

* After the Revolutionary War the first national Thanksgiving Day proclaimed by George Washington was November 26, 1789. Abraham Lincoln, urged by Sarah J. Hale, revived the custom officially in 1863, designating the last Thursday in November as the date.

H. Du Boise was present at the party. No doubt his departure from the neighborhood will be much lamented. It was refreshing to hear Miss Lane enjoys such excellent health, and improving as years pass by, in reposing into that state of single blessedness that all ladies much dislike to bear.

Mr. Woodhull is still with you and will give you a sermon today. It is a long time since I have heard a sermon. It must be since last August in Virginia. They say we have a chaplain, but he has not made his appearance.

The coming weeks will decide the operations this Fall. We have every reason to believe they will be successes. At any rate we hope so, and thus close the war by next Spring. Excuse the ink, etc. I remain, your afft. Cousin,

R. T. Van Wyck

P. S. My stew is done and I take my dinner. 2 P.M.

EDITOR'S NOTE:

That November of 1863 President Lincoln issued a Proclamation asking that the people observe Thanksgiving in spite of the war:

"The year that is drawing toward its close has been filled with the blessings of fruitful fields and healthful skies," it began. "To these bounties, which are so constantly enjoyed that we are prone to forget the source from which they come, others have been added" – "extraordinary blessings." He goes on to say that in the midst of a terrible civil war, yet look at the blessings: we are at peace with all others save the Rebels, and inch by inch they are being pushed back, and that despite the "needful diversions of wealth and strength from the fields of peaceful labor to the national defence," the population has been expanding and there is so much wealth and energy left that all the mines have been worked as usual and the farms cultivated and new lands cleared.

"No human counsel hath devised, nor hath any mortal hand worked out these great things. They are the gracious gifts of the Most High God who, while dealing with us in anger for our sins has, nevertheless, remembered mercy. It has seemed to me fit and proper that they should be so solemnly, reverently, and gratefully acknowledged as with one heart and voice by the whole American people.

"I do therefore invite my fellow-citizens in every part of the United States, and also those who are at sea, and those who are sojourning in foreign countries, to set apart and observe"...the day of Thanksgiving. And he asks the people, while they are giving thanks, "to commend to God's tender care" all those who have been good enough and brave enough to fight for their country..."all those who are dead on the field of honour and have gone to a world of glory," and he asked them also to pray "that the wounds of the nation may be healed."

To Robert Johnston

Normandy, Tenn.
Dec. 5th 1863

Dear Robert,

Yours of the 22nd has been received. Need I say it was welcomed, it was more than that, for it seemed like meeting a friend in a strange land. Mother, upon whose correspondence is my chief reliance to keep alive my fondness for home in its gleanings of news, etc., besides gratifying my selfish passion to occupy in their perusal the many leisure hours. Once in a while a neighbor comes in our shanty to talk about the news, which I am always ready to hear and discuss.

Since the date of your letter you have received the joyous announcement of our great success in these parts. Burnside's heroic resistance against Longstreet; Grant's, Hooker's, and Sherman's complete rout of Bragg's army. This has made the newspapers interesting. In the meanwhile, the old Army of the Potomac has made again one of its old strategistic [*his word*] movements, the results of which seems quite as mysterious as formerly. However, these blows have effectually released Tenn. and Ky. from Rebel rule, thereby narrowing their territory in men and means, assuring us that we are progressing by hard blows toward an effectual subjugation of the South. The sooner the better t'would suit me.*

Perhaps you noticed the 2d division of the 12th Corps under Gen. Geary participated to great advantage in the late battle. By a strange fatality their position would have been our own, the 1st Div.'s, had it not been for the rivalry of the two Generals, resulting in the success of Geary, the senior. We had almost reached Chattanooga when ordered back, the 2d to take our place. Our position is decidedly preferable to the front (save the glories), even that is taken with a great deal of discount on the scale of health. We will get there soon enough.

---

* In a series of battles at Chattanooga on November 23-25, Union forces under Gen. Grant (appointed head of the Western armies on October 10) succeeded in driving the Rebels out of the Mississippi Valley. These actions set the stage for Gen. Sherman's Atlanta campaign by opening the gateway to the Deep South.

I have seen some of the best farming land in this State and Ky. that one would wish to behold. The more we approach the Southern boundary of the State, the more hilly and mountainous, but all along the streams, and they are very numerous, the soil is very fertile. With the cultivation of the East here, it would be one of the best sections of country to live in.

Geo. Burroughs came on from New York a few days ago. He seemed fully recovered in health, but acts homesick. This is said to be a very sympathetic and contagious disease, but my digestion remains the same for all palatable viands.

For variety a few weeks ago my comrades and myself took a stroll outside the picket lines, and introduced ourselves to a stray flock of sheep, selecting three fine ones, singly bearing them on our shoulders, marched into our quarters. The fries, roasts, and boils followed each other in quick succession till they all vanished, and that was not long. We had made an arrangement with an old settler to bring us in a wild turkey for Thanksgiving which he tells me frequent a spring near his house in quite a flock. But he did not bring it. I have seen them near the R.R. track in search of the scattering <u>corn</u> that falls from the cars, bringing many a bullet after them.

Chicken, butter, eggs, bread, and cake are brought into camp in rather small quantity—of the former—and any amount of the latter. The vendors are those "snuff-chewing angels" perched upon some aged horse or mule that our correspondent for the *Eagle* gave so glowing a description of. Indeed, this life is fast making bachelors of us. For as to cooking, baking, washing, and mending, the aforesaid females bear no comparison to our skill.

Hoping our pleasant times here will continue and that I may have many opportunities to write you from this place, desiring to be remembered to your Mother and Uncle, I remain you afft.

Friend   R. T. Van Wyck

P. S. Jacob G. Montross is looking finely. Says if we remain here, would feel satisfied. We both are looking for a box said to have been sent the 13th of last month. I hope we will get it by Christmas or New Year's.

Normandy, Tenn.
Dec. 14th '63

Dear Mother,

Yours was received the 12th. Enclosed I found the C. Plaster and

Comb. The latter of which, coupled with your healthy suggestion that "an ounce of preventive is better than a pound of cure" was truly welcomed. The truth of the matter is this: I usually carried a towel, soap, comb, and glass in the skirt pocket of my coat all through the marches last summer, and whenever an opportunity offered by coming across a spring or stream of water I could always make myself comfortable. From such arduous duties the old comb has "played out," making it necessary for me to replace it the best way possible.

So far the cold weather has been slight, the ground scarcely frozen. At present the rain has just left us and beginning to be cold.

I was sorry to hear of the death of Mrs. Van Brunt,* following so quickly the death of her husband. Their genial hospitality upon my city visits will always be remembered. But particularly to those friends directly connected and associated with them will this separation be keenly felt.

I am much indebted to Father for his letter giving me the <u>farm</u> news, etc. I hope they might be more frequent. The box sent so long ago has not arrived. Jacob has written home as to the receipt, giving his father the necessary instructions to find out what is the matter. It is quite likely at Nashville, to which place we have written, hearing nothing from it. I hope it will at least be our Christmas box, if intended to be disposed previously.

The army and political news are soon digested amongst us and of late have been highly favored in the regularity of the dailies from Nashville and Louisville, giving us the President's Message, and the relapse of the Army of the Potomac into its old malady, the lockjaw (as R. Johnston says).

We (that is, the Army of the Cumberland) I am proud to say have been more successful of late. Whether it is directly attributable to the importation of the 150th from the Army of the Potomac, and a little of the combination of some of its notorious strategistic [sic] ideas with some of the vim of the Western men, or directly the reverse, I do not know. Our <u>base</u> seems secure yet, and I hope will be till Spring, when perhaps we may be found marching in the opposite direction—homeward bound.

With much love to all I remain your afft. Son

R. T. Van Wyck

---

* The Van Brunts are relatives of his mother.

P. S. I have received the *Harper's* and the papers. Tell the Other House folks [*the Van Vechtens*] their papers have been received, although I have been negligent in acknowledging them as I should.

New Year's Day 1864
Normandy, Tenn.

Dear Cousin [*Sarah*],

May this be a substitute for a call, and my wishes to you all for a Happy New Year. It always seems this day is fated to be cold and bleak, for we are now experiencing the coldest day of the season, the ground closed with the frost and a thin coat of snow barely concealing the earth, which previously has been in a favorable state for constructing earthworks for defense.

I presume I can rightly conclude of the fine sleighing, of the attentive watching down the lane for the many comers in their "turn-outs" to pay their compliments to both young and old—at Fishkill with you.

My stability of present comfort is hung upon such a feeble thread, that of course I couldn't tell what during the next two months will turn up to interfere with our fine arrangements in Winter quarters, but as yet know nothing to the contrary [*against*] remaining here during the Winter.

The Winter season of Society meetings, evenings' entertainments has commenced in earnest with you, and the many events that give an unending torrent of talk and gossip are unknown [*here*] and perhaps [*are*] <u>now</u> above my comprehension since my sojourn in the Wilderness hasn't been improving my "civilized tendencies." <u>Our</u> programme of the evenings consists of a Prayer meeting, Singing school, and a declaiming Society organized by our <u>new</u> Chaplain.

I have received all the papers sent me, and just received *Harper's* for Dec. from Mother. Reading matter of all kinds is much wanted. Don't wait till your letters are answered before you write another, if anything turns up interesting. My stationary living forbids it upon my part.

Remember me to GrandFather and the rest of the family. With much love I remain your aff. Cousin

R. T. Van Wyck

177

2nd Jan.

I received a letter informing me of Mr. Delevan's death, and also of GrandFather's ill health. Also stating the very cold weather. We here till yesterday thought of going out in our shirt sleeves; to wear an overcoat [*seemed*] preposterous.

Tullahoma, Tenn.
Jan. 4th, '63[*sic*] ['*64*]

Dear Mother,

I received yours, as a "New Year's [*greeting*]," the 1st. At which time we were favored with the coldest weather of the season, and the old settlers here say the coldest since the past ten years. But now it is all over and it is quite moderate again. GrandFather's declining health quite took me by surprise and pain, inasmuch as my connection in the army prevents the possibility of seeing him again. The death of Mr. Delevan, although at the time of [*my*] leaving home his life hung upon a slender thread, I had quite forgotten [*about it*] till your letter announced his death.

We remain much the same, as upon my last letter, except the time passes slowly and very monotonous. Shanty building gave us something to do, besides our employment upon the Stockade, both of which seem completed. A description of the latter by a correspondent of the *Eagle* has not passed your notice: Such a conglomeration of barroom slang and little wit would be readily observed. I suppose it is intended to bring the 150th into notice again, since the next Presidential election will leave a vacancy for Congressman, an eligible one for our Colonel. Such men don't scruple to pull so insignificant and dirty a ruse as that was intended to be. During this repose of the army, matters of that kind are forgotten. We are nearing the half of our allotted period of enlistment and the time will not seem so long when we begin to turn the scale, yet I am in hopes that period will be really short.

That unfortunate box – if you could know how much it is commented upon, its arrival would certainly be no small matter of talk for Co. "K." As every train approaches from the "North," its announcement is usually indicated with "I'll go and get your box." A few things – paper for one – wouldn't come amiss.

This might find you in the city. With much love I remain your afft.

Son   R. T. Van Wyck

P. S. Normandy instead of Tullahoma. My mistake.

EDITOR'S NOTE:
    R. T. Van Wyck omits mentioning that on January 1, 1864, he was pro-
moted to sergeant.

Normandy, Tenn.
Jan. 14th, '64

Dear Mother,
    I received your letter this morning. I have delayed writing, expect-
ing to hear every day how GrandFather is getting along and that he yet
lives. I am pleased to hear how little pain he suffers and that his
approaching end is so peaceful and happy. Great changes will have
taken place in the neighborhood, perhaps ere this letter reaches you;
the speedy summons of Mr. Delevan and the death of GrandFather
will leave quite a blank in the place, particularly the latter.
    New Year's ushered in with a keen perception of Old Winter
made us keep close to our shanties but now the icy shackles are loos-
ened and [we] are now enjoying fine Spring weather.
    The war items are uninteresting and there seems a great calm like
as before a great storm, which undoubtedly will open in the Spring
with sanguine expectation of success and with all the available power
the Govt. can hurl against the Rebs. The reenlisted men after having
returned, recuperated by their short furlough, will give fresh vigor to
the contest. We will by that time mass a large army at this point
strong enough to drive everything before us. I may mention, as a
rumour, that the 12th Corps is to be detached from this army and join
an expedition getting up in New York for aggressive movement along
the coast, or a concerted plan upon Richmond by way of the James
River. I cannot vouch for its authenticity. Time will tell.
    The box has not arrived yet. I think it never will. Hoping to
hear from you soon, I remain your aff. Son   R. T. Van Wyck

Normandy, Tenn.
Jan. 18th, '64

Dear Mother,
    I received yours, mailed the 11th, yesterday. I was glad to hear,
again, how GrandFather is doing. The event of his death will leave

179

a blank in the family which time only can efface. Everything connected with the farm, his zeal and interestedness [*his word*] pertaining to it, as well as his free and disinterested counsel and advice to those in trouble in the neighborhood will make his death keenly felt. You mentioned also the death of Mrs. Cotheal [*?*] and the severe illness of Wesley Pierce, both of which were items of great interest; the latter will leave a family almost in destitute circumstances.

No material change has taken place since I last wrote you, except the weather has become mild and Springlike. The frost which at no time has entered more than two or three inches [*in the ground*], has now become drawn out and it is every way pleasant and agreeable.

Our new Chaplain, whom I mentioned in one of my previous letters, is a late graduate from the Seminary, but is applying himself zealously at his work. He makes no pretensions and is becoming much liked by the boys.

An annexation of three Companies from what was once the 145th N. Y. Vols; they being equally distributed throughout this Reg't; our Co. received 12 men, thus making our Reg't of good effective strength.

I hope to hear soon if any change takes place.

With much love I remain your aff. Son

R. T. Van Wyck

Normandy, Tenn.
Jan. 26th, '64

Dear Sarah,

Your penciled note I received a week since. I am fully aware of the anxiety you all must feel in witnessing (if it must be so) the death of our beloved [*grand*] parent. His happiness and joyous expectancy are abundant consolation for us, while the separation will leave a great void never to be filled. It seemed now how opportune my furlough was last summer, but then I little realized so grievous a change would take place. My communications from home are few and far between, especially now when you are so absorbed in home duties.

That special home visitation (the box—alas!) has never reached us. I am not in absolute need of any of those things: but you know the pleasure any of those things would give me.

No change has taken place in young society [*there*] abouts. The death of Mrs. Cotheal [*?*] was rather of sudden character. Although generally known as an invalid, her disease was not thought t'would take so serious a turn.

We remain much the same, luxuriating in good health and spirits, anticipating to move by Spring. This latter supposition is never discussed, time will show. I regularly receive the papers which afford much reading matter, to while away the time upon picket [*duty*]. This latter institution comes once in every third or sixth day: of twenty-four hours each. Not very hard when one gets used to it. Remember me to all. I remain, your afft. Cousin

R. T. Van Wyck

P. S. I wish you all a Happy New Year.

Normandy, Tenn.
Jan. 28th, '64

Dear Mother,

Yours of the 19th and 21st came to hand this morning. I was glad to learn that Fred had arrived at "Wickope Hd. Quarters" having survived the elements, [*and*] "Van Brunt's Barracks" inclusive. His visit is different now than formerly, and unattended with the mirth and pleasure of former days.

GrandFather's strength and constitution seems almost to conquer the disease, and his tenacity of life is marvelous. I had almost thought his death had occurred by the non-arrival of a letter, and am daily looking and anxious to hear how it has gone with him. The incessant nursing and attention, although tiresome, will not be regretted by anyone. I am sorry my own situation renders this duty impossible.

The photograph of Julia Elmendorf, you will please keep. My securities against a total obliteration of it by rainstorms, etc., are small. She must have altered somewhat since I saw her last. An acknowledgment of the favor I suppose is unnecessary.

The *Atlantic* for December came to hand. A good number it was. The papers from the other house come regularly. When not noticed by me they may, like some of my letters, be detained upon the road but eventually come. Nothing like reading matter, I assure you. We might stay here a good part of the Spring but can't tell much about it. Soon the Spring campaign will commence, then the papers will be sought after by everyone.

Hoping to hear from you soon, and will endeavor to write weekly, if not oftener. With much love, I remain, your aff.   Son

R. T. Van Wyck

P.S. The box, if detained in New York and not reshipped, you had better use up the eatables, and the shirts you will please retain till I write for them, when they can be sent by mail under the new postage law (for soldiers, packages under two lbs.) at small cost. And ask Father if he will please remit ten dollars ($10).

Normandy, Tenn.
Feb. 12th, '64

Dear Mother,

Yours of the 3rd came to hand yesterday. I thereby learned of the death of GrandFather.* How lonely it must be now, at the "other house;" he who was always present and was always interested in everything going on, now is gone. How does GrandMother seem to be? I suppose very nervous, and must feel the bereavement very keenly. I hope she will be treated with the utmost kindness by the family, and am assured she will be. From this grievous change by death many matters will be altered in that family household, and a total change will take place throughout.

That long-looked-for "box" has at last arrived this morning. Strange to say, everything, with the exception of a few things, were in good order. The things you sent me particularly so. A few apples and a loaf of bread for Jacob were spoiled. We have been exemplifying

---

* General Abraham Van Wyck was born in Fishkill on July 8, 1774. His maternal grandfather, Col. John Brinckerhoff, was a great friend of General Washington. According to family records, "whenever Washington could, he would accept the hospitality of this old home and would spend days together with the Colonel and his family, of which General Abraham was the youngest grandson."

He inherited part of the original tract of land purchased by his paternal grandfather, Theodorus Van Wyck, in 1726 from Madam Brett, and to this he added more by purchase. In 1802 he built the house nearer the road, "the other house," in which his daughter Louisa Van Vechten and her family, including Sarah, also lived. He was active in the State militia from 1800 to 1822 and served in the War of 1812 as Lt. Gen. of the 6th Regiment, 2nd Brig., N.Y. Detached Militia.

The family genealogy states that "General Abraham was a man of great influence, exceptional ability and sterling integrity, and his advice was often sought and referred to, and no one's opinion in the community on any subject of business action carried greater weight than his. He had a marvelous faculty of seeing, in an emergency, the precise thing that should be done and he was much in demand in the settling of estates ... During the Civil War he was fearless and outspoken in behalf of the Union." He died on February 3, 1864.

the question now before the debating society: "Whether there is more pleasure in anticipation than in realization;" which allow me to say we have had rather too much of the former, and so far the practicable effect of receiving the box much the best of the two. I intend reserving my shirts (which are fine ones) till the hot weather commences, without I am obliged to sacrifice my present ones. Jacob had given the box up for lost, and was taken quite aback upon its delivery; while his exclamations of pleasure bordered somewhat upon the <u>humorous</u> or ridiculous, I don't know which.

Captain Scofield arrived here yesterday morning. It seems it never "rains but what it pours." All the home matters come all in a heap. Your paper and envelopes came by him. He might have given you some pleasure in telling you of some of his doings by giving him time enough to get things out, or if he did not unfortunately recall his exploits in his early days (1813)! Your satisfaction might have been somewhat like my own, to hear what is doing in Fishkill <u>now</u>, and let the biographer recall his historic life in those eventful times.

I received a letter from Uncle Anthony this morning, from Madison, Wisc. He states Aunt Margaret and the children are boarding at Kenosha and that he visited Davenport about Christmas and New Year's, but he did not enjoy himself much, nor did Aunt M., for they were both sick. He comes down from Madison* once in three or four weeks. There will not be a long session as there is little business to transact.

The three companies have returned from their foraging excursion to levy <u>that</u> tax upon a County where three men were shot by guerrillas not long since. Upon returning and within a short distance from Tullahoma, and as two soldiers of our Reg't [*George Lovelace and John Odell*] were alone in advance of the Reg't, they were attacked by a party of twenty guerrillas and were <u>found</u> <u>shot</u> as their comrades came up. Their bodies were brought up with the Reg't today. What course

---

* Anthony Van Wyck had been successful in his quest for election to the Wisconsin State Senate. According to family histories, Anthony Van Wyck was one of the notable men to bear the family name. Of a most trustworthy character, generous to a fault, warm-hearted and interested in all with whom life brought him in touch, combined with a graceful personality and keen intellect ... no man ever won more friends wherever he lived. He was also a highly-accomplished man with a deep interest in history and languages. He went west to Wisconsin where he spent eight years in the legislature, and later was judge in Kenosha County for sixteen years.

will be pursued next seems undetermined as the Col. feels concerned, as it reflects some discredit on his command of the party. As you have sent me this large sheet I might punish you often by long letters. Express my thanks to the <u>girls</u> for their contributions of writing materials, and tell them that I recognize by their <u>favor</u> that letters can be concise as well as voluminous. I expect a letter soon.

With much love I remain your afft. Son

R. T. Van Wyck

P. S. I have repeatedly been obliged while upon guard, to time the relief, to borrow a watch from my tent fellows. And should we have received my last pay [*I would have*] made a purchase of one, costing from fifteen to twenty dollars. I wish Father, if not much trouble, to send me one by mail, of no more value, and I would be extremely obliged.

Normandy, Tenn.
Feb. 13, '64

Dear Sarah,

I have just received your letter Jan. 7th (being missent), Co. "K" not being distinctly marked.

So GrandFather is dead. A life well spent in usefulness, and having been blest with a mind vigorous to the last. GrandMother—poor woman!—will miss him most, but who will not miss him?

This paper and envelope you sent by the Captain comes very acceptable; also the material sent me in the box by you. Express to your Mother my thanks for those mittens. I regret my inability to do them justice this Winter, but at any rate I appreciate her kindness in sending them. We have had a delightful winter, as I have repeatedly intimated to you.

The papers you send usually arrive and are much thought of. The magazines as well. This Winter has been just the reverse [*for you*] of [*the*] last in the visiting and amusements. Nothing has turned up or you would have told me. As <u>you</u> have limited the content of my correspondence by the [*small-sized*] sheets [*which she had sent him*], I will be obliged to close. I remain your aft. Cousin,

R. T. Van Wyck

Normandy, Tenn.
Feb. 24th '64

Dear Sarah,

I much thank you for your letter giving me an account of GrandFather's illness and funeral. It must be very lonesome now for you and Anna, deprived of company; a strong contrast to the previous year, when gaiety was so the order of the day.

The Kip family I have heard nothing of recently, except that Isaac was looking for a settlement* again. He will find it difficult to get one as good as the one he left. Dennis Wortman I saw in the papers has been called to the First Dutch Church in Philadelphia, a position of much importance. He is getting along finely in the estimation of the literary public.

Frank Kip I suppose is now in New York pursuing his studies. Will Andrews I have lost sight of, but undoubtedly he is somewhere sharpening and brightening himself up for the great contest in the world. Besides them are the Hoyts and Jacksons, giving evidence of talent, who are rushing into the professions as a matter of course, I suppose.

Well, which of the number mentioned are you following intently through his career? Excuse me for asking you so positive a question, which I hope you may answer by an outward ceremonial act. . . .

Tell Mother the *Harper's* came to hand, and also your [*news*]papers. We remain here without any material change. The weather fine. Winter almost gone and only another one to pass in the service. Where will that one find me?

With much love to all, I remain your aff. Cousin

R. T. Van Wyck

Normandy, Tenn.
March 1st '64

Dear Mother,

Yours of the 21st ult. from Brooklyn came to hand yesterday. At which time we were visited by an unusual quantity of rain, lasting throughout, and a great part of today. The snow-topped [*railroad*] cars coming from the North afforded abundant evidence that you have received a quantity of snow. Thus much [*concern*] for the

---

* Isaac Kip was an ordained minister.

weather, which till recently has been favorable for the advancing army, in the South now [*there*] will be great sufferers from this storm.

Father has written me about the will, and I thought it a more favorable and equitable arrangement than I expected. Aunt Susan or Mr. Lane might seem disposed to grumble, by not having the old homestead after the death of Aunt Louisa, and by not having the privilege now to share [*it*] with her. Does the dissatisfaction which you allude to refer to her, or to home?

The Sanitary Fair in Brooklyn I presume has been a great success. We receive Sanitary assistance from that association, in the shape of onions, and I always associate this latter article in my mind when the society is mentioned. At present there is not a sick man in our Reg't, a contrast to last year this time in Baltimore. It's strange, too, for [*picket*] duty exposes the privates every third night to weather the storm, such as last night's.

A strange incident happened last night, upon picket. As the Spring months were ushered in – precisely at 12 m. – a quail came fluttering from the bushes and alighted close by the fire, thus indicating a desire to "give itself up." I accordingly secured it by tieing [*sic*] its legs, prudently thinking it might take to itself wings and pass our lines again. This ominous circumstance, happening at such a time, would lead one to infer that Secession would become "played out" and "would give itself up" during the Spring months, similar to the example before me. So we thought, and we clipped its wings, like <u>slavery</u> will be from the <u>Rebs</u>, and letting it make itself at home in the shanty, domesticating and cultivating its good qualities; so we hope secession will become [*tamed*]. That was the "sign of the times" we saw upon picket.

I answered Fred's letter some time since. I am sorry he has not received it. *Harper's* for February came yesterday. With much love I remain your aft. Son

R. T. Van Wyck

P. S. I didn't wish to reflect anything unpleasant when I mentioned as being the recipient of the onions from the Sanitary Commission.* I have learned to like onions much better than I used to, for finding them so excellent a corrective of the digestive organs, they are much sought after.

---

* The Sanitary Commission was the forerunner of the Red Cross, brought into being mainly by the women of the North. The fairs were a way of raising money.

Normandy, Tenn.
March 15th '64

Dear Cousin [*Sarah*],

Your note of March 5th came to hand yesterday. We are now discussing the <u>pro</u> and <u>con</u> of the removal of this Corps and the Eleventh to old Va. again, as well as arranging war matters generally for the ensuing summer. The conclusion usually arrived at is the urgent necessity of remaining at this place as long as possible. We are not over-anxious to leave it, I assure you, for we have learned by sore experience the effects of marching during the Summer season.

Besides, from frequent excursions into the country for some of the luxuries of life, such as eggs, butter, etc., we have become acquainted with some of the people whose hospitality is irresistible, particularly the <u>ladies</u> (commonly called angels)–occasionally one is seen of considerable beauty.

In our Company there is one person whose proficiency in vocal music is remarkable. He, with several of the Co., gave the miller (who has several daughters) a benefit a few nights ago. They, in response to the patriotic hymns, gave us some of their Secesh melodies.

The weather is fine, a few weeks of the like, everything will be out in <u>bloom</u>. The news from Fishkill is cheering. A move is on <u>foot</u> to connect another family with the Kips. They seem very much alike in temperament and disposition. I am much of the opinion [*that*] long engagements are not just the thing for them, or for the family. So you have my opinion of the other representation, nothing derogatory to him, but just my course of action precisely. Since the question is asked how _____ [*blank*] would do? Perhaps it would be time enough when you can have the privilege to answer it. If such should be the case, it will soften this present disappointment. I didn't know [*if*] you was afraid of tiring me [*but*] you could mention perhaps [*if*] you have got it all arranged.

Write soon. Remember me to Van Wyck. I remain your aff. Cousin.

R. T. Van Wyck

P. S. For fear I might disclose <u>this</u> secret you mentioned, <u>please</u> destroy this letter as soon as received.

Normandy, Tenn.
March 18th '64

Dear Father,

Yours of the 1st inst. was received the 12th. I had previously been informed by a notice from the Post Master at Nashville of the receipt of a registered package, which I imagined was the watch. I have received it this morning and it seems exactly the thing I wanted.

J. Montross was visited by his cousin from the 13th Ill. (Brinckerhoff Serene)[*his name*] a few days ago. I think you must know him. He staid a long time with his uncle John Brinckerhoff in the Winter of '59. He enlisted at Sandwich, Ill., in the Spring of '61 and now has only two months to serve. He is a sergeant of the same company as Aben Brinckerhoff and participated in all the battles of the Mississippi.

I received a letter from Uncle Anthony this morning. He says the family are all well but that Howard [*his son*] met with an accident that will injure his eye permanently. The pupil has lost the power of contraction almost. He says he leads a dull life away from his family.

Military matters here remain much the same. A company of engineers came here this morning to construct a blockhouse upon the site of our Stockade. The object undoubtedly is to decrease the amount of force here. As a Company of 30 will be as strong as a hundred and fifty now is, we possibly will leave upon its erection. The papers intimate the removal of the Eleventh and Twelfth Corps to Va. The Potomac Army thus reinforced will, under Grant, make another demonstration upon Richmond, which I hope will be successful.*

Jacob's furlough has not been returned <u>approved</u> yet. It being necessary to go through so much form, the pleasure must be extreme to compensate for the trouble.

Spring seems to hold off long. A few cold days seem to follow weeks of sunshine. I suppose Mr. Briggs remains with you still and is making preparation for the coming summer; while here nothing

---

* On March 8, 1864, President Lincoln had appointed Gen. Ulysses S. Grant as the new General-in-Chief of the Armies of the United States. Grant immediately reorganized the Union forces by ordering into active service the thousands of men who had been funneled into backwater jobs, and to ensure that the armies would operate as a dependable team he appointed to key posts men upon whom he could rely. He gave his own place as Chief of the Western Armies to Gen. William Tecumseh Sherman, while he himself took to the field with Meade's Army of the Potomac in Virginia.

prevents the farming out-of-doors operations to proceed through the Winter. I have sent some seeds with the cotton as it is picked.

I have received the Brooklyn <u>Eagles</u> containing the latest from the fair at Brooklyn. Now we will see what New York will do. With much love I remain your aft.

Son

R. T. Van Wyck

Normandy, Tenn.
March 21st '64

Dear Mother,

Yours of March 14th containing more sad news arrived this morning. It was of so sudden an occurrence that you all must have been taken unawares.* She had certain failings, but undoubtedly was a good wife for Van Wyck, whose habits were not often very domestic, or if so, not of congenial taste and inclinations–so I have thought.**

They say we are agoing to leave here and are to be removed to the RailRoad running parallel with this from Nashville to Huntsville, or somewhere there. You will see our present locality – only seven miles north of Tullahoma – and our future might possibly be some fifty miles to the West. But <u>rumor</u> and <u>hearsay</u> are old liars, and I have given you this for just what it is worth.

Last Saturday evening, the evening appointed to inaugurate a course of lectures in connection with a debating society (by the author of those articles from the 150th N. Y. Vols. which you have seen in the Poughkeepsie *Eagle*, and signed MRW) and he made quite a sensation. That is, he first made a sensation by getting greatly inebriated and then submitting to a sobering process till able to deliver something like the specimens you have seen in the paper. He is captain of Co. "D." A friend of his, a Major upon the staff of Gen. Slocum, was as much so as himself, and who came up to hear his friend speak, but could not help saying a word for himself once in a

---

* The apparently unexpected death of Sarah's sister-in-law, Mary Van Vechten.
** The family records state of A. Van Wyck Van Vechten, Sarah's brother, that "Faithfulness was the keynote of his character; faithfulness to his parents, to his wife, to his children, to his church, his college, his profession [*lawyer*], his clients, his friends, his God. He numbered his friends by the hosts and maintained his interest in numerous organizations" throughout his long life. He did not remarry. It may be that the lack of domesticity Richard comments on refers to the marked conviviality of his temperament.

while. I have received the *Eagles*, and was glad to hear it, the fair, resulted so handsomely.

Remember me to all at home. I remain your aff. Son

R. T. Van Wyck

Normandy, Tenn.
April 10th '64

Dear Sarah,

I have received your letter from New York. I have quite a mind to scold you, and could give you a long letter upon the religious necessity of being cheerful, happy, etc., but I am afraid it would be distasteful to you. At any rate you must find the demonstrative grief of the children* and the impressive subdued grief of Van no way tending to a contented mind.

Don't think I speak harsh and unfeeling, but believe me, despondency only adds to the burdens of those whom it is your duty to relieve by a cheerful and happy frame of mind. If I can help it I don't allow myself to get in such a state, and everything goes smooth and easy. I am confident my present condition is due to affecting the bright side of every position and circumstance, and were I to weigh and treasure all the unpleasant ills of life I would need more transportation than my two shoulders could carry.

I owe you an apology for eliciting that candid confession between you and Isaac, for from Frank's proposed matrimonial alliance I thought there would be no accounting for the brother's (so bad taste). My old friend <u>Louise</u> follows closely in the routine of fashions and will soon be put upon the retired list. I was here agoing to add a message to her—but would you have delivered it? It might lead to the correspondence we thought of.

Our Corps (12th) is joined to the 11th and [*is*] called the 1st Corps of the Army. I will soon instruct you as to the direction of my letters: for the present, the same as formerly.

Remember me to Van and the children. I remain your

afft. Cousin
R. T. Van Wyck

---

* Her sister-in-law left behind two girls, Marie and Effie, respectively, aged six and nine.

Normandy, Tenn.
April 25th 1864

Dear Mother,

I received your letter last evening. It seemed a long time in coming, I thought, owing to some delay in the mails. The death of Herman Lee took me by surprise. He seemed so admirably situated to enjoy life, just married, and surrounded by everything to make him happy. But death visits alike the civilian as the soldier. He probably thought of his mother and wife as a preventative to joining the army in any capacity, without the consideration of the result of his death.

The settlement of the property will cause some trouble, more or less. It will not be lightened if Uncle Henry is much interested, or the other spirit, Mr. Lane. How does Van Wyck seem to get along looking after the Van Vechten interests?

I suppose the farmers are all busy in farming operations just now. So will we be – for we leave here tomorrow morning at 8 o'clock for Tullahoma, then we will be joined by the rest of the Brigade or Division, destination unknown, surmised Vicksburg, overland march, or Va., overland march, or what is more probable, the Front, Lookout Valley,* by marching. At any rate, you must not think where we are going till I can write again on the route.

I make use of a common expression by saying "we have put in two winters very comfortably," and we can't grumble much if the summers are spent in active duty; for my part I am tired of staying so long in a place and hail the prospect of a change, no matter what. The Reg't that relieves us, the 31st Wisc., has been out as long as the 150th N. Y., but cannot show any particular action or engagement, have lost a large percentage of men by sickness; but are treated like green troops by us. Thus it is, it becomes necessary to have a Summer Campaign for some material for the boys to talk about next Winter, if for no other good.

Don't wait for answers to your letters, as the communication for receiving mail matters will not be good. I will write as often as possible but I will rely upon you as my correspondent in chief. Sarah writes once in a while but I should get out of the way of writing letters were they the only ones to answer.

---

* R. T. Van Wyck's guess of their destination as Lookout Valley, on their way "to steal a march upon Atlanta" was an accurate one.

Love to all, I remain, your aft. Son

R. T. Van Wyck

EDITOR'S NOTE:

As head of the Western armies, General Sherman received orders from Gen. Grant to go after Gen. Johnston's rebel army. "You I propose to move against Johnston's army," General Grant wrote to Sherman on April 4, 1864, "to break it up, and to get into the interior of the enemy's country as far as you can, inflicting all the damage you can against their war resources. I do not propose to lay down for you a plan of campaign, but simply to lay down the work it is desirable to have done, and leave you free to execute it in your own way."

General Sherman thereupon instructed his own three army commanders, Generals McPherson, Thomas, and Schofield, to make immediate preparations for a hard campaign. "The great question was one of supplies," he wrote in his *Memoirs*.* "We should have to repair the railroad, use it, and guard it...To make the troops as mobile as possible and make the strictest possible orders in relation to wagons and all species of incumbrances and impedimenta whatever," each soldier and officer was required to carry on his horse or person food and clothing enough for five days. To each regiment was allowed but one wagon and one ambulance and to the officers one pack horse or mule. Tents were forbidden to all save the sick and wounded. "I doubt if any army ever went forth to battle with fewer impedimenta...Neither Atlanta, nor Augusta, nor Savannah was to be the objective, but the army of Joseph E. Johnston, 'go where it might.' I fixed the date of May first when all things should be in readiness for the grand forward movement."

Thus began General Sherman's terrible march of attrition through the South to break the back of the Rebellion.

On April 26, 1864, as his regiment left for the field, R. T. Van Wyck began keeping a pocket diary which has survived, water-logged and mildewed but still legible:

April 26. Left Normandy, Tenn., encamped near Tullahoma seven miles distant. Day pleasant and marching not over-burdensome, but found the night cold and quite a change. Attended a pleasant prayer meeting. The active life of camp exilerating [sic] upon my spirits.

---

* *Memoirs of General W. T. Sherman,* Written by Himself, D. Appleton & Company, 1875, Vol. II, pp. 8-26.

April 27. Remained here today. Lessened our clothing. Sent our overcoats to Nashville in charge of John Montross. The 150th making preparations of leaving on the morrow. Expect a long march ahead and hard work.

April 28. Reached Decherd today. Passed first six miles through blackjack forest soil, then latterly the country grew better as we neared our encampment for the night, distance 13 miles. Suffered much from the heat and marching. But turned in for the night with hopes of a good sleep.

April 29. The first four miles passed through some fertile country till we began to ascend a span of the Cumberland Mt. Suffered much from heat and want of water. Encamped for the night at an old camp. Rained hard during the night – wet through. Passed 8th Cdm. Corps. [*Gen. Sherman's corps*]

April 30. Continued the march en route for Bridgeport, Tenn. [*Alabama*]. Passed over a bad tableland six miles and then descended to the valley once historic in Jackson's campaign. Watered by a deep stream called Battle Creek. Scenery splendid. Distance during the day 18 miles.

May 1. Continued the march down the valley till we made the junction with the Tennessee River, then traveled in a west direction till we came to Bridgeport. Crossed the River and went up the right bank of the river six miles to Shell Mound adjacent to a saltpeter cave and fine stream of water. Distance 14 miles. Weather fine and country beautiful.

May 2. Left Shell Mound and marched eight miles to Whiteside at the beginning of the Lookout Valley. Weather cold but clear. Every day brings us nearer to the difficulties of the holding of Chattanooga. Dead mules and horses are abundant evidence of the former state of things.

(Letter in pencil)

White Side [*sic*] on the line between
Tenn. & Ala.
May 2d, 1864

Dear Mother,

Since my last letter in which I mentioned our departure from Normandy, Tenn., we arrived here this noon, or more definite–2 p.m. We have come so far 73 miles and are within eight miles of

Lookout Valley and a little farther off from Chattanooga. Most of the country – especially within a day's march from Bridgeport, and in an East-by-South direction from Decherd over the Cumberland Mts. and down into the valley of Battle Creek, named from Andrew Jackson's exploits in Indian warfare – most of the country is beautiful, wild and sublime.

So is the scenery about Bridgeport and toward Chattanooga, but the evils of war has marred much of the surrounding loveliness. The vegetation is more advanced, especially in the valleys, blossoms and flowers abound in wondrous profusion, the sweet-scented shrub grown in gardens north is found growing wild on the hillside, but it does not counteract the stench arising from the dead mules and horses starved and worn out last fall and winter; every few yards brings one to view and they have not been very particular to bury them, for they have MacAdamised the road with them by throwing over [them] a little earth. The waggons [sic] pass over them when they drive in the harness.

[All] this shows the cost and difficulties enabling us to maintain our position at Chattanooga before the RailRoad was completed. Now it is very different, now abundant supplies arrive without the loss of so much life to animals as well as man. The most direct road to Chattanooga was once said to be that one where you can see the most [dead] mules. If this is not the most direct, I don't wish to see the other.

I don't know how this massing of troops, or in what organization this movement is intended to produce, but I have been informed that three columns will attack the Rebel army at once, each consisting of two Corps. The one under Hooker, the 14th, the 11th and 12th, or by consolidation, the 20th. It is said the 20th Corps now contains upwards of seventy Reg'ts, or 85,000 men, the 14th Corps consists of at least 20,000 men, so you must have some idea of the army in front three times this amount.*

---

* Three western armies were put under General Sherman's command: the Army of the Tennessee, under General McPherson with 35,000 men; the Army of the Ohio, under General Schofield with 15,000 men; and the massive Army of the Cumberland, under General Thomas, 50,000 men; amounting, in all, to over 100,000 men. *Memoirs of W. T. Sherman, op.cit.*

Richard T. Van Wyck's regiment, under Colonel Ketcham, was now incorporated into the 20th Corps of the Army of the Cumberland, under General Joseph Hooker as corps commander.

The weather is fine and undoubtedly before long you will hear of some news in Va. as well as here. I stand the marching much better than anticipated when I set out, and much better than last Summer. I received a letter from Sarah in which she says Fred, called up at 47th St. from the T____ D____? received my letter in answer to one addressed from Fishkill. I have taken this opportunity to pencil this note, hoping you will excuse it. I know you would if you knew the circumstances of my situation. Don't forget to write often. Send some postage stamps. Love, from your afft. Son

R. T. Van Wyck

EDITORS NOTE:
As hard as Gen Bragg's siege of Chattanooga was on Gen. Rosecrans' Union army the previous summer and fall, it took a disastrous toll of horses and mules who died by the thousands from starvation and overwork.

May 3. Marched en route for Rossville 16 miles and passed to the base of Lookout Mt. through Lookout Valley by Hooker's Hdqtrs. Came right through a short distance of Chattanooga to the south. Got a good view of it.

May 4. Marched to Chickamauga Creek 10 miles over the battle-ground of last summer. Saw the indications of the awful struggle. The country more level. The forest interspersed with pine and the trees not very dense. Soil a sandy loam. Few houses or indications of a farming community.

May 5. Crossed the river and was detailed to guard the Brigade Waggon [sic] trains and marched within five miles of Ringgold [Sherman's front line headquarters]. The soil would richly repay cultivation. Weather fine. Concentration of forces for battle. It can't be long deferred.

EDITOR'S NOTE:
May 5th was D-Day, the day set for the simultaneous advance of both General Grant's and General Sherman's armies against Generals Lee and Johnston. On the fifth of May General Sherman rode out to Ringgold, and "on the very day appointed by General Grant from his headquarters in Virginia the great campaign was begun...I had near me only my personal staff, with about half a dozen wagons–and no wall-tents, with a very small mess establishment...because I wanted to set the example and gradually convert all parts of

that army into a mobile machine, willing and able to start at a moment's notice, and to subsist on the scantiest food." *Memoirs, op. cit.,* p. 31.

Although Atlanta lay only 100 miles south of Chattanooga the way led through the mountain ridges of northern Georgia. The Union forces met their first repulse in the high cliffs before Dalton where the Rebels, under the command of Gen. Joseph E. Johnston, had entrenched themselves. Sherman then sent forces south to outflank the enemy at Snake Creek Gap, but the Rebels had blocked the mouth of the gap at Resaca, where another battle ensued.

May 6.* Remained in camp today and attended to sundry necessary articles, washing, etc.

May 7. Left camp at half-past four. Marched four miles in a south direction, then turned to the east and crossed a mountain ridge in a direct line for Dalton. Encamped at a place called Trickam 10 miles from Dalton. Climate hot, roads dusty.

May 8. Spent the day upon picket in front of our Brigade. Day pleasant. In afternoon a reconnaissance by the 3rd Div., 20th Corps, of a Brig. of Infantry and a Brig. of Cavalry. They drove the enemy and occupied the ridge to the front and was very successful.

May 9. Remained in camp during [*day*] but awaiting orders to move. An artillery duel was seen on an adjoining mountain. No result obtained as I know of.

May 10. Left camp at half-past twelve A.M. and marched 16 miles, part of which way in a due south direction, then east to a gap. Arrived at ten o'clock A.M. Left at five o'clock P.M. and marched 10 miles in an easterly direction to a point seven miles from R.R. going to Atlanta. Rebels are in retreat.

May 11. Remained in camp all day. Flooded out last night and the day cold and rainy. News from the front encouraging. A line of battle eight miles long to prevent a retreat of the Rebs to Atlanta. In the afternoon changed our position to a better place for camping.

May 12. Remained in camp all day. Day pleasant but cool. Concentration of troops is fast going on.

---

* General Thomas's troops including the 20th Corps under General Hooker were already in position, his advance being as far as Ringgold. May 6th was given to Generals Schofield and McPherson to get into position. *Memoirs,* p. 32.

EDITOR'S NOTE:
Well aware of the importance of letters from home to morale, the army tried to ensure that even the most scattered outposts received their home mail. Postmaster General Montgomery Blair's use of the railroad in getting mail to soldiers was first put into effect a year earlier during the Vicksburg campaign, with the blessings of both Generals Grant and Sherman. The latter's Army of the Tennessee is credited with proving that mail could be sorted on fast trains and distributed in transit under the most difficult conditions, thus inaugurating the system which later became the regular U.S. mail service. *Sherman, Fighting Prophet,* by Lloyd Lewis, N.Y., 1932, p. 170.

(Letter in pencil)

May 12th '64

Dear Father,
We are now in the rear of the enemy, some fifteen miles south of Dalton. The night of May 9th, at which time I received your letter, we marched with a rest of five hours, till eight o'clock the following night, starting at half-past twelve, distance 30 miles. Everything looks lovely and works well. The Rebs are hemmed in, and we must take part of their army anyhow, if not the whole. We have had some rain but it is pleasant again.

I would write more but the mail goes off this minute. But write often. Address:

> Co. K   150th Reg't. N. Y. Vols.
> 2d Brig.   1st Div.   20th Corps
> Cumberland Army

and I will receive it, but all letters with the old direction as well.

I remain your aff. Son

R. T. Van Wyck

We have heard of the victory upon the Rapidan by Gen. Grant, it's glorious news. Send me 2 handkerchiefs by mail, if you please.

EDITOR'S NOTE:
On May 12th Sherman had concentrated his entire force at the gap at Resaca, which the Confederates had strengthened with three miles of trenches and reinforced troops. During May 13th, 14th, and 15th General Hooker's men led a series of massive attacks against deadly Rebel fire. Eventually the Union forces began to out-flank the Rebel lines, and General Johnston prudently retreated further south, while Gen. Sherman entered Resaca at daylight on the 16th.

GEORGIA
1864—1865

I saw the Rebels at Resaca come up to the charge cool
and firm, but this mass with their officers waving their
swords and heroically marching up to the cannon's
mouth with such gallantry, it gave us no small opinion of their courage.

–R.T. Van Wyck

Bring the good old bugleboys, we'll sing another song;
Sing it with a spirit that will start the world along,
Sing it as we used to sing it, fifty thousand strong.
While we were marching through Georgia. Hurrah! Hurrah!
We bring the jubilee! Hurrah! Hurrah!
The flag that makes you free!
So we sang the chorus from Atlanta to the sea,
While we were marching through Georgia.
–*Marching Through Georgia*

By the summer of 1864, it was apparent that a few more strategically placed blows would end the Confederacy and the war.
Northern sentiment in favor of continuing the war, however,
remained fragile.

Grant and Lee seemed to be at a stalemate before Petersburg,
and Sherman was about to begin the final phase of his advance upon
Atlanta. The Union armies in the Eastern and Western Theaters,
under the commands of Grant and Sherman, respectively, moved
with confidence and concert of action. The two generals were thor-
ough soldiers and firm friends who rejoiced in each other's successes. Their willingness to cooperate was a vital factor in the success of
their overall attack plan.

Any serious setback to Sherman's campaign might result in a further loss of public confidence and support for Lincoln's war aims.

The Democratic party, with McClellan as its nominee for president, led those who wished for peace or despaired of victory. Lincoln's own party began to question his policies and motives. With the presidential election due in November, even Lincoln's most ardent supporters began to express uncertainty regarding the likelihood of his re-election. On August 23, Lincoln wrote and sealed this gloomy prophecy:

> It seems exceedingly probable that this administration will not be re-elected. Then it will be my duty to so co-operate with the President-elect as to save the Union between the election and the inauguration, as he will have secured his election on such ground that he cannot possibly save it afterward.

Despite attempts by Horace Greeley and others to secure peace without further force of arms, Lincoln remained steadfast in his belief that peace could be assured only on the condition of absolute surrender, with no turning back from enforcing the prohibition of slavery in every part of the Republic.

*****

The 150th had marched and fought for eighty-five miles since leaving Chattanooga. Following the battle at Resaca, the two opposing armies of Sherman and Johnston engaged in combat at New Hope Church, Kennesaw Mountain, Muddy Creek and Kulp's Farm, with Sherman driving Johnston inexorably from point to point, to the very gates of Atlanta.

Atlanta was of vital military importance because of its network of railroads which extended to all portions of the Gulf states. It was also the center of manufacturing for government supplies, munitions and materials. In 1861, Atlanta's population was estimated at fifteen thousand. The terrain around the city was barren and uncultivated, but twenty miles south, towards the river valleys of the Chattahoochee and Etowah, there was rich fertile farmland. The capture of Atlanta, the South's gateway, would deal a crippling blow to the rebel cause.

On July 5, 1864, from a position on a high ridge overlooking the Confederate lines, the 150th NYVs caught their first view of the rooftops of Atlanta. By mid-July, Sherman's Army had successfully crossed the Chattahoochee River and established bridgeheads on its eastern bank. Johnston, finding himself outwitted and strategically defeated, withdrew to Atlanta before he could be cut off from it. On July 17th, Jefferson Davis, his patience at an end, removed Johnston from command in favor of a "real fighting soldier," General John Bell Hood. On July 20th, the impulsive Hood attacked the Union forces at Peachtree Creek, only to be repelled. Further unsuccessful attacks from Atlanta's defenses, on July 22 and July 28, lost him 12,300 troops to the Union's 4,353. The forty-two-day "Siege of Atlanta" had commenced.

During the following six weeks, Atlanta suffered a tremendous pounding from the Union batteries. Almost every garden and yard in the city had its cave or bomb-proof shelter for protection.

By August 4, Sherman's lines were within 250-300 yards of the enemy's works. After one more unsuccessful try to break the siege (at Jonesborough on August 31st), Hood retreated south of the city under the cover of night. At 8 o'clock on the evening of September 2nd, with Major General Henry W. Slocum at the head of the main column, the 20th Corps entered the city from the north and west to take possession of the rebel fortifications.

The fall of Atlanta shifted popular opinion and political support to Lincoln, resulting in Lincoln's landslide re-election in November. Sherman had saved Lincoln, and by saving him, sealed the fate of the South.

On September 8th, the people of Atlanta were notified that they must make speedy preparations to leave the city. All who were loyal to the Federal cause were to be sent to the north, while rebel families were to be sent at least thirty miles to the south under a flag of truce to the care of General Hood.

Hood tried to divert Sherman's attention that autumn by striking north through Tennessee and Kentucky, but Sherman had anticipated that move and had dispatched General Thomas with 35,000 men to Nashville. On December 15th, Hood's Army of Tennessee was completely broken at the battle of Nashville. The remnants of the once-proud Confederate Army of Tennessee, now with less than 7,500 effectives, dispersed. Some were sent to Mobile, Alabama, some to Mississippi. Others were reunited in the Carolinas with General Joseph Johnston for one final fight against

Sherman.

Upon leaving Atlanta, Sherman ordered the city torched to remove it from the war for good. On the morning of the 15th of November the 14th, 15th, 17th, and 20th Corps organized into right and left wings and moved out with a total of 62,000 men, 2,500 wagons, and one piece of artillery for every thousand men. It was an entirely refurbished army, selected from men who were battle-tested and hardened by long campaigning. The 150th, 2nd Brigade, 1st Division, 20th Corps was part of the Left Wing, together with the 14th Corps, under the command of General Slocum.

Sherman's expedition and "scorched earth policy" sought to destroy central Georgia's war-supporting agricultural economy. On November 19th, the 150th reached the picturesque town of Madison, population 2,000, where they learned of Lincoln's re-election. After destroying all the works around the train depot and railroad track, the regiment turned southward towards Milledgeville, Georgia's state capital. Sherman's left was now threatening Augusta; his right, Macon; his real objective was Savannah.

The country lying between Madison, Covington and Milledgeville was a perfect garden, with farmyards well-stocked with hogs, poultry, corn, grain and sweet potatoes. The foraging parties had no difficulty in replenishing the Commissary Department. On November 24th, the regiment proceeded in a southeasterly direction without serious incident until the column reached the Montieth Swamp, a few miles from Savannah, where the division's 3rd Brigade had to attack and destroy rebel fortifications on the road.

While suffering from short rations in the inhospitable marshes, the 150th was transferred to Argyle Island, one of the delta islands in the Savannah River, lying opposite the city. At high tide the island was subject to shelling from Confederate gunboats.

On December 13th, with the help of the Union fleet, Sherman's forces captured Fort McAllister, which commanded Savannah. General Hardee refused to surrender the city, but on the night of December 20th, the movement of retreating rebel troops across a pontoon bridge to the South Carolina side signaled his stealthy evacuation. After a nine-day siege, Savannah formally capitulated at 5:00 a.m. on the morning of December 21st, to great jubilation in the North.

Three weeks after the fall of Savannah, Sherman, sensing that the end was near, prepared to drive north through South Carolina and into North Carolina.

Over the past eighteen months, Van Wyck had witnessed much of the devastation and suffering resulting from "total war" which targets its destructive force on civilians, soldiers, home and property, without discrimination, causing Van Wyck to reflect in a letter home how thankful he was "that the horrors of war and devastation is so far removed from our own pleasant homes ... The destruction of everything useful or ornamental was the order of things."

J.C.Q.

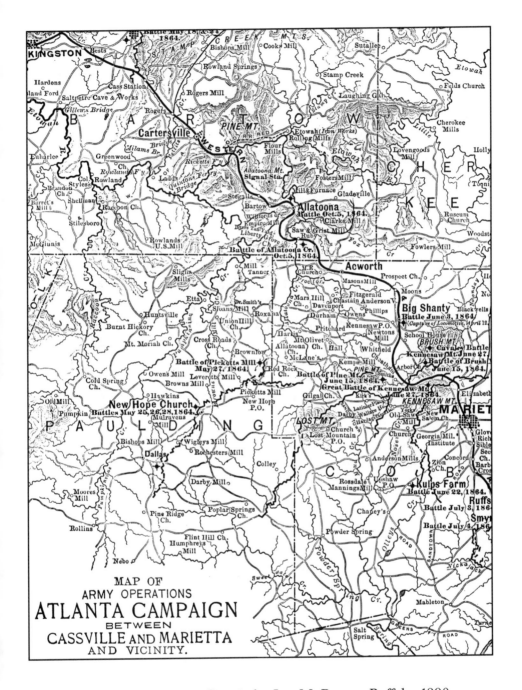

Mountain Campaigns in Georgia, by Jos. M. Brown, Buffalo, 1890.

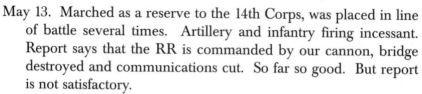

May 13. Marched as a reserve to the 14th Corps, was placed in line of battle several times. Artillery and infantry firing incessant. Report says that the RR is commanded by our cannon, bridge destroyed and communications cut. So far so good. But report is not satisfactory.

May 14. Acted as a reserve to the army in any quarter, was moved about several times. But finally did a very successful attempt to prevent a capture of a battery on the extreme left. Fighting throughout the [day] hard. Our brigade repulsed a brigade of Rebs in the above attempt.*

May 15. Engaged behind a breastwork a column of Rebs at Greenspine Station and totally routed them after an hour and three quarters' engagement.

May 16. This morning found the enemy gone in full retreat. Crossed over to the left flank in pursuit, saw but little of the enemy's proceedings and should say they got off in good order. Encamped at night at the river which crosses the RR at SugarLoaf Gap. Country poor and more open.

May 17. Crossed the River Coosa and marched toward Calhoun where the RR crosses the river. The soil better and some good plantations are passed during the day.

EDITOR'S NOTE:

On May 18th the Union troops engaged the Rebels at Cassville, and General Johnston had to retreat further south to the high ground at Allatoona. Once again Sherman tried a flanking movement to the south, only to find the Rebels already entrenched at New Hope Church.

May 18. Travelled in a southeast direction fifteen miles. Saw some excellent land. Old cotton fields planted to corn and sown with wheat. Said the rapid march was to intercept a waggon [sic] train and did not encamp till 10 p.m.

---

* General Sherman notes in his *Memoirs* (p. 36) that "Hooker's Corps had also some heavy and handsome fighting that afternoon and night on the left, where the Dalton road entered the entrenchments, capturing a four-gun entrenched battery with its men and guns, and generally all our men showed the finest fighting qualities."

(Letter in pencil)

May 18th '64

Dear Mother,

I was in the battle on the 14th and 15th and a merciful Providence has again spared me. No one was killed, one from our company was slightly wounded, and the Adjutant very severely.*

Our day's fighting (that is, the 20th Corps) got the Rebs in retreat toward Atlanta, and we are in hot pursuit. The weather is fine and we are hoping to be successful as Grant in Va. to totally annihilate his forces. How soon another fight will come off I cannot tell.

I hope you will write often. As I cannot answer promptly you must not think it singular. With much love I remain your aff. Son

R. T. Van Wyck

May 19. Remained in camp till 2 P.M. and marched four miles in a south direction. Came into line of battle and scoured the country a mile or more till we came to the enemy posted on a commanding range of hills. Worked at breastworks most of the night.

(Letter in pencil)

Camp 20th A.C. Near Kingston, Ga.
May 19th '64 (1 P.M.)

Dear Mother,

I have embraced this opportunity to give you another line. I had so far shown my good intention to write when we were ordered to move.

May 20th, 3 P.M.

Since yesterday we moved four miles by a series of skirmishes and line of battle to intercept a body of <u>Rebs</u> covering the main army of the enemy and occupying a place called <u>Cassville,</u> three miles east of Kingston. I thought a fight was before us as we threw up breastworks, planted cannon, etc., all night, but when morning came nothing was seen of the enemy, although they were erecting like fortifications till nearly morning.

This <u>village</u> is the finest yet seen in <u>Ga.</u>, in a rich cotton district, fine dwellings, public institutions, streets well laid out, and among

---

* The three men wounded at Resaca, GA, on May 15, 1864, later died of their wounds: Thomas W. Wright, Benj. A. Harp, and Folsom Richardson.

many of the houses good libraries of excellent works evince the character of the place. But the enemy had not vacated the place more than a quarter of an hour before a perfect sack was instituted by our troops. The owners it seems had shared the same scare as the rest of the Rebs and had followed them, so there was no one to stay the hand of the <u>destroyer.</u> Everything in the eating line was first used, then came cotton sheets, blankets, ladies' dresses and toilets, hats, etc., and finally epistolary correspondence of some of the <u>fair</u> <u>ones</u> with the gallant and chivalrous Southerners. These were highly interesting. They little expected such a disposal of letters or they would have committed them to the flames. After the boys were satiated in this work a guard was placed in town to prevent further destruction.

I should say the army has made a clean sweep of things as they have <u>advanced</u>. I don't write this in justification of these acts but to illustrate the manner how an army is supported in an enemy's country, or partly so.

Last evening makes the third skirmish we have had by our Brigade since the commencement. Although the one at Resaca might be considered a good fight I have enjoyed good health so far and feel first-rate. This is the first day's rest we have had since April 27th and yet it is hardly sufficient to wash up, etc., as we go on in the morning.

Yours and Father's letters of May 10th and 11th came to hand today. They were well received, I assure you. Nothing is so acceptable just at present as to receive letters from home. I had heard in one of the letters from home how Isaac Kip and one of the Miss Van Vechtens (Miss Sarah) were getting talked about. She denies any engagement between them, but perhaps at that time the contract had not been entered upon, which at a more subsequent time I might have the pleasure to hear. It would not be objectionable to the family on either side.

We don't expect to come up with the Rebs till we come to Atlanta. If they are as good at fighting as in running we would have a poor show here, anyhow.

Strawberries are in season and peaches are as large as the end of your thumb. Wheat and Rye are in blossom, but poor cultivation is universal. (No negroes seen as yet, all moved South.)

I feel grateful to a merciful Providence who so far has spared my life amid all the <u>dangers</u> of the last few weeks, besides giving me my present good health. I do hope I may be spared to return home again. Write soon, your afft Son

R. T. Van Wyck

P.S. I don't doubt your prayers are answered in my behalf.
I received *Harper's* for April, and send me the May No., if you please.

May 20. Remained at breastworks at Cassville till 2 P.M. and went into camp nearer the village. Spent the rest of the day in washing and resting. The town suffered a perfect sack by our troops, leaving nothing unturned. No citizens remaining to stay the hand of the destroyer.

May 21. Remained in camp all day. Nothing of interest occurred. Weather fine and health good.

May 22. First Sunday in a long while in which we had the pleasure to remain quiet. The country looks fine and has been well cultivated, and every indication of a thriving community.

May 23. Left camp this morning at half-past four and marched fifteen miles to and across the river south of Kingston. Day hot and oppressive. High Tower River, so called. [*Etowah River*]

May 24. Left camp at four o'clock and marched over a high tableland to a place called Huntsville and encamped. Weather still hot. Rained during the night and prospects of cooling.

EDITOR'S NOTE:

On May 25th a bloody battle took place at New Hope Church (the "Hell Hole") with heavy Union losses. By now both sides had brought up their main forces. On May 28th at Pickett's Mill the Union 4th Corps and 14th Corps advanced against the Rebels. They were cut down by the well-entrenched Confederates, and Sherman had to move back to the rail lines. Nevertheless, his assaults had forced the enemy to abandon Allatoona and to retreat to Kennesaw Mountain. Sherman's advance slowed under heavy rains in mid-June, but on June 27th in the blistering heat he launched the battle for Kennesaw Mountain against the Confederate's fortified position.

May 25. Left Huntsville at eight o'clock and marched in a south direction four miles and countermarched to support the 2d Div.

[*at Dallas*]. And under a severe cannonade and musketry fire an hour and a half.* Rained during the night and went to the river at 10 P.M.

May 26. Remained quiet during the day expecting orders to advance. The Rebs relatively holding the same position as the preceding evening. We have planted cannon and silenced two of theirs by sharpshooters.

May 27. Position same as yesterday. The stream called PumpkinVine [*Creek*] flows to our rear. And this fight might be called by that name. [*It was called instead Pickett's Mill.*]

May 28. Removed a hundred yards to the left and quietly awaiting orders. Musketry constant during the day. I was aroused from sleep by the rapid discharge of small arms during the night. Position the same as on previous days.

May 29. Sunday was unusually quiet, more so than any previous day. Attended a prayer meeting in the morning. But about 11 P.M. a desperate attempt was made to carry our works and for a time the musketry was terrific, but they were finally repulsed.

May 30. Day passed like the preceding ones. A noisy musketry firing throughout the day. We were anticipating a similar attack as upon the former night but it passed without a disturbance.

May 31. In the same position as on the previous days. Nothing of any moment occurred. Day pleasant and health good. The country from Huntsville more sterile than I have before seen. It seemed a succession of valleys and ridges wooded by pine and blackjack [*a common oak of eastern United States with a black bark*].

June 1. Moved about nine o'clock to the left. Encamped for the night on a stony hill. Short of rations but obtained them during the night. Weather still continues fine.

June 2. Moved camp about half-past three A.M. and marched half a mile to a strong fortification. There seemed a great concentration of troops at this point and in all probability would have been [*firing*] had it not rained hard. But everything quiet. Detached to build a bridge, finished at 12 P.M.

---

* James Elliott, John Grad, Charles LeClaire, Samuel Myers, and Henry W. Story of the 150th NY Volunteers were killed in action at Dallas, GA, on May 25th. Isaac I. Blauvelt and Isaac Smith died of their wounds shortly afterward.

June 3. Returned from bridge building about 9 A.M., found the Reg't. in the same position. Weather looks threatening with a little rain. Very little firing along the lines. Some hot firing during the night.

June 4. Had a quiet night's rest. Moved camp about five o'clock P.M. to the advance lines in front. Weather rainy and somewhat unpleasant. We seemed to leave the ridges and entered some nice farms of rich soil but poorly cultivated.

June 5. Continued the march to the left and encamped for the night, distance two miles. Enemy said to be on the retreat. Weather rainy. Wheat is sown upon old cotton fields. Some looks well if put in properly.

June 6. Moved still farther to the left and advanced in line of battle. Built breastworks, then out skirmishing, but no demonstration made by the enemy. Rations short. Weather rainy but health good.

June 7. Remained in same position till near night when we moved a hundred yards to the left. Drove two days' meat up front and are living famously. Weather still rainy.

June 8. An opportunity was given us to wash up as we were to remain in camp all day. A mail received and sent off. [*No letters of this date extant.*] Distance from RR only four miles. Rations will come up without difficulty now. CC from Kingston 35 miles.

June 9. Still remain at this place. Nothing of interest occurred. Weather rainy. Cavalry reconnaissance developed the position of the enemy in small force on our front.

June 10. Expected momentary to leave but still remained all day. The 23rd Corps passed to our front. No matter of great interest occurred. Rained in hard showers during the day.

June 11. Moved at 11 o'clock and threw up works within shelling distance of the enemy. Two men, one killed, the other wounded by a shell. [*Henry L. Stone and Henry C. Winans, who died the next day.*] Weather very rainy. Hard work made by it as we were obliged to make our works strong.

June 12. Completed our works during a hard rain which poured down unceasing all day. The enemy quiet.

June 13. Still rained during the day with a cold northeasterly wind. Everything about the same. A few cannon placed in position bearing upon a hill, the commencement of a chain of hills running in a southwest direction.

June 14. A brisk cannonading upon the Rebel works. Was detailed for picket. A sharp musketry fire kept up all the afternoon, accompanied with artillery. We finally succeeded in taking the hill [*Pine Hill*] without much loss. Lt. Gen. Polk (Rebel) said to have been killed with a shell.*

June 15. The last two days dry and pleasant. Was relieved from picket and followed my Regt. which went into action about four o'clock P.M. All [*the line*] was under fire. No one was injured in it.

June 16. Remained all day under a perfect rain of balls of shot and shell. An artillery duel in which we seemed to be victorious. During the night we retired from the works and we pursued.

June 17. Followed the pursuit this morning. The Fourth Corps skirmished quite heavily with the enemy. Built breastworks at nightfall. Rained hard during the night.

EDITOR'S NOTE:

Gen. Sherman notes in his *Memoirs* (pp.55-6), that the men of both armies "became extremely skillful" in constructing breastworks. To spare his own men he later organized "pioneer corps" of the freedmen who escaped to his army, and who "became very useful to us during the rest of the war" by working at night while his soldiers slept. They were paid $10 a month.

Confederate Gen. Johnston used slave labor to the same end, having them build fortifications well in advance of his lines to prepare for his next strategic retrograde move.

(Letter in pencil)

Near Marietta, Ga.
June 17th '64

Dear Mother,

Yours of May 28th, also of June 4th came to hand a day or more ago. I would have answered sooner but we have had active times again. The afternoon of the 15th our corps drove on the Rebel skirmishers in front, and attacked the enemy upon one of their range of breastworks; the second Div. advanced within a hundred yards of their works, and as usual under cover of darkness constructed a work of their own; some loss was sustained, of course.

---

* General Leonidas Polk was formerly Episcopal Bishop of Louisiana. When Union troops reached the top of Pine Hill the next day they found a sign left by the Confederates: "You goddam Yankees have killed our old Gen'l Polk". *War So Terrible,* J.L.McDonough and J.P. Jones, W.W. Norton, N.Y., 1989, p. 177.

In the meanwhile we were posted upon the flank. But yesterday an artillery duel commenced, we having arranged several batteries commanding their position. As fast as one position was taken by the Rebs, it was soon silenced. However, they treated us to shell and shot, by no means inviting. We lost in the Reg't. by chance shots and shells, 4 killed* and as many wounded. They left their works this morning about two o'clock and retired to another of their lines of defense long ago constructed like the present one.

Our first success took place upon the [*June*] 14th by the cooperation of the 14th, 4th, and 20th Corps in planting batteries around and ashelling the Rebs out of a Mountain commanding the R.R., thus enabling Gen. McPherson to cross the river to flank their position.

June 20th. Since the above we have had from day to day a succession of sharp skirmishing in which three or more of our men were wounded. Besides, it has been the rainiest times I ever saw, pouring down incessant, and almost impossible to get dry for days in succession, this making the mud no way pleasant. I would have finished this letter before if I thought I could keep it dry while writing.

The result of the last week's conflict has given some ground to us, although strongly defended by breastworks of the best character. They yield stubbornly to our artillery which keeps up a constant shower of shell and grape upon them. Apparently thus far we much excel them in this area of the service.

I have received your *Harper's* for May and June, also the papers from the Van Vechtens. They used to write me, but I suppose as I have been unable to answer their letters, I am not again favored.

I suppose the country looks fine. I see very little of cultivated land recently. It seems to be a grand bushwhacking fight on a grand scale. I must close this in time for <u>mails.</u> With much love I remain your Aff't Son

R. T. Van Wyck

June 18. Remained at breastworks all day. Rained hard all day. Enemy said to be retreating. Fourth Corps said to be following them up.

June 19. Sunday. Moved in order of battle. Detailed to construct bridges. Rained hard. A busy day for the Sabbath.

---

* Pvts. Daniel Glancey, William R. Phelps, Cornelius Sparks, and Henry Sigler.

June 20. Left at four oclock and was relieved by the Fourth Corps. Marched still further to the Right joined by the whole division. Rained during the night and day.

June 21. Built breastworks and had a treat of a liberal use of water. Rained hard. Had a good night's rest.

June 22. The Rebs massed their force against us and attacked our skirmishers, driving them in. A hard fight occurred lasting an hour and a half of steady musket fire. They were repulsed with great slaughter. Lieutenant of Artillery and several privates killed.*

June 23. Remained in camp all day in same position [*near Marietta*]. We received reinforcements by a division. Had a good night's rest undisturbed. Nothing of importance occurred. Weather fine.

(Letter in pencil)

Within sight of Marietta, Ga.
June 23d '64

Dear Father,

I received your letter, also that of Mother's this evening (that is, that of June 14th). I have the opportunity to announce that a severe fight occurred last evening, or rather afternoon, in which the Rebs were repulsed (a whole Division) by part of two Brigades, our own [*2d*] and the 1st. The circumstances were these: in marching towards the left flank, the 20th Corps to connect with the 23rd Corps, our Division found a gap held by some Reb cavalry defending a ridge commanding the main road to Atlanta, thus no time was to be lost to obtain it. Our whole force was deployed to secure as much ground as possible by building breastworks on the [*June*] 21st, part of which force held, as skirmishers, our present position upon which the battle was fought.

The morning of the 22nd we quickly strengthened our forces and marched to this position to relieve them. The importance of this position was so vital to the Rebels that from prisoners come in [*we ascertained*] that a whole Corps, that of Gen. Hood's, was sent to dislodge us. We had no sooner come in line of battle than we could hear the Rebel cheers driving on our skirmishers in front, but as fortune

---

* First Lt. Henry Gridley, and Pvts. James Todd, John Sweetman, James E. Davidson, and John Simon. Two days later, Pvt. John Hart was killed on picket duty.

favored us, being screened by underbrush, we had time to convert a rail fence into a breastwork in the meantime while a battery came in. The Rebs, seeing the battery and seeing a small force directly in support of the battery putting up works for defense, thought no time must be lost. And before many moments elapsed a whole Division came pouring down upon us. I saw the Rebels at Resaca come up to the charge cool and firm, but this mass with their officers waving their swords and heroically marching up to the cannon's mouth with such gallantry, it gave us no small opinion of their courage.

We saw them at a distance but had no orders to fire till they had approached within three hundred yards, when the battery opened with grape and canister.* Even this did not recoil them momentarily till they had received seven or eight volleys of musketry. The battery now opened upon the next lines of support, they recoiled. The front line now being isolated from the base, it took advantage of a little ravine to shelter itself from the hot fire. We found our ammunition was getting short and every precaution was taken to save it should they attempt another rally to charge; at the same time everyone must see his man before he fires. This state of things lasted two hours. The men cut off [from their lines] were popping at us, we lay concealed behind works, and but two lives were lost, and few wounded. Lieut. Gridley of Co. A [was] killed, the smartest officer in the Reg't.

If we had a support we would have taken five or six hundred prisoners, but for fear a charge upon them would not be successful, it was thought prudent to let well enough alone. During that night the enemy were taking off their killed and wounded, which from prisoners' reports, amount to 2,000. The skirmishers advanced beyond the scene of the conflict directly in our front. All the boys went down. A great many dead were left behind, the ground for several acres covered with blood and stripped clothing.

[Letter continues in ink]

June 24, '64. It being too dark to finish this last evening I will merely add that we finished or strengthened our works the night of the 22nd, expecting momentarily an assault, but we waited patiently throughout. The next day (23rd) we were glad to see the 3d Div. filing in front and establishing another line of works. So we have named this place Ft. Confidence from our ability to hold it.

---

* Shot composed of small metal fragments which covered a wide target area.

I had no trouble to sleep last night for it being the first night in a long while when it didn't rain, or [*there wasn't*] some night march, breastworks, or something else to disturb us. For the last two weeks we have more properly a right to be classified among the amphibious animals, for to have dry clothing on is a curiosity. However, I remain in first-rate health, and the tendencies leading to my sickness last summer entirely removed. I feel rather better than when I started from Normandy.

As to the issue here it seems to be all one way – that is, a determination to succeed. So far we have driven the enemy from every position, not so much by assault as by flank movements and the good use of our artillery. We have not had the positions for the use of artillery equal to the Rebs till recently. Why they failed to use it I can't understand. Now we are getting on the same footing and if they can't reply to it, they must leave. Think of taking Burroughs Mountain by placing batteries around it and throwing shot and shell to the top. I saw just such a mountain captured a few days ago. The Rebs made short work pulling up their tents and taking cover. A cannon was brought to bear upon us, but was soon dismounted by a few well-directed shots.

I have given you a long letter upon war subjects, but my desire for a peace and cessation of hostilities is no less strong. Many are the hours of sorrow and mourning, not to be forgotten in one generation, but the next will derive the benefit of it. I have so far been spared, thanks to a merciful Providence. The future is known and ordered by His all-wise power, and He doeth all things well. So come what may, it is all for the best.

I don't know as I want anything specially. A <u>blouse</u>, as it is called, that is, a loose, dark-blue flannel coat, would be a good substitute for the one I wear, [*which*] is tattered. The opportunity to draw from Govt. will not be till the campaign is over. Besides this, two pairs of cotton drawers. Both articles might be sent by mail, but you must judge of the cost.

I have acknowledged the receipt of *Harper's* for May and June, [*news*]papers, etc. Burroughs is sick, but not dangerously. Montross says it is not as agreeable here as at home, the food included, but he is well. I am glad to hear from home often. I will write as often as possible. With much love, your aff't Son

R. T. Van Wyck

June 24. Remained here during the day. Nothing of importance occurred. Weather fine.

June 25. Remained in camp. Nothing of importance occurred. Weather fine, etc.

June 26. Moved camp about four o'clock in the morning to the right of the Second Div. as reserve. Passed a quiet Sabbath and anticipated a long stay.

June 27. Left camp about four o'clock A.M. directly in rear of 2nd Div. who advanced upon the Rebel works. Shifted camp about five o'clock and settled permanently down.

June 28. Remained in this position all day.

EDITOR'S NOTE:

On June 27th in 90-degree heat Union forces opened fire on the Rebel position at Kennesaw Mountain. The Union's center columns under Gen. Thomas were mowed down, and Gen. McPherson's attack from the left on Little Kennesaw was thrown back, but Gen. Schofield's forces on the right established a bridgehead. While Sherman was reinforcing this position, Johnston once again slipped away to another fortified position further south in front of the Chattahoochee River. The battle of Kennesaw Mountain was considered a Confederate victory with losses of 808 killed or wounded to some 2,500 Union casualities, but by now the Union's forces had fought their way past the mountains and were in position to prepare for the assault on Atlanta.

During the past year the Confederates had turned Atlanta into a fortress, encircling the city with miles of trenches, rifle pits, and redoubts that were too strong to be assaulted. Rather than waste his men against the fortifications, General Sherman decided to besiege the city and starve out the Rebel army, now under the command of General Hood, who had replaced General Johnston. *Memoirs, op. cit,.* pp. 80-81.

(Letter in pencil)

In the Field,
June 28th '64

Dear Mother,

We remain in much the same position as when I wrote you last, except a little more to the left. The enemy is strongly entrenched in our immediate front and so are we. Yesterday the 14th Corps charged upon their works but nothing decisive resulted. Likewise, the 2d Div. of this Corps extended their lines, or advanced them nearer the enemy. I don't know how matters stand because our line of battle is so long that it is out of hearing of cannon even with us placed in the center of it.

Various rumors are current, from being ordered to have on hand five days' rations in haversack, and five in the waggons [*sic*], and from this it is conjectured that an expedition is for us. Today I embraced an opportunity to wash all my clothes and mend them, and with the few articles I drew from Govt. I feel decidedly better. So you need not send me the things I sent for just at present. The weather is hot, and I am afraid the season will not allow much active operations during next month, if the capture of Richmond or Atlanta is not accomplished by that time. But we will hold our own here and drive the Rebs South of the Tallahatchee river at any rate.

I received the *Harper's Weekly* and [*the*] *Frank Leslie.** The illustration of the saving [*of*] the 5th Ind. Battery by the 3d Brigade of the 1st Div. is a good one. Our Brigade was to the right of the Battery and directly in front of the Reb line of battle, but did not fire. The [*sight?*] of that Brigade was quite sufficient to scatter them. But the others [*accounts*] of the Battle at Resaca [*are*] very erroneous, particularly that of taking out the cannon from the fortifications by Geary's 2nd Div., also that of the capture of the colors of the 38th and 58th Ala. Reg'ts., the first of which was taken by the 27th Indiana of our Brigade. Well, opportunities offer often to exhibit such feats, and much oftener than we like sometimes.

The country does not look beautiful now, and almost upon the border of the haying season. I remain in first-rate health. Will write you again soon. I remain your Aff. Son

R. T. Van Wyck

Letter from J. G. Mason to A. V. W. Van Vechten
46 Pine Street, New York

Written on letterhead of
OUR COUNTRY   **OUR HOMES**
CINCINNATI SANITARY COMMISSION TO OUR BRAVE SOLDIERS
Woods of Georgia near
Kennesaw Mountain, June 28/'64

Frank Leslie's Illustrated Weekly.

Dear Sir,

Your letter was gladly received at Kingston. It does one good to receive letters out here so far from civilization. You can hardly imagine how far beyond the reach of home and social restraint the army is. There is no society here, for most of the people have left with the Rebel Army. The portion remaining is so utterly demoralized that the only influence is to contribute to the licentiousness of the Army. The evil of war is not to be estimated by the number killed and wounded. Its horrors do not consist only in the ghastly wound, the shattered limbs, the mangled and bleeding body. Horrible as these are, there is yet something connected with war even more horrible: the wound of a pure soul, the shattered and ruined character. These are to me the greatest horrors.

The number of souls killed and wounded are to be recorded before the greatest evils of this war are to be summed up. This list will be long, I fear. I would not intimate that there are no good influences here, none who do not go into the multitude to do [good]—the Christian Com., the chaplains, the lovers of Christ in the ranks of whom I have met just a few. And I wish I could add without exception the Sanitary Com. are doing a good and noble work. The Sanitary Commission I was somewhat disappointed in the character of her Agents.

In its infancy but little respect was paid to character in the employment of Agents. Consequently many unworthy men insinuated themselves into the work. While I remained in the rear at the supply station I was painfully impressed with this fact. I regretted that I have come out. I found that I must associate with men not only irreligious but open haters of religion and absolutely licentious.

However, since I have come to the front I find the character of the agents very different. Several of them are Ministers. The one with whom I mess is a minister which, of course, makes it very pleasant. I now have the same opportunity of doing good as have Agents of the Christian Commission.

Latterly the policy of the Commission has been changed so that more care is taken in selecting men of character. I enjoy the work here very much. I have under my care of 4th* Corps A.C. [*Army of*

---

*In his letter of August 12, R.T. Van Wyck refers to Mr. Mason as being with the *14th* Corps Sanitary Delegation.

the Cumberland] I make out daily the reports of the wounded and see that they are fed and clothed. Supply them with reading matter. Talk with the wounded. Write letters for them, and make myself general-ly useful.

My headquarters are about a mile and a half from the line of bat-tle. Not much danger except occasionally a wandering shell comes flying around us seeking whom he may devour. Yesterday our Corps assaulted the enemies' works and were repulsed into some loss. The Enemy occupy the Kennesaw Mts., two high peaks between our forces and Marietta. They are strongly fortified there. We cannot take it by storm. We must flank them, which I think is the design. Hooker's Corps is ordered to advance with three-days' rations. Our forces lie in the form of a horseshoe around the base of the Mountain. The 4th, 20th, and 23rd Corps lie on the right and have done most of the fighting.

Very sincerely yours,
J. G. Mason

R. T. Van Wyck's journal resumes:

June 29. Remained here all day. Assisted in getting out the pay-rolls.
June 30. Mustered for pay. Moved camp about 8 o'clock P.M. a quarter of a mile. A heavy shower but cleared off pleasant.
July 1. Cleared a space for a camp and put up quarters for a stay. Weather fine.
July 2. Remained in waiting all day. Nothing of interest occurred.
July 3. Left camp about half-past four and followed the retreat of the Rebs four or five miles. Weather fine.
July 4. Moved and planted a battery in expectation of giving the Rebs a shelling but they moved off. We followed about five o'clock and encamped a few miles to the right.
July 5. Continued the pursuit of the Rebs to the River [*Chattahoochee*]. Encamped on an elevation commanding a view of Atlanta.
July 6. Marched to the left and came upon works of the Rebs dis-puting the passage of the river. Weather fair and everything going on agreeable. Detailed for picket.
July 7. Passed the night in front of the enemy upon skirmish line.

The rest of the day upon reserve. Day fine. Rebs friendly, exchanged [news]papers and tobacco.

July 8. Remained in camp all day, washing, etc. Weather fine. News unimportant. Arranged tents and prepared to settle down.

July 9. Encamped still at this place. Various rumors of departure current in camp.

July 10. Broke camp at two o'clock A.M. moved two hundred yards to the right, remained two hours and reoccupied our old camp. A slight shower towards night, but the day pleasant and agreeable.

July 11. Remained in camp all day. Nothing of interest occurred.

(Letter in pencil)

Near Atlanta, Ga.
July 11th '64

Dear Sarah,

I received your letter of the 26th ult. yesterday. Must not be surprised if paper is a little soiled or if the envelope looks [as] if it had seen hard times, for between rain and perspiration writing materials scarcely survives. You are informed repeatedly from home of my whereabouts, so I need not discourse upon war topics at any length, except to say that Atlanta, the goal of the summer campaign, is within sight.

We have arrived here after successive skirmishes and fightings of nearly sixty days' duration. <u>Providence</u> has so far smiled upon our army that so far we have caused the enemy to evacuate its strongholds, yet the expenditure of life less than at Gettysburg. It has been by no means small [however], for the heat of the season acts unfavorably for the wounded.

The news from home quite interesting, particularly that of F. Kip and Miss G. Bartow. I didn't suppose the match was viewed with much favor by Dr. Kip's family. It is a strange affair, anyhow. No less strange than his brother's, however, which, by the by, allow me to say that if you are possessed of the Kip <u>mania</u>, let their examples induce you, of that irresistible offer, to have it immediately consummated. The young lady by being so committed upon her love affairs is not likely to have soon an adviser. How does Miss N____ A. escape the gauntlet of offers, enjoyments, etc., for so great expectations as hers, together with an attractive form, is not likely to go unnoticed. Besides, there is Miss E. Brinckerhoff, of great expectations, both of which seems to be put in the cold by all the excitable young gents. I will warn all of that latter class, if any of such have any serious intentions, they had better improve the present opportunity. For when I get home I will have cheek enough to do anything desperate.

The country now looks fine and now you are expatiating upon the luxuries of garden produce, strawberries included. What has become of the Andrews, William and Susan? Possibly their headquarters are at Wethersfield, Conn.

Remember me to Aunt Susan, Mr. Lane, and all the rest of the family. With much love I remain your aff. Cousin

R. T. Van Wyck

July 12. Spent same as yesterday. Weather fine but hot.
July 13. Spent same as on the preceding. Weather still continues fine. 2nd Mass. moved camp to a more comfortable situation. We all making preparations for a stay.
July 14. Remained in the same place. A heavy shower during the night.

(Letter in pencil)

Near Atlanta, Ga.
July 14th '64

Dear Mother,

Your letter of July 7th I received last evening. I was glad to know the suspense relative to the last battles have been relieved. I have written you so recently and having suffered no change of camp since, I cannot give you much new.

We remain encamped much the same as at Kelleys Ford, Va., our bunks raised a foot or more from the ground, tents regularly pitched in streets artificially shaded. A detail from each company sent out every day upon picket, returning the next [*day*]. The advance link is along the Chattahoochee River, only a hundred yards in width. The exchange of [*news*]papers, tobacco, etc. [*with the Rebs*] goes on to a greater extent than ever before and besides this, much talk and sentiment.

A mutual understanding seems to exist between the two parties as to firing, and when Johnny Reb thinks it his duty to fire he intimates to Yank to "lie low," and vice versa. Our officers seem to encourage the intercourse, believing it does much to demoralize the enemy as they (Rebs) are heartily tired of the war and are becoming convinced of the failure of their cause. They have not got Richmond news for the last week which shows the communication is interrupted by Gen. Grant. We have received news from that quarter long in advance of our papers, by way of Atlanta, getting the daily about one or two o'clock, much in advance of our own.

I heard a good joke yesterday: in answer to several interrogatories passed between the pickets, one of which was, "Who commanded the Federal Army?" answer "Gen. Sherman." "Who commanded the Rebel Army?" answer "Gen. Sherman," because when he moved, they had to move. The boys seem to like the picket duty first rate and much prefer to be there than in camp.

The advance of the Rebel raiders into Md. and Penn. will cause some excitement among the shoddies in New York, for without they defend themselves, Gen. Grant will not withdraw his attention from Petersburg or Richmond.

I anticipated the dearth of labor in our section of country. I hope you may succeed this year, for I do strongly believe something decisive will result from this summer campaign, and with the return of the army a general collapse will take place in everything. The wet weather which continued up to the 22nd of June seems to have left us. We have been thus favored by water in great abundance converting every ravine into a running stream.

I countermanded the order for the articles of clothing, for the quartermaster has furnished us again with new clothes. I was much surprised to learn that Mr. Lane was so moneyless. Van Wyck can't like this much. There is money somewhere to travel upon, it seems. I hope to hear from you soon again. I remain your aff. Son

R. T. Van Wyck

July 15. Still remained here.

July 16. Remained here. Weather fine. A shower during the night.

July 17. Left camp around 3 o'clock P.M. and crossed the river a mile above our former encampment, passed over to the left of the RR and marched on the other side of the river to the left four or five miles.

July 18. Left our former encampment about 3 P.M. and marched four miles in a south direction to flank Atlanta in the distance. No signs of the enemy in strong force.

July 19. Resumed our march about five o'clock and marched direct for Atlanta, distance three miles. We remained here three miles from Atlanta.

(Letter in pencil)

East of Atlanta, Ga.
July 19th '64

Dear Mother,

I write this morning to acknowledge receipt of that coat and drawers, which are splendid articles. At first, since I had countermanded the sending of them, I had drawn from Govt. such as I needed. [*Then*] I thought I would sacrifice my present ones, but through the kindness of the Colonel I got the package carried by the waggon [*sic*] till I need them.

[*I understand that but for*] the delay of my second letter and the promptness of your meeting my request, you would have deferred sending them for the present. But they are truly welcomed, and I can put them to excellent use. Don't think I sent for them to gratify a whimsical notion, for the small amount of clothing we are able to carry with us, and the wear and exposure, as well as the privilege of [*not*] always finding a supply of water puts cleanliness out of the question, and it is expected Govt. must issue frequently such articles as needed, but in the early start of this campaign the impression seemed to exist that if we got our rations we must stand it to go barebacked into Atlanta, therefore my request. It is all right now, I can have them carried, and give yourself no uneasiness but what they will be judiciously applied.

We moved from our camp where we had remained seven or eight days, on the 17th, crossed the river to the left, and marched in a Southeasterly direction and continued the march yesterday and momentarily expect to resume it this morning. We are no nearer Atlanta than before, but by this move expect to flank the Rebel breastworks protecting the city, which are said to be strong. We don't think so sanguine of getting into Atlanta just at present, but by a little maneuvering the thing will be accomplished.

Our summer work undoubtedly will not end there, not until we drive them into Va. I hope Va. matters will look brighter, it much encourages the Rebs to hear that a demonstration is marching upon Washington. I have confidence of the ability of the garrison at that city to hold it; a change by taking Petersburg would be a fine thing to prevent it.

I expect to hear soon from home. That coat fits first rate, it couldn't be better if made to order. If you have the No. of the size, preserve it. Such quality of stuff is rarely seen in the army, especially among the musket carriers (privates). Remember me to all at home. I remain your af't Son

R. T. Van Wyck

July 20. A severe attack was made by the enemy this afternoon and severely repulsed by the whole line. We lost many in killed and wounded throughout the corps.*

July 21. Remained in camp all day and attended to the dead and wounded. In the afternoon was moved to the advance line and held that position all night.

(Letter in pencil)

Within Three Miles of Atlanta, Ga.
July 21st '64

Dear Mother,

I received your letter of July 12th about the same time I mailed one acknowledging the receipt of those articles of clothing (July 19th).

So you have our situation, with the exception of adding that yesterday afternoon we witnessed one of the desperate encounters during the campaign. It seems that Hood, who now commands the Rebel army via Johnston superseded, supposing, from the heavy force of ours on each flank (one of which was Gen. McPherson, only within one inch and a half from Atlanta) that our center must be necessarily weakened, concentrated their forces and attacked our forces about the time we were meditating an advance upon theirs. But

---

* On July 17, Confederate Gen. Jos. E. Johnston was replaced by Gen. John Bell Hood. Since Hood was known to be "bold to the point of rashness," the Union army realized this change meant "fight," and Gen. Sherman cautioned his soldiers to "be prepared always for battle in any shape." Nevertheless, both Generals Sherman and Grant considered the wily Gen. Johnston their most dangerous opponent. *Memoirs*, p. 72.

they were sorely disappointed to find us so strong in force, although the dense underbrush permitted them to approach the works without being seen. Our works, however, were very poor indeed, and the exposure cost many men their lives,* as I saw them this morning — but the well-directed fire of our men soon checked the advance of the enemy and forced them to retire in much disorder.**

I don't know what next will turn up, but if Hood takes his army along as well as Johnston [*did*] he will deserve great praise, for they are much disheartened and discouraged.

I am glad to learn that you are all well and that haying is progressing favorably. Your letters are a great pleasure to receive, and I am glad Sarah has overcome her prudish notions and written me, which letter I received about the same time as yours.

I will write soon again. With much love I remain your aff. Son

R. T. Van Wyck

July 22. Having found the enemy deserted their works the skirmishers were advanced and we immediately followed. We soon came upon their works but did not get into position till towards three, but subsequently moved and advanced during the night.

July 23. Remained in same position till towards night. Were then detached to advance our works in front of 2nd Brigade which we completed during the night.

July 24. Resumed our works and finished them. At night feint was made for an assault in which we gave the Johnnys a scare.

July 25. Remained here during the day. At night the Johnnys tried our trick upon us and made us come into our works lively.

July 26. Same as on the preceding day. Nothing of interest transpiring.

July 27. The 13th N.J. made a rally in front of our works and beyond the picket line to burn some buildings. They were quite successful, captured thirty, killed seven, and wounded eight in their lines.

---

* From 150th Vols.: Bernard Connolly, Stephen Simmons, Nathan C. Hedden, John E. Pultz, Thos. Burnett, James Horton, Henry Dykeman. Richard Hyde was wounded and later died.

** The blow fell mainly on Hooker's corps which had crossed Peachtree Creek, when without warning, the enemy came pouring down upon them. Hooker's whole corps fought on open ground and lost about 1500 men to the enemy's 400 dead. *Memoirs*, p. 73.

(Letter in pencil)

In Front of Atlanta, Ga.
July 27th '64

Dear Mother,

I received yours of July 19th yesterday. Since my last letter and the battle of the 20th which I wrote you about, we have advanced a mile or more, if not two, built works, etc. Our cannon over our works in rear have been sending minute messages [*every five minutes*] into the heart of the city in the shape of shot and shell. They have heartily answered like compliments and given us no small amount of shell, but doing us no harm.

You have heard of the death of Gen. McPherson,* and also of the capture of Gen. Hardee, as well as our success in establishing the lines around this side of the city. The Rebs must fight desperately to pierce our lines or to get off with whole bones.

In answer to your questions, the first of which is "My Promotions:" Made Corporal Oct. 11, 1862, promoted to Sergeant Jan. 1st, 1864. Second: Engaged in the battle of Gettysburg July 2d and 3d, 1863; of Resaca, Ga., May 15th, 1864; of Dallas, Ga., May 25th, 1864; of Lost Mt., June 15th, 1864; to the right of Kennesaw Mt. and near Marietta, June 22d, 1864; in front of Atlanta, July 20th, 1864.

The skirmishes occur daily, and I have quite lost track of them, for in advancing the picket [*line*] they act as skirmishers, and are now called the skirmish line. "What special service performed?" None, in the sense it is meant, except as being one of the million muskets acting offensively upon the enemy. As to health, never ask for better. The rest you will fill up, only not put too much to it.

---

*On July 21st Confederate Gen. Hood had sent a corps on an all-night march to attack the exposed south flank of Gen. James Mcpherson's Army of the Tennessee, but the Union forces were well protected and exacted much damage on Hood's corps. However Gen. McPherson, who was Sherman's favorite subordinate officer, lost his life when he rode by mistake into Rebel lines and was shot down as he tried to get away. His horse came back "bleeding, wounded, and riderless," followed within an hour "by an ambulance bearing McPherson's body." *Memoirs*, p. 77.

Sherman had seen Gen. McPherson not only as "a noble gallant gentleman and the best hope for a great soldier," who might well out-distance both Grant and himself, but as "a man qualified to heal the national strife" after the war. *Sherman: Fighting Prophet*, op.cit., pp. 299, 387.

We are having a spell of dry weather, not unpleasant or at all like the dryness and heat you speak of. So much wet weather in the early season has given us a fine campaign.

You might have heard of a sensational report of the occupation of Atlanta, but you must know that it is erroneous by this time. But perhaps before this reaches you, you might credit it, for we have got them in a pretty tight place.

I have received *Harper's* for July. The *American Messenger* I received through the chaplain. I have also received *Frank Leslie* and "Our Country." I received a letter from Uncle Anthony yesterday. He is well but says his crops are light in consequence of the weather. Write often. With much [*love*] I remain your aff't Son

R. T. Van Wyck

July 28. Still remained in same position. We made an ineffectual attempt to advance our lines but failed. Weather fine. General Hooker leaves the army upon his own request*.

July 29. Upon picket in front of our own works. Some brisk skirmishing but was not assaulted or did [*not*] attack the enemy's rifle pits. Was relieved at 6 P.M. Weather looked rainy.

July 30. Remained in camp behind or in our trenches. Advanced our skirmish line and gobbled up some hundred or more Rebs. Weather fine.

July 31. During the night the enemy shelled our works continuously till sunrise when they discontinued for the day. Therefore the Sabbath passed off very quiet. No change in the position of the two armies except from reports that "McPherson's Army"** has secured the RR leading south. Since crossing the Chattahoochee River the country bears evidence of better cultivation, soil being more fertile. Yet from Marietta I have found it by no means sterile.

---

* He was replaced by Gen. Alpheus S. Williams, and then by General Henry W. Slocum.

** Army of the Tennessee, which was now led by General Otis O. Howard. General Hooker, feeling he should have received this command, resigned in protest at being bypassed. Over the past two months, feeling superior in rank and experience to Generals Schofield and McPherson, Gen. Hooker had become troublesome by acting outside of orders. A month after resigning, he said in a speech at Cincinnati that "Sherman had run up against a rock at Atlanta," and that the country should prepare itself for disaster in that quarter. In any case, Sherman found in Howard a most able and satisfactory commander.

(Letter in pencil)

Letterhead:
AGENCY OF THE U. S. SANITARY COMMISSION
The United States Sanitary Commission establishes a Depot of Hospital and Sanitary Supplies in charge of a competent Agent at every post within our lines, following up the advance of the army. Our agents will use every exertion to secure the sure delivery of letters to soldiers, sent to their care.

Siege of Atlanta, Ga.
July 31st, 1864

Dear Father,

My letter of the 28th gave you the special news of change here. We hold relatively the same position as then, except we have had several sorties upon the enemies' pickets and gobbled up a hundred or more. This has drawn the enemies' <u>guns</u> upon our position which has confined us closely to the trenches.

We have (as I have been informed) surrounded the city, cutting the R.R., etc. The citizens have left the city, but unfortunately many women and children were killed by our shells, owing to the desperation of their commanders, Hood, who treated with scorn the summons of Sherman warning him to surrender the city or he would shell it. How long this state of things will last I don't know, perhaps several weeks. We will get the best of them yet, without something unforeseen turns up. I hope the campaign will end upon the taking of this city.

Many amusing scenes occur during these times. J. G. Montross, whose proclivities for eating and whose carefulness to keep out of harm's way [*is*] equally as great (which necessitates considerable exposure [*in order*] to cook) puts him in much trouble. Often one meal will suffice for all day. The health of the men excellent, however.

I am sorry to hear of the drought in the East. It must affect the pasture for fattening the cattle, but I presume the wheat has not been affected as much as the oats. Now is a good opportunity to make money, and indebtedness defrayed, with greenbacks [*which*] is considerable different to what it will be, or has been in the moneyed circles. The shoddy men have had a good time of it, but easy comes, easy goes. So it was in the early stages of the Rebellion, but such a class of men come to grief at last. I do believe there are many who have accumulated considerable amounts of gold in the Confederacy, but to get it out, that is the question.

I suppose the estate is about settled and everything satisfactory. Mr. Lane and Aunt Susan are striving to make themselves happy by traveling (as I have been informed). Theodorus V. W. and family is diverting themselves amid the "Tons" at the watering places, etc. I am glad to receive letters from home. I remain with much love, your aff. Son

R. T. Van Wyck

P. S. Tell Mother to send me a fine comb, or what she may term a "trap."

EDITOR'S NOTE:

Always careful of his men's lives, and wishing to avoid the wholesale slaughter attendant upon attacking a well-fortified Atlanta, Gen. Sherman had no choice but to settle down to a long siege of the city.

Aug. 1. Very quiet along the lines. No news in camp. Weather fine.
Aug. 2. The day passed like the preceding.*
Aug. 3. No change in camp. We remained same as on preceding day.

(Letter in pencil)

Siege of Atlanta, Ga.
Aug. 3d '64

Dear Sarah,

I received your letter yesterday. You see the extra sheet of paper is just the thing. How well you anticipated my wants.–

It is very delightful to hear of your sociable picknicks. Would it be possible for me to come down to such a diet as you had then set before you! Give me an opportunity of trying, I can soon tell you.

In your letter you spoke of H.–possibly meaning Hasbrouck DuBois–intending giving a few weeks of leisure at home. In the absence of an equal number of gentlemen to the young ladies, his coming will be a relief to the other gallant sex. I received a letter from F. Kip a few days since. I take it he is ready for the Theological Seminary, having passed at the N. Y. University. He mentions little

---

* Pvt. James W. Chambers of Co. B was wounded, and died Dec. 28, 1864.

news, but I am obliged to him for the favor. I suppose Dr. Kip's house is crowded now with friends and his own family. They are a happy-go-easy set.

We are fencing in by daily stages this stronghold of Rebellion with this great army. We have lived here under musketry and artillery fire for ten or more days. The noise of shells bursting and bullets wizzing [*sic*] through the air has got to be of little consequence, as little more than that of a movement on a R.R. or any common-place occurrence in camp. A few nights since I pitched my tent out-side the trenches, being more comfortable, it being quiet along the lines. But towards morning I was awakened out of my sleep by a quantity of dirt thrown upon my tent by a shell, and a few moments after a shell went through a tent adjoining my own. I thought it was best to move from there. The boys told me shelling was going on all night but I must have slept through it, as I knew nothing of it. What can't we get used to?

I have reason to be thankful to be preserved amid such continu-al danger. I have so far escaped injury or death, thanks to His all-protecting arm, trusting the future will be ordered for the best. Whether permitted to return home or killed — it will be all right.

I hope you will write often. Often I can't answer, but every chance I will improve.

Remember me to Anna and the rest of the Family. I remain your aff. Cousin

R. T. Van Wyck

Aug. 4. Prepared to move our breastworks a few hundred yards in front. A detail was employed most of the night.

Aug. 5. Commenced work at 3 A.M. and soon made the works ten-antable. Pitched our tent and occupied it. Weather hot and sultry.

Aug. 6. The day overcast was not as hot as yesterday. Nothing new on the lines.

(Letter in pencil)

In the Field near Atlanta, Ga.
Aug. 6th '64

Dear Mother,

I received yours of July 25th, [*on*] Aug. 4th. I assure you it bright-ens a happy hour to get a letter from home and hear what is going on. In like manner you are relieved from the suspense in getting one of my letters and knowing all is going on well as yet. The Army here, so little is known except what is official, and having been very successful with only a smaller proportionate army to contend against, I suppose the people at home are commending us highly—or the Gen. (Sherman) [*his parenthesis*] in command – for so skillfully managing it.

We are still drawing the lines tighter around the city, having advanced our works and enabled the right and the left wing to meet. They say McPherson's army* holds, or will obtain at all hazards, the Macon R.R., the only avenue of supplies. These roads were interrupted by some of our raiding parties some time since. At present a large force of cavalry is moving toward Macon and Americus to liberate the prisoners there imprisoned, said to number twenty thousand. Spare arms is taken along to arm them, besides ambulances and hospital stores for the sick. If not able to return will make direct for Pensacola from there to New Orleans, and take transports up the river. This is mere hearsay, however, but before many weeks you may hear more about it. It comprises Stoneman's whole force. The dismounted cavalry are in breastworks upon the flanks.

No one has greater reason to become disaffected as regards the management of the war to its duration, etc., than ourselves, and how disappointed we all were that it did not end agreeable to our expectations months since. But to see the magnitude of war operations and the vast amount of territory to be subdued [*we realize that*] we know little about it; but having got the Rebel army in a tight place after three years of toil and suffering, the army have much dislike for the Secesh to get off with whole bones because a few Rebel sympathisers [*sic*] up north are either called upon to run the same risk as ourselves, or are interfered with in shoddifying the Govt. or are taxed to bear the expense. Such ones forget that there are persons in the army who are not only taxed to support the war, but are taxed to pay the commutation levied by the civil authorities to screen many from the draft.

If this army is to be recruited to continue its effective force, those at home who have done so little should be the last to grumble. It is a poor argument for the opposition to advance – this last call. It is but an echo of the Southern leaders to get as much clemency as

---

* The Army of the Tennessee, now led by Gen. Howard, was evidently still thought of as "McPherson's army."

possible in a new administration, for I believe the South cannot be held together much longer than the next presidential election and are ready to come back to the Union as much as Jeff[*erson Davis*] dislikes it, and is willing [*wants?*] to be left alone. This is an expression of every Rebel prisoner or deserter I have seen yet.

I mailed a letter to F. Kip in answer to one I received from him. He sent me his ferrotype.* They are small, about the size of a postage stamp. I should like yours and Father's. And tell the girls at the other house to send me theirs. They can't give much trouble to get taken. However, they are new to me. I received a letter from Uncle Anthony a few days since. Were you disappointed in the appearance of Aben's** wife taken from photograph? I am glad he sent them home.

Can you read my letters? I am obliged to write in pencil. When I get settled down I will use ink. I am due seven months' pay, amounting to $130. As no sutlers are allowed I have little use for money but a small amount I had on hand at Normandy has sufficed till the present, but I should like to have some on hand for an emergency, and would be much obliged for five or ten dollars. I remain your aff. Son

R. T. Van Wyck

P. S. I will happily receive any inquiries for such ferrotypes – am not particular, but especially prize those I have mentioned.

EDITOR'S NOTE:

When Gen. Sherman sent two cavalry forces to destroy the Macon railroad supplying Atlanta, Gen. Stoneman begged permission to ride onto Macon and free the Andersonville prisoners. When both cavalry forces were routed and Stoneman taken prisoner, Sherman blamed himself for letting his "natural and intense desire" to rescue the prisoners overcome his military judgment. *Sherman: Fighting Prophet, pp.402-3.*

Aug. 7. The day quiet, passed off without much noise upon picket. Weather fine.

Aug. 8. Nothing unusual occurred. Day showery and hot. Still continued the siege of the city. Am ignorant how it progresses, but rumor says favorable.

---

* A tintype, a photograph made on a thin iron plate.
** His brother, Abraham Van Wyck.

Aug. 9.   Still in the same position.
Aug. 10. Still in the same place. Weather still showery.
Aug. 11. No change in our situation. Rain in showers.
Aug. 12. In the same position. No change.

(Letter in pencil)

In the Front of Atlanta
Aug. 12th '64

Dear Mother,

I received your letter of Aug. 2d yesterday. Was quite surprised you had not heard of the engagement of the 20th July in which our Reg't. was engaged. Of this I wrote you in a letter bearing date July 21st or 22d. I do not know which, but subsequent letters have convinced you of my welfare.

The weather is showery and not as hot as might be, although encamped and exposed to little fatigue in the sun, I have not a fair opportunity of judging, but sometimes our thin canvas coverings are a slight protection from the hot sun. Our subterranean abodes under the breastworks are much cooler and afford a good refuge in midday, while the outside elevated tents and benches are much the best sleeping apartments.

The battery in our rear which has till recently kept up a constant fire upon the city and forts have shifted more to the right and with it the enemy have changed the range of their guns, giving us little fear of their shells. But hardly a night passes without some alarm is given by a heavy skirmishing going on between the pickets. Fortunately I have been on picket but once here on the advance lines, at which time the Rebs were very pacific and permitted some exchanges. The next day they were just like wasps and a person had to lie low to save <u>his</u> <u>bacon</u> (himself). We have heard of the capture of Mobile*–if that is so, we will have gunboats up the Alabama if not up the Chattahoochee River to threaten their rear and cut off supplies. They will threaten Macon, at any rate.

The [*R.R.*] cars are bringing supplies of ammunition up to the works, also large guns, etc. Our commissary department is not much better than it has been, but quite sufficient to answer our requirements at present. The light articles, such as dessicated [*sic*] potatoes,

---

* Admiral Farragut had captured forts in the bay, but the city had not yet been taken.

vegetables, beans, rice, allowed us by regulation and given us before, cannot be obtained for us. One lb. of hard bread, 1 lb. of fresh beef or in lieu, 1/4 lb. of salt pork or bacon, with coffee and sugar, constitute our ration per day. It is quite surprising to myself to find one in such good health upon such a coarse diet. And how my three-day rations disappear long before they ought to for my own good seems to be a great mystery to me when I reflect how great an antipathy I had against salt meats generally.

Montross has been suffering from fever and diarrhea and has looked decidedly bad, but I am happy to say he is better, and he says he is improving. I obtained four biscuits by bribing a cook upon a R.R. engine, the first bread rations Montross has taken in a week. And the first soft bread (biscuit) I have seen since leaving Normandy. He has received a little assistance from the Sanitary Commission, but slight indeed. I must look up that Mason (Van Wyck's friend) of the 14th Corps Sanitary Delegation. For the little articles they can give cannot be obtained elsewhere by enlisted men for love of no one. And if he has much regard for Van Wyck he can ration me as well with his goods and I will laud his excellence to V.W. as good as words can express.

Say nothing to the Montross family about Jacob, he is well enough to write himself. If he does not, he probably does not wish to let his folks know he is sick or has been. The intimacy between V. W. and Hasbrouck DuBois might land V. W. into some good family for a wife, and by so doing lead his friend (H. D. B.) the same way. They at the other house would like to settle that for him, I suppose.

The mail has just now come in. I have received *Frank Leslie's* for July 30th. Mr. Voorhees and family are possibly now with you. What does Mr. Voorhees now think of the war? If active enough? or tired of it? and longs for peace upon any terms? The future is certainly dark and mysterious but evidently for some good purpose, that is, <u>peace</u>, so much desired by both sides cannot be arrived at without a committal to some of the first principles of our Republic and would bring this war to an end without any good resulting from the vast sacrifice of men and treasure. Time will unravel this and bring it all right, I hope.

Excuse me for writing so tedious a letter. I hope to hear from home soon again. With much love I remain your aff. Son

R. T. Van Wyck

Aug. 13. Weather hot and sultry. No change in affairs here.

Aug. 14. Still in the same place. Health good. Weather hot and oppressive at midday.

Aug. 15. Still the same.

Aug. 16. Reported that RR cut at Dalton. No mail for two days. Rations full as yet. No change with us here. Weather dry and hot, showers in afternoon.

Aug. 17. Still the same.

Aug. 18. No news of any importance or any change in our situation.

Aug. 19. Upon picket to relieve a Sergt. sick – for only twelve hours. The enemy quiet and showed themselves numerous upon their rifle pits. Commenced firing towards night. Severe battle upon the left.

Aug. 20. Still the same. Various rumors as to moving. Some indication of going back upon RR. Weather rainy, showery.

Aug. 21. Passed a quiet Sabbath. Quite rainy. Nothing new and no change with us.

(Letter in pencil)

> In front of Atlanta, Ga.
> Aug. 21st '64

Dear Mother,

I received yours of Aug. 9th yesterday. The delay was owing to the track being torn up by guerrillas between here and Chattanooga. It seemed as fast as repaired, some part of the long line was put out of order, and we had no mail matter for four days. So long a cessation has not occurred in a long time. This <u>cracker line</u>* is looked to with much anxiety by the boys, who would recommend the detailing of this corps to the duty of keeping it open, but Sherman "doesn't see it." However, as long as we receive our usual rations, everything will go on well.

We have received reinforcements to the amount of twenty or thirty thousand, which has enabled us to secure the Macon R. R., the R. R. of supplies for the Rebs. This was not obtained without a struggle, for the 17th corps is said to have repulsed [*them*] through repeated assaults, after which followed it up with a charge, thus establishing their lines.

---

* Railroad supply line.

While upon picket day before yesterday I got a glimpse of what might once have constituted some of the beauties of Atlanta – the fine residences in the suburbs, some of which were not totally demolished by shells or stripped of lumber, but the Rebs had converted the greens in front into bombproofs and cut lines of rifle pits through them. We saw their opperations [*sic*] from our lines, about half as far as [*it is from our house*] to the "other house," except a ravine between. They, like ourselves, have given up picket firing, and exchange various articles with us, but are kept strict by their officers and are very suspicious that we may not play some Yankee trick upon them. Two picket lines were gobbled up slyly by us since we came here, numbering in all over two hundred men, and very likely they can spare no more men just at present.

I am sorry the hot weather has so enervated your system, but with the cheerful service of Aunt Mary and the Voorhees family you may improve, I hope. I will write soon again.

The inflation of prices and corresponding profits looks handsome. There is not much fear of a depression just at present, particularly for farmers.

Love to all. I remain your aff't. Son   R. T. Van Wyck

Aug. 22. Still the same.
Aug. 23.* No change. A large mail arrived today.
Aug. 24. No change.

(Letter in pencil, badly faded)

In Front of Atlanta, Ga.
Aug. 24 '64

Dear Mother,

I received yours of Aug. 16th last evening. It seems unaccountable that so long a time elapses before you receive my letters, while only seven days is taken for your letter to reach me.

Nothing new later than I last wrote you a few days ago. We still batter away at the city with siege guns and it does seem to me that scarcely a house remains uninjured. When I wrote you I said we had possession of the Macon R. R., the vital one to the enemy, but

---

* On Aug. 23 Pvt. Willis D. Chamberlain of 150 N.Y. Vols. was killed.

that is a mistake, our lines hold the R. R. to Montgomery, branching from the Macon R.Road.

Kilpatrick* made a circuit of Atlanta and returned yesterday. He destroyed the R. R. waggon [sic] trains, captured a Brigadier and eighty men. He met with much resistance and was obliged to cut his way out several times. Many of his men lost their hats and seemed worn out. But the raid only has the same effect that the guerrillas are continually making upon our R. Road – we fix the track up again, and they will do the same; if we cannot hold the road they will still hold out. I have observed they are very sparing of their artillery, and ammunition boxes, if the latter are found, bears a very late date, and undoubtedly the resources of the Rebs are taxed to the utmost to make up the deficiency of loss of the use of the Atlanta armories and foundries.

I went in search of Mr. Mason, delegate of the Sanitary Commission, but was unsuccessful in finding him. I heard there had been persons visiting the different Hospitals of the 14th Corps from that body, and I suppose he must have been one of them. It does little good to send persons on such missions if they do not send agents to every division in the army of their own who are not hoodwinked by the medical department, or blinded by the respect of epaulets to do their duty impartially alike to the soldiers (privates) as to the soldiers (commissioned).

My observation has convinced me that rascality nowhere is [as] rampant as in the medical department, whose powers as disburser of Sanitary stores has been supreme. The chaplains are sometimes made agents, as our chaplain in the division of our own, and perhaps he gives the sick and wounded the preference, and if anything is left, those who have got the most cheek get it. He has been more susceptible to the solicitations of officers and [those] shirted with nice colored shirts, etc. This cheeky set, whose provision by the Govt. is ample to furnish them and is alike in the subsistence department to much improve their condition above the private soldiers. But he that can sponge the most comes out the best. He has as good a right to

---

* Gen. Judson Kilpatrick, a 28-year-old West Pointer, was head of one of Sherman's three cavalry units. General Sherman himself was unenthusiastic about the cavalry's effectiveness in disabling a railroad properly. He now decided it was time to put into operation his original plan for a "grand left wheel around Atlanta," in order to decoy Gen. Hood out of the city.

have as those who have received, and therefore they all go in pell mell. They can't insult the agent, for he has established the precedent.

An incident occurred at his tent when a member of our own company was present. An officer came in and asked the chaplain for a pair of drawers, particularly a light, nice pair, but the chaplain demurred, saying they were intended for the sick. The officer said a plug of tobacco would suit the sick persons present (who saw the transaction) much better than the drawers, and he would give one dollar into the hands of the chaplain for their benefit as compensation for them. He had no money but promised to pay – that will be the last of him and the articles. So you see how the matter is. I don't condemn the institution by no means, but I must say that the Sanitary Com. are negligent in not sending authorized agents into every Division of the Army who are not connected with the Military Department in the slightest – who are honest men, incorruptible, and who will band themselves together to systematize the distribution of the stores to give it to those who need it and say <u>no</u> to those who have no right to ask it.

You have seen letters in the papers stating that the neglect of the sick to be furnished with various articles (which often there is much truth in) would never occur. I am agoing to r____[?] <u>my</u> <u>face</u> for some stuff tomorrow to see which of <u>us</u> is intended the articles are sent to, but I don't think I will succeed well. A little imagination to state [*I have*] a poor appetite, indigestion, helps materially, but in both instances my appearance will belie me, and in the former [*my appetite is*] much too good for my rations.

I have just returned from the Ist Div. Hospital where I obtained the 4 lbs. of potatoes I asked for and received. ("Us" means anyone who is lucky enough to obtain upon asking anything they may by chance have on hand (after providing for the Medical Department and supervisory attendants, the sick and wounded, and the balance distributed to the Reg't in the field) as far as they will go. This latter policy is in all Divs. except our own, wholly in the hands of the Medical Department who sell the stuff to sutlers, pocketing the funds, or [*giving it*] to their favorite officers.*

---

* Gen. Sherman notes in his Memoirs, "I several times gained the ill-will of the agents of the Sanitary Commission because I forbade their coming to the front unless they would consent to distribute their stores equally among all." (p. 302)

I am agoing to send Uncle Anthony the order of exercises at the Hopewell Church. As you say, the policy of H. DuBois by Miss Ann Bartow I am not competent to judge, but the style of the former is not unlike the man.

As I have given you a long letter I must close. Have you received the letter asking for money? I notice the papers sent to J. Montross come with the one-cent stamp from Johnsville. I wish you would send [-- ?] and packages of envelopes can be mailed for one cent an ounce, if rolled up, tied tightly, and expressed at the end, or marked "writing paper."

Remember me to Mr. Voorhees and family, if with you, and to Aunt Mary. Write soon. I remain your aft. Son

R. T. Van Wyck

P. S. Yours of Aug. 17th I received today with the $10 and the "trap" comb. I am glad you looked favorably to the ferrotypes and will soon send them.

Aug. 25. Made preparations to move which were accomplished about nine o'clock P.M. Marched in retreat to the RR bridge over the Chattahoochee River.

Aug. 26. After taking up our line built breastworks. Heat almost unbearable. Showers in the afternoon.

Aug. 27. Improved our camp and settled down in comfortable quarters. Weather fine.

Chattahoochee River
Aug. 27th '64

Dear Mother,

In closing my last letter I acknowledged the receipt of yours of August 17th, with the $10 and comb enclosed. The 25th we marched in retreat, that is, the left flank of our army consisting of the 4th and 20th Corps were thrown back to the river,* our div. of the corps

---

* The 20th Corps drew the least hazardous assignment in Sherman's flanking movement: to hold the railroad bridge across the Chattahoochee River a few miles outside of Atlanta, and to keep an eye on Hood's army inside Atlanta, while the main Union army stole silently out of the city on August 25-26. When the Rebel skirmishers found the Yankee lines deserted the whole city rejoiced that Sherman was gone, but his army was now busily destroying the city's main supply lines on the railroads to the east and south of Atlanta. *Memoirs, op.cit.*, pp. 104-9.

holding the works on the south side of the river, the other Div. continuing the connection by R. R. to the right and also to the left, while the 4th Corps could be spared to assist the right (extreme) to sever the [*Rebel's*] communication with Atlanta by the Macon Road. This perhaps is what is called a movement by the right flanks, and another change in the programme to take Atlanta by flank.

Our Reg't is a quarter of a mile from the R. R. Bridge and within a few hundred yards of the river, and if the Rebs don't trouble us much, we will have a nice time. The river is a nice place for bathing, it has a rapid current, a person crosses without swimming, but impossible for troops and artillery. The R. R. Bridge is a great structure, there is also a waggon [*sic*] bridge and pontoon, so it is making the north bank quite a depot for supplies, and by the daily arrival of sutlers, bakers, the place is going right ahead of the city of Atlanta (that part of it where we held a few hundred yards of breastworks), for noncombatants are not apt to get within range of shells and bullets.

We retired in the night, slyly keeping our fires up, bands playing, so that the enemy would not think something was up, and did prove successful, for the enemy did not observe the pickets when they left.

I have written you from all the information that I can glean, but do not know how authentic it may be. We anticipate to lay here some time, many of the Reg't are looking for the paymaster and I don't know who would reject him. I gave you in my last a long letter upon Sanitary matters, and even this <u>war</u> letter can't be very satisfactory, for a retrograde move is an indication of ill success, but be cheerful, for army men are nohow despondent about it, and I hope before long you will hear good news.

I hope you are getting a good share of the cooling showers, now of daily an occurrence here. But yesterday was the hottest day for us of the season and I don't know what we should have done if the shower had not come up to cool us. We were up all night of the 25th, and all day yesterday we were building works, this coming after a season of inaction, was not at all pleasant.

I am glad the girls at the other house are having such pleasant times with the young clergymen. I suppose with the friends now staying with you they together will get up some picnic – I wish I was there to be counted in. I wish you would tell anyone I am not exclusive in the reception of these ferrotypes, and I was rejoiced that V.

W.'s [*Van Wyck's*] children are the first volunteers, and that now if I am to see all my friends I will not have to resort to a draft.

I will write you soon again. With much love I remain your Aff't Son

R. T. Van Wyck

EDITOR'S NOTE:

When Gen. Sherman began his flanking maneuver on the night of Aug. 25, Gen. Thomas was worried at his cutting the army off from its supply base with only ten days' rations. Sherman, however, had timed the march to coincide with the ripening of the corn, which his men roasted every night. Thus Gen. Hood, thinking Gen. Wheeler's cavalry had cut the Union supply lines, was fooled into believing a starving Union army was abandoning the siege. It wasn't until Aug. 30 that Hood realized Sherman was attacking, not retreating. *Sherman: Fighting Prophet, op. cit., pp 405-6.*

Chattahoochee Bridge
Aug. 27th '64

Dear Cousin [*Sarah*],

I received yours of August 17th while seven miles nearer the Rebel capital, Atlanta. I am here after a night march in which our left flank fell back to the river, part of which, one corps, was transferred to the right flank to demonstrate upon the Macon Road to Atlanta. But ere this reaches you you will know much better than I do now what this movement was for.

I can imagine what nice times you and Anna are having with the young people and how many of them envy you your luck, or rather your irresistible qualities to please the young clergymen. And from other sources I am inclined to think it is mutual, but to satisfy myself I have often seriously thought of writing GrandMother about it, her keen observation is very reliable upon such subjects. Frank K. did not communicate to me his heart troubles, perhaps he thought I might not sympathize with him or with the substitute policy, Mrs. Lee for Miss Bartow, or any other fanciful design of his. He sent me his ferrotype and I hinted in my letter that I would be extremely happy to receive any other members of the family. It would seem forward to particularize so I merely styled them "my friends."

I wish you would mention to Miss Sarah [*Kip*] I am collecting a ferrotypic album (that is, of my pocketbook, the depletion of which the paymaster has paid little attention to, and having been led nowhere near the insidious portals of sutlers' shops and pie bakers, I have found little use for if I had money) and by Frank sending <u>his</u> gave me the idea to reorganize matters, and I would have a treat, every time I took out my pocketbook it would do me about as much good.

Mother has already asked you to send me yours and Anna's. If I knew how common a matter they were I would ask you to solicit some of the young ladies for me. I am not particular about the young ladies, either; your Father, Mother, GrandMother, Aunt Susan, Mr. Lane (<u>all</u>), I would be happy to receive. I would be glad to hear from you about it.

With much love to all I remain your aft. Cousin

R. T. Van Wyck

Aug. 28. Still the same.

Aug. 29. Still the same.

Aug. 30. Still the same.

Aug. 31. Mustered for pay today. A reconnoitering party [*that*] went out toward Atlanta discovered the fact that only a small force holds Atlanta of Militia only.

Sept. 1. Last night quite chilly, but during the day the weather fine. Nothing of importance. News came of the nomination of McClellan for President 1865. Party spirit strong <u>for</u> him (Dem.). *

Chattahoochee R. R. Bridge
Sept. 1st '64

Dear Sarah,

Yours of Aug. 23rd with your ferrotypes enclosed I received this morning.

Your birthday experience with your ferrotype has given me an opportunity to have an opinion as how fast "old age" is coming on with you. How truthful I may be I know not, but you look much older, and the fine times in the gay and social circles has not stayed the effects of months of time, while Anna, on the contrary, is warding off famously the fatal effects to youth and beauty of that great

---

* August of 1864 was a very low point in the Civil War. General Grant was bogged down at Richmond and Sherman in front of Atlanta, while public sentiment for "peace at any price" was proliferating. On August 30th the Democratic National Convention, meeting in Chicago, drew up a peace platform and chose McClellan as its presidential nominee. It was evident President Lincoln very badly needed a victory in the field, and Gen. Sherman very much wanted to give him one.

destroyer, <u>time</u>. Her recipe is worth knowing. To know how to take life easily is a great perfection.

Accept my thanks for the ferrotypes. I prize them highly, I assure you. I think Anna's is excellent, yours not as well as might be. I have written you about some more ferrotypes, those of your Mother and GrandMother, etc.

Today is the commencement of Autumn. I can hardly conceive how the Summer has passed. As we left Normandy in April, the vegetation seemed to advance as we marched south. The <u>Harvest</u> season passed till finally the ripening of corn and the hazy appearance of the air indicative of the season has settled over us. The active life has made us unconscious of the flight of time and the commencement of the campaign seems but as yesterday.

Nothing new since I wrote you. In a reconnoitering party we ascertained the Enemy had left Atlanta to check Sherman, who is marching towards Macon. As a consequence only a few Militia and cavalry now confronts us at Atlanta.

Will you go to Becon [*sic*] Mt. while the Voorhees, etc., family are staying at our house? If V. W.'s little girls have their ferrotypes ready to send me, tell them I am looking for them daily, and it will please me greatly to get them. Effie is becoming quite a lady and Marie not much behind. Van Wyck comes up weekly, I suppose.

Remember me to Aunt Susan and Mr. Lane, and the rest of the family.

From your aff. Cousin,
R. T. Van Wyck

Clipping enclosed:

[*Correspondence of the Louisville* Journal]
EPITAPH OF A WAR HORSE

Before Atlanta, Geo., Aug. 14, 1864

In the midst of such perpetual fighting as has been going on around the doomed city of Atlanta for weeks, one would not hope to find other than serious faces among the combatants, nor expect to see fun rollicking among the graves of the heroic dead. Yet, in war as in peace, the better part of man's nature shines out in many a comic act, illustrating the fact that war fails to blunt the finer feelings or mar the jollity that cannot be circumscribed by events. These reflections were suggested by an incident that occurred yesterday. While walking along a portion of our lines my attention was attracted to a grave, which was newly made, and from its "make-up" led me to think that it must be the last resting place of a General, or some other man of note. Fancy my surprise when I read the following epitaph on the headboard:

> Here sleeps poor Billy, little gray,
> In camp, on march, so frisky and gay;
> Now, alas! he sleeps alone,
> Without a feed or sculptured stone
> To glad his hide or tell the tale
> How Quartermasters ever fail
> To furnish grub, when e'er they can
> To weary horse and starving man.
> Know this truth, old honest Abe
> That Billy sleeps like sucking babe,
> The victim of this sordid crew,
> Who fill their fobs with spoils from you.
> The only mourner at his head
> Is sable John, who never fed
> The faithful beast when he could shun
> The dreaded sound of hostile gun;
> The brush and comb he cast aside
> Through mercy on the horse's hide.
> But now he fills a lonely grave,
> Where oats nor corn can no more save.
> Here let him rest from sound of gun,
> Secure from jest and vulgar pun.
> He, living, was the soldier's pride,
> And for the want of care he died.

On inquiry I found the noble animal whose misfortunes were so pathetically apostrophized, belonged to Colonel Halpin, 15th Kentucky. "Billy," it appears, was the Colonel's fancy nag, and when he fell the gallant Colonel had him buried and the history of his misfortunes put at his head. This is but one of thousands of funny things that occur from day to day, while rifles and their whizzing messengers plunge into the ranks of the enemy and artillery thunders death among the victims of the god of war.

Chaplain G.

Sept. 2. Remained in camp till around 4 o'clock and ordered to march towards Atlanta which we entered about eight o'clock.

EDITOR'S NOTE:

By the time Confederate General Hood discovered the whereabouts of the Union forces they were entrenched at Jonesboro, twenty miles south, and he hurriedly sent his troops there to engage them in a fierce battle, at the end of which the Rebels lost 1,725 men to the less than 200 for the Federals.

General Slocum and his Twentieth Corps, camped along the Chattahoochee River, heard great explosions within Atlanta the night of September 1st and when he went forward to investigate he found the Rebels had blown up their ammunition and supply stores before evacuating the city. Thus on September 2nd Gen. Slocum's troops found themselves entering Atlanta unopposed.

"Atlanta is ours, and fairly won," Sherman reported. A grateful President Lincoln extended to General Sherman and to "the gallant officers and soldiers of his command" the nation's thanks for the capture of the city of Atlanta. Gen. Grant wired Gen. Sherman that he had ordered a salute by every battery facing the enemy "in honor of this great victory." *Memoirs,* pp. 108-110.

Chattahoochee R. R. Bridge
Sept. 2d 1864

Dear Mother,

There being some irregularity in the mail I thought I would inflict another letter upon you. My last letter was dated from this place, but how long we may remain here I do not know. Sherman's army, consisting of six Corps at the time we fell back from the fortifications around Atlanta, marched south towards Macon. The Rebel Army followed suit, thus leaving Atlanta held only by Militia and a Brigade of cavalry. It is reported that Atlanta is ours.

Sept. 3d. Atlanta, Ga. I will conclude this letter in assuring you that I am now writing you from Atlanta itself. The first Brigade had three hours the start of us. We left our camp upon the Chattahoochee about four o'clock and reached the south side of the city (Reb. fortifications) about eight o'clock last evening. As I was so unfortunate as to pass through the city in the night I could form but a poor idea, but sidewalks, paving stones, brownstone fronts, polished marble residences, has led me to conclude it is a fine city.

The citizens (women) came out and gave us water and seemed glad to see [us], but I don't know how sincere they may be. But I think they are glad to come out of their underground abodes where they have been living for six weeks. Our Brig. (2d) band gave them some music of the right sort, and took possession of the first-class Hotel (furnishing their own rations) about as large as the Gregory House, Po'keepsie, but opposite a splendid park, where the 2d Massachusetts had encamped for the night. Although the city soon was under provost guard, the desire of the soldiers for tobacco, and the mutual feeling [*which*] soon existed between them and the guards allowed them to search for it. They found any abundance of it. A box of tobacco is now worth $100 to $150, sutlers' prices. Our Reg't obtained as many as 25 boxes and cigars, it seemed almost everyone had a box strapped upon his knapsack, besides everyone had one in his mouth. It would be impossible to attempt any strategistic [*his word*] move just at present, till this stock is gone, for the Rebs would discover the move by the column of smoke.

You have got a more deffinite [*sic*] or detailed account through the papers of the destruction of property destroyed by their evacuation, the damage to the city by our shells, and the loyalty of the present inhabitants, better than I can give you; besides the available service to the govt. of the vast amount of machinery remaining for the manufacture of ammunition, etc. A bakery and any number of sutlers have commenced business, the place being occupied only twenty-four hours. The siege now being over, the city will draw supplies from the surrounding country. I hope we will remain here, for they will be the right kind of supplies for us.

Sherman has moved south toward Macon, thus flanking Hood out of here. It is reported that Hood's army is cut in two and much demoralized. They say Ft. Morgan has gone up, and Mobile with it. I think McClellan's stock will go down, will it not?

I soon hope to hear of Richmond in our possession, then I will be confident the end is not far distant, when we can all go to our homes. I don't know how long we will stay here, but not long. It rained hard all day and is now raining. I hope to hear from you soon. I remain your aff. Son

R. T. Van Wyck

P. S. The boys say lots of Johnny's are coming in. They say the Confederacy is played out.

[*In pencil*]: 107th N. Y. Vol. were the first Federal troops that entered Atlanta. They belong to our Brig. 12th, and were sent out early of the morning of the 2d of Sept. to act as skirmishers.

Sept. 3. Prepared our quarters and went into camp by the east of the city. Raining continuously all day.

Sept. 4. Nothing of interest occurred. The church bells ring and seemed to remind one of home. The Sabbath seemed not forgotten by the citizens of the city.

Sept. 5. Took a pass and went downtown. It begins to thrive with northern industry already. Hospitals are being established to give our soldiers an opportunity.

Sept. 6. The waggon [sic] train under Sherman begins to arrive in the city preparatory of the main army returning [*from the great flanking movement that had enticed Gen. Hood out of Atlanta*].

Atlanta, Sept. 6th '64

Dear Mother,

I presume your letters or letter is captured, as I have failed to receive one in some time. My last letter of the 3d has given you our present position. I visited the city yesterday and was glad to see the buildings in such a good state of preservation, although all were more or less injured by shell and solid shot, particularly the large brick stores and buildings. One large stone house of polished granite (variegated), costing in good times $100,000, had only a piece taken out of the kitchen by solid shot. As I passed, the music of a piano indicated occupants. I have been told it is getting to be quite an officers' resort already.

But it is amusing to see the changes that a certain class that never owned at any time more than half a doz. chairs, a table, and bed who move into a large house and have hardly an article of furniture for each room. The former occupant in such cases has followed the Rebel army. But Govt. is fast getting matters settled, northern tradesmen are already in the place with quite an assortment of goods, and in a few weeks the place will be going again.

This city is considered the most healthy city in the South and the large buildings are being fitted up for Hospitals. The Sanitary Department have a good building, etc. The citizens admit they have suffered more from their own army than ours. The line of rifle pits around the city has taken with it the destruction of fine buildings for the protection of men in the trenches, and the same material as we are now constructing into summer shanties.

I suppose the papers are comparing the success of Sherman with the position of Grant in Va., or rather the failure of Warren to hold the Weldon R.R. or the whole of it. I think soon Richmond will be evacuated as the main production of supplies have come from the States already in our own possession. The occupation of the whole of this State will take place this fall. I will send you some old Reb.[*news*]papers I found downtown. They are dirty – they got wet during the shower and are much soiled. Much of the matter you have seen in the Northern papers.

I wish you would send me some postage stamps, and also that Father would send me $10. I had hoped the PayMaster would have been with us, but the situation of the army seems to retard our pay.

With much love I remain your aff. Son   R. T. Van Wyck

Sept. 7. No news of importance. The R.R. being cut renders us ignorant of what is going on in the <u>States</u>. Weather rainy.

Sept. 8. The 4th and 23rd Corps arrived today. The former is encamped about four miles out of the city. The latter is to go to Decatur, Ga. Weather cloudy and threatening rain.

Sept. 9. Early in the morning the waggon [*sic*] train commenced moving out of the city (of the 4th Corps). Prepared to receive General Thomas, but were disappointed.

Sept. 10. Went on picket this morning.

Sept. 11. Returned to camp this morning. Prepared to break camp and moved at half-past twelve to an interior line of works. Received a large mail, the first in a week. Two letters from home and one from Aunt Mary.

Sept. 12. Commenced erecting shanties of better quality than any since leaving our Winter quarters.

Sept. 13. One year ago today left Kelleys Ford, Va., for Rapidan. Still resumed our house building. Abundance of good material but hard labor to obtain at hand.

Sept. 14. Completed our work upon our quarters. We have every assurance of making a long stay of it here. Weather delightful – cold toward morning.

Atlanta, Ga.
Sept. 14th '64

Dear Mother,

I received yours of Aug. 27th and of Sept. 1st [*on*] the 11th. The delay was consequent upon a <u>cut</u> of the R.R. between Chattanooga and Nashville. And my inability to answer your letter sooner is owing to a move of camp nearer the city, where we were obliged to erect substantial quarters, much like those at Normandy, in anticipation of making a long stay of it. My letters home are possibly delayed for the same reason of the rupture of the R. R.

But for the last few days I have experienced a busy time in getting up my shanty. All the troops except this Division have left the city, and this Div. are massed east of the city. As the scrabble for boards has been great, those that were fortunate enough to secure a lot at first had much the shorter distance to carry them. But the last perhaps were not much the losers, for soon the vacant houses of good style (noble mansions) were carried off in pieces, those who had completed their houses except for a door or light, obtained a grained or venetian door, when perhaps their sides of the houses would be of rough barn boards, or the floor of planed fine material and the rest of rough exterior. One would see a strange medley in going through the camp.

I am glad to say I am again in comfortable quarters, with all probability of staying a few months and possibly all winter. Sherman, in general orders, said that all the troops would rest for a month to receive pay and clothing and till another campaign was planned; preparatory to entering a fine Winter campaign. The latter we do not take to ourselves, or do not wish to be included in. I suppose when Grant takes Richmond and Granger or Farragut takes Mobile, we will think a move is on foot for us.

I received a letter from Aunt Margaret.* They have hired a house in Kenosha for the winter. They are all well, except Howard, who has a bad influenza. I feel greatly honored in getting her unexpected letter. I am going to ask them for their ferrotypes. I am daily looking for yours and Father's. I hope they haven't been captured. I suppose you wouldn't like to see or know your faces were filling an artist gallery at Macon.

I was glad to receive the cuttings from the papers. As McClellan has refused the nomination upon the Peace platform,** the road is clear for Lincoln now. That is another victory for those who are

---

* Wife of Judge Anthony Van Wyck.
** Gen. McClellan repudiated the peace platform of the Democratic Party, but he remained the Democratic nominee for president.

anxious to sustain the Govt, as much so as Atlanta. I will write again in a few days. With much love I remain your Aft. Son

R. T. Van Wyck

Sept. 15. Still the same. We further improved our camp., etc. Mailed a letter home.

Sept. 16. Still the same. First Dress Parade.

Sept. 17. Inspection by Capt. Thompkins of Brigade. Weather fine. Prepared for a review on the morrow.

Sept. 18. Marched through a rainstorm two miles and got soaking wet. Felt disagreeable the rest of the day.

Sept. 19. Weather cleared up warm, dried our wet clothes, etc. Received a home mail. It was truly welcomed.

Sept. 20. Division review today. Weather indicated rain, but passed Gen. Sherman's HQ's and also Gen. Thomas. It was highly satisfactory to all concerned.

Sept. 21. A heavy rain set in all day. We remained quiet all day. Nothing of interest occurred.

Atlanta, Ga., Sept. 21st '64

Dear Mother,

I received yours of Sept. 14th today. I would have replied to yours of the 11th, which I received a day or two ago with the writing paper upon which you see before you if I had not written so recently. But your letter today was doubly interesting to me, inasmuch as it contained those ferrotypes I have been so long looking for. I think yourself and father are looking very well indeed, and are faithful pictures. You don't know what a home feeling it gives me to look at your faces.

In answering Aunt Margaret's letter I have asked for hers, Uncle Anthony's, and the children's, so I will soon have a family collection. Why couldn't Fred and Aunt Mary send me theirs? or will they? The R. R. is all right between here and the States. Morgan is killed and Wheeler* is looked after, so they need not be afraid of the ferrotypes seceding to parts unknown if they should address them to me.

---

* Generals John Hunt Morgan and Jos. Wheeler were Confederate cavalry raiders of fearsome reputation. It was said that Southerners considered Wheeler's cavalrymen as worse plunderers than Sherman's troops.

I am glad you had so splendid a trip to Lebanon Springs, and that the company [*was*] so delightful. With the addition of Fred, Mr. and Mrs. Sherwood, and _____V. B[*runt?*] you must have had fine times. The Shaker theology, I take from a series of sermons published in the Louisville *Journal*, might be taken as a burlesque upon the marriage doctrine, if not advocated with such a perversion of the Scriptures and earnestness. It is no wonder it never gained ground in the country. They are models of industry and thrift.

We remain in the same position. Our shanty possesses a stained door with stylish knob, a sash in rear of three panes of glass, roof of canvas or thin muslin, floor of planed and grooved material, sides of odds and ends of barns, fences, window shutters, etc. Bunks, I desire to speak more fully, are shelves more or less smooth, two on one side and one on the other (there being three of us) and an alleyway between, a table at the foot of the two tier of bunks, opposite of which part of a settle [*a bench*] I transported upon my shoulders from a Female Seminary, which we draw up to the table where we eat or write. Our Shanty is 10 by 6 ft.

I have said nothing of various little shelves for kettles, bottles, soap, all but provisions are variously conspicuous. The latter we have special spite against Wheeler and Co. for so curtailing, while others contend that he may keep the Road cut if he chooses, we can look at our rations when hungry, till Farragut opens the way to Mobile.

The kitchen furniture is daily increasing, we are in worse situation than when we had abundance to cook and nothing to do it with. But I must leave this important subject for another letter and close this, after which I will lay myself upon the shelf for eight or ten hours, and tomorrow take a look into the *Harper's* for Sept., *Frank Leslie's* and the Po'keepsie *Eagle* you sent me.

Many thanks for your ferrotypes. I remain with much love your aft. Son

R. T. Van Wyck

Sept. 22. Michael Burns died of diarrhea. We buried him in cemetery adjoining 1st Div. Hospital. He was sick only a few days.
Sept. 23. Received six recruits for this Co.K. Weather rainy and disagreeable. News unimportant. Troops fast coming in to fill up depleted organizations.
Sept. 24. Still continued rainy and disagreeable. News unimportant.

Sept. 25. Chaplain of 3rd Wisc. preached near camp. Weather fine. News from Va. cheering, particularly from Sheridan.*

Sept. 26. Commenced drilling the recruits. Still the same. Anxious for the paymaster to pay us.

Sept. 27. Still looking for the paymaster. R. J. Hevener returned to Regt. Weather fine.

Sept. 28. Went on picket. Day pleasant although it threatened rain. Nothing of note occurred.

Atlanta, Ga. Sept. 29th '64

Dear Mother,

I acknowledged the receipt of your and Father's ferrotypes by letter mailed the 22d inst. I have feared it met with misfortune and has not reached you, as the guerrillas are very numerous between here and Chattanooga. Besides, I have been waiting daily for the Paymaster to come over with the greenbacks. He has been with us for a week past, but eight months' accounts are very tedious to look after. Therefore, in view of this, [*in order*] to send home by check part of this amount, I have delayed writing. I should like to know whether you have sent the ten dollars I wrote for, and at what date you mailed the letter. If not sent upon receipt of this, do not send it.

I have understood that the Adams Express Co. brings through boxes at the rate of $10 per hundred pds. from New York. I have been thinking that a box of fifty pds. would come very acceptable, if containing a leather portfolio (not of paper and glue that comes apart upon getting wet), two pair of woolen stockings, a towel, a piece of <u>Castile</u> soap, filling [*the rest*] up with eatables such as you sent last winter, of dried fruits, butter, sugar, tea, chocolate, and a few boxes of condensed milk. I will send in a few days some money, from which take out the necessary

---

* On September 19, 1864, General Grant sent Gen. Philip Sheridan moving south to Winchester, VA, to chase down the Rebel army, and despite mishap and bungle he rallied his men in a series of fierce encounters. Gen. Jubal Early, however, inflicted much loss on Union troops and got his army clean away. Sheridan continued through the Shenandoah Valley till he had it in his possession, making of the South's principal storehouse a desolate wasteland. *Bruce Catton's Civil War*, pp. 632-45.

In his *Memoirs* [*Vol. II*] Gen. Grant noted that "these two campaigns [*Sherman's and Sheridan's*] probably had more effect on the November presidential election than all the speeches, bonfires, parades in the North."

expenses. I think if this could be expressed from New York it wouldn't meet with the ill success of the one of last winter.

We are cheered with the news from Va. of Sheridan. Rumors of a peace negociation [*sic*] is said to be in progress but I presume it is all fiction. The mail comes through so very irregular we are not sure of anything that we hear.

The army is at rest, except a part sent to the rear to guard the Road. I don't think anything is to be done yet awhile, and we are waiting for the Va. Army to effect the capture of Richmond.

How the presidential election will affect matters and things I don't think anyone knows. Lincoln is now upon the increase while McClellan is on the wane. I think the farmer is all right. I will write soon again. In the meanwhile I hope your letters will come to hand all right. I remain with much love, your afft. Son

R. T. Van Wyck

Sept. 30. Received eight months' pay today. Mailed a letter written 29th and enclosed $120.
Oct. 1. Sent off my letter. Also took a check of Capt. Cogswell for $100.
Oct. 2. Nothing new today.
Oct. 3. Sent a check of $100 to James Van Wyck [*his father*].

Atlanta, Ga. Oct. 3d '64

Dear Sarah,

In answer to yours of Aug. 23rd upon the celebration of your twenty-fourth birthday, and also in acknowledgment of yours and Anna's ferrotypes, I made the necessary comment and expressed my obligation for the favor bestowed, etc., I hope. But owing to the R. R., I suppose, I have heard nothing from you whether such letters of mine were received or no. So in writing another letter I certainly cannot answer any of yours, but must write upon some uninteresting subject connected with the Army culinary department exce[—— ?] or speculate upon the engrossing topic of talk at Fishkill – Marriages, Betrothals, Tea Drinks, etc., taken from here and there a little circumstantive [*his word*] evidence aided largely by the imagination either to acquit or convict any poor <u>subject.</u>

You may judge of my embarrassment in penning this letter, by glancing at my introductory first sentence of such length, such errors cannot speak well for my schooldays. I once heard of a certain Landlord whose preparation of dried apples were the only article of diet he set before his guests. I never believed till after this Summer's campaign how much truth could be taken in the case. The deceptive properties of a hardtack under the influence of water is truly marvelous. This has often constituted a meal, and happy were we to get even that sometimes, and a fried, swelled hardtack may be called a strategistic [sic] flank movement to prevent starvation. But we are doing better now decidedly, and can say we are doing finely and expect to thrive soon again when the R. R. is open.

Mother tells me Mrs. Elmendorf has been staying at your house. Miss Juliet had got to be quite a young lady, I suppose. You have had no lady friends staying with you this summer. I hope I may hear from you soon, and by that time perhaps I will find something acceptable to write. With much love I remain your aff. Cousin.

R. T. Van Wyck

Oct. 4. Nothing new transpired.

Oct. 5. Moved to the Marietta Road to protect the north side of city. This we did towards night.

Oct. 6. Remained in camp during the day. It rained hard.

Oct. 7. Was detailed upon fortress. Work[ed] upon fortifications. Day pleasant and agreeable.

Oct. 8. Weather changed quite cold during night, making the fires agreeable to sit by in the morning.

Oct. 9. Still continued cold and a little disagreeable.

Oct. 10. No trains through from Chattanooga and no mail for two weeks. Weather still continues cold.

Oct. 11. Moved early, about half-past four, upon a foraging expedition,* accompanied by four hundred waggons and one brigade of Infantry besides ourselves. We traveled about twelve miles without getting anything much, encamped for the night.

Oct. 12. Filled part of the waggons [sic] with corn, cotton, etc. After marching and guarding the waggons we returned to the same campground as on the previous night.

---

* With their rail lines being continuously broken by the Confederates their flow of supplies were halted; hence the necessity for foraging expeditions on the countryside.

Oct. 13. We completed filling the remainder of the waggons, as well as did considerable private foraging upon our own account. After which we returned to within five miles of Atlanta reached here.

Oct. 14. Today, [up] about 4 o'clock A.M. and started for the city which we reached noon. We took up our old quarters upon the East side of the city temporarily for we were ordered to the other side tomorrow. We found a large mail.

Atlanta, Ga., Oct. 14, '64

Dear Mother,

By politeness of the Colonel I have written this letter to be sure of at least one of my many letters getting through. I have not heard from home since the 14th of Sept. and now having sent by letter a bill of $20 dollars and a check of $100 dollars I should like to hear from it as soon as possible.

At the same time our mail matter has collected at Chattanooga owing to the trouble on the R. R. This afternoon I hear that several car loads of mail for the Corps has arrived and being distributed to the various Regts. We just returned from a foraging excursion 25 or 30 miles Southeast from here into the corn district of the C. S. A. We left here on the 11th and returned today (noon) having traveled the whole distance since yesterday, four o'clock. I assure you I feel almost dead from want of sleep.

Our force consists of two Brigades of Infantry, a Reg't of Cavalry, and a Battery. We brought into camp 565 (six-mule) loads of corn, to say nothing of foraging on private account of sweet potatoes, honey, sorgum [sic], squab, hogs, sheep, etc., and it is said we have lived high. I did think so myself till last night's march put it all out of my head. This has been a very successful attempt to supply ourselves from the country South. I saw one hundred loads of corn gathered in less than two hours. How would it seem for a Dutchess Co. farmer to take his afternoon's sleep, when upon getting up to find his fifty-acre corn field disappeared, not scarcely a husk or ear remaining. I believe he would have some idea of the devastation of war. With the exception of a slight brush of the advance guards, we were unmolested.

The Colonel, being a Repub. candidate for Congress, has obtained a leave of absence for 40 days. He goes home tomorrow. I have also sent my vote to Father to fill the eighth day of Nov. next. He will understand from the envelope how he will manage it.*

Previous to the raid we made for supplies we moved our quarters to the north side of the city. We are agoing somewhere tomorrow to camp. It seems when we get everything fixed up we move again.

But I got five letters today, four of yours of the 19th, 21st, 27th, and Oct. 1st and one of Sarah's of Sept. 26, also the Handbills, Po'keepsie *Eagle*, etc. I cannot answer each but will in future. Our shanty (curiosity shop) is like living in a basement and looking at a brownstone front on the opposite side of the street. We will have a trial soon again of shanty-building, I suppose. I will write soon again. I remain, with much love, your aff. Son

R. T. Van Wyck

P. S. The cuttings of papers you sent me, I have seen some of them before I received yours. I would like to have a *Weekly Tribune* sent regularly. I also received the ten dollars $10.

Oct. 15. We left camp about noon bag and baggage and after repairing our old tent we made our way for the Front House to get supper. Eighteen [men] that was there.

Oct. 16. Sunday today I was detailed upon picket. Weather cold and windy. Duty not fatiguing.

Oct. 17. Was relieved from picket about 10 o'clock A.M. No news of any account is occurring. Sherman still fighting with Hood between here and Chattanooga. Hood in Snake Creek Gap between Sherman and Schofield.**

Oct. 18. Weather still continuing cold. Remained in the same place. Guerrillas upon RR between here and bridge.

Atlanta, Ga.
Oct. 18th '64

Dear Cousin [*Sarah*],

Your letter of Sept. 25th reached me upon my return from a raid towards Macon for corn and cotton. It would have reached me sooner

---

* Not all states used absentee ballots; soldiers from some states were granted leaves of absence to go home and vote, while other states sent commissioners to collect their soldiers' vote, and a few made no arrangements at all for the soldiers to vote.
** Gen. Sherman had taken off with part of his army to chase Gen. Hood northwards.

if the communications between here and the States were always unin-
terrupted; at present there seems a strong desire with Hood to try
some of our supplies at Chattanooga, whether in deference to our
coffee, beef, or hardtack for a change from his corn meal and pork, I
don't know which. But at any rate we are not anxious for him to
have it without a fair exchange, and accordingly 565 waggon loads
of corn and cotton was brought in last Friday, and Sunday another
expedition started out for the same purpose. We are living in <u>hopes</u>
of better times in the commissary department, and also that our own
mail will be in good order.

I have ventured to write this, hoping it will not meet the fate of
several others to you, by lodging in some Corps mail department till
everything is right. I have received your [new] ferrotype, it is a good
one. I have not enclosed your first [one]. I suppose you have no
objections to my keeping both.

This letter will possibly find you administering domestic affairs in
47th Street. You also have the delightful task of superintending the
early tuition of two young ladies.* I do believe in view of such task and
a review of old school days you begin to feel <u>old</u>, a natural recurrence
to anybody. But don't borrow trouble or think no one else has nothing to look after or think about, for everyone has his or her burden to
carry through this world – it may be real or imaginary. A cheerful disposition to throw off fancied ill and not make much of trouble when it
comes in reality, is everyone's duty to do, if we should enjoy life as [it]
is meant for us to do. Hasn't every picture a bright side? Should we
be continually looking at the dark side? These "some things which you
wish I could know" and which are making you old, if not important to
write about, why think about it? Why let every would-be pleasant
hour be blasted by the thought so unpleasant. Am I right or am I mistaken? It is the principle I go upon.

These young ladies whom you solicited for me their ferrotypes I
have failed to receive as yet. I am doubtful whether I will get any.
Young ladies are not apt to grant such a request except by personal application. But many thanks for your kindness in so doing. If successful I
will write you. Give me your address. I have forgotten it. Remember
me to Van and the children. With much love I remain your aff. Cousin

R. T. Van Wyck

---

* Sarah's young nieces.

P. S. My friend Miss S. K. treats me quite ungraciously by withholding her ferrotype. "Actions speak louder than words," if words are often the most noisy.

[*Written on a separate piece of paper, in pencil*]
Don't feel offended by what I wrote about your ferrotype. To look "old" does not imply you have become prematurely so, but is too candid an expression to be used to a young unmarried lady. Photographs – ferrotypes, are sometimes great libels.

Oct. 19. Remained still in the same place. Operations still progressing favorable in the rear.

Atlanta, Ga.
Oct. 19th '64

Dear Father,
Since my return from that <u>raid</u> and at which time I received your letter of Sept. 17th we have been at our old business of looking from various places from the fortifications around Atlanta for something to turn up. Our senses of <u>seeing</u> and hearing are no way tasked compared with that one of smelling – for horses, mules, and cattle lie around as thick as flies in Summertime. Perhaps in view of such waste of raw material, and that generally by no great effort of the olfactory nerves, one is expected to imbibe as much [*nourishment*] equal to the deficiency in rations now existing, turning the waste into an economical adventure for the Govt. But we are sensibly feeling the effects of the cutting of the R. R. in the deficiency of forage for our transportation, and we hope by successive raids to prevent the entire extinction of the stock till the communications are in good shape.

The position of the contending armies you know as much as myself. Report says Hood is between Sherman and Schofield, the latter has 15,000 thousand men at Chattanooga.

The proposition of Mr. Way to operate with grapes upon the ground east of Daniels might be a good one, so far as profit as a crop is concerned, for from what you have written me about Robert's he will derive mostly the proceeds of his farm from this crop alone. But I am in no great favor with the cropping or letting business–except in case the property is to remain inactive. Mr. Way is capable, industrious, and so far as his experience goes, much better than anyone I know of. But in his place he will assume one half of the cost of vines and be to all the labor of attending them, and will realize half the proceeds. The former will not amount to over two or three hundred dollars now. The labor will not exceed half the value of the crop of potatoes upon the land before the vines come into bearing, and will be continued much to the injury of the vines – if not objected to by you.

And now, as to fertilizers, manures, etc., the <u>principal</u> <u>cost,</u> nothing is said about. It isn't expected that the original strength of the land [*will be*] able to withstand continuous crops of potatoes and the vines to improve. Your teams [*of horses*] and perhaps men will bring charcoal bottom from the mountains or from the farm rather than have the vineyard not to thrive.

So in the former you save the three hundred dollars and the cultivation of the vines not to exceed $150 a year–more, not to forget you only receive half the proceeds, while in the latter you assume the whole of the crop of potatoes equal to the first cultivation, and finally the proceeds of the vines commensurate with all the trouble, cost, etc.

Mr. Way doesn't own the land, but he gets as much from it as yourself, if <u>let</u> [*leased*] to him. But with the care of a large farm it is difficult to give that close attention to the grape to insure its success. You often, with as good a farmer as Mr. Briggs, have some reason to complain on him.

The R. R. through Fishkill Village will make quite a place of it. John Green's place (Mr. Jackson's old place) has a good situation for a Hotel, which that far-sighted individual will not omit doing. The Hopewell route will suit the people in that part of town. I don't think it will benefit them as much as they think, for except for the value of their land, society will be more one of cash, [*from*] the newcomers from the city, than one of themselves. Mr. Cortelyou is now contented with his purchase. He was at first dissatisfied with it. This R. R. will be a good market for your wood upon the mountain, and will be sought after.

Have you heard from Aben since the draft? This Reg't might have gone Democratic, all except for Congressman: the McClellan element has been quite in the ascendant.* We will soon know who

---

* Although the army still had great affection for Gen. McClellan, they turned against him when they realized he was running on an appeasement ticket, and they felt that to vote against Lincoln was to vote against the Union which they were fighting to preserve. In the end, they voted by a large majority for Lincoln and the war's continuation. In Sherman's army, 86% of the soldiers voted for Lincoln. *The March to the Sea and Beyond,* by J.P. Glatthaar, pp. 46-7.

will be the chosen <u>one</u>. I think there are but a few who look for a settlement of the war to release us much before the expiration of our term of service next Fall. The first month of the last year [*of service*] is almost gone. But with lots to do in making inroads into the enemies' country, time flies fast.

How is Bentley doing? Has A. Skeel left Davenport? I received a message from Mrs. Otis. She still is sanguine that the national forces will triumph at last. I presume she still is living in Brooklyn. I am glad Uncle Anthony is releasing himself from this embarrassment. Is it through the Skeels, or otherwise? Aunt Margaret says Dr. Hoffman is a surgeon in the U. S. Army.

If you have not sent that box, put in one of my thick vests; if sent, never mind it. I hope I may be able to enjoy the box when it comes.

Write me often about what is going on upon the <u>farm</u>. If I seldom mention it in my letters it isn't because I never think of it, for I always have it in mind. I hope to hear from you soon.

With much love, I remain your aff. Son

R. T. Van Wyck

Oct. 20. Our camp was considerably altered by constructing chimney, etc.

Oct. 21. Weather cold and wintry.

Oct. 22. We received a through mail, first since the 14th. In the afternoon was ordered to leave to support the foraging party gone down into the country. We marched to 12 o'clock P.M. [*A.M.*] Marched 15 miles.

Oct. 23. Continued the march 15 miles or more southwards and left around the crossroads leading to Jonesboro and encamped for the night at Decatur six miles from Atlanta.

Oct. 24. Resumed the march in the morning and took up our quarters in our camp upon North Marietta Street.

Oct. 25. Repaired our shanty and made it quite tenantable. Day pleasant, etc.

Oct. 26. Still made ourselves secure by further repairs. Received a mail and a letter from home. Weather threatens rain.

Oct. 27. Rained hard all day.

Atlanta, Ga.
Oct. 27th '64

Dear Mother,

I received your letter of Oct. 6th postmarked Fishkill, and also one postmarked Brooklyn of October 14th. The former I received as the Reg't was ordered to leave in hot haste to support a raiding party then thirty miles distant who were threatened by a large body of Rebel cavalry. Such foot races does well enough when you have the whole day before you and a probability of getting a night's sleep, but in this case we started at three o'clock P.M. and marched about twenty miles by 12 o'clock and resumed the march early the next morning.

In the night's march we passed over the same ground as on the previous raid, but during the morning followed the trail of the expedition and came up with it, returning about 10 o'clock A. M. with 150 waggons [sic] all loaded with corn, besides numerous private buggies and light carriages loaded with chickens, hoggs [sic], honey, cows, cattle, etc. They had apprehended no danger, and hardly welcomed us for making fifty miles in thirty-six hours, enabling them to bring in their booty safely. We did not fare so well [with] sweet potatoes as upon the previous raid, for then we were cooking at every halt, either wasting or otherwise, but this time we hadn't time to look for them.

The result of election will be known soon, perhaps before you receive this.

I had stopped here [in this letter] to look after some <u>tallow</u> to fry my beefstake [sic] but alas, I came away disappointed. No one would ever accuse the poor animals slaughtered of carrying with them a superabundance of that substance. So it is boiled (beef) muscle daily, enough to make us sick of <u>flesh</u> in such shape; but our necessities overrule all objections.

I am in first-rate health and weigh 160 lbs, so you see I am doing well. I have received the Po'keepsie *Eagle* and read the letters from W. R. Woodin, the 150th's correspondent. He represents the spoils (Commissary) as first-rate here, and I don't think he has much overrated the matter. I have received *Harper's* for October.

In your letter you spoke of an intimacy between Miss Jennie Polhemous and Anna and Sarah for certain reasons.* You neglected

---

* Probably as a candidate for marriage with their recently widowed brother, A.V.W. Van Vechten.

to write how it is being returned upon the gentleman's part, if such attentions were reciprocal. I believe she is said to be a good <u>business lady</u>, so if the solid charms were the inducement for the first, perhaps the want of a domestic manager will be the second inducement.

The weather has been cold and windy for a week past, today it rains. The forest trees are changing fast with the <u>frost,</u> but so far a fine <u>Fall</u>. If my letters are interesting I am glad to know they are so. The time spent in writing them is pleasant to me, assured they will meet with a prompt answer, for letters received now are or have been the only connecting link with civilization. I will write soon again. I presume this will find you at Fishkill. With much love I remain your aff. Son

R. T. Van Wyck

Oct. 28. Was detailed upon fatigue, building fortifications.

Oct. 29. Rumors of an early leave, destination unknown. Preparation for a fifty-days' campaign.

Oct. 30. Detailed upon picket. Day quite pleasant and passed off agreeable.

Oct. 31. Mustered for pay. Great moving of trucks. The HQ's Army of the Cumberland moved to the rear. We anticipated to follow. Preparations for an active campaign of fifty or ninety days and requisitions for clothing, etc., to be filled out.

Nov. 1. Went downtown on a pass. Took dinner at the Front House. Great activity prevails in town consequent upon the arrival of trains from Chattanooga with supplies

EDITOR'S NOTE:

During the last two weeks of October, 1864, General Sherman ordered a medical weeding-out process of his troops to ensure that he had only the best men for his new campaign, soldiers so inured to hardship that disease would be sloughed off.

Without such extraordinary veterans the General's March to the Sea, and his forthcoming March through the Carolinas would have been impossible. The British military historian B. H. Liddell Hart has described these soldiers as "probably the finest army of military workmen the modern world has seen," and the Confederate General Jos. E. Johnston has been quoted as saying, "There has been no such army since the days of Julius Caesar."

Sherman's veterans were self-reliant and cool-headed; men who, often without officers' guidance, knew how to position themselves in the field, outflank a Rebel force, or conduct an orderly retreat from a tight corner. They would rush to the sound of gunfire through bog or field or forest, dig themselves in, and hold on until reinforcements arrived. These veterans knew the cost of frontal attack and instead used flanking maneuvers whenever possible. Above all, they had learned how to protect themselves behind anything that would deflect shot. They could dig in under fire as quickly as moles, grabbing a few fence rails or slashing down a sapling or brush, and then scooping out a ditch behind it to shelter in, piling up the dirt in front for instant earthworks. They were, in short, absolutely crack troops who could live off the land, feed themselves, make their own roads as they went, survive in all weather, and improvise almost anything they needed.*

Atlanta, Ga.   Nov. 1st '64

Dear Mother,

Since my last letter there has been various rumors and changes among the troops in town. The Hdqtrs. of the Army of the Cumberland has been removed to Chattanooga. The Army of [the] Tennessee (23rd Army Corps, Gen. Schofield) is coming to relieve us. The Army of the Cumberland meditate upon a campaign to Montgomery, and Jackson, Miss., while Sherman with the Army of [the] Mississippi (13th, 16th, and 17th Corps), with two divisions of the 4th Corps, are pushing Hood towards Mobile.

Again, it is said upon good authority that we (20th Corps) are agoing to march through the C[onfederate] S[tates] of A[merica] to Charleston or Savannah...Any of these reports you may believe, but I know we have orders to prepare for fifty days' campaign. It may be either by way of Huntsville, Ala., or direct from here to Charleston.

Now we have had one of Sherman's rests: that is, going upon foraging raids, building forts and fortifications; and consequently feel fresh to enter a Winter Campaign. Of course, we haven't moved yet, so when we do I will write. The business in the city has quite revived by the arrival of through trains; they are bringing in supplies at a great rate. This we are glad to see.

Nov. 2nd. The campaign, instead of being fifty days is increased to ninety days, as clothing for that time is immediately issued, and an extra pair of shoes is ordered to be carried along. But still we may remain here.

---

* *The March to the Sea and Beyond*, op.cit., pp. xii, 15, 19-20.

Weather is rainy and cold. I imagine you are having some such weather, except more cold. The face of the country must look dreary and barren with you; here the forest leaves are slightly affected with the frost and with the exception of the ruins of war everywhere around it would appear quite pleasant.

I hope to receive a letter soon, before we leave, if <u>we</u> <u>do.</u> With much love I remain your afft Son

R. T. Van Wyck

Nov. 2. A cold rainstorm set in and continues during the day.

Nov. 3. Still continued cold. Rumors of leaving.

Nov. 4. Very cold and windy. Frosty ice during the night.

Nov. 5. Left camp about four o'clock and encamped about three miles upon the Macon Road for the night.

Nov. 6. The order was countermanded and we returned to our old camp, reached it about night, found it in the same condition we left it. Had service in the morning.

Two Passes:

Camp 150th N. Y. Vols.
Nov. 1st '64
Guards and Patrols
Pass Sergt. R. T. Van Wyck from eleven o'clock A.M. to one o'clock P.M. to visit Atlanta, Ga.

Signed by:
John S. Scofield*
Capt., Co. K 12th[?] Regt.

A. B. Smith
Maj. Com'd'ng

By Command of Col. E. Acarnian[?]
Com'd'ng Brig.
by
William Wattles

---

* Capt. John S. Scofield is not to be confused with General Schofield.

Camp of the 150th N. Y. Vols.
In the Field near Atlanta
Guards and Patrols
Pass Corpl. Jacob G. Montross of Co. "K," 150th Regt. from 8 o'clock
A.M. until one o'clock P.M. to visit 1st division Hospital, 20th Corps.

Signed by:
John S. Scofield
Capt. Com'd'ng Co. "K"

Appr'd
J. H. Ketcham
Col. 150th NY Vols.

(Letter in pencil)

Atlanta, Ga. Nov. 6th '64

Dear Mother,

We are on the march. That is, we started yesterday afternoon and encamped three miles outside of the city, towards <u>Macon</u>. I have embraced the present opportunity this morning to write, perhaps the last for a few months, as we undoubtedly will be off for Macon, Charleston, or for Mobile in twenty-four hours.

The evacuation of the city seems the settled conviction upon everyone's mind, all property of any consequence is being taken to the rear preparatory to leaving the city, while this expedition will launch out into the enemy's country to subsist upon the land. It will be a great undertaking, accompanied with much danger of being gobbled up, to say nothing of hard work and hard fare, but then if it succeeds, will be one of the greatest raids of the war.

The drum is beating for Sunday service, it is rarely we are benefited by our chaplain, and the future cannot assure us of the privilege. He is having a slim audience. The wind blows cold and chilly from the south, the boys little like leaving their fires, to say nothing of their general proclivities to the contrary.

I expect to hear soon from you by the troops bringing up the rear with the mail after we have been out a few days. I will not have the pleasure of seeing that box, but then <u>perhaps</u> I may get it by New Year's, and then be in a position to enjoy it. I must finish, with much love to all, I remain your afft. Son.

R. T. Van Wyck

Nov. 7. The weather continued rainy. No news of any account transpiring. The arrival of the 15th and 17th Corps at the river.
Waggons came in for supplies.

Atlanta, Ga. Nov. 7th '64

Dear Father,

My last letter upon the 6th informed you of the movement of this
corps upon a raid. Immediately mailing the letter, I soon afterwards
received the order to fall in and return to camp, when it was too late to
rectify what I then stated, the order being countermanded for what reason I don't know. But there seems to be a general belief that the expedition is only temporarily delayed. When I got back to camp I received
your letter of Oct. 28th, informing me of the safe arrival of the check, etc.

I suppose by this time the box is on the way. Well, I may return
from this raid about the time the box will get here, if not more expeditions than the one we had last winter. It will run the chances of my
getting it anyhow, even if it is probable we were to stay here this winter, so let it come.

I am glad Mr. Briggs has made a purchase of a farm in Sullivan
Co. He is a deserving, hard-working man and I dare say he has not
misapplied the opportunity of the past few years to start himself. The
applications for the situation [*replacing him*] will be much sought, I
dare say. I am glad you have concluded to only let it for one year,
and I hope by that time to get out of the service and assist you in the
management of it.

The horse, which you value at $300, must be getting along in
years. I hope you will make him earn his living. Such stock, if
employed upon the farm, will be improved and can be employed
usefully, the younger [*horse*] the same – without you seem disposed
to sell him, which you can do as well as he is, as to break him in. I
wish you could have some of the mules for working stock that are
starving to death here by the hundred. You never saw a dead mule
and rarely a dead horse. Here our roads are McAdamized with them
–creeks, springs, rivers, houses, barns, everywhere, they are living
dead about, the whole country is putrid with them. But this is the
consequences of the <u>war</u>, unavoidable.

I have just written to Aben. All letters will reach me and I will
be glad to receive them. With much love I remain your afft. Son

R. T. Van Wyck

P. S. I forgot to mention of a couple of Handkerchiefs in that box. Be so kind as to send them by mail.

Nov. 8. Awaiting a movement with orders for immediate departure. Still threatening rain.

Nov. 9. Was alarmed by a demonstration made by Reb cavalry and sent out to look after them, but returned unsuccessful. Heavy shower during the night.

Nov. 10. All quiet in camp. Weather remaining cold.

Nov. 11. Still the same.

Nov. 12. [*Illegible.*]

Nov. 13. The consolidation of the army and the passing through of the 15th and 17th Corps. Was detailed tearing up RR to the Bridge. The Macon Depot torn down and Gov. buildings burnt.

Nov. 14. Remained in camp during the day. Expecting to leave. The works of destruction still going on.

EDITOR'S NOTE:

General Sherman left Gen. Geo. Thomas at Nashville, with a force of some 70,000 men to defend Tennessee against any attempts by Gen. Hood to retake it. On Nov. 15, after evacuating all civilians from Atlanta and putting the city to the torch, Gen. Sherman marched southward with an army of some 60,000 veterans, to "ruin Georgia" and to reach the coast 300 miles away.

General Sherman's Orders for the March to the Sea

"The two general orders made for this march appear to me ... so clear, emphatic, and well-digested, that no account of that historic event is perfect without them, and I give them entire ...:*

Headquarters Military Division of the Mississippi,
In the Field, Kingston, Georgia, November 8, 1864

The general commanding deems it proper at this time to inform the officers and men of the Fourteenth, Fifteenth, Seventeenth, and Twentieth Corps, that he has organized them into an army for a special purpose, well known to the War Department and to General Grant.

It is sufficient for you to know that it involves a departure from our present base, and a long and difficult march to a new one. All the chances of war

---

* *Memoirs, op.cit.,* pp. 174-6.

have been considered and provided for, as far as human sagacity can. All he asks of you is to maintain that discipline, patience, and courage which have characterized you in the past, and he hopes, through you, to strike a blow at our enemy that will have a material effect in producing what we all so much desire, his complete overthrow.

Of all things, the most important is that the men during marches and in camp keep their places and do not scatter about as stragglers or foragers, to be picked up by a hostile people in detail. It is also of the utmost importance that our wagons should not be loaded with anything but provisions and ammunition. All surplus servants, non-combatants, and refugees, should now go to the rear, and none should be encouraged to encumber us on the march. At some future time we will be able to provide for the poor whites and blacks who seek to escape the bondage under which they are now suffering. With these few simple cautions, he hopes to lead you to achievements equal in importance to those of the past.

By order of Major-General W. T. Sherman,

L. M. Cayton, Aide-de-Camp

November 9, 1864

1. For the purpose of military operations, this army is divided into two wings, viz.: The right wing, Major-General O. O. Howard, commanding, 15th and 17th Corps; the left wing, Maj.-Gen. H. W. Slocum commanding, the 14th and 20th Corps.

2. The habitual order of march will be wherever practicable by four roads, as nearly parallel as possible, and converging at points hereafter to be indicated in orders...

3. There will be no general train of supplies, but each corps will have its ammunition-train and provision-train, distributed habitually as follows: Behind each regiment should follow one wagon and one ambulance ... The separate columns will start habitually at 7 a.m., and make about fifteen miles per day, unless otherwise fixed in orders.

4. The army will forage liberally on the country during the march. Each brigade commander will organize a good and sufficient foraging party, under the command of one or more discreet officers, who will gather near the route traveled corn or forage of any kind, meat of any kind, vegetables, corn-meal ... aiming at all times to keep in the wagons at least ten days' provision for his command, and three days' forage. Soldiers must not enter the dwellings of the inhabitants or commit any trespass; but they may be permitted to gather

turnips, potatoes... and to drive in stock in sight of their camp. To regular foraging parties must be intrusted the gathering of provisions and forage at any distance from the road traveled.

5. To corps commanders alone is intrusted the power to destroy mills, houses, cotton-gins, etc.; and for them this general principle is laid down: In districts and neighborhoods where the army is unmolested, no destruction of such property should be permitted; but should guerrillas or bush-whackers molest our march, or should the inhabitants burn bridges, obstruct roads, or otherwise manifest local hostility, then army commanders should order and enforce a devastation more or less relentless, according to the measure of such hostility.

6. As for horses, mules, wagons, etc., belonging to the inhabitants, the cavalry and artillery may appropriate freely and without limit; discriminating, however, between the rich, who are usually hostile, and the poor and industrious, usually neutral or friendly. Foraging-parties may also take mules or horses, to replace the jaded animals of their trains, or to serve as pack-mules for the regiments or brigades. In all foraging, of whatever kind, the parties engaged will refrain from abusive or threatening language, and may where the officer in command thinks proper give written certificates of the facts, but no receipts, and they will endeavor to leave with each family a reasonable portion for their maintenance.

7. Negroes who are able-bodied and can be of service to the several columns may be taken along; but each army commander will bear in mind that the question of supplies is a very important one, and that his first duty is to see to those who bear arms.*

8. The organization at once of a good pioneer battalion** for each army corps, composed if possible of negroes, should be attended to. This battalion should follow the advance-guard, repair roads and double them if possible so that the columns will not be delayed after reaching bad places.

9. Captain O. M. Poe, chief-engineer, will assign to each wing of the army a pontoon-train, fully equipped and organized, and the commanders thereof will see to their being properly protected at all times.

By order of Major-General W. T. Sherman.

---

* Although General Sherman did not use Negroes in combat many assisted the army as teamsters, servants, grooms, and laborers.
** These Negro pioneer (labor) battalions were to receive their meals and $10 a month pay.

Nov. 15. Broke camp about half-past five and marched about 10 miles to Stone Mt. Day pleasant and cold...[*remainder illegible*]

Nov. 16. The Regt. on picket during the night. Commenced marching towards Yellow River at 1 P.M. and reached it about 11 o'clock, distance only 10 miles, but were delayed on account of waggon train.

Nov. 17. Resumed the march towards Augusta about half-past 10 o'clock and still kept as guard to waggon train, and went into camp about 12 M. and immediately was detailed upon picket.

Nov. 18. Was detailed to forage for the Regt. and after a very fatiguing march for 20 miles reached camp at 4 A.M. next morning– within a mile or more of Madison.

Nov. 19. Passed through the city of Madison. I found it the most beautiful city of the South. We encamped for the night five miles south of the city. We feasted upon potatoes and fresh meat, any quantity of it.

Nov. 20. Left camp about half-past eight and marched 10 miles to within a few miles of Eatonton. It rained hard during the night.

Nov. 21. Started marching in a drenching rain and marched about 12 miles. Mud heavy and deep. Passed through Eatonton.

Nov. 22. Passed through Milledgeville and encamped east of the city. Marched 13 miles within city. Abundance of horses and mules procured for the Army.

Nov. 23. Remained in camp all day.

Nov. 24. Broke camp early in morning towards Sandersville, distance 10 miles.

Nov. 25. Resumed the march early in the morning and made 10 miles still on the Savannah road. Met the enemy early in the day. A small enemy force. [*Wheeler's Confederate cavalry*].

Nov. 26. Skirmished with Reb cavalry till noon. Passed through Hendersonville about noon. Marched south and reached the Macon and Savannah RR at Station No. 13 and tore up a mile or more of RR.

Nov. 27. Marched 16 miles to next Station. Weather fine and somewhat hot. Name of the place Davisboro.

Nov. 28. Marched to next Station, 10 miles [*between*] Stations.

Burnt RR all day.* Country flat and surface water in great abundance.

Nov. 29. Resumed the march and destroyed 10 miles of track. Foraged during the day and quite successful. Considerable cultivated land between the stations, but the country low and swampy.

Nov. 30. Marched N.E. and crossed the Ogeechee River. Plantations of large size of Rice[*fields*]. Country low and unhealthy.

Dec. 1 Continued the march towards Millen Junction but the land marshy. We made little progress.

Dec. 2. Reached within eight miles of Junction (Millen). Bad roads. Weather still continues fine.

Dec. 3. Crossed the RR above Millen and marched in a due East direction some five miles and encamped in a beautiful grove of pines.

Dec. 4. Resumed the march in the morning. The country since crossing the RR is level, gradually descending – less rough and good traveling, made 15 miles east from RR.

Dec. 5 Remained in camp all day. Marched about eight o'clock P.M. about three miles. Roads bad.

Dec. 6. Marched directly south eight or ten miles. Roads still bad and becoming more so. We follow the course of the Savannah River.

Dec. 7. We marched still in the same direction towards and arrived at Springfield, distance 10 miles. Roads getting better.

Dec. 8. Was detailed with the rest of Company as foragers. We were successful for <u>ourselves</u>, but the waggons not coming up we were delayed and night found us ten miles in rear of our division.

Dec. 9. Joined our Div. and marched a few miles. We came upon a Fort garrisoned by 300 men. But the men got away and escaped.

Dec. 10. Marched 9 miles and intersected the RR to Charleston. Continued the march till we confronted the fortifications and but

---

* Sherman's army became masters at destroying railroad tracks. The wooden ties were pulled up and set afire and the middle sections of the steel rails were heated over these fires and then wrapped around a tree, or with the help of a giant wrench they were twisted out of shape or formed into the letters U and S. Bent rails could be hammered straight again, but the "Sherman [*neck*] tie," i.e., the twisted rails, had to be reshaped at steel mills. *The March to the Sea and Beyond, op. cit.*, pp. 137-8.

a few hundred yards of Savannah River. One Company (C) captured a steamer. Rainy and camping bad.

Dec. 11. Under orders to move but remained in same position during the day. Troops were moving in position during the day. Troops were moving in position around the city. Weather turned up cold during the night.

Dec. 12. Advanced our lines much nearer the enemy upon better drier ground. Rations short. Nothing but meat and coffee. Captured a gunboat. Still cold.

Dec. 13. Nothing heard from the fleet and the opening of our cracker line. Weather still cold. The Rebs still shell our position. We don't answer in return but have kept seemingly quiet.

Dec. 14. Was detailed upon picket. Nothing occurred. Was relieved at night. No rations still from the fleet though the cracker line is open and communications open to the fleet.

Dec. 15. Went in search of something to eat. Visited the rice mills. Could not get any except what was unhulled.

Dec. 16. Was ordered down to one of the Islands in the river (with the rest of the Brigade). The Rebs shell us considerable but did no damage. We were hard at [hull]ing rice all day and lived again.

Dec. 17. The Colonel returned, got a mail, and prospect of rations and likewise sent a mail. A heavy dew last night, like rain. The enemy quiet today.

(Letter in pencil)
Noted on envelope by recipient: First letter received after Marching through Georgia.

In front of Savannah, Ga.
or on Harrison's Island, S. C.
Dec. 17th, 1864

Dear Mother,

I received yours of Nov. 6th and 16th by arrival of steamer and joining our communications at this point.

This is the first opportunity of writing you, and the intermission [was] greater than at any time yet. The details of the expedition you will get more complete by the newspaper reporters along. We pushed steadily forward, encountered no enemy till we neared this point, lived famously upon sweet potatoes, pork, chicken, turkeys, etc., an abundance of everything we wanted as the country was rich in everything. We passed through Madison, Milledgeville, destroying R.R. and ruining the country generally. I would like to give you a long letter, but this must suffice at present.

I arrived <u>here</u> some days ago in good health and <u>no</u> <u>worse</u> than a good <u>scrubbing</u> and a suit of clothes would make me.

The Colonel [*Ketcham*] has arrived, mail came, and our rations (which were merely <u>nominal</u> and has been scanty since coming into the <u>swamps*</u>) will be issued tomorrow in full. So these good things are enough for one day - - -

I am now writing in one of the negro shanties upon one of the rice islands, four miles from the city. A gunboat (Rebel) comes up every day and throws us a few shells, with that exception we have nothing to do but <u>pound</u> out rice from the hull, which I assure you keeps me well employed to get more than I can <u>eat</u>.

I will write you soon again. The box you know I would like much but if I am going around all winter I can do without it. Two shirts I would much like and wish them sent (by mail or otherwise) if you could do so. It is quite warm at present. It is hot in the middle of the day (disagreeable).

With much love I remain your afft. Son

R. T. Van Wyck

P. S. I will inquire about boxes and then let you know.
I have received the *Weekly Tribunes* up to Nov. 26th.

Dec. 18. In afternoon was detailed to construct fascines** from reeds and laid down a bridge of them which proved highly satisfactory to HQ.

Dec. 19. Moved early in the morning to relieve the Iowa Mil. and 3rd Wisc. Regt. who were ordered to advance the lines [*across the Savannah River*] into S. Car. In afternoon went to work at our fascine building.

Dec. 20. Still at work at fascine. No news from Savannah. Weather threatens rain. A shell from gunboat killed a man in breastwork

---

* Rather worse than "scanty," according to his notebook.
** Long bundles of sticks (or reeds) bound together, used in filling ditches, strengthening ramparts, making retaining walls or bridges, etc.

likewise a musket ball killed Noah Wixon of Co. H.*

Dec. 21. The city surrendered this morning about 5 A. M. We were ordered (Brigade) to recross to the Georgia side of river, but the wind and tide made it difficult for the boats.

Dec. 22. Still continued crossing. The weather continued cold. We marched for the city about 4 P. M. and encamped along the river a mile from the city.

EDITOR'S NOTE:

After his troops surrounded Savannah, Gen. Sherman found he first had to capture Fort McAllister. This was done on Dec. 13th by Gen. Hazen with help from the Union fleet. The 25th and 20th Corps were then sent to place siege guns in position in the lowlands around the city and to build a supply depot and a pier and roads leading to them through the swamps. Gen. Hardee's forces holding Savannah were small and Sherman wanted to take the city before the garrison was reinforced and before the winter rains totally bogged down his army. On Dec. 18th Sherman sent Hardee an ultimatum, but Hardee refused to surrender. However, on the morning of Dec. 21st skirmishers of the 20th Corps found that Gen. Hardee had evacuated the city during the night. [*R. T. Van Wyck and his brigade were nearly caught by the retreating Confederate forces – see next letter.*] On Dec. 22nd Gen. Sherman sent a telegram to: "His Excellency President Lincoln. I beg to present you as a Christmas gift the city of Savannah, with one hundred and fifty heavy guns and plenty of ammunition, also about twenty-five thousand bales of cotton. [*Signed*] W. T. Sherman, Major-General." *The General Who Marched to Hell*, by E. S. Miers, N.Y., p. 272.

Dec. 23. Busily engaged getting up our shanty. Did little towards it.

Dec. 24. Made a voyage up the river in search of lumber, etc. Was disappointed in the disposal of it.

Dec. 25. Christmas Sunday. Still at work to get out of the weather, which looks threatening rain. It rained hard during the night but escaped a drenching.

Dec. 26. Completed our shanty, built a chimney, etc. Could not find time to write home. Our rations do not come in as plentiful as anticipated, but soon perhaps everything will be remedied.

Dec. 27. Wrote some letters. The weather still continues fine. Felt settled down in my shanty.

---

* Pvt. William A. Palmatier of Co. C was also killed in action this day.

EDITOR'S NOTE:

On Dec. 24th Gen. Sherman received an official report of the great battles of Dec. 15-16 at Nashville where Gen. Thomas defeated Gen. Hood's army. "General Thomas's brilliant victory was necessary to mine to make a complete whole" [*of the March to the Sea*] by removing the main threat to his rear. *Memoirs*, op. cit., p. 219.

Savannah, Dec. 27th '64

Dear Mother,

Yours of Nov. 29th came to hand some days since, but oweing [*sic*] to business (that of necessity) I could not reply sooner. My last hurried letter has not more than informed you of the safe arrival in this port, only minus certain articles of clothing which it is useless to mention, inasmuch as they forsook me in such manner and condition that I hardly think a ragpicker would much rejoice at the finding.

We had a good time, much better than I anticipated, for after getting 25 or 30 miles from Atlanta we found sweet potatoes and pork in abundance, and as we did the foraging on private account we found it necessary only to get supplied about 3 o'clock P.M. to last us for supper and breakfast. But latterly the plantations were of larger size and fewer and we were obliged to get as we could find.

I got a view of Southern institutions, which I am assured if [*they*] could be presented to some of the Southern rights men north would convert them. It has already turned the minds of all with us, and all agree, if it is admitted that a negro is a human being* their condition is not a wit [*sic*] better than our domestic animals. There are plantations where the slaves are well taken care of, but I have seen them with no more to help themselves than you would find in a pig sty. As we neared the Savannah River they blockaded the roads and followed us by the thousands.

But of all, the most miserable situation is that of the rice plantation. The land is overflowed and hardly a foot of it but what is protected by an embankment – here they live and work. The surface of the country is a gradual descent from Atlanta to the ocean; from Milledgeville, a brake is not used upon the wagons, but in and around that place and at Madison I saw some of the most fertile land

---

* He is quoting from one of the arguments put forward in the Dred Scott case of 1857-8 which held that since the Negro was "only two-thirds human" he was not qualified for freedom.

which the Confederacy can well boast of. But when we reached the Macon & Savannah R. R. we struck the sand and the country became sterile.

Soon after mailing my last letter the brigade were ordered to cross the river into South Carolina. The morning of the 21st the Rebs discovered that this movement threatened their communications and evacuated the city. A great danger soon threatened us, for we were only a mile from the pike upon which the whole Rebel army were marching out and a river between our own communications (this side). They attacked as we attempted to cross over in boats which became unmanageable on account of the wind, but night coming on, we got across. Col. Ketcham got wounded and some two or three more.

We are a mile north of the city and got pretty good quarters, and I hope we can make a stay of it. The box it would be best to keep for the present. I have not been down to the city yet. I am told the inhabitants take the capture with better grace than the citizens of Atlanta. The stores will open and business commence, a cheering news for the Rebs. I suppose we will be off for Charleston as soon as the men are provided with clothing, etc., and I hope that will be our last campaign.

Thanksgiving day we left Milledgeville for the Southern R. R.– but I had chicken, though we lived famously in that section of country. Christmas was a very fatiguing day here. I often think of the comforts of home, but one thing we have the best of you, while you are shivering over a fire, we have nice April weather, a thunder shower is now passing over.

I have received a letter from Aben, and from Uncle Anthony, both are well. I am looking for another mail. I remain with much love your Aft. Son.

R. T. Van Wyck

Co. K, 150th Regt. N. Y. Vols.
2nd Brig., 1st Div., 20th Army Corps
Sherman's Army*

Dec. 28. No material change in programme. A corps review is daily
looked for.

---

* Note that it is now "Sherman's army" in the minds of his men; it is not an official designation.

Savannah, Dec. 28th '64

Dear Cousin [*Sarah*],

Yours of Nov. 7th I received some days since. You were prepared for this intermission of correspondence, knowing of Sherman's march from Atlanta, and were looking forward to the time when I could communicate from the seaboard. We reached here Dec. 11th and invested the city, but the city did not fall into our hands till the 21st.

I enjoyed myself first-rate, much better than anticipated, although at times the marches were fatiguing. How thankful I am that the horrors of war and ensueing [*sic*] devastation is so far removed from our own pleasant homes. Many were the times I have seen splendid mansions, even after the lawful appropriation of subsistance [*sic*] therein contained, given over to the plunder of the soldiery. The destruction of everything useful and ornamental was the order of things.

Our camp is a mile from the city up the river in the <u>midst</u> of a forest of <u>live oak</u>, under which moss-covered branches we have put up quarters. The climate is much like April, a shower has just passed over and the appearance of the country is much like it at that season at home.

From a letter from Mother you spent Thanksgiving at home. I dare say you enjoyed yourself well, except you missed the noise and excitement of city life, which is becoming more agreeable. You spent a very agreeable visit to Englewood, and I am glad you found the Messrs. Van Brunts attractive and fascinating young men. It gives you a view of society in New Jersey. You must be forming many pleasant acquaintances in and around 47th Street. I take the *Tribune*, and if you wish to escape detection you must suggest <u>that</u> publication [*announcement of her engagement*] in the other dailies.

Dec. 29th. Being interrupted I could not finish my letter yesterday. I don't know whether I can add much more interesting. I have so often wished myself home <u>sometimes</u> that I have got hardened to the feeling, but now only nine months to <u>put in</u> and then I will be out of service. Remember me to Van Wyck and the children. With much love I remain your aff. Cousin

R. T. Van Wyck

Dec. 29. Weather still cold and disagreeable. No news of importance.

Dec. 30. The Corps review [*of his troops by Gen. Sherman*] took place today. I also received a mail. Rumor says we are to be detached from the Corps (20th).

Dec. 31. After muster in and inspection, were ordered to move our quarters to the right of the 1st Brigade. Thus giving us another busy time for New Year's on the morrow. The weather cold and bleak for these parts. Was detailed upon guard over the old camp.

Recipe for Blackberry Brandy: to 2 qts. of blackberry juice, put 1 1/2 lb. of white sugar, 1/2 oz. of cinamon [*sic*], 1/2 oz. of nutmeg, 1/4 oz. cloves, 1 oz. allspice. Let it boil a few minutes, and when cool, add one pint of brandy. [*Blackberries were the prime remedy for diarrhea.*]

1865

Jan. 1. Was upon guard all day. Did little to seeing to a chimney and shanty. Weather still cold.

Jan. 2. Occupied the time in putting up a shanty and completed it, all but a chimney.

Jan. 3. Completed the chimney today and got partially arranged. Can find little time for reading.

Jan. 4. Still the same.

Jan. 5. Still the same.

Jan. 6. Was detailed upon fatigue at noon.

Jan. 7. Still the same.

Savannah, Ga.
January 7th 1865

Dear Mother,

I wish you a "Happy New Year." Yours of Dec. 10th came to hand a few days since. We are getting ready for another campaign, probably against Charleston. The defences [*sic*] of the city are in progress and as we daily work upon the fortifications many suppose we will remain to garrison this place.

Again, many are looking for a "soft thing" from the political influence of Col. Ketcham, to obtain [*for himself*] through the War Department a detached post of duty where the duty would not prevent him from being with his Reg't inasmuch as his <u>wound</u> will force him to resign if called into the field. [*See note at end of letter.*]

Thus matters rest, except the talking about rations, clothing, etc., which are coming in slowly. The weather has been fine, for the past few days, very warm. I don't know as I ever spent Christmas and New Year's so miserable as the past. The first shanties we built and were getting settled down when we were ordered to tear down and remove a quarter of a mile distant, bringing it upon New Year's Day, a miserably spent one.

I have received *Harper's* for January. I read of the fine sleighing, skating between Christmas and New Year's. The contrast is a strange one, while here if upon any morning the stopper of the canteen gets stuck, we think it is very cold. The city is fast becoming reconciled to Federal laws, as the population is more foreign than of native population. They begin to rejoice at the change of power.

I am looking forward to a letter, although I do not deserve one for my delinquency in not answering you sooner, but I hope to write soon in a few days. With much love I remain your aft. Son,

R. T. Van Wyck

P. S. I wish Father would send me $10, also some postage stamps.

Editor's note:

Col. Ketcham was seriously wounded and "unable to join his command again in active service. At Atlanta he had been promoted to Brigadier-General by Brevet, and subsequently for conspicuous bravery, to rank of Brevet Major General." *History of Dutchess County, op. cit.*, p. 197.

Jan. 8. Started for church but owing to the lateness of the hour did not get a seat. Quite a pleasant day.
Jan. 9. All quiet today. No news of any importance.

Savannah, Ga.
January 9th, 1865

Dear Father,

I received yours of the 21st ult. yesterday. I am surprised you have not heard of my arrival or had not received my letter of Dec. 12th, but have ere this known of my situation, I hope. You seem to know how well we succeeded from the papers. We have suffered no change since my last [*letter*] to Mother a few days since, but are looking forward for some move <u>daily</u>. The 17th Corps took transports for Beaufort some days since and it is presumed we will quickly follow in that direction. (I seem to keep my usual good health and balance at 159 lbs.)

My *Weekly Tribune* has come to me up to Dec. 17th and in my next I will get the general army news. There is a paper published here but little outside of Department matters are printed, and even that is much restricted. The old topic of <u>peace</u> through Rebel and by the Rebel Government is being revived again. Of course, we think the bottom is fast falling out of the C.S. A., but their [sic] may be many a hard knock yet to bring them to terms. We think the next campaign will be the most effective one yet, and as represented to us, will be a speedy one.

You have had good sleighing part of the time, I suppose. The accounts from the North are that King Frost reigns in all his glory. I am sorry that I cannot have the pleasure of that box, but I [agree] with you that it better be kept where it is than sent, for the present. The express office is just opened in town, and if we are fortunate [enough] to remain here, I will let you know, and then you may send it.

Our rations are coming in slowly and for the little luxuries the sutlers have, a person must cover them with greenbacks. Fortunately we have had abundance of rice, most of which time has been our constant food. I am afraid some of the Dutchess County people have been reading that piece in the Dec. No. of *Harper's*, "After Petroleum," and believed that along the Fishkill Creek and under the Mt. that fluid could be found.* I hope so, too, and enough to lubricate business in that section. The Waldrons have so vivid an imagination that they suppose they are now burning <u>oil</u> from their own deposit upon their farm. Blivmer [?] has made the most sensible arrangement with his property.

I intend to write Aben and Uncle Anthony immediately. I have been so situated that during the day something or other has so occupied my time, and when night comes, without candles, I only can read by making a large fire and hard work at that, but I have got a few candles now and I will make up for lost time. I think I got all your letters and I am glad to receive them. With much love I remain your aff. Son,

R. T. Van Wyck

Jan. 10. Still the same.

---

* The "discovery" of oil deposits in Fishkill turned out to be a hoax.

Richard T. Van Wyck's letter to his cousin Sarah E. Van Vechten, dated December 4, 1862, in which he writes "The effect of war is to petrify the heart." *Collection of the East Fishkill Historical Society.*

Richard T. Van Wyck's writing box which he carried throughout the war. *Collection of the East Fishkill Historical Society.*

Richard T. Van Wyck's canteen and cartridge box plate.
Collection of the East Fishkill Historical Society.

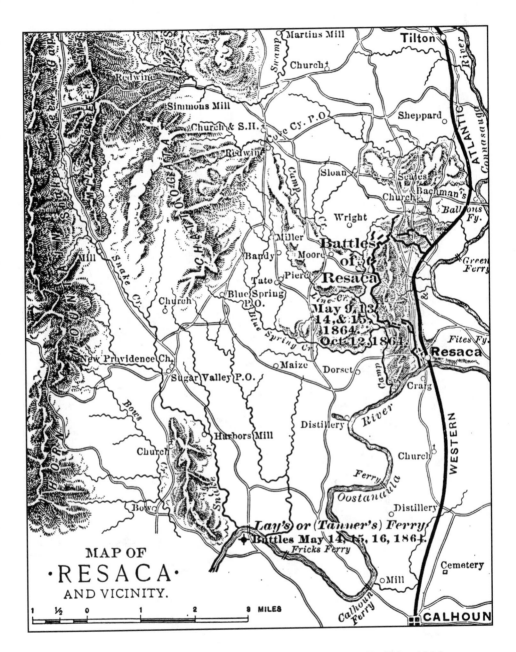

Mountain Campaigns in Georgia, by Jos. M. Brown, Buffalo, 1890.

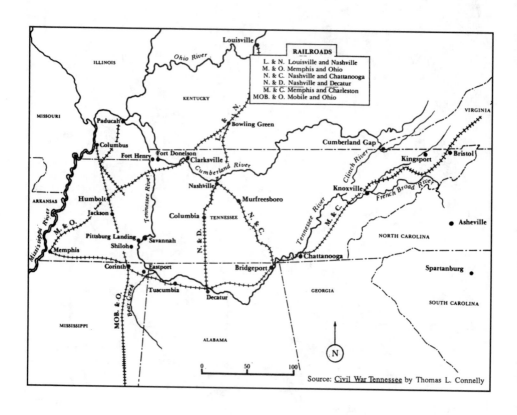

RAILROADS

L. & N. Louisville and Nashville
M. & O. Memphis and Ohio
N. & C. Nashville and Chattanooga
N. & D. Nashville and Decatur
M. & C. Memphis and Charleston
MOB. & O. Mobile and Ohio

N

0   50   100

Source: Civil War Tennessee by Thomas L. Connelly

Battle of Resaca, May 14-15, 1865. *Mountain Campaigns in Georgia* by Joseph M. Brown (People's Press). *Collection of John C. Quinn.*

Company A 150th New York Volunteers. First Lieutenant Henry Gridley is seated in the middle of the front row. Gridley was killed in action, shot through the heart, at Kulp's Farm, Georgia, on June 22, 1864. Van Wyck described him as the "smartest officer in the Regiment." *Courtesy of Dutchess County Historical Society.*

The Siege of Atlanta, Georgia, July 22–September 1, 1864.
Frank Leslie's Illustrated Newspaper. Collection of John C. Quinn.

Sept. 14, 1864 letter from Richard to his mother. *Collection of the East Fishkill Historical Society.*

Confederate Army Evacuating Savannah, Georgia, December 20, 1864. *Frank Leslie's Illustrated Newspaper. Collection of John C. Quinn.*

Battle of Bentonville, North Carolina, March 20, 1865. *Frank Leslie's Illustrated Newspaper. Collection of John C. Quinn.*

Sherman and His Generals. Left to right, standing: Major
General Oliver Otis Howard (Army of the Tennessee), Major
General William Babcock Hazen (2nd Division, 15th Army
Corps), Brevet Major General Jefferson Columbus Davis
(14th Army Corps), Major General Joseph Anthony Mower
(20th Army Corps). Left to right, seated: Major General John
Alexander (15th Army Corps), Major General William
Tecumseh Sherman, Major General Henry Warner Slocum
(Army of Georgia). At the close of the war, when the 150th
was ready to be mustered out, General Henry W. Slocum
commented, "No regiment goes home with a better record.
They are an honor to the service and to our State." *The
Massachusetts Military Order of the Loyal Legion and the U.S. Army
Military History Institute. Collection of John C. Quinn.*

Grand Review of the United States Army at Washington City, May 23, 1865. *Frank Leslie's Illustrated Newspaper. Collection of John C. Quinn.*

Richard T. Van Wyck's pocket diary, 1864-1865, which he carried throughout the campaigns with Sherman. *Collection of the East Fishkill Historical Society.*

Richard and Sarah (Van Vechten) Van Wyck. *Collection of the East Fishkill Historical Society.*

Samuel V. Van Wyck and Edith A. Van Wyck, Richard and Sarah's children. *Collection of the East Fishkill Historical Society.*

Sarah with daughter Louisa, who died in infancy. *Collection of the East Fishkill Historical Society.*

Edith A. Van Wyck, Richard and Sarah's youngest daughter, born August 13, 1879. *Collection of the East Fishkill Historical Society.*

(top) James Van Wyck, the oldest son of Richard and Sarah.
Collection of the East Fishkill Historical Society.
(bottom) Richard T. Van Wyck. "Taken & Finished in 10 min.
@ LeRoy's GEM Gallery, 78 Water St. (cor. Third),
Newburgh, NY." *Collection of the East Fishkill Historical Society.*

Mrs. Richard T. Van Wyck (Sarah Van Vechten) in spirited old age. *Collection of the East Fishkill Historical Society.*

CAROLINAS—NEW YORK
1865

We received the painful news of the <u>Murder of</u> President
Lincoln and Seward and were it not an official communication to Sherman from the War Department, would
not believe it. The country cannot have its cup of pleasure in view of the end of the war unalloyed. God, having preserved him to us, and brought about the wishes
of every patriot, has taken him away.

–R.T. Van Wyck

As the year opened, Richard T. Van Wyck's unit had crossed into
South Carolina about twenty-four miles from Savannah. The senior
commanders on both sides recognized that the war, which had covered more land area and been more destructive of life and property
than any recorded in American history, was entering its final days.
On the 15th of January, Fort Fisher, North Carolina, the South's last
port, fell to the Union. In Washington, on January 31, 1865, Congress
voted 119 to 56 to pass the Thirteenth Amendment to abolish slavery, then sent it on to the states for ratification.

On January 17th, General William Tecumseh Sherman, with the
passion of a crusader, turned the two columns of his Army of the
Tennessee–60,000 officers and men–northward through the
Carolinas. The 150th, Slocum's Army of Georgia, 20th Corps,
remained part of the Left Wing.

During the next two months, the regiment met little resistance and
continued to live off the land. The two wings of Sherman's Army
destroyed railroad tracks, stockpiles of ammunition, factories, mills,
cotton, and an incalculable number of private homes, barns and stores.

The pent-up anger of the Federal troops against South Carolina,
whose firing upon Fort Sumter had precipitated the war, could not be
restrained. So great was the hatred, Van Wyck wrote to his mother,
that it seemed impossible "to stay the hand of the destroyer ... despite
orders to the contrary." The back roads of the Southland were
clogged with tens of thousands of Confederate refugees, bundles on

their heads, children in arms, men on mules, women in old wagons, and many with little to eat.

On February 11th, the regiment started across country for Columbia, the capital of South Carolina, arriving on the outskirts during the afternoon of the 16th. The city was defended by a small Confederate force and fell on the 17th. By the next morning, much of the city had burned to the ground, the result of high winds and the burning of cotton by drunken Federal cavalry soldiers.

At dawn on February 18th, the regiment resumed the march to Fayetteville, a journey of about two hundred miles, during which they used pontoons to cross flooded rivers, corduroyed marshes, survived exposure to cold spring rains, and experienced occasional skirmishing with rebel forces. Three weeks later, on March 11th, they reached Fayetteville. The next day, to the cheering of a throng of soldiers, a Union steamboat, the first to arrive since the fall of Fort Fisher, brought badly needed supplies and letters from home. General Sherman instructed the skipper of the steamer to remain at Fayetteville until nightfall, providing his staff and men with the opportunity to write dispatches and letters home.

Jefferson Davis had appointed Robert E. Lee General-in-Chief of what remained of the Confederate Army, and in early March, Lee restored General Joseph E. Johnston, Sherman's old nemesis, to command the remnants of Hood's and Hardee's shattered armies in the Carolinas—16,000 infantry and 7,000 cavalry.

According to Sherman's plan, the Left Wing, which included the 150th, was to advance northward to Averasboro. From there, the column would head east toward Goldsboro via Bentonville to unite with 40,000 more Federals under Major General John M. Schofield. On March 16th, General Johnston sent Hardee's corps to fight a delaying action near Averasboro. At 6 a.m. that morning, the 150th was in the line of battle. This engagement was the longest, lasting until late in the afternoon, and, in some respects, the hardest the regiment was in.

Early in the afternoon of March 19th, Confederate infantry attempting to stop Sherman's advance at Bentonville crashed through segments of the 14th and 20th Corps and routed an entire division. The 150th was rushed to the scene, along with other reinforcements from the 20th Corps, to secure the center and left flank of the Union line until the enemy finally broke off the attack.

On the morning of March 20th, the regiment resumed the march to Goldsboro, arriving on March 24th and taking their position in the line of works on the Weldon Road. Fifty days out of Savannah, the 150th had covered over four hundred miles of rough terrain in wretched weather, crossing swollen rivers and navigating "impenetrable" swamps. After the battles of Kinston, Averasboro and Bentonville, Sherman's combined four corps and Schofield's two totaled 90,000 effectives, twice as many as had set out on what Sherman called "one of the longest and most important marches ever made by an organized army in a civilized country."

In the Eastern Theater of the war, after a last desperate effort to break Grant's Petersburg lines had failed, and he found that his escape west was blocked by General Sheridan's cavalry, General Lee surrendered his army at Appomattox Courthouse on April 9, 1865. News of Lee's surrender reached the 150th near Smithfield, North Carolina, on April 12th. "We have hurrahed ourselves hoarse as step by step we have neared the end of bloodshed and battle," Van Wyck wrote to his mother, "still the all-absorbing subject is, how soon will we get home." The war was not quite at an end for the Dutchess County Regiment, however, for they were still in pursuit of General Johnston.

Johnston realized that the Confederate position was hopeless, and to prevent further loss of life he offered to negotiate a truce. The 150th had reached the city of Raleigh, North Carolina, when it learned of the assassination of President Lincoln. Two weeks later, on April 26th, the same day that General Johnston surrendered his 25,000-man army to General Sherman, the funeral train with the flag-draped hearse car carrying President Lincoln's body moved up the Hudson River on its way to Albany and Springfield. Every station along the line was crowded with people and draped in mourning. Sherman's Carolinas campaign was concluded, and the war had ended for the men of the 150th. On April 29th, the regiment was ordered to proceed to Washington to be mustered out of service. In nine days, they marched from Raleigh to Richmond, a distance of 170 miles. News of the regiment's homeward journey and anticipated arrival spread quickly throughout every village and town in their home county. The *Poughkeepsie Eagle* Daily Log of May 4th appealed to the local citizenry to receive their returning regiment, the "Pride of Dutchess", with a warm and momentous reception.

*****

On the Federal side, the total number of men called into military service during the war to save the Union was 2,656,533, of whom nearly 200,000 were black. About 1,400,000 were in active service, and 60,000 were killed in the field. Another 30,000 were mortally wounded, and 184,000 died in hospitals and camps. Three hundred thousand Union soldiers perished during the war, and it is supposed the Confederates lost an equal number. During its service, Van Wyck's regiment lost 108 men who were killed in the field, mortally wounded, or died of disease. Of the 1,200 men listed on its rolls, about 450 came home with the regiment at the close of the war.

The 150th New York Volunteer Infantry Regiment was discharged from United States service on June 8, 1865. On the following day, they arrived in New York City. There, they boarded the steamer *Mary Benton* and came up the Hudson River on June 12th. The regiment's great reception at the landing in Poughkeepsie, and the demonstrations of the 50,000 people who were waiting to greet them was reported by the *Poughkeepsie Eagle* in its June 13th issue:

> June 12, 1865, will henceforth be a great day in the annals of the City of Poughkeepsie and of Dutchess County, being that on which the 150th Regiment of New York Volunteers was formally received on its return home from the war which crushed out the great rebellion. Decidedly the great attraction of the day was the noble 150th Regiment itself, and never before did any organization so completely take up the attention of the masses as did the brave veterans. Warworn in appearance, their faces browned by Southern suns, their steady, measured step, the expression of their countenances, every one of them seeming to exclaim, "I have dared to do all that becomes a man," was a picture never to be witnessed again in the streets of this city. Every inch of ground over which they moved was consecrated by their tread. Thousands of bouquets were hurled from windows and house-tops at the regiment in every street they passed through, and the enthusiasm along the

route as the regiment passed was unequalled. Old men wept tears of joy at the sight. The procession was the largest ever gotten up in this city.

J.C.Q.

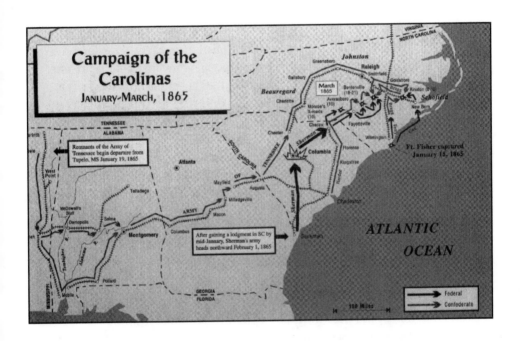

Last Stand in the Carolinas: The Battle of Bentonville, by Mark L. Bradley, Campbell, 1996. *Courtesy of Savas Woodbury Publishers.*

Written on the letterhead of:
THE U. S. CHRISTIAN COMMISSION

**Sends this Sheet as the Soldier's Messenger to his home.
Let it haste to those who wait for tidings**

General Sherman's Army
150th N. Y. Regt. Ist Div. 20th Army Corps
January 10th, 1865

Dear Mother,

I received your letter of Jan. 5th stating [*that*] the anxiety of my long continual silence had considerably abated by receiving my first letter from here.

The news from Fishkill about the marriages of William La Due and Isaac Kip were new things for me, and that the winter was passing off so pleasantly with the snow-coated ground and fine sleighing. Oh! dear, it made me shiver to think of you all bundled up in furs. Why, our <u>new</u> campaign commences tomorrow against Charleston (marching northward) and with nothing more than my summer outfit of Woolen blanket, Rubber blanket, shelter tent, a change of clothing (1 shirt, 1 socks, 1 Drawers) writing material, frying pan and hatchet, one day or more rations, these I carry in my knapsack.

The clothing that I wear is simple enough: cap, coat (blouse), pants, and shoes (no overcoat). I slept well by the picket fire with only my rubber around my shoulders last night. I write this to make you feel more comfortable as you sit over the fire at home, and lend you to think that this weather would pass for mild September weather at home.

The boys are merry over their expected departure for South Carolina tomorrow. The most of them are tired [*of it here*] and want to be off for Charleston or somewhere.

I received yours of Dec. 22nd. It must have been mislaid somewhere. I received that package of handkerchiefs, etc. My shirts have not come yet. I am not in urgent need of them, they will come along soon. I hope as I get nearer home our mail facilities will be better. I feel as if I am getting nearer home. One hundred miles to Charleston—all these count.*

---

* General Sherman writes that he gave out, "with some ostentation ... that we were going to Charleston or Augusta," but had long since made up his mind to waste no time on either, aside from playing on Rebel fears and thus keeping their forces concentrated in those cities, rather than on his front and thus making his path "more difficult and bloody." *Memoirs*, p. 253.

Give my love to all inquiring friends. With much love I remain your aft. Son

R. T. Van Wyck

Jan. 11. Still the same.

Jan. 12. Still the same

Jan. 13 and Jan. 14. [*No entries.*]

Jan. 15. Was upon picket. Weather quite cool but not uncomfortable. Got a mail from home.

Jan. 16. [*No entry.*]

Jan. 17. Broke camp and crossed into S. Car. We marched 10 miles to Fort upon Hardee's Plantation. We relieved the 3rd Division, who advanced as far as Hardeeville (10 miles) upon the Charleston Sw. RR.

Jan. 18. Left camp about 1 P.M. and marched about 10 miles in a N. E. direction. Road good, and country fine and level.

Jan. 19. Marched three miles. We found Hardeeville upon the bank of the river. The weather rainy. A gunboat and transport came up the river. Indications of a disagreeable time.

Jan. 20. Rained all day. Remained in camp all day.

Jan. 21. Rained all day. The ground saturated with waters around about.

Jan. 22. Sunday. Still rainy. No move yet. Wagons stuck in mud three miles from Savannah H.Q. 1st Div. truck deserted upon rice island.

Jan. 23. The weather continues stormy. But in the afternoon cleared up, toward night cold and windy. We are in the same position.

Jan. 24. Still the same cold wind.

(Letter in pencil)

Three Miles from Hardeeville, Ga.[*S.Car.*]
Tuesday, Jan. 24th '64[*sic*] ['*65*]

Dear Mother,

Yours of the 12th came to hand this morning. I am expecting the shirts, etc., by next mail. No papers have come yet. My *Tribune* I have received only up to Dec. 17th. The *Harper's* I have acknowledged.

Since writing you Jan 17th,* at which time we crossed into South

---

* Letter not extant.

Carolina, we have had a wet time. The first two days [we] did first-rate, but before the large train of wagons could cross the Island along the river the rain came on and almost swept them into the Atlantic. The mules and men were just able to get off.

In the meanwhile we were busy enough in heaping up sand at this point to get out of the rain and flood. Of course, no move can be made at present. The transports bring supplies up to us.

We have remained here since the 19th (24 miles from Savannah). If we had stayed in Savannah two days later, the rain would have prevented us from starting at all and we would have been comfortably housed from the weather.

I am much indebted for your budget of news in the neighborhood. The family and select sleigh rides are affording food for the tongue (as of old) while the fingers are busy in contributing for charitable purposes. It confuses me a little when you mention about snow, etc. The winter is passing swiftly away. I will write soon again. This must suffice for the present. Mail leaves in half an hour.

With much love I remain your afft. Son

R. T. Van Wyck

EDITOR'S NOTE:

On this march Gen. Sherman aimed to break up the railroads of North and South Carolina and to unite his army with Gen. Grant's outside Richmond. He faced several armies: Gen. Hardee's in Charleston, remnants of Gen. Hood's near Augusta, plus Gen. Beauregard's and the cavalry of Gens. Wheeler and Hampton which he was on the alert to keep from joining forces against him. But his biggest worry was that Gen. Lee would break out of Richmond and waylay him somewhere between Columbia and Raleigh.

He therefore made arrangements for naval and army reinforcements at strategic places along the sea coast, including evacuation of his troops by sea, if necessary, while Gen. Grant also alerted Gens. Thomas and Canby to rush to Sherman's aid if he was overwhelmed by superior forces.

Despite heavy rains, flooding rivers, and muddy roads he kept his men on the move in order to reach the railroad junction of Goldsboro, N. Car., where he could receive supplies and reinforcements before joining Gen. Grant. *Memoirs, op.cit.*, pp. 255-6, 271-2.

Jan. 25. Cold and windy.

Jan. 26. Thursday. Moved camp in the afternoon some three miles or more toward Augusta.

Jan. 27. Friday. Moved at nine o'clock, delayed on acct. of obstructions and did not make only three miles.

Jan. 28. Broke camp early upon a reconvitance [*his word*] party of
our Regt., but were allowed back and moved camp about 12 midnight five miles and encamped for the night.

Jan. 29. Sunday. Moved at nine o'clock. Skirmished with enemy
and passed through Robertville, four miles.

Jan 30. Encamped here all day, went upon a foraging expedition,
was met by the enemy pickets.

Jan. 31. Still in the same position. Weather fine. Washed and prepared for a campaign.

Robertsville, Ga.
[*Robertville, S.C.*]
January 31st, 1865

Dear Mother,

My last letter [*was*] written near Hardeeville during a spell of wet
weather. Since then we have marched leisurely along driving the
Rebel cavalry before us, our own Brigade and often our Reg't in the
advance.

The country as we advance up the river becomes more fertile,
large plantations handsomely arranged, and houses luxuriously furnished. No poor class of people are met with. The slaveholders and
the slaves only have been the occupants, but the former have deserted, scarcely two or three whites I have seen upon the twenty or thirty farm houses I have visited. They have taken all except their furniture, all provisions except a little corn, and all live stock. This place
is as large as Johnsville, a fine Church and many fine residences, but
not a soul could we find upon entering. The road intersects here, one
to Beaufort, one to Branchville, one to the river about five miles distant.

We started upon the Branchville road yesterday to see what forage could be obtained. The party consisted of a Lieut. and thirty-five
men. Other parties have encountered the Rebels, and as one plantation was stripped would drive them off another, and consequently
we had to go some distance into the Rebel lines. A party of strag-
gling men (mounted) had approached to the most distant plantation
when the Rebs rallied in force (just as they were going into the barns
and [*collecting*] bacon, chickens, hoggs [*sic*], etc.) and drove them back

pell mell into our ranks. We started for the Rebs, who skedaddled in great style. We rescued one and brought off a wounded man, besides getting loaded with everything we wanted.

The left wing (14th and 20th Corps) are concentrating at this point between here and the river, forty miles from Savannah. If we approach Branchville in this direction we will find something to contend with in the shape of cavalry, said to be three Divisions (one Corps) . If our objective point is Augusta we will follow the river closer.

I am looking for a letter in the mail now from the boat in the river, but as the outward mail goes out at one o'clock I cannot wait till then and will write soon in a few days. With much love I remain your afft. Son

R. T. Van Wyck

Feb. 1. Brigade drill in afternoon and a mail.

Feb. 2. Broke camp in morning and marched in a North direction, distance ten miles, obstructions in the way. A slight rain during the night.

Feb. 3. Raining during the day and encamped early in afternoon. Plenty of forage. Hams and chickens.

Feb. 4. Started at eight o'clock with the wagons and marched about 12 miles. Many handsome places upon the way. Day pleasant and country undulating.

Feb. 5. Sunday. Marched twelve miles towards R.R. (Charl. - Aug.) and within a few miles of Barnwell. Country not quite so fertile. Day pleasant.

Feb. 6. [*No entry.*]

Feb. 7. Broke camp and marched six or seven miles. Stormy and cold. Was detailed upon picket. Reached R.R.

Feb. 8. Marched towards Augusta and distant R. R. five miles and returned to [*illegible*]. Day pleasant, cool. Plenty of forage—hams and chickens, etc.

Feb. 9. Remained in camp late in day, only marched two miles towards Augusta. Came in camp late at night.

Feb. 10. Destroyed R. R. all day and marched five miles toward Augusta.

Feb. 11. Broke camp early and marched toward the Edisto River, N. E. Camped about 8 p.m. Distance ten miles.

Feb. 12. Broke camp about 9 a.m. and marched to the North Edisto River, distance about 12 miles. One mile from water.

Feb. 13. Sunday. Crossed the river and marched about ten miles to the [*illegible*] town of the Orangeburg Pike.

Feb. 14. Marched four miles and waited for the 4th Corps to meet [*us*]. Weather rainy and disagreeable.

Feb. 15. Marched to Lexington Court House ten miles. Weather still continues disagreeable.

Feb. 16. Marched toward Columbia, encamped a few miles of the river.

Feb. 17. Marched up to the crossing over of a branch of the Sumter and crossed during the night.

Feb. 18. Broke camp and marched seven miles toward Broad River.

Feb. 19. Arrived at Broad River. Country much sterile caused by the presence of the 14th, 13th, and 17th Corps.

Feb. 20. Sunday. Crossed Broad River [*at Alston*] and marched six miles. Country better and good living upon the enemy. Some very rich land.

Feb. 21. Marched due North. Still continuing forward.

Feb. 22. Crossed the [*Catawba*] river and encamped. Our foragers brought in 35 mules and horses and abundance of flour and meal.

Feb. 23. Marched to Rocky Mount [*Post Office, S. Car.*], distance fifteen miles.

Feb. 24. Travelled only a few miles and encamped [*at Hanging Rock*].*

Feb. 25. Remained in camp all day. No move. The roads are in bad condition by the heavy rains. It rained hard all night.

Feb. 26. Sunday. Remained in camp till towards night and marched five miles. Roads bad.

Feb. 27. Started early in morning and marched three miles and went into camp for the night.

Feb. 28. Started from camp about 1 p.m. and marched about ten miles. Roads in bad order. Got in camp late at night.

Mar. 1. Marched towards Chesterfield some 15 miles. Country sterile.

---

* The pontoon bridge over the Catawba river at Rocky Mount P. O. (South Carolina), was washed away by floods leaving the 14th Corps stranded, so Gen. Sherman halted the 20th Corps at Hanging Rock to allow time for the 14th to cross over. *Memoirs, op. cit.,* p. 289.

Mar. 2. Reached Chesterfield, the county seat of Chesterfield district some five miles south of N. Car. boundary. Distance 18 miles. The Rebs made a show of resistance [*Gen. Butler's cavalry*].

Mar. 3. Remained in camp till late in the day, when we were ordered forward and only did five miles and encamped for the night.

Mar. 4. Broke camp 2 P.M. and marched toward Great Pedee River five miles. Weather unpleasant.

Mar. 5. Sunday. Remained in camp all day. Day pleasant and quite warm.

Mar. 6. Marched to Cheraw and crossed Pontoon Bridge. Got in camp about 12 midnight.

Mar. 7. Broke camp early in morning and marched fifteen miles to the RR nearly completed between Raleigh. Country sandy and sterile.

Mar. 8. Marched fifteen miles through a hard rain all day. Got into camp late at night wet through and through.

Mar. 9. Marched with waggons and still rained hard and was detailed to corduroy the road.*

Mar. 10. Roads most miserable. Forward fixing roads, etc. Went into camp in good season.

Mar. 11. Started upon a forced march for Fayetteville and marched eighteen miles.

Mar. 12. Remained in camp and sent off letters home.

Letter in pencil on the letterhead of:

THE U. S. CHRISTIAN COMMISSION
Sends this Sheet as the Soldier's Messenger to his home.
Let it haste to those who wait for tidings.

[*Fayetteville, N.C.*]
General Sherman's Army
150th N. Y. Regt, 1st Div., 20th Army Corps
March 12th, 1865

Dear Mother,

So long ago you have heard from me. I suppose no little wonderment and dread has been entertained as to my safety and situation.

---

* Laying down a base of fence rails, split saplings, etc., on muddy roads to support the weight of wagons and artillery.

We left Savannah upon the 17th of January, but during a stress of bad weather upon the Savannah River (Hardeeville) which I communicated to you; with that exception, it has been nearly two months of genuine active service. Our line of march was through Blackville upon the Augusta & Charleston R. R., cutting the R. R. at that place; from there we crossed the Edisto River and marched directly for Columbia, the capital, which city surrendered to the 15th Corps.

We crossed the two branches of the Santee River and marched directly for Winnsboro, destroying the R.R. at that place. We still continued to march in a north direction and crossed the Wateree River, where we marched due east through Chesterfield and Cheraw to Fayetteville upon the Cape Fear River where we reached communications.

We have not suffered for want of food, but for days the rain would pour down. We still pushed through corduroy[ing] as we went, [making] miles upon miles of road, fording streams when not deep, building bridges and laying down pontoons, and living upon the country so classically. I think this campaign will bear the palm of any other campaign during the war. South Carolina is no more. The scope of travel of all corps could not be very much less than from fifty miles [apart] and whenever a house was found deserted it was burnt down. From Savannah to Branchville scarcely a house remains standing. Those that do remain are generally of the poor whites of which there are only a few. So great was the indignation among the rank and file that everything that would burn was fired.* Charleston and Wilmington have fallen during our travels.**

We are to remain here a day or two and march on to Goldsboro and New Bern, after which we will operate with Grant's army.

We expect a mail during the day and if I get another chance I will write again. Write as often as possible and I will get your letters.

[This letter is unsigned]

---

* The men in Sherman's Army felt that South Carolina was the state that had provoked the war; hence, in the words of an Illinois man, burning everything they came near "not under orders, but in spite of orders." The men had it in for the state and they took it out their own way. In his *Memoirs* Gen. Sherman wrote; "Somehow our men had got the idea that South Carolina was the cause of all our troubles; her people was the first to fire on Fort Sumter, had been in a great hurry to precipitate the country into civil war; and therefore on them should fall the scourge of war in its worst form".

** Charleston was evacuated by Gen. Hardee on Feb. 17 and taken possession of by Gen. Foster's troops. Wilmington was captured by Gen. Terry on Feb. 22. *Memoirs*, p. 289.

Mar. 14. Remained in camp all day. Was detailed for picket during the night.

Mar. 15. Moved early in morning and marched 14 miles. Was sent again to support Kilpatrick and marched through mud five miles.

Mar. 16. Encountered the enemy [*Gen. Hardee's infantry and cavalry*] early in the morning and fought all day but did not suffer great damage.

Mar. 17. Marched a few miles and encamped for the night.

Mar. 18. Crossed a marshy river and marched five or six miles.

Mar. 19. Marched ten miles and came up with the enemy [*Gen. Johnston's whole army*]. A severe battle was fought by the 14th Corps in which they were repulsed and a total life saved by the arrival of the 20th Corps.

Mar. 20. Moved to a position in the Brigade. In the afternoon made an observation of the enemy's lines.

Mar. 21. Remained in camp all day. The enemy threatened our lines but made no attack. [*By the next day Gen. Johnston was gone, leaving all roads clear.*]

Mar. 22. Started early in the day for Cox Bridge over the Neuse river and made ten miles.

Mar. 23. Marched for the Bridge and arrived at 11.

Mar. 24. Arrived at Goldsboro today and took up our position in the line of works upon the Weldon Road.

Mar. 25. Making a permanent camp.

(Letter in pencil)

Goldsboro, So. C.[*North Carolina*]
March 25, '65

Dear Mother,

We reached here yesterday after much trouble. I wrote you at Fayetteville the 12th. We started from there the 14th and came upon enemy the 16th, and a severe fight ensued in which our Brigade bore a principal part.*

We marched the previous night through the mud and water up to our knees to support Kilpatrick, whom we were to support upon the morrow. The cavalry commenced the attack but it became soon evident of the strength of the enemy who were in superior numbers

---

* First Lt. David B. Sleight, Pvts. John Cass and Wm. J. Wallin of 150th Vols. were killed.

against cavalry–although we drove them three miles. We were reinforced by the rest of the Division and the 3rd Div. of our Corps. Captured six hundred prisoners and several pieces of cannon. The enemy left our front during the night and we did not come upon them till the 19th, about 45 miles west of Goldsboro and within a few miles of Smithfield.

In the attack the 14th Corps leading the advance made a <u>bad</u> position of their lines of <u>battle</u>, and were exposed to a flank movement which the enemy, taking advantage of, threw them back in great disorder upon our <u>Brig.</u>, but we were able to organize them again before the enemy were upon us. The 3rd Brig. and 1st coming upon the scene meanwhile, the Rebs made seven ineffectual attempts to get through and were repulsed with much loss. The enemy was attacked by the right wing of the 15th and 17th Corps upon the 20th and 21st [*of March*] and they made a clear thing of them, capturing prisoners and recapturing some of our own men.

As the enemy were making for Raleigh we made for this place, finding portions of the 23rd, 24th and 25th Corps getting the R.R. in order (from New Bern) and also Williamston to furnish us rations. The cars are in town <u>now</u> and I will send this pencilled letter, hoping to follow it up with another as quick as possible.

The last letter I have received from home bears date of Jan. 12th. So when I get my mail I will get a large one, I hope. I have enjoyed good health and it has quite surprised me to think what I have gone through with. But a kind Providence has so far shielded me from all <u>harm.</u>

We expect to have a rest of 40 days to get ourselves fitted up again. I wish you would send me twenty ($20) dollars. Remember me to all –with much love I remain your aff. Son

R. T. Van Wyck

Goldsboro, March 28th, '65

Dear Mother,

I received such a budget of letters from home that I am at a loss how to answer them. I am exceedingly thankful to receive, after so long a time in ignorance of what is going on either at home or abroad, those letter and papers. Aben has also favored me with a letter, quite cheerful for him, but there seems, <u>I</u> <u>infer</u>, a little trouble in his congregation, but I hope his knowledge of human nature will <u>now</u> bring him all right.

Uncle Anthony seems in his letter to be much absorbed in his duties as senator. And with all my letters received, I have found great pleasure in the news they carry.

Sarah V.V. has given me accounts of the young people's doings in the neighborhood. I have been so long away from such cheerful scenes that I begin to feel <u>old</u>, and would imagine that were I to return again I could only be a passive <u>member</u> of those amusements. The arrival of my *Weekly Tribune* has posted me up. By the by, when does my subscription run out? If possible, give me the benefit of it till Sept.

I suppose Sherman's success has kept down any feeling among a certain class in favor of <u>Peace</u> upon any terms, and has increased the true Union sentiment to give them peace when they lay down their arms. I hope to receive in a few days the northern press relative to Sherman's operations. He has fulfilled what was expected of him, to wipe out South Carolina, of which the ashes of her towns and country plantations can attest. It will take years to populate her again. So great the hatred, it seemed impossible to stay the general destruction going on, despite orders to the contrary. I think the Western troops more zealous to have a hand in the work than the Eastern. We found Union people in North Carolina, but I fear they were not deeply impressed with anything good of us, for we lived necessarily upon the country, and thousands of families were rendered destitute. This plan of Sherman's to strip the country where he goes has given rise to a band of foragers (called vulgarly, bummers*) forty from each Reg't, commanded by a commissioned officer mounted upon horses or mules, which they were to capture. They are a fearless set of men, ruffians at home.

Our detail after its organization captured some sixty horses and mules by getting in advance of the main column after which, by combination with other details, they cleared the road of small bands of Reb cavalry. They usually returned to their Reg't every night escorting several loaded carts of meal, bacon shoulders, and hams, without they had secured a mill and are grinding up corn. They find most of

---

* In addition to the regular foraging parties sent out by each brigade each morning to bring in supplies, the army was surrounded by a horde of stragglers, including deserters from both armies, whose purpose was looting. All of these men were included in the generic term of "bummers," and they ravaged the South.

the meat buried, which these individuals show great tact [*in sharing*] (perhaps from past associations) and have given us generally a good supply. At present they are running a mill eight miles from here, and getting meat 30 miles from here. If we had depended upon our own efforts to obtain food we would have starved. We get Govt. rations at present; with what we receive from that source we have abundance.

As to clothing, we did better than upon the Savannah campaign. That is, we wore our shirts longer before throwing them away. Soap played out. When we chanced to pass the Negro troops from New Bern, there seemed to be a striking resemblance. We have already received a new outfit of clothing and feel comfortable. I wish a light felt hat (size 7 2/8) could be sent me by mail. The shirts being sent by express they reached Savannah after our departure, but I suppose I will get them here.

In regard to Col. Ketcham's address to his Reg't, I hardly know what to think of it. It was meant for publication and for the Dutchess Co. people. He is a politician and his modesty isn't much to boast of, so to those that know the man, it may bear of much construction. As we get a mail every day I hope to receive many letters from home.

With much love I remain your aft. Son

R. T. Van Wyck

Goldsboro, March 31st '65

Dear Sarah,

I have received your two letters soon after my arrival at this place. I am happy to know you are keeping up the reputation of the country in enjoying yourselves during the Winter months by contributing of your industry to some charitable object. As much good is adduced in the general good feeling of chat and merriment by meeting together as by the former.

Being a <u>sober-minded</u> individual I have given this moral to your doings, while you, upon the contrary, are much puzzled to know how Miss Lizzie Brinckerhoff, Miss Adriance, and a numerous host of your acquaintances have turned sewing Societies into such good account. I am afraid you are getting to be such a fastidious individual in matters of that <u>sort</u> that unless a person can wear a parson's gown, a professor of medicine, or that of law, he need not appear at <u>court</u>. I hope to speak a word for those gallants at Hopewell and

Gayhead, members of my profession (not my present one), and am very sorry their attentions have not been appreciated heretofore.

Engaged in active life, isolated from the world, I have little thought how my cherished idols one by one have eluded my grasp. But then to console my thoughts under such great misfortunes, my companion the rheumatism, suggests the query: how is he to be accommodated if taken into the concern? Having added bad to worse by being absent I am resigned to my lot, but if you can find anyone to take care of a rheumatic (young) old man, just such a one would suit me, if any.

You have heard all the war news by the papers and I will not write you about it. I expect some of your letters are now on the way for me, I hope. Mother writes me that you have been spending some time at Dr. Kip's as company to Miss Sarah. It must be lonesome at that house now, so many have gone. And perhaps, before this reaches you, you may be in 47th Street, as I have not heard from home since the 14th. If so, remember me to Van Wyck and ask him to write me. With much love I remain your afft. Cousin

R. T. Van Wyck

Goldsboro, N. C.
April 3rd, 1865

Dear Mother,

Your weekly letters come in irregular, that is, the first last. I am thankful to receive them. There seems in camp great talk about peace just now, particularly the move made in Rebel Congress, relative to the report of Lee, about the condition of the [Rebel] army and also the report of the peace commissioners to Washington. I hope something will be effected by them, to accept the Union as it is. I believe the war is kept alive by the officials at Richmond, particularly by Jeff[erson Davis], who is reluctant to abandon his situation, which in the event of the failure of the C. S. A., he will be little thought of by his own people.

At any rate, it admits a great deal, and stimulates the spirits of troops wonderfully by admitting the weakness of the enemy and their inability to resist us at all points. Upon the other hand it reveals to the Southern army their own situation and who are now waiting for their own government to act in the matter, their failure to do so will only devolve upon the army to give themselves up and go to their homes, and thus settle the matter which could be done honorable at Richmond.

Our army here is undergoing considerable change preparatory to going into another campaign. The three divisions, right, left, and center, have two Corps each. The right consist of the 15th and 17th Corps under Howard. The left 14th and 20th Corps under Slocum. The center 23rd and 24th Corps under Schofield—so reported. Our own Corps suffers a change in command, also our Division. We do not know how long we shall remain here, or where or in what direction we shall go, but as the Rebel army under Johnston is intrenched at Raleigh we might possibly go in that direction.

We get abundant supplies, and by Gen. order shall have all the food the rich granaries of the North can bestow. But we are excited to hear what the Rebs are inclined to do, the papers (late and daily) come very irregular, and when one is received it goes the round of the Brigade. We still are very incredulous, so much has been said about peace almost upon first entering into the service that we now only look to the expiration of our time, thinking little of the result of our service, which must to your mind seem almost the end of the war. I hope and pray it might be as near as [Confederate] Vice President Stephens says, that is, will take place before the 1st of May.

We are getting over our troubles of sore bones, etc., after resting, washing, and getting clean clothes, and begin to drop into the monotony of camp life again.* How it must sound to you to say "the luxury of clean clothes," but with us it is a common expression.

I look for the mail which comes promptly, to see if it gives me something besides camp matters to think about. If the trees overhead were other than Pine I could tell you how far advanced the season is. But upon the 20th of last month the Peach trees were in blossom, and the winter grain growing fast and looked splendid. Since leaving Savannah we have met nothing but Pine forests, except here and there an area of corn land, then travel into the forest for miles.

---

* Sherman's army had fewer illnesses than all other Union troops, and while his men reached Goldsboro tattered and weary, they were found to be in exemplary physical condition, fit and healthy, and some even had gained weight.

The 150th N.Y. Vols.'s casualties in the Civil War were 108: 46 men killed in battle and 62 died from disease. *History of Dutchess County*, op. cit., p 197.

In Nor. Car. we were almost sure to wade a swamp between each Plantation. But one section of country was <u>hilly</u> (that was near Winnsboro, S. C.), the rest of our travel so level that one hill as steep as that one at the White Bridge a curiosity. Such a one we found near Columbia. I could say a great deal about Southern soil, but it is enough to say that all of it would not equal the State of Ohio or Illinois.

I have understood J. Montross has received a furlough to go home from Nashville. He seems very fortunate in that respect. I don't suppose we will see him in the field again. He will manage to put his time in, at Nashville Hospital.

With much love to all, I remain your afft. Son

R. T. Van Wyck

Special Field Orders No. 54

Headquarters Military Division of the Mississippi
In the Field, Smithfield, North Carolina, April 12, 1865

The general commanding announces to the army that he has official notice from General Grant that General Lee surrendered to him his entire army on the 9th inst., at Appomattox Court-House, Virginia.

Glory to God and our country, and all honor to our comrades in arms, toward whom we are marching!

A little more labor, a little more toil on our part, the great race is won, and our Government stands regenerated, after four long years of war.

W. T. Sherman, Major-General Commanding

(Letter in pencil; very faded)

Raleigh, N. C.
April 15th '65

Dear Mother,

I reached here from Goldsboro the 13th, leaving on the 10th. We found the city evacuated by Johnston, who is making his way West. I fear we will have to follow him, and he has got such a good pair of legs our chances are uncertain to intercept him this side of Georgia. I have been told our next communication will be the Savannah River (a little north of the old rought [*sic*] last Spring).

The Bummers have been organized again. We received the news of Lee's surrender the 10th. I suppose you think the war is over. I suppose the hard knocks are done with, but we will be obliged to follow the remnant of the enemy, like so many hounds, from one state to another.

I did not suppose I could send a letter through, but I think now the R.R. is open to Weldon and also to Goldsboro. We made a start this morning, but we were ordered back. I hope we will not have to go.

I am in good health (first-rate). Weather has been fine, warm, and the country is decidedly the most fertile part of the State, and looks splendid.

With much love I remain your aft. Son

R. T. Van Wyck

Special Field Orders, No. 56*

Headquarters Military Division of the Mississippi,
In the Field, Raleigh, North Carolina, April 17, 1865.

[*Gen. Sherman*] announces, with pain and sorrow, that on the evening of the 14th instant, at the theatre in Washington city his Excellency the President of the United States, Mr. Lincoln, was assassinated by one who uttered the State motto of Virginia. At the same time, the Secretary of State, Mr. Seward, while suffering from a broken arm, was also stabbed by another murderer in his own house, but still survives, and his son was wounded, supposed fatally. It is believed, by persons capable of judging, that other high officers were designed to share the same fate. Thus it seems that our enemy, despairing of meeting us in open, manly warfare, begins to resort to the assassin's tools.

Your general does not wish you to infer that this is universal, for he knows that the great mass of the Confederate army would scorn

---

* *Memoirs*, op. cit., p. 351.

to sanction such acts, but he believes it the legitimate [*inevitable*] consequence of rebellion against rightful authority.

We have met every phase which this war has assumed, and must now be prepared for it in its last and worst shape, that of assassins and guerrillas; but woe unto the people who seek to expend their wild passions in such a manner, for there is but one dread result!

By order of Major-General W. T. Sherman,

L. M. Dayton, Assistant Adjutant-General

EDITOR'S NOTE:

On April 17, Gen. Sherman had been on the point of leaving Raleigh by train to discuss surrender terms with Gen. Johnston when he was handed a decoded wire from Washington informing him of President Lincoln's assassination. He had immediately sworn the telegrapher to secrecy, fearful that the news would leak out before surrender could be effected, inflaming the Union army to incendiary acts and causing the breakup of Johnston's army into rebel guerrilla forces which would ruin all chances for the restoration of the Union.

Gen. Johnston was equally devastated by the news. "Mr. Lincoln was the best friend the Confederacy ever had," he said, calling the assassination "the greatest possible calamity for the South."

On his return that evening Gen. Sherman was extremely careful in breaking the news to his army. First he had the streets of Raleigh cleared of all soldiers, ordering them back to their regimental camps, and on informing them of the dire news he explicitly exonerated the Confederate army of any hand in the affair in order to keep tempers cool. During the following suspenseful hours he and his officers kept a close watch on the troops until the danger of any spontaneous retaliation had passed. *Sherman: Fighting Prophet, op. cit.*, pp. 534-537.

(Letter in pencil)

Raleigh, N. C.
April 18th, 1865

Dear Mother,

My last letter upon the 14th, at which time I thought of a forward movement in the direction of Hillsboro directly west from here, would be the next step. But here we are yet. Johnston has been reported to have surrendered, his communications west are cut by Stoneman. We started in pursuit of him, but the order being countermanded, we concluded that negotiations are passing between him and Sherman as to the surrender, and looking forward every moment to that result.

We received the painful news of the <u>Murder</u> of President Lincoln and Seward, and were it not an official communication to Sherman from the War Department, would not believe it. After having fought these traitors in fair fight and in every phase, we will undoubtedly have to meet them as guerrillas and assassins, but woe to them in the latter. The country cannot have its cup of pleasure in view of the end of the war unalloyed. God, having preserved him to us, and brought about the wishes of every patriot, has thus taken him away. I do hope his successor, the Vice President, will do honor to the position.

I do hope we can be mustered out of the service soon. We all expect it. I never saw quite as happy a set [*sight?*] as a number of rebel Prisoners in our hands who expected to go home, too.

The city is half the size of Po'keepsie, has a State house, an Insane Asylum, and an asylum for the deaf and dum [*sic*]. It is well laid out and has been a quiet inland city, inferior to Atlanta in size and business. How long we shall remain here I do not know, but I hope the next move will be for <u>home</u>.

We are anxious for a mail. Will get one as soon as R.R. is in order to Goldsboro. With much love I remain your Aft. Son

R. T. Van Wyck

(Letter in pencil)

Raleigh, N. C.
April 19th, 1865

Dear Father,

I received yours of Apr. 3rd, also one from Mother of the 5th. Enclosed I found $20 dollars. With the same mail a package containing my hat also arrived. The shirts sent by express have not reached me. If I come within reach of the express agencies I may get them, but never mind. I am not in pressing need of them at present.

They say "negotiations are still pending between Johnston and Sherman." We remain still the same. No steps are taken to lay out a camp, but remain almost the same as when we settled down the first night one week ago. So from that we hardly expect to go farther into the interior.

The weather has been splendid, trees in full leaf. Hundreds of acres of corn planted just coming up is left with no one to take care of [*them*]. The Rebs conscripted all the men, and Sherman frightened the remainder away. As a general thing we found agriculture, although of different style than with you, much better than in Georgia and in Tennessee. The soil where it is rich and fertile becomes with their management highly productive. The grapes do not flourish here as they do north, and when a field becomes exhausted it is not turned over to grass but returns to forest again. Farther north in Tenn. they have not that difficulty, but the grapes flourish.

I am glad Uncle Anthony is being appreciated and is to open a law office. I am sure he will succeed. I am hoping today's mail will bring some news of the assassination at Washington. I have been hoping it would turn out a false rumor. I will write soon again.

With much love I remain your aff. Son
R. T. Van Wyck

(Letter in pencil)

Raleigh, N. C.
April 21st, 1865

Dear Mother,

I received yours of the 11th today. You have had heretofore the advantage of me in getting informed of captures, surrenders, and possibly of the final suspension of hostilities with a view to Peace from the Potomac to the Rio Grande. But yet the end is at hand, and although we have hurrahed ourselves hoarse, as step by step we have neared the end of bloodshed and battle—still the all-absorbing and important subject is how soon will we go home. We ought to be content to rest upon our laurels for the summer, with no dread prospects of a fight ahead and with a fair prospect of getting home with whole bones, but then a restless spirit seems to pervade the whole army of volunteers—and I am sure it is infectious for I have taken the malady badly. Your letter does not help me a mite.

We are waiting the return of General Cox (messenger from Gen. Sherman) from Washington, then we can guess how soon we will get home. The army is not as economical as last Winter, and if they are possessed with a passion to lessen expenses they cannot do it much better than to let us go.

I cannot realize it is all over, and will not till I get home again. With much love I remain your Aft. Son

R. T. Van Wyck

(Letter in pencil)

In the Field, 17 miles
West of Raleigh, N. C.
April 26th, 1865

Dear Mother,

We left our camp yesterday morning and are here today. It is one of the incomprehensible acts of this drama. It is reported that the proposal of Johnston's surrender having been rejected and none but unconditional surrender accepted. Still again, there are negotiations still pending between Grant and Sherman with Johnston, that to enforce the claims of their demands we have moved to within striking distance. We little expected to move in this direction, but were conjecturing whether the old sort of transportations home would be taken (that is, "leather"), or by transports and R. R. As a mail goes out this morning I conclude we will not go far in this direction, for if we follow Johnston we have got to be <u>fast</u>.

Just one year ago today I left Normandy, Tenn. We have made a good trail through the Southern states and marched many hundred miles. Another hundred miles or two will complete the circuit and end my three years' tour. I wouldn't recommend the route for one will see the country now with unfavorable circumstances (South Carolina and Georgia).

We are fearful another line of policy will be adopted by the President now. We attribute this rejection of the Surrender of the Confederate States Government due alone to [*President*] Andrew Johnson. It may not be, however, but only the expression of the public sentiment North. We are looking anxiously for something to turn up. I remain with much love your aft. Son

R. T. Van Wyck

EDITOR'S NOTE:

When he met with Gen. Johnston to draw up surrender terms, Gen. Sherman ended up granting concessions that were far too sweeping. He felt he was offering the peace of reconciliation that President Lincoln had wanted. Secretary of War Stanton, who wanted harsh terms for the defeated South, rejected this armistice in such a manner that it caused a public furor over Sherman's motives, for which Sherman never forgave him.

General Grant urged him to offer Johnston more limited terms; this truce was duly signed on April 26. Thus Sherman, whose troops had ravaged the

Southland, imperiled his career in his effort to befriend the South after the war, seeking its reconciliation with the Union.

A few weeks later he wrote to a friend at the U.S.Sanitation Commission: "...I have always desired that strife should cease at the earliest possible moment. I confess without shame I am sick and tired of fighting. Its glory is all moonshine; even success the most brilliant is over dead and mangled bodies...[*and*] the anguish and lamentation of distant families...

"...And, so far as I know, all the fighting men of our army want peace, and it is only those who have never heard a shot, never heard the shrieks and groans of the wounded (friend or foe), that cry aloud for more blood, more vengeance, more desolation..."*

(Letter in pencil)

Washington, D. C., or
Bladensburgh[*sic*], Maryland
May 25th, 1865

Dear Mother,

I think I have not acknowledged the receipt of two of your letters, both of last month. I have been quite negligent in this respect and have been too sanguine of throwing down the pen, hoping to be with you at an early period. But then abundant opportunity will ensue before that happy time will arrive (probably ten days), and yours will be received.

I saw T. Van Wyck, Polhemus Van Wyck, and <u>son</u> of T. Polhemus, also Theodore, son of L. Van Wyck yesterday. They came to Washington to see the view of Meade's and Sherman's armies. They could not recognize me when the 150th passed the White House, but came to camp towards evening.

I was delighted to see them, I assure you. I was wondering while passing through the city and glancing down the dense throng of citizens, if there was any that I could give a good hearty shake of the hand to. They have some idea of our army by this time if they viewed the procession throughout. They were very anxious to know the manner of attacks and advances, and it gave me pleasure to inform them, although time passed so rapidly I had little time for home inquiries, etc. Van Wyck Brinckerhoff lost his wife – how sudden and how great an affliction it must be for him.

---

* *Sherman and His Campaigns*, by S.M. Bowman and R.B. Irwin, New York, 1865.

The box of Jacob's that he talked over, sighed after, and continually wished for so long and anxiously at Atlanta arrived at camp a few days ago, being delivered by the express co. to the Reg't to dispose of. Geo Burroughs and myself took possession of it and found few articles in a damaged state (cheese, rice, and half a dozen biscuits only). We daily commiserate with Jacob in his unfortunate absence and thank our own good fortune that here we are partakers of his bounty. I assure you <u>such</u> food isn't hard to take.

We hope we have pitched our tents (for a regular camp) the last time. We are five miles from Washington on the Baltimore and Wash. R. R. and hope we will get transportation when our time comes. How soon that will be I don't know.

I have some money now, but if we should stay here will need some. Send me five dollars. I will receive it if sent immediately by return of mails. Love to all from your aft. Son

R. T. Van Wyck

EDITOR'S NOTE:

A Victory celebration was held on May 23 and 24, 1865, in the form of a two-day Grand Review of the Union Army.

General Sherman was concerned about how his battle-worn veterans would look in comparison to the spit-and-polish troops of the Army of the Potomac, renowned for their close-order marching, practiced to perfection during the eight-month stalemate between Gen. Grant's and Gen. Lee's armies at Richmond, while the rough-and-ready Westerners who had fought their way through a thousand miles of treacherous swamp, thicket and piney woods, had not had time for any drilling in over a year. Besides, their blue uniforms were faded, their hair long and their beards unkempt, they wore dashing slouched hats, and their boots were worn and dull.

On the first day of the Grand Review the crowd responded wildly to the smart-stepping smartly uniformed Army of the Potomac, giving General Meade a thunderous ovation. But General Sherman need not have worried. When his Westerners swung down the avenue the next day with their "proud, rolling swagger," they took the crowds by storm. Each division was preceded by its corps of Negro "pioneers" armed with their picks and shovels, keeping perfect step. When Sherman's lean, weather-beaten veterans appeared, all skin and bone and muscle under their bullet-torn flags, draped now with flowers, followed by their war-riddled ambulance corps, and then by assemblages of Negro camp followers on mule-drawn wagons strung with pots and pans and hams and chickens, they presented so vivid a picture of their bitterly won campaign through the heart of the Southland that they stole the show.*

And then—it was noted by thoughtful observers—this great army, which could have made the world tremble, suddenly evaporated. The soldiers turned in their arms and dispersed, melting into the countryside as they returned to their homes and families, and the army was no more.

> Bladensburg, Maryland
> Camp of the 150th N. Y. Vols.
> June 1st, 1865

Dear Mother,

I suppose you are daily expecting my <u>arrival</u> at home inasmuch as no letters have been received of very recent date. I didn't suppose so long a time would elapse before the realization of that blissful event, but our incompetent and neglectful officers are dragging through this allott[*ment*] business to settle up every individual account prior to the muster out of the Regimental organization, and it seems to me from this progress so far that a week or more will be consumed before the muster out will be accomplished, to say nothing if delayed by transportation, here or on the way.

But then we live better than at any camp since being in the service and ought to enjoy ourselves much better than at any other period. The privilege to visit the City of Washington has generally been embraced by most of the troops, no papers being required. But after today applications to visit the city has to go through the <u>long list</u> of Brig. Gen. and Maj. Gen. for their approval. It is curious to hear the comments of the <u>men</u> upon the Public Buildings. They have never seen the like of them before. Since the grand review of the Army the papers have been very meager of interesting items. Sherman's official letter to Grant will set matters in a better light with the Southern people. I hope it will have a good effect. I may have the opportunity to write home again.

I remain with much love your afft. Son

> R. T. Van Wyck

---

* *The Civil War: Red River to Appomattox,* by Shelby Foote, N.Y., 1974, pp. 1015-1017, and *Memoirs, op. cit.*

Camp 150th N. Y. Vols.

near Washington or Bladensburg, Md.
June 3rd, 1865

Dear Mother,

I am induced to write once again to acknowledge the $5.00 and also the letter from Uncle Anthony.

In anticipation of the return of the 150th a great fuss is being made to receive the "brave heroes." I hope they will not inflict so great an imposition upon good nature that they must have us paraded through the streets of Po'keepsie.

Well, in speaking for myself, I speak for every enlisted man, that they wish to get quietly to their homes at the earliest practicable moment. Were it not that payment is to be made upon our arrival, I would despair that the 150th would reach that place as an organization. We will get home next week, anyhow.

As it will be uncertain at what moment we will start I don't see how the committee of arrangement will organize their forces of fire companies, etc., upon such short notice. I should not wonder that a day will be set apart for such celebration, if so, a favorable opportunity will occur for this member to avoid that performance.

With much love I remain your afft Son

R. T. Van Wyck

Written in pencil on the envelope by his mother:
"The last letter received. The writer arrived home the 10th of June, 1865, on Saturday evening, well in mind and body."

A final postscript:

Kenosha, Wisc., Dec. 7th, 1865

Richard T. Van Wyck, Esq.
My Dr. Nephew,

I owe you an apology for my long delay in thanking you for your Photograph and for the Book you sent me. The first was especially gratifying, even without the War "tan" and the last has been as pleasant as anything could be next to your own letters, which are yet to me more valuable.

Let me urge you again to make memoranda, if you have not yet done so, of your journeys and Campaigns. You have been nobly associated with some of the most interesting events of this great War—by far the most important event of our age, and in future years it will be very interesting to refer to many incidents which in time you will forget. Now is the time to record them.

You have had a fine rest—a pleasant summer, and now for the next campaign. What is it to be? Sherman's boys don't rest long. What about the future? I was gratified to learn from your father a few days since that he was making arrangements to give you the Brinckerhoff Farm. Should this be decided on, you are doubtless preparing for its charge.

Were it not rather inquisitive I might inquire if the female department had been provided for? If there are no young girls left in Dutchess I can assure you there are some very good and attractive ones in Wisconsin – "noteworthy observation" before final choice. So come and see.

We are all well. This is Thanksgiving and very pleasant in every respect but the absence of one's kin. We have remembered among the mercies of the year your own safe return. It was often my prayer for you, Dear Richard, when you were on that long and terrible Campaign before Atlanta, that you might be spared by God, and that by lifelong devotion to His cause, you might attest your gratitude for His guardian care. Life is short, Dear Richard. Let us do what we can without delay.

I hope to hear from you as often as you can write. With much love to your father and mother, and warmest interest in your happiness,

Very affectionately,
Anthony Van Wyck

P. S. Please ask your father if Bentley sent him any money the 1st of December as agreed?

Two years later, on October 3, 1867,
Richard T. Van Wyck and Sarah Van Vechten were married.

A clipping from a New York newspaper carefully preserved in R. T. Van Wyck's copy of "General Sherman's Memoirs":

RECEPTION TO GENERAL SHERMAN

Nearly Four Thousand Veterans Pay Their Respects to the Late Head of the Army

In the Bowery near Houston Street, under the Germania Assembly Rooms, is the hall of Koltes Post, Grand Army of the Republic. Last evening 2,000 men in uniform of the Grand Army crowded the hall and the passageways leading to it, and in their midst stood the victor of many a hard-fought battle, William Tecumseh Sherman. General Barnum, in the name of the Grand Army, welcomed the General. As Gen. Sherman turned to reply, 2,000 voices were raised in one wild shout of welcome that shook the rafters and drowned the music of the band playing some old war song. As the General looked over the faces of those veterans and heard that shout, his eyes flashed brightly beneath the bushy eyebrows, the color mounted to his cheeks and he stood erect and straight as an arrow. When the enthusiasm had subsided the General said:

"I am always glad to meet soldiers. In other days I commanded you, but now you command me. Since those years in which we fought together, I have traveled over many parts of this country and have seen its growing greatness. I have seen towns, where but a few years ago there was only an adobe hut on a barren waste, which now have their electric lights and their Grand Army Posts. And in the places I have found that the Grand Army men were the judges, the prominent men and the successful men of business. The Grand Army has done a great work and I believe that since the war closed, since those old days of marching, countermarching, you have more than payed the country back in civilization alone for the $13 a month you used to draw. You and I have fought the same battles. We fought the same battles at Chattanooga and at Atlanta and we are fighting the same battles now. The battle of right against wrong, the battle of intelligence against ignorance, the battle of progress and of destiny. Wherever and whenever I hear that soldiers wish me to be with them, that wish is my law. I can no longer command you but you can always command me."

This speech was not delivered without frequent interruptions. At almost every sentence applause and hurrahs broke forth. These outbursts would be succeeded by intervals of almost breathless silence, the soldiers listening with the closest attention to every word that fell from the lips of their beloved General. At the close of the speech the band struck up "Marching Through Georgia," and in a second everyone was singing it. Then General Barnum raised his hand and said, "Comrade Tums will sing 'Marching Through Georgia,' and we and the band will join in the chorus." Mr. Tums sang the song and after every verse the chorus rang out: "Hurrah, hurrah, we bring the jubilee!"

At its close Gen. Barnum said: "We had intended to hire a larger hall and make a more formal affair of this reception, but General Sherman said no. He wanted to come down here where he could be with the boys." "Hurrah for the General!" shouted someone, and three such cheers were given as that hall never heard before. "I wish," continued Gen. Barnum, "that I could remember that other "Marching Through Georgia," which goes:

> Proud, proud, was our army that morning
> That stood by the cypress and vine,
> When Sherman says, "boys, you are weary,
> This day fair Savannah is mine!"
> Then sang we a song for our chieftain
> That echoed o'er river and lea
> And the stars in our banner shone brighter
> For Sherman had marched to the sea.

The veterans then thronged around General Sherman and shook him by the hand. Another Post, with drums beating and flags unfurled now marched into the hall, out of which those who had already paid their respects to the General passed. So, all the evening, veterans of the Grand Army came and went, until nearly 4,000 men had paid their respects to General Sherman.

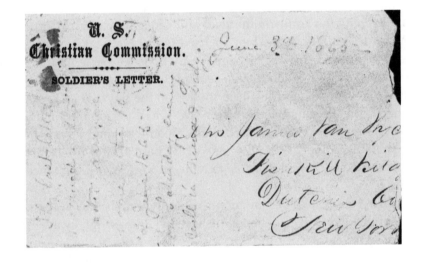

The faded inscription in pencil, written by Richard T. Van
Wyck's mother reads, "June 3d 1865-The last letter received.
The writer arrived home the 10th of June 1865 on Saturday
evening, well in mind & body." *Collection of the East Fishkill
Historical Society.*

Epilogue

Richard Thorne Van Wyck was born on August 5, 1838, on a farm of his ancestors in a hamlet in East Fishkill, New York. His forebears came from Utrecht, Holland, in the 1600s and settled on Long Island; later, in 1736, two grandsons of Cornelius Barentse Van Wyck established themselves in Dutchess County in the mid-Hudson valley.

His father, James Van Wyck, was a farmer, a graduate of the Polytechnic Institute in Chittenango, New York, a noted school in those days. It was said of him that "one saw the excellence of his character the more closely one became acquainted with him; it manifested itself not only in clear words and eloquence of speech, but in his kindness and gentleness of manner which made you feel he was a friend of God and of man."

James rebuilt the family homestead and brought his bride, Cornelia Ann Van Wyck, there. She died when Richard was three, and he and his older brother, Aben, were cared for by the family housekeeper until their father's remarriage eight years later. His second wife, Elizabeth Van Brunt of Brooklyn, New York, became a true mother to the boys. The family records say of her, "This excellent and amiable wife was a person of rare ability and unusual accomplishments, and a cordial welcome awaited those who visited their hospitable home." From the tone of Richard's letter to her there is no doubt in the reader's mind of her beneficent and loving influence on her stepsons.

Richard Van Wyck lived in an era when the family was at the center of most people's lives, even when kith and kin moved far away. Richard's brother, Aben, had moved to New York City to work at the law and ended up pursuing a career as a minister in Michigan. His uncle, Judge Anthony Van Wyck, had in his youth journeyed by horseback from New York to Alabama. Later, for reasons of health, he spent four years in Europe, and thereafter lived the remainder of his life in Wisconsin, interrupted by a sojourn in Marietta, Georgia.

But these outlanders seldom lost touch with their home towns and their families, and distance was no insurmountable obstacle to long visits. At the heart of familial continuity there is often a dominant figure to provide a focal point, such as the old General Abraham Van Wyck, Richard's grandfather who, as a boy, had known George Washington; or an exceptionally warm-hearted and concerned person such as his Uncle Anthony, or A. Van Wyck Van Vechten, his cousin, who is credited with having a special talent for friendship, or Richard's stepmother, whose abiding concern for the family is reflected by Richard's responses to her letters.

When the war was over, Richard returned to his farm in Dutchess County and two years later he married Sarah Van Vechten on October 3, 1867, the anniversary of his father's marriage to his stepmother. For their honeymoon Richard took his bride on a pilgrimage to the battlefields of Gettysburg, now silent and at peace. Sarah bore him five children, of whom only the eldest, James, and the youngest, Edith, survived into maturity. Two, Louisa and Richard, died in infancy. A fourth child, Samuel, showed such keen interest in his father's war service that his parents took him to Gettysburg when he was thirteen. He died two years later, in May of 1892.

Earlier that year Richard T. Van Wyck suddenly became ill and died on January 2, 1892 at the age of fifty-three. He and Sarah had been married for nearly twenty-five years. His wife said of him: "He was well qualified to enter into public life, but was naturally reserved, disliking all efforts on the part of others to bring him into prominence. Born with high religious principles, together with a high sense of honor and the courage of his convictions, he won the confidence of all with whom he came into contact." His fellow soldiers remembered him as a man who went out of his way to be kind and encouraging to his comrades.

The following is taken from his obituary in the *Fishkill Journal* of January 6, 1892:

> The death of Richard T. Van Wyck was learned with profound sorrow on Sunday morning.
>
> Mr. Van Wyck was a successful farmer and fruit grower near Johnsville in the town of East Fishkill. In October last the family moved to Fishkill Landing for the winter for the purpose of being nearer the schools [for his children]. Mr. Van Wyck occupied the Hall place, and it was there he died from pneumonia on Saturday evening at 6 o'clock.
>
> His death was a shock to the community. He was highly esteemed in his native town and he will be greatly missed. Words are inadequate to console the afflicted family in their deep grief, so sudden was the end of the head of the household.
>
> A veteran of the war for the Union, he enlisted for three years in the 150th Regiment in 1862, going from private to First Lieutenant. A man of quiet turn,

> he seldom talked of his war record except when he
> was with some of his old war comrades, but he used
> his time and influence in recruiting for his regimental
> company in his town and was successful in getting a
> number to enlist.

The fact of his recruiting for his old regiment is evidence of the pride he took in his war service. The veterans of General Sherman's campaign knew well that they had been part of a remarkable army which had accomplished a great and terrible work.

His men rightly felt that only Sherman's Army, so ably prepared and so bold in execution, could have undertaken this excoriating task of attrition. After they returned to their ordinary lives and after the horrors of war had dimmed, the fact that they had intrepidly served their country at a fateful time in its destiny remained for the men of Sherman's Army a shining thread in the somber tapestry of the Civil War.

V.H.K.

Po'keepsie Oct. 10, 1862

Dr Father

"By politeness of Alexander Bartow" I will write you that we will leave tomorrow at 2 o'clock. I have been staying at the Gregory House and am somewhat privileged to do so, but it will not last long. I have been thinking of meeting the regement [sic] at N.Y. or Baltimore. I have not decided on whether I can do so. Jacob G. Montross* is now with us and is very pleased with the arrangements. He has asked for no position; but we are expecting a change as quick as we get to our destination.

I am in hope of seeing Mother in N.Y. if possible. I saw [Rev.] Mr. Woodhull** on Thursday and several of Fishkill freinds. I believe there is nothing I want from home with the exception of that brandy, but I can possibly make up for the deficiency in N.Y. I am glad we are going so soon. I will write you as soon as I get to our place of destination. Much love to all

from your afft son
R. T. Van Wyck

P.S. I shall possibly take my citizen's clothes with me.

Baltimore November 7, 1862

Dear Father

I have just returned from guard duty down in Baltimore. Guarding the Conscrips [sic] for the County of Maryland. Leaving here last Monday night and returning here last night. The winter has come upon [us] in earnest just now. Last evening cold and wintry and near morning it commenced snowing, which at the present time has acquired the depth of three inches. This seems to make camp life very uncomfortable, and corre-spondence a somewhat difficult undertaking on account of the state of one's fingers.

The irregular quartermaster's stores....has impaired my funds to an extent connect-ed with sums advanced or loaned to certain parties, and I am obliged to ask for rein-forcements to the amount of fifteen or twenty dollars. In view of being called off again and out of reach of the items allowed us, there being no alternative but to make it up by private purse.

I am in hopes the Regt. will take quarters in some barrack and I will endeavor to get one of the camp stoves in use here. An extra blanket would not come amiss now. We were mustered the 1st for payment but how soon it will be made I don't know. There is so much ceremony to go through that the present use of it is very desirable. In the future I will husband it better if I can.

J. G. Montross is on the sick list, not very bad, however. I think he is sick of this life. He finds it extremely difficult to satisfy his appetite. He will see worse times to come. Give my love to all, from your son,

R. T. Van Wyck

Camp Belcher [sic] Bal. M. D.
Nov. 14, 1862

Dr. Father

I received your letter yesterday. I hope it did not inconvenience you upon the call for that money. I will let the blanket remain till we go into Buildings. As I was about writing you I had received a call from John Pudney,*** now living in the city here.

---

* A friend from the hamlet of Johnsville [now Wiccopee].
** Former pastor of the Presbyterian Church at nearby Brinckerhoff.
*** A neighbor at home.

Accidentally Jacob G. Montross met him in the street and of course introduced himself yesterday. Whereupon he immediately called here this morning and invited us to spend the evening with him. I shall avail myself, once more, of making a call and glad of the opportunity. He knew the Captain and I hope we shall see him often. He says he has been living here since Oct. His business is the trunk & India Rubber Store. He is the first acquaintance I have met since I have been out.

You have possibly heard of our removal to this present Camp. It possesses great advantages over our former one. And still our present quarters are far superior to the majority of Regts. in the surrounding [area].

The political aspect of the country is very disheartening to a firm basis of government in the future; but is felt here as an indication of a speedy termination of the controversy by a recognition of the Southern Confederacy and a Compromise Act. This winter will surely decide the matter.

I have received a letter from Aben* and also from Uncle Anthony. The former is much better settled than formerly, and the latter is burdened with cares and his mind much distressed. He is exempt from draft, I suppose. If not it will go hard with him. He cannot stand the exposure should he go, and substitutes are hard to find if he felt disposed to get one. No one should be obliged to go under such circumstances. I hope Robt. Johnston will get an exempt. Rachel, I hope, is well and should you see her, tell [her] I called to see her before I left but she had not returned from her visit. Remember me to all. Tell Bray I would not advise him either way, to come here or remain where he is. If he is positive he will be drafted he is better off here. I believe Jacob G. Montross has written to him about it. Having answered Mother's letter, you know my situation here

From your Son
R. T. Van Wyck

Mother in her last letter revived my attachment to that horse. If you have not sold him I was foolish in thinking of selling him.

Baltimore Nov. 28, 1862

Dear Mother

Excuse the above display in a letter like this. But thinking the representation of the grounds and camp of the above regiment is almost similar, it will give you a good idea of our present situation. You will notice Co. K street, to the right of the encampment, and our tent to the right of the street, the first one. You also see the commissary and sutler's buildings upon the right and the hospitals upon the left; while to the rear, out of view, are the cook houses. The barracks are in the rear of the tents, upon the highest elevation. The first row of tents in rear are the captains, Left[enants]. and in rear of those, the field and staff. The small tents in the distance are not placed in our encampment. The parade you see is a ceremony identical in every respect to ours, every day in the year. Usually the last duty of the day.

I received your letter today giving me an account of your keeping the 27th. It often surprises me how speedy the transit of letters. I thought of you often during the day. To me the Thanksgiven [sic] of [the] past year and the present one of 1862 are truly two different days. The first found me in Fishkill enjoying the society of friends, while the latter with its endless monotony, reminds me of the old fireside and abundant good things at home. However, for a wonder, we were left to ourselves during the forenoon, and in the afternoon blank shots were fired to get the boys used to the report, after which the

---

* Abraham Van Wyck, his older brother who had entered the ministry and was living in Michigan.

Chaplain addressed the Regt. There appears to be a great amount of practice in firing. There possibly might be some truth in the report you wrote me, in our destination to some southern part. But I am confident but few of the officers are knowing it. Capt. Scofield* is superintending the buildings together with a number of our company who are mechanics. This shows he would not interest himself in this enterprise, or would not be allowed to do it, if our departure is so close at hand. I am in favor of a speedy erection of the building, or to go to some warmer climate. I have attempted to do some writing and was prevented by the climate. As it is, this evening, I can get along quite comfortable.

The prayer meeting for the week was held upon Thursday evening. Many a fervid prayer went up for an acknowledgment of our blessings, and a happy issue of this struggle upon which we are engaged. If we should leave I will give you timely notice, but need not feel at all anxious about it, for I am fearful it will not take place. Give my love to all from

Your Son   R. T. Van Wyck

P. S. I forgot to mention for Thanksgiven we had some delicious <u>Salt</u> <u>Pork.</u>

To his cousin A. Van Wyck Van Vechten

Camp Belger, Baltimore, Md
Sunday, Nov. 30th, 1862

Dear Van

As I was sitting in my tent this afternoon pondering upon your much-welcomed epistle, I thought from my last ill-directed letter that a prompt answer would not be objectionable. My tent fellows have not returned from Church at Baltimore and glad am I that I did not accompany them for I have been the recipient of four letters this afternoon. Beside, from the blissful silence which now reigns in tent, of such seldom occurrence, it is a pity it should go by without being improved. There is a little of duty upon Sabbath morning, but after inspection, we are excused from further duty during the day, except dress parade at 5 o'clock. Till then we voluntarily attend Church in Camp at Eleven, lasting an hour, after which we occupy the time as best suits us. Liberty is granted to attend Church down in the city, but I have not taken with it, for the reason our own service is not as well attended as it should be, and needs a better representation from our own Church-going people to make it popular or induce persons of no Church tendencies to attend. They say, "it's an ill wind that blows no one no good" and but for this I could not here have this privilege to thank you for your heart-stirring letter.

In your pursuit of business and your necessary knowledge of human nature, you see life in a station just above me, persons possessing all the polish, intelligence, and wickedness of the world and one of it. While here it is undisguised without the deception, without the interested guise of business, to sin. Why shouldn't it be so, or why shouldn't there be something to mar our enjoyment of temperal [*sic*] pleasure in the many great national blessings which we have formerly enjoyed, in the many pleasures of friends and friendly intercourse; in situations which our lot has not been cast, to combat with poverty or engulf us in riches - neither has affliction been at our door, and but for sin discoverable in every pursuit of life to make us miserable, we would not have those longings for a better and a just perception, and appreciation of it, by not striving after it.

To be sure, I was a little tinctured by ambition when I first entered. But when I found how happy I could make myself by the society of few about me, in this situation, I feel very much satisfied. Since I last wrote you we have moved camp to this place, called

---

* Captain John S. Scofield of Company K.

Camp Belger, in a grove four miles north of Baltimore. We are now erecting Barracks. Till they are ready for us, we will make the best of our tents to withstand the cold winds. So far so well, sleeping on the floor of our tent, quite as comfortable as softer pallets. We anticipate going into winter quarters here. Much love to your wife and family,

From your Cousin,   R. T. V. W.

P. S. Geo. Burroughs, Chas. Burroughs' son, is one of my tent fellows.

Camp Belger   Jan. 5th   [*1863*]

Dear Father

We have returned back to this place again. Arrived here Friday night. A pleasant excursion for New Year's it has been. Today (Monday) I am going with Major Smith to Washington to guard some convalescence [*sic*] soldiers back to their camp who have been in the hospitals at Baltimore.

I have a black frock dress coat home which if I could get you to take to Green's at Fishkill Landing, that he may alter and cut it down for a military coat, it would much oblige me. The coat, if he will be careful to preserve the coat front, that it may not be difficult to button up. Make it a little larger than would suit me when home, for I have heavy wollen [*sic*] clothes underneath. Besides, it was difficult to button then. He will no doubt know how to make the alteration. When he completes it, if he will enclose it in heavy hardware paper, and express it to Balt. The expense will not amount to over 50 cents. When I have time I will write more fully about my doings here. With much love to all, I remain your afft Son

R. T. Van Wyck

To Sarah E. Van Vechten with an enclosure of pressed leaves

Camp Belger, Jan 10th, '63

Dear Cousin

I inclose that relic I omitted in my previous letter.

Nothing has turned up interesting. We are looking for our pay on Monday next. This gives us opportunity to smooth some of the rough edges of camp diet. I remain your afft Cousin,   R. T. Van Wyck

Baltimore Jan 18th 1863

Dear Father

I received your letter the 16th and was surprised to hear that you had not heard from me in so long. But I hope by this time you have some idea of my whereabouts. When I last wrote you, I had taken up my quarters in the old building adjoining the hospital, and at the present time you will find me still there. It has not been as pleasant as expected, my not having the opportunity of having more than four hours off duty at a time to give me the pleasure of spending at the reading rooms, which was the great consideration of coming down.

But the license given and abuse of which that has made brutes instead of men of almost the whole number here, has induced me to get back again into my old quarters, which I expect to do in a few days. Nothing has transpired yet to give a coloring of transpiring events, and your letter informing me of the state of feeling politically, is too true in all circles, including the army in the field.

If you have not noticed it, you will find a very interesting letter in the *Times* of the 16th from its correspondent at Fredericksburg, whose company I had the pleasure of meeting on my way to Washington, he having been returning from a leaf [*sic*] of absence since the battle. I find from what I have ascertained that his account of the feeling in

Camp and among the people at Washington is too correct. It is to be hoped, however, that something will turn up in our favor before long. The army, suffering from the neglect of government to promptly pay the men, but which I have little reason to complain of, as we have received our pay up to the first of Nov. but not on the first of Jan., which has somewhat discommoded me. If you can send me fifteen or twenty dollars in Treasury funds, it will greatly oblige me.

The winter from accounts with you has been very mild; it has been very favorable for our duty and at times quite like Spring. Give my love to all, from your Son

R. T. Van Wyck

Baltimore Jan 21st, '63

Dear Mother

I thought I would answer your letter received today, at the Reading Rooms upon my being relieved from duty: but it is raining so hard just at present I would defer going.

No change has taken place since I last wrote you, except that I realize my privilege of going to the reading rooms at least five-sixths of my time, and with the exception of the noisy, uncomfortable sleeping and living quarters I would like my position very much, and would not desire a change. I have not yet decided which course to take, to remain here or return to camp. I have the power to do so.

The money Father sent me is very acceptable. Indeed, he quite anticipated my wants which I stated to him in my last letter, but this is quite sufficient for the present. I observe the changes death has made in our midst at home and elsewhere. I am happy to hear of Fred once more. He will undoubtedly like it much better now than formerly.

As I last wrote you upon my conversation with Allard Anthony, I saw him on his return from Washington again. He has imbibed the universal depression feeling toward the affairs of government. He says the despotic government of Jeff Davis is much better than Seymourism* in New York State.

I was for the first time since leaving home, in, and attended Church, last evening. How homelike and pleasant it appeared to me, you have but a faint idea. I think if I remain here I will in future improve the opportunity. Give my love to all at home,

from your Son   R. T. Van Wyck

Letter addressed to Mrs. James Van Wyck, no salutation.

Union Relief Rooms, Baltimore
Feb 23rd

I received your letter Saturday, but not having anything special to communicate I deferred writing till something turned up. I might make an incident of meeting a Fishkill friend or acquaintance (if such could be called) Chas. Varack, the grandson of Chas. Jackson, and the fortunate young gentleman who succeeded in getting a commission in the 1st N. Y. Mounted Rifles down at Suffolk.

As I was at the Norfolk boat[yard] Sunday morning upon tutching [sic] the pier, whom should I meet but Varack, leading or directing his horse ashore, and immediately made his acquaintance. He told me he was going to the Eutaw [?] house. After my return I went there. The circumstance of bringing his horse home attracted my attention, as to what purpose he could be leaving his command. From his story, he says he resigned on acct. of such hard duty enjoined upon him and getting tired enough of soldiering.

From the statement of one of the Regt. who knew him, says it was a forced

---

* Gov. Horatio Seymour of New York State was a Copperhead, i.e., an appeaser in favor of accommodating the Confederacy.

resignation; the reason, drunkenness and incapacity or incompetency–the prevailing misfortune in the army. He (Varack) gave me a windy account of the offers made him if he would only stay. That he could have the captaincy and finally upon the offer, of going upon the Staff of Gen. Dodge, (lately made a Gen. from a Col.) which he had not decided to accept as yet.

The truth of the Private's statement, time will show. He [Varack] went to Washington last night and will be at Fishkill during the week. His kindly offer of taking anything home for me makes me feel a conscientious ill treatment of him of telling you what he would want to conceal.

We have had a severe snow storm and now the streets are almost impassable. We are Brigaded, called the 3rd Maryland Brigade of the 8th Army Corps. What difference it will make with us, I do not know. The Gen. commanding is "Briggs." The boys are speculating upon the least suspicious action that is taken indicating a forward movement, supplying the want of consistency in all cases by vivid imagination. So it is not best to tell you of any of these news, etc.

I received a letter from Frank Kip yesterday. Isaac must have a nice time of it down in Louisianna [sic], the climate is so mild.

We will return back to camp positively in a week, or by the first of March. Fred is not opposed to the President's Proclamation,* is he? Love to all from   your afft. son
R. T. Van Wyck

Belger Barracks   Balt.
March 10th, 1863
Dear Mother

I received your letter yesterday, also one from Robt. Johnston giving me some outside gossip of the neighborhood which I was very much pleased to hear, together with his comment upon the times.

Tell Father I was over today to see Flora Temple,** that far-famed animal of race track notoriety, now owned by William McDowell who was suspected of seccession [sic] principles, which, from the cold civility we met with show that he is only a time-serving man. His grounds were very handsomely laid out, something like the residences on the [Hudson] River, and showed much luxury. The stables were very handsome and accommodated many said to be fast steeds, but did not suit my eye. I have revived my love of horses lately it seems, and you must excuse me for this diversion.

Tomorrow we are examined by Gen. Briggs, with what effect it will have I know not. Since my last, we have moved up to the Barracks, and the change is agreeable from the light duty, etc.

Belger Barracks, Balt.
March 19th, 1863
Dear Mother,

In reading an old magazine which says, "It is not necessary that every human being should soar: but then he must not clip his wings, " I was reminded forcibly of the construction given my non-acceptance of Sergeantcy [sic], which others commented so much upon. It is represented that "I am clipping my wings" to a commissioned office. I certainly at that time did not so regard it, but did it for the purpose of attaining it. Directly, it was the thing, but indirectly it would seem poor policy, and "my excuses rather

---

* The Emancipation Proclamation.
** A famous trotting horse.

frivolous." The captain's suggestion upon which I acted insured his endeavors to obtain for me the office lately vacant, but the odium for his antiquated notions among the young officers at headquarters failed to have any influence for me. His zeal to further my interests is unquestionable.

My blind indifference to the confirmed fact that all men are not honest, honorable, and upright [*did not help*], while my own diffidence does not make amends in toadyism to smooth over their dishonesty or want of faith, so common here. I regret my folly in being so communicative upon these things without giving them the full particulars. It will be a lesson for me in future to keep such affairs to myself. It is a difficult matter for one not interested in war matters to know how things are conducted, and what conscientious scruples would in one [*case*] and not [*in*] another [*help*] to obtain anything [*one*] sought. For instance, a liberal use of money would enable me to go on speedily and clear the road of many obstructions.

This has been a source of great disquietude to me since being in the army: to feel by some cause or other [*that*] it is expected of me to promote myself. I design to let things take their way and give myself no trouble about it. Not but what I feel very thankful that my friends are so solicitous for my welfare. I do not know what it might be – pride, the prevailing infirmity of this branch of the Van Wyck family, or the want of that successful qualification noted as "cheek."

However, if one in his course through this life receives a competence of all its enjoyments it does not follow that he should be thirsting for position and should be imbued with an unquenchable popular ambition, nor should he be groveling with the lowest because he is averse to competition, but the Robinson Crusoe idea of the extremes is mine: "Where with a happy contentment to choose between poverty and riches, one glides gently through life using but not abusing the many blessings which surround us."

Such views are out of place here, where everyone is expected to reap some reward for public service, as [*it is*] also safe for me to moralize now, for power is a great perverter of virtue or reason. Again I don't feel quite as patriotic as formerly, and the sanguine tendencies of public individuals, when much biased by their interests, [*make it*] extremely difficult with such conflicting opinions to judge how things will terminate.

That we have a higher power governing and controlling the course of events is a blessed assurance. And also, to each of us individually [*we have*] a Friend and Comforter, by whom we expect to be able to be made acceptable for that kingdom where the wicked cease from troubling, and the weary are at rest. May all those whom we so love at home meet there, too, is the prayer

of Your Afft.
Son
R. T. Van Wyck

To V. W. Van Vechten

Belger Barracks, Balt.
April 11, 1863

Dear Cousin,

Your letter I received today. So fine a position as an officer in Cavalry has been my "ne plus ultra" of military ambition. My notorious passion for horse flesh has always led me to think it would more accord with my habits, tastes, etc., than infantry: but there are some movements which I would have to inform myself upon. Confidence and aptness to learn are considered the essential qualifications: which [*in the former*] my past six months' experience has made me feel equal for any emergency; while in the latter I could not underrate myself and think I am the dullest.

I wouldn't decline any position, but if the Cavalry wants recruits I feel sanguine of doing my country some good in that capacity.

The Colonel suggested to me that if a letter of recommendation to any General, official, or to others would avail me, it is at my service. Besides, a Major Haynor [*Haynes?*] a staff officer of Gen. Schenck's formerly of Gen. Wool's staff, under whose command I was placed at the Union Relief, would cheerfully give me a recommendation to Gen. Wool, or to anyone that may seem fit. If these would have an influence, I will obtain them.

In the meanwhile, I await an answer, and if Cavalry is feasible I will try to post myself to enable me to pass the necessary instructions. Under great obligations to you I remain your

Aft. Cousin
R. T. Van Wyck

To Robert Johnston

Belger Barracks, Balt.
Apr. 11th, 1863

Dear Friend,

I received your letter today and [*it*] was truly welcomed. I admit I showed no soldierlike action in becoming disheartened by the course of events that savored of the adroitness and intrigue of politics. From this discovery I took measures to get a position in some other Regt. in some capacity as a Commissioned officer. In answer to inquiries from Allard Anthony and Van Wyck V. V. in New York I have been much encouraged with [*the*] feasibility of the undertaking, particularly if the conscription is ordered.

Van Wyck V. V., whose acquaintance with military men in the city is somewhat extensive, wrote me today saying that "an opportunity might offer more readily in the Cavalry. How would that suit you? You would be obliged to pass some instructions – perhaps."

Upon which I wrote him that Cavalry had been my "hobby," although in infantry I was better informed, but if there should be a likelihood of getting one, which he will write me [*about*], why, I will post myself in the theory, and endeavor to pass the instructions. I am getting more "brass" than formerly and will use a little of it.

As to the draft, everything is in the dark as yet. When anything I can do in that way by influence with Governor Seymour or with the Secretary of War I [*will*] have everything ready as soon as the appointing power is known.

I wrote to Van Wyck that I could obtain some excellent recommendations from Col. Ketchan and Major Haynes [*Haynor?*], staff officer of General Schenck, to such ones as he may seem fit.

I prefer the Cavalry service in many respects to infantry, but I will consider myself very fortunate to attain such a position. What think you about it? In the meanwhile I rest in hope that something will turn up favorable, thanking you for your kindness in furthering my interests, and desire to hear from you often about it. With much love I remain your affct.

Friend
R. T. Van Wyck

P. S. Thank you for the *Atlantic Monthly* of April. It comprises many excellent articles in this No. It came just in time to follow the March No., which I have been reading, in which [*there was*] an excellent piece called "A Call to My Countrywomen." I endorse this sentiment.

Belger Barracks, Balt.
Apr. 20th, 1863

Dear Cousin [*Sarah*],

Your last letter written in New York to me is still unanswered. My negligence is attributable partly to business matters and some duty. You are now home again, enjoying the fine Spring weather of sunshine and showers, after the recreation of visiting, party tea drinking, etc.

A letter from Aunt Mary disclosed the fact of a joint letter, written by you all, that was to be sent me while during your stay in Brooklyn. But this interesting epistle, since its failure [*to appear*] has been quite a disappointment.

There is nothing new in War matters here, and indeed my pen will have to employ itself upon some farfetched subject to finish a letter, for generally gossip [*about*] war matters are lies and [*gossip*] upon home speculations mere trash for me to write about, but to hear [*about*] is very entertaining.

My 'carte visite' you write me about, give yourself no trouble. You are not likely to meet the inquirer again very soon, and when I get promoted and can show more brass buttons; which would be more acceptable to her than me, the embodyment [*sic*] of good health – like the [*photo*] last winter I sent home, I will send <u>her</u> one. Upon this promise I will endeavor to get hers in my next letter to her. Ritie is very pretty. Is she?

Health is the main consideration in War. To be an invalid here is of all things the most unenviable. While in Health you are buoyed along by the bustle and excitement, and time passes swiftly and imperceptibly by.

But the blessed assurances of the Bible to comfort one in despondency arising from persons appointed to trust from unwarranted merit, particularly applicable is the 37th Psalm and the 31st and 24th also, without which t'would go roughly indeed.

Love to all. Hoping to hear from you soon, I remain your

Affectionate Cousin
R. T. Van Wyck

To A. V. W. Van Vechten

Belger Barracks, Balt.
April 25th 1863

Dear Cousin

Before I last wrote you, I had not made the necessary pecuniary arrangement. In the meanwhile I have received information from Father that funds to the amount of $500 or upwards will be placed at your disposal to be so used as you see fit.

But I am somewhat ignorant of how much money or in what way I could advise you to proceed. I was in hopes, however, that a lieutenantcy [*sic*] would not cost more than that sum, inclusive of outfit. But if alone, all right.

I hardly know whether it is very commendable in me to be so desirous of getting out of the ranks. But I have been so far satisfied with my present position and now I think I have served my time out in the enlisted ranks, and to take a step [*up*] in the ladder, should it come in the way of regular promotion, would be very desirable.

As it is, the past six months will make amend for this irregular course, and when I am assured the road is blocked here, I feel I am in the right to go some other way. I know that I am intruding upon your business in assisting me, but hoping I can repay you in future, I remain your afft. Cousin

R. T. Van Wyck

To A. V. W. Van Vechten

Belger Barracks, Balt.
May 2, 1863

Dear Cousin,

I received your letter today. I am sorry I will not be able to come on sooner than the latter part of next week. And perhaps not till the first of the week after.

I hardly think I will be so fortunate as to get an Adjutancy of a regiment; still, it is not much better than a lieutenancy. However, I would not throw away your labor in your effort for me, by refusing it. Much more, I cannot fail to appreciate your kindness to me, and remain,

Your Affectionate Cousin,
R. T. Van Wyck

46 Pine Street, New York
May 8th 1863

Dear Father:

I arrived in the city this morning and had expected to be with you today. But <u>this</u> business with Van Wyck required my presence tomorrow and will try to come up in the 3 o'clock <u>train</u> <u>from</u> <u>New</u> <u>York</u>–then that is Saturday. And perhaps you can meet me at the <u>depot</u>. If not in that train, in the one following.

I have just been over to Brooklyn and found Mother had just left for home. Hoping to see you soon, I remain your afft.

Son
R. T. Van Wyck

To Robert Johnston

46 Pine St. N. Y.
Tuesday May 12th

Robert,

I have succeeded in getting a position as Second Lieutenant in [the] First Regt. Seymour Light Infantry, and have as good as a commission already. But I am in the service and would require to be mustered out to take this position. A letter from your friend, S. Smith, to the Governor stating my position at present and requesting him to authorize my muster out or discharge to take that position as Second Lieut. in this Regt., also stating my character, etc., and what[ever] he may choose to add. This letter of his to the Gov., together with one from Col. Ketcham, will effect something, I am sure.

You will please send me at Baltimore this letter of S. Smith [so] that I may be able to <u>come</u> <u>on</u> perhaps in a few <u>weeks</u>, that is, hoping this influence will have the desired result in my <u>discharge.</u>

I am sorry to give you this trouble, but hoping in the future I may thank you in person I remain your afft.

Friend,
R. T. Van Wyck

P. S. The Commission I have that is not the one in regular form, which I will get when the Regt. is mustered into service.

46 Pine Street
12th May 1863

Robert,

I have thought it <u>best</u> that family, etc., would take my <u>letters</u>, yours from S. Smith and the one from the Col. – in person to <u>Albany</u>. So if you would send it to his address, 46 Pine St. (A. V. W. Van Vechten) you would greatly <u>oblige</u>. Matters of this kind are often neglected in the multiplicity of business, and to bring the matter up in person would be <u>very</u> advisable, which he has kindly consented to do, for me.

Your Friend,
R. T. Van Wyck

To: Brig. Genl. J. T. Sprague
Adj. Genl., New York
Albany, N. Y.

HeadQuarters 150th Regt. N. Y. Vols.
Belger Barracks, Balt.
May 13th 1863

Sir:

Corporal Richard T. Van Wyck of Co. "K" 150th Regt., N. Y. Vols., informs me that he has been promised the position of 2nd Lieut. in Col. Henry F. Liebenan's Regt., First Seymour Light Infantry, and requests a letter from me.

Corporal Van Wyck has been a member of my Regt. since September last, and I am happy to bear testimony to the faithful and efficient manner in which he has discharged his duties. He is a young man of high moral character and is in every respect capable, and worthy of promotion. I am Sir,

Very Respectfully,
Your Obedient Servant
J. H. Ketcham
Col. 150th Regt. N. Y. Vols.

Belger Barracks, Balt.
May 16th 1863

Dear Cousin [*Sarah*]

Again at camp. I hope you will not think it strange if I tell you that it seems quite homelike–the noise of the drum and of the men hurrying to and fro, which has so ingrafted itself into my thoughts and being; to have other impressions would be ridiculous.

Besides, the home trip, upon reflection seems but as a dream,* a counterpart of scenes of the like: wrapped up in my blanket in sleep, and [*dreaming*] that I saw you all well at home, which really was the sum and substance of my visit. However, I am in hopes of seeing you all before many months pass by. Again, the country and the camp look so beautiful. The large forest trees fully leafed and the air so balmy that for one to feel blue he must court unpleasant thoughts, while everything is the very <u>reverse</u> that surrounds us.

I did not see the <u>friend</u> I proposed seeing while in the city, but was prevented. Fred was over in Brooklyn: to spend the evening with him was a sufficient substitute for so delicious society I had in prospect. If another occasion offers for me to gratify this curiosity to see her, and should my suggestion meet with a ready assent, will give my spare moments some interesting matters of reflection which perhaps some of her letters contain. How nice t'would be just at this moment to answer her letter and give her such a glowing description of camp life, go into raptures about the weather and this delicious climate–Oh! it makes me miserable to think of my inability to do so.

---

* He never did get up to Fishkill, as he had to stay with relatives in the city to see about his commission. See page 90, letter dated May 20th, 1863.

I will exclude the thought till I come home again. Much love to all. I remain your Afft.

Cousin,
R. T. Van Wyck

(On legal paper)

Recommendation
for promotion
on behalf of
Rich'd T. Van Wyck

Signed by
Hon. Augt. Schell
& Sam'l. Sloan, Esq.

New York, May 18th 1863

To His Excellency Horatio Seymour
Governor of the State of New York

Richard T. Van Wyck of Fishkill, Dutchess County, in the year 1862 enlisted as a private in the 150th Regiment of New York Volunteers, desiring to understand fully his duties as a soldier. After about nine months' close attention to the duties of the Service, he is desirous of procuring the position of Second Lieutenant in the First Regiment of Seymour Light Infantry (N. Y. Vol.) Col. H. F. Liebenan commanding. There seems to be nothing to prevent his taking that position except the authorization of Your Excellency to muster him out of the 150th Regiment.

The letter of Col. Ketcham of the Regiment last named gives good recommendation. The undersigned familiar with his family associations or personal qualifications cordially recommend said Van Wyck to the consideration of Your Excellency in the above matter.
(signed) Sam Sloan
Augustus Schell

To A. Van Wyck Van Vechten

Tuesday, May 20th 1863

Dear Van,

I got a letter from Richard, written on Tuesday last, but which I did not receive till the last of the week. I went to see Mr. Smith yesterday. He will do all we wish him to in the matter. Offered a letter to the Governor and the Adjutant Gen.

He wishes more specific information than I could give him from Richard's hurried letter to me. Which is it that Richard most wants – to get mustered out of the service or have the Commission secured to him at Albany?

Write me also the name of the Reg't he is going in and the name of the Colonel and what state of forwardness it is in, also the rank he now has in the 150th Reg't and any other facts you know about it, and I will send your letter to Mr. Smith and he will write at once.

Mr. Smith wished all these facts. You know how rigid "red tape and routine" are in all these matters.

Richard wrote to me as though the commission was secured to him already. Please write just how the matter stands and what has been done thus far.

Please answer this at once and I will forward to Mr. Smith and send his letters to you with as little delay as possible.

Excuse this scrawl, it is late and I am just home from a long ride to Putnam County.

Yours sincerely,
Rob't Johnston

To Robert Johnston

Belger Barracks, Balt.
May 26, 1863

Dear Friend,

Your letter I received previous to leaving on furlough remains unanswered. Since returning to camp, however, and thinking over my visit home; to give my friends and <u>you</u> particularly so much trouble in my effort in bettering myself in my situation as a soldier, it would ill become me not to feel grateful for your kindness in furtherance of my plans, when circumstances have so embarrassed my personal action here.

Indeed, believe me, I am a great debtor to my friends in this matter and have learned to appreciate and esteem their friendship.

My apology for the limited statement of my wants which the exigency of the case demanded: [it] was an undue haste to give the business a start before I left, which [departure] was close at hand, or otherwise I could have put the matter before you in a proper way.

It promises well to succeed, the only obstacle now is the proper evidence that the company I am to join already contains forty men, which I am sure can be easily adjusted.

Here matters go on in a quiet easy way, to enjoy this life of idleness and ease and become quiet observers of all passing events takes time to become such passive creatures; but then some take to it as to the manor born. With much love, I remain your Afft

Friend
R. T. Van Wyck

To A. V. W. Van Vechten

Belger Barracks, Balt.
June 20, 1863

Dear Cousin,

I received your letter the 17th with the one before referred to. I am sorry to say I have not taken any action on the matter except farther than an interview with the Colonel, who advised [me] to let it be for the present, and that under the existing circumstances in this department Gen. Schenck would throw the matter aside in a summary manner. And his extreme nervousness forbids any possibility of any personal interview with him except his personal friends and these upon business connected with this trouble in Md.

I think the Col. will present the matter before the General as soon as the matter has subsided a little. I have been unable to attend to the matter before, on account of marching to sundry places about here. I am in good health yet and rather enjoy this activity. I am in hopes that when we see the Rebels we will draw as good aim from our new Enfield rifles as we have so long drawn from the Subsistence department.

With much love I remain your

Af't. Cousin
R.T. Van Wyck

(Enclosed with the letter was a clipping from a Baltimore newspaper:)

Military—The 7th New York Militia, Colonel Marshal Lefferts, yesterday after-noon left their quarters at the Continental Hotel, Holiday Street, and marching to Fort Federal Hill took possession of the same in accordance with an order issued by Gen. Schenck. There were about five hundred muskets in the col-umn, which will be considerably increased in the course of two or three days. On Monday afternoon their celebrated band, led by Prof. Grafful, is expected to arrive here, and we may, therefore, expect some fine musical treats on the occasion of the evening dress parades.

The 150th New York Volunteers, which moved from Camp Belger to Fort Marshall, returned from that post last evening, and are now in part occu-pying their old quarters. The companies of the 5th New York Artillery, Col. Graham, which have been garrisoning Fort Federal Hill, have been ordered elsewhere.

Kellys Ford
Aug. 2nd 1863

Dear Mother,

I received your letter this morning and also the five dollars. Send the remainder in about two weeks. Sorry you have not got all my letters as punctual as formerly, but there is trouble in getting them off here. I have got all your letters, I guess. I'm glad always to receive them. I must hurry to get this off, for the mail closes and I must <u>hurry</u>.

With much love, I am well, your
afft. Son
R. T. Van Wyck

EDITOR'S NOTE:

"[*After Gettysburg*] the [*150th*] regiment then joined in Meade's pursuit of Lee's army, marching and countermarching until August 1st, when it crossed the Rappahannock at Kelly's Ford, and supported as skirmishers the cavalry, who drove the enemy. During the month of August the regiment lay in camp and many of the men were sick with acclimating fever. There were 250 cases in the hospital with typhoid and malarial fever."

The History of Dutchess County, op. cit., p. 196.

Kelleys Ford, Va.
Aug 13th 1863

Dear Father,

I received the money day before yesterday. Just now there seems to be an indica-tion of getting our pay. There is nothing new in our movements. I suppose we are wait-ing for the conscripts and at the same time watching Lee in his movements, besides recruiting the army after long marches. As to myself I feel quite as good as ever now, although at our first coming here I was little the worse from the fatigue, etc.

I am glad you are closing up the Hay season, and lately have had good weather. I give you this letter to acknowledge the receipt of the money, and am doubtful whether you will receive this immediate, from your absence to Po'keepsie.

With much love I remain your afft. Son

R. T. Van Wyck

Kelleys Ford, Va.
Aug. 17th 1863

Dear Father,

350

Since I last wrote you we have been paid off. I will remit $20, a check to your order on the Falkill [?] Bank, Po'keepsie. It can be cashed in Fishkill, as Mr. Sleight is well known in the County.

As we are likely to be moving about I thought it best to send that amount home and if I need it before getting paid off again I will send for it.

We don't expect to remain here a great while, and perhaps several months.

With much love, your afft. Son

R. T. Van Wyck

P. S. Please write me when you receive it.

To A. V. W. Van Vechten

Kelleys Ford, Va.
Sep. 5th 1863

Dear Cousin,

We still remain at this place taking our position in the line of pickets extending from Culpeper and Fredericksburg to Richmond along the Rappa-hannock. We are dependent as much upon the papers for news as yourself, even in our own department.

The Regt. has suffered very much from sickness, perhaps diminished to one half of the effective men that came with us. My health has been quite good, although I have had an attack of the prevalent camp dysentery, but am now all right.

From Father I learned that you are still working for me in New York to effect a Commission. Many thanks for your kindness in thus pursuing such a difficult enterprise. I would therefore take any notification of your success as an agreeable surprise.

Address me as before (3rd Reg., 1st Div., 12th A. Corps, Washington, D.C.) and I will be sure to get it no matter where the Regt is posted.

With much love to yourself and family I remain, your afft. cousin,

R. T. Van Wyck

Kelleys Ford
Sept 15th 1863

Dear Cousin [*Sarah*],

I am glad to find you have been enjoying yourself so much this summer. Now that the draft is settled and selected many of the gallants of the Fishkills, those who remain will not have this bugbear to mar their social enjoyment of the fair ones. You are better posted in the doings of the army than myself, except what comes under my own personal knowledge and observation.

Last Sunday morning I witnessed the crossing of the river of the cavalry force of Kilpatrick's, numbering some 4,000 in all. Since then we hear they reconnaissanced the country in the direction of Culpeper and found that the enemy were moving their forces to reinforce their army to the South and the Southwest.* We don't expect to remain here very long, although extensive preparations are made to make ourselves comfortable.

Last week in taking a walk about the country I called at a farmhouse and asked for some milk to drink and was entertained by a vigorous onslaught upon the Feds from a specimen of secessionist fair one. I paid 20 cents a quart for milk, and this thrown in. You can't imagine how we are situated here. We expect to get nearer to Richmond before the winter sets in, where we can command some of the luxuries without the fabulous prices.

---

* These events affecting the Western theatre of the war were to alter the course of Richard Van Wyck's career in the Union army.

I see that Tyding and Aben Van Wyck have been drafted, also Garret DuBois. I suppose they possess the lucky $300 and therefore will not aid us with their assistance.

Write soon. I remain your afft. cousin

R. T. Van Wyck

Tullahoma, Tenn.
Oct. 23rd '63

Dear Mother,

I received your letter of October 2d last evening. You have not received mine of recent date since my arrival in this place. We are again upon the move again— Destination Stevenson. Fortunately for me I have the prospect of car transportation instead of as the Regt. by marching.

We have had some unpleasant weather and had made preparation of making this place our winter quarters. But in this we are disappointed.

I cannot from want give you much of a letter. But if Father will in your next send me ten dollars I will get it in the course of time.

It is impossible to tell when I can get my next letter from you. But hoping things will be made more smooth one of these days I remain, your afft. Son

R. T. Van Wyck

Normandy, Tenn.
Christmas Day

Dear Mother,

Your letter I received yesterday. Upon its reception I was busily engaged in again moving and transferring my shanty about a quarter of a mile distant. As a consequence it has somewhat deranged my calculations for a dinner today, but not as much as I anticipated. Two Chickens were awaiting execution for several days and were sentenced to be wasted today for dinner. So you see I have endeavored to have a respect for the day, under difficulties of moving and police duties.

You could not have received my letter previous to the mailing of yours. I am sorry to hear of GrandFather's ill health. The weather must be cold with you, while here it has scarcely frozen the ground, and withal been very pleasant thus far. Some of the boys have slept out and are now doing it without suffering any inconvenience.

The box has not arrived nor has the *Atlantic Monthly* you sent me. The former we are not looking anxiously for, expecting to hear of its miscarriage, but when it comes we are assured everything will be in good order from the substantial nature of the contents. Jacob remains philosophical upon the subject and not saving his appetite on that account.

There is nothing of worth to narrate here, and we scarcely know what is going on elsewhere, except from the same channels as yourself. There seems no indication of a move to the front; but if at all, will be on the line of R.R. towards Nashville. I hope we can remain with some comfort here this Winter, then in the Spring I am ready for a tramp. That is, if the war goes on.

Your mention of the yearly pork appropriations of sausage, etc., reminds me of the small one we bought for New Year's or the Holy Days. With the repeated roasts we will have, [it] might indicate our anti-diet sentiments. Now that Isaac Kip has cooled off his glorious determination to serve his country he has learned by this time "to let well enough alone." I have received all the papers you sent me.

With much love I remain your Afft. Son.

R. T. Van Wyck

Normandy, Tenn.
Feb. 6th, '64

Dear Mother,

Yours was received today (Saturday) of the 29th. I expect to hear by every mail of the possible death of GrandFather who now is so low. By Capt. Scofield I will get some news from home, as he has favored you with a visit. His furlough will expire next Tuesday, or rather, his leave of absence.

No news here, everything is just the same as formerly, and very monotonous. We have signs of the guerrillas occasionally along the railroad, but never coming near enough to get a look at them.

Jacob and myself are looking out for that box. A great number have come lately and we learn the express co. are endeavoring to put all the goods through now on hand to be forwarded, so we can't be long awaiting, we hope.

As I go on Picket [*duty*] tomorrow I have embraced this opportunity to write a few lines before the week closes. I hope you will not fail to send the magazines and papers.

I remain your aff. Son   R. T. Van Wyck

P. S. I am much obliged for Father's letter. There is nothing I could wish more than a few skeins of thread just at present. You will think your [*writing*] paper is of all things most necessary, judging from the present sheet. It will be truly welcomed.

Normandy, Tenn.
Feb. 26th '64

Dear Father,

I received your letters, the 24th inst. I found the thread, which was just the thing: for not giving you the color I did not much expect it would be suitable.

To me the disposition of GrandFather's property by his will seems a very equitable arrangement. Uncle Henry* might possibly be possessed of more of it than the rest, which undoubtedly will ease his mind from the fear he will not get his part, and so keep peace in the family.

Does that Western indebtedness look much better than formerly? Or does Uncle Anthony assume the interest of it? And also about that affair of Bentley's, which I hope is coming out all right. The purchase of the Secore property by Joseph Sherwood will make one other addition to our Church.

How is Mr. Delevan's will arranged? And do the Sisters continue to live upon the farm? Many alterations will, I suppose, be made in the neighborhood during the year. As Aunt Louisa** will still continue to live at the old homestead, will GrandMother live with them? And also, Mr. and Mrs. Lane?***

Weather is fine, and Winter seems to have left us, as indeed it nearly has. The farmers have sowed their oats, planted potatoes, and many garden articles, so you can imagine how far the season is advanced with us. No prospects of moving from here as yet, and as furloughs are given out, that time might be far in the future. Jacob G. Montross has made application for furlough and will probably receive one in a week or more, thus giving you an account of our place and Winter doings. I hope he will be successful in getting his furlough.

I made mention of a watch in my former letter to be sent to me. If you would do

---

* Henry is Gen. Van Wyck's eldest son, brother of Richard's father, James.

** Louisa (Van Wyck) Van Vechten, Sarah's mother, sister of James Van Wyck.

*** Susan (Van Wyck) Lane is another aunt, sister of Louisa and of Richard T.'s father, James.

anything in the matter you can send it by him when he returns. This watch should not cost more than twenty ($20) dollars or less than fifteen ($15) to be good.

I hope to hear soon from home. With love I remain you afft. Son

R.T. Van Wyck

Normandy, Tenn.
Monday, March 7th, '64

Dear Mother,

Just one week ago today found me in this identical spot, attending to this duty of the service, upon picket. Then, the rain poured down incessant throughout the twenty-four hours; today, however, it only showers and the sun alternately casts a ray upon our forlorn condition, and relieves a certain chilliness of the climate. Still, this is a favorable season for thinking, for not always reading matter holds out and our thoughts unconsciously take a retrospect of the past and speculate as to the future.

I do always think of home and wonder how much trouble you borrow on my behalf; for considering your views of civilized life as regards health and comfort, you might think with a shudder in your <u>cold</u> <u>climate</u> how this can be endured. When I wrote you last summer in Va. how a mere shadow I had become from the severe marching, and how the removal to this State had benefited me, I can say <u>now</u>, instead of the living anatomy I then presented, I am glad to say just the reverse in every way and shape, not troubled with colds in any way or shape, which I attribute to a plentiful bestowal of Govt. luxuries in the right place.

Thus the Winter has passed swiftly and comfortably and Spring with gentle slowness and balmy breezes inspires us to meet the future cheerfully. I would like well enough to get a furlough so that we could compare notes of the past year, but that furlough is next to an impossibility and given only in exceptional cases. J. Montross has one in prospect, but there is much doubt as to his success.

The Colonel [*Ketcham*] is <u>now</u> in Dutchess Co. upon leave of absence. Many inquiries will be made after the Reg't and members of it. Thanks to a kind Providence he has not the painful duty to tell of the usual fatalities of the service; as this Reg't has been remarkably preserved throughout, without any derangement of Regimental or company commandant.

The Brooklyn *Daily Eagle* with the description of the Sanitary Fair came to hand. I did [*not*] know which to admire the most, either the description so ably written or the things there represented. Taking it altogether it must have been a splendid affair. Then New York seems not to be behindhand in this charitable enterprise.

Tuesday, March 8th, '64

P. S. Upon being relieved from picket I found a letter from you of Feb. 29th, Brooklyn. I am glad to hear the watch is to be obtained. A subsequent letter of mine advised the forwarding it on by Jacob Montross, but you will know soon after the receipt of this letter whether he can have that privilege or not. If not, you can send it by mail or by Adams Express Co., which[*ever*] of the two you would think most likely to bring it safely to its destination.

With much love to all I remain your aff't. Son.   R. T. Van Wyck

EDITOR'S NOTE:

Well aware of the importance of letters from home to morale, the army tried to ensure that even the most scattered outposts received their home mail. Postmaster General Montgomery Blair's use of the railroad in getting mail to soldiers was first put into effect a year earlier during the Vicksburg campaign, with the blessings of both Generals Grant and Sherman. The latter's Army of the Tennessee is credited with proving that mail could be sorted on fast trains and distributed in transit under the most difficult conditions, thus inaugurating the system which later became the regular U.S. mail service. *Sherman, Fighting Prophet,* by Lloyd Lewis, N.Y., 1932, p. 170.

Normandy, Tenn.
April 21st, 1864

Dear Mother,

From some cause or other our mail does not arrive as punctual as formerly. Or it may be that you think us moved, the name of the organization changed, a letter would not reach me. As to the latter, let me say we are the 150th Reg't still, are in the 2d Brig. of the 1st Division of the 20th or 12th Corps, I don't know which. An official order has it the former, while much talk at headquarters seems to think the latter is the No. of the Corps, but nothing official indicates the latter.

We are having the finest kind of weather, the trees are coming out in leaf, and the nights are warm and agreeable. We may move to Va., but I think that is not designed for us at present. The campaign will open soon with force and vigor in Va.; as all seem to look there, it wouldn't be unlikely for this army in view of this diversion to steal a march upon Atlanta.

Hardee has moved his Corps to Va. to support Lee. There is a great army in front and constantly increasing in every particular: Cavalry, Artillery, and infantry.

J. G. Montross writes me the farmers are getting large prices for their grain just at present. Butter will get to be as much of a luxury with the working classes on acct. of price, as it has been to us. Now it is entirely gone. No sutlers are allowed in this army.

I have nothing more to write. Write often, I will inform you if we should leave at the earliest opportunity. Direct as above. I remain your

Afft. Son
R. T. Van Wyck

(Letter in pencil)

Eight Miles from
Atlanta, Ga.
July 8th '64

Dear Mother,

I received your letter just upon mailing my last. Since which time we have had the pleasure to follow the Rebs to the River. Although they have breastworks here on this side of the river and we the same, we are looking forward to soon occupying Atlanta. From a view I obtained of the city from a treetop they seem to have thought much of it, for work upon work cover the plains, but we will come [*via*] some flank operation upon them.

Today was the anniversary of GrandFather's birthday. Now everything is changed. Frank Kip seems not to be unlike his brother in his inconstant devoted affection towards the feminine sex. It does not surprise me in the least. It was a foolish affair anyhow. Miss G_____ need not moan over the affair in the least, for it is some of the work of her own doing, or partly so. Don't you think so? I am glad Uncle Anthony has partly paid his indebtedness. How much better he will feel. The young ladies who have the Kip favor must marry them before they have a chance to change their mind.

The weather is getting hot. I fear it will prevent much active operations for some months to come. Night before last the Rebs were very friendly and exchanged [*news*]papers. Since the retreat from Marietta we have taken 4,000 prisoners, if not more. They are much demoralized.

As the haying season is about commencing you will not fail to keep me posted, as all communications are gladly received. I remain with much love your aff. Son

R. T. Van Wyck

Atlanta, Ga.
Sept. 3d '64

Dear Mother,

I sent a few days ago some money enclosed ($20). I got a check upon the Po'keepsie Bank for $100. In either case there is considerable risk, but in the latter much less as the money from Nashville is guaranteed [*but*] the Company assume no risks from here to there. The mail has failed to bring up any of your letters since Aug. 14th.

The R. R. is torn up at Tullahoma and also upon the R. R. from Tullahoma and also upon the R. R. from Nashville to Huntsville. A large portion of our army have gone to the rear to keep the Road open, and we expect soon to be in a fair way of keeping regularly posted and supplied with everything, rations not excepted. With this exception, there is nothing new.

Many rumors daily reach us of the possibilities of Peace at an early day, but how authentic, or how near our forces in Va. have scattered Lee's army, thereby giving us peace upon the crushing of the Rebellion, has given us much talk in Camp. The Reg't has received seventy-five recruits of one-year men. A decidedly better class than the old ones, both physically and morally better men. We will then, with the convalescents returning, have a large Reg't again.

I will write soon again. I remain with much love, your aft. Son

R. T. Van Wyck

P. S. Please give me Aben's address. Is it the same as formerly–Middletown, Michigan?

Atlanta, Ga. Sept. 17th '64

Dear Mother,

When last I wrote you I had hardly got settled down in my new shanty. I therefore answered your letter hurriedly, for such great enterprises (private) as erecting one's habitation and embellishing it with the style of a great city will allow of no hindrance.

Besides, having received no letters since then, I have given them another perusal and I think this might reach you soon after your return from the L. Springs. I hope you have had a pleasant time among the Shakers. Such little trips divert the mind from everyday life and freshen it for the future. Mr. Voorhees and family undoubtedly left a blank in the society at home, and the noise of the children will be much missed.

The tea drinking has become quite a mania with the girls at the other house. They have taken to it very naturally I am sure, having always had so good instructors in their own family. The girls do not travel this Summer, how is that? Mr. Lane and Aunt Susan find no trouble to worry a few short months at fashionable places – money cannot be as much of an item with Mr. Lane as formerly.

For the past two Sabbaths we have heard the bells of the city from our camp, but unable to get a pass to visit them, or attend church.

The citizens by order of Gen. Sherman are obliged to go South, if they have any friends in the Southern Army or if not otherwise employed here. An armistice of ten days has gone into effect to enable those to go South, and to allow such as Hood is sending north. Geo. Burroughs says he took advantage of it while guarding a waggon [*sic*] train freighted with refugees to enter the Reb. lines, he took dinner with them of better quality of food than abounds with us.

I am hoping the Express Co. will be able to forward boxes by R. R. soon, for then I will be sending for some stuff. When that is fixed and we have better assurances of making a long stay of it, I will write for a small box. We likewise hope to do better in the way of rations as soon as the Roads are cleared. It is reported by the Colonel that we will receive eight months' pay Monday. I hope that is so. I hope when the mail comes through from Nashville I will receive a letter from home. Love to all, I remain your aff. Son

R. T. Van Wyck

BIBLIOGRAPHY
Virginia Hughes Kaminsky

American Heritage Picture History of the Civil War, by Bruce Catton, New York,1982.
Battle Cry of Freedom: The Civil War Era, by James M. McPherson, New York, 1988.
Bruce Catton's Civil War, 3 volumes The Fairfax Press, New York, 1984.
Civil War Battles, by Curt Johnson and Mark McLaughlin, New York, 1977, 1981.
The Civil War: A Narrative, 3 volumes, by Shelby Foote, New York, 1958-74.
The Civil War: Strange and Fascinating Facts, by Burke Davis, New York, 1982.
The Common Soldier in the Civil War, by Bell Irvin Wiley, Indianopolis, 1943.
Descendants of Cornelius Barentse Van Wyck and Anna Polhemus, by Anne Van Wyck. Tobias A. Wright,New York, 1912.
The Fiery Trail: A Union Officer's Account of Sherman's Last Campaigns, Ed. by Richard Harwell and Philip N. Racine, Knoxville, 1986.
The General Who Marched to Hell: Sherman and the Southern Campaign, by Earl Schenck Miers, New York, 1990.
The History of Dutchess County, Ed. by Frank Hasbrouck, Poughkeepsie, New York, 1909.
The Life of Johnny Reb, by Bell Irvin Wiley, Indianapolis, 1943.
The Life of Billy Yank, by Bell Irvin Wiley, Indianapolis, 1943.
The March to the Sea and Beyond: Sherman's Troops in the Savannah and Carolinas Campaign, by Joseph T. Glatthaar, New York, 1985.
Memoirs of General William T. Sherman, 2 volumes by Himself, New York, 1886.
Patriotic Gore, by Edmund Wilson, New York, 1962.
Personal Memoirs of U. S. Grant, 2 volumes, New York, 1885.
Sherman and his Campaigns, by S.M. Bowman and R.B. Irwin, New York, 1865.
Sherman: Fighting Prophet, by Lloyd Lewis, New York, 1932.
The Shipwreck of Their Hopes: The Battle for Chattanooga, by Peter Cozzens, Univerity of Illinois Press, Urbana and Chicago, 1994.

John C. Quinn

Abraham Lincoln: The True Story of A Great Life, 2 Volumes, by William H. Herndon and Jesse W. Weik, New York, 1916.
"A Fair To Remember: Maryland Women In Aid of The Union," by Robert W. Schoeberlein, Maryland Historical Society Magazine, Volume 90,

Number 4, 1995.

American Civil War Reports As Recorded In Harper's Weekly, by Sidney Rudeau, Verplanck, 1994.

An American Iliad: The Story of The Civil War, by Charles P. Roland, Lexington, 1991.

The Annals of America: The Crisis of The Union, Volume 9, by William Benton, Chicago, 1972.

The Army of The Cumberland, by Henry M. Cist, New York, 1882.

A Short History of The Civil War, by James L. Stokesbury, New York, 1995.

As Seen From The Ranks, by Charles E. Benton, New York, 1902.

Atlanta And The War, by Webb Garrison, Nashville, 1995.

Atlas For The American Civil War, by Thomas E. Griess, Wayne, 1986.

Ballads and Songs of The Civil War, by Jerry Silverman, Pacific, 1993.

Battle Cry of Freedom, by James M. McPherson, New York, 1988.

The Beards' New Basic History of The United States, by Charles A. Beard, Garden City, 1968.

Brother Against Brother, by James M. McPherson, New York, 1990.

Brothers In Arms, by William C. Davis, New York, 1995.

The Brothers' War, by Annette Tapert, New York, 1988.

Bruce Catton's America, by Himself, New York, 1993.

Bullet and Shell: The Civil War As The Soldier Saw It, by George F. Williams, Woodbury, 1882.

The Centennial History of The Civil War, 3 Volumes, by Bruce Catton, Garden City, 1965.

The Civil War: A Narrative, 3 Volumes, by Shelby Foote, New York, 1963.

The Civil War: An Illustrated History, by Geoffrey C. Ward, New York, 1990.

The Civil War In Maryland, by Daniel Carroll Toomey, Baltimore, 1983.

The Civil War Sourcebook, by Philip Katcher, New York, 1992.

Civil War Tennessee, by Thomas L. Connelly, Knoxville, 1979.

Civil War Wordbook, by Darrel Lyman, Pennsylvania, 1994.

"Collecting Civil War Letters," by John C. Quinn, Northeast, Hudson, 1995.

The Confederacy Is on Her Way Up the Spout: Letters to South Carolina 1861-1864, by Roderick Heller III and Carolynn Ayres Heller, Athens, 1992.

Confederate Letters and Diaries: 1861-1865, by Walbrook D. Swank, Shippensburg, 1988.

The Daily Journal, Newburgh, April 10, 1865; April 11, 1865; April 15, 1865; April 17, 1865; April 22, 1865; April 24, 1865; April 26, 1865.

Dear Friend Anna: The Civil War Letters From a Common Soldier From Maine, by Beverly Hayes Kallgren and James L. Crouthamel, Orono, 1992.

Dear Wife: Letters of a Civil War Soldier, By Jack C. Davis, Louisville, 1991.

Divided We Fought, by Hearst D. Milhollen and Milton Kaplan, New York, 1952.

Douglas Southall Freeman on Leadership, by Stuart W. Smith, Shippensburg, 1990.

"The Dutchess County Regiment," by David Topps, Gettysburg Magazine, Issue 12, Seymour, 1995.

The "Dutchess County Regiment" In The Civil War, by Reverend Edward O. Bartlett, D.D., Danbury, 1907.

Early American Steamers, Volume 2, by Eric Heyl, Buffalo, 1956.

Early American Steamers, Volume 2, by Eric Heyl, Buffalo, 1964.

Early Photography at Gettysburg, by William A. Frassanito, Gettysburg, 1995.

Edmund P. Platt Diary, by Himself, Dutchess County Historical Society Special Collection, October 1862.

Encyclopedia of The Civil War, by John S. Bowman, Greenwich, 1992.

Field of Battle: The Civil War Letters of Major Thomas J. Halsey, by K.M. Kostyal, Washington, D.C., 1996.

The Gazette, Rhinebeck, May 31, 1864; July 5, 1864; July 26, 1864; August 9, 1864; August 30, 1864; September 6, 1864; December 6, 1864.

Generals in Blue, by Ezra J. Warner, Baton Rouge, 1964.

Generals in Gray, by Ezra J. Warner, Baton Rouge, 1964.

Gettysburg: A Battlefield Atlas, by Craig L. Symonds, Baltimore, 1992.

Gettysburg: Culp's Hill and Cemetery Hill, by Harry W. Pfanz, Chapel Hill, 1993.

Gettysburg: The Confederate High Tide, by Champ Clark, Alexandria, 1985.

Gettysburg: The Second Day, by Harry W. Pfanz, Chapel Hill, 1987.

Great Battles of The Civil War, by John MacDonald, New York, 1988.

Growing Up In The 1850's: The Journal of Agnes Lee, by Mary Custis Lee deButts, Chapel Hill, 1984.

The Hard Hand of War: Union Military Policy Towards Southern Civilians, 1861-1865, by Mark Grimsley, New York, 1995.

Hard Tack and Coffee, by John D. Billings, Boston, 1887.

Historical Sketch: With Exercises at Dedication of Monument and Reunion Campfire of 150th New York Volunteer Infantry, by William R. Wooden, Poughkeepsie, 1889.

Hospital Sketches: An Army Nurse's True Account of Her Experience during the Civil War, by Louisa May Alcott, Old Saybrook, 1993.

Hospital Trains of The Army of The Cumberland, Volume 51, Number 3, Tennessee Historical Quarterly, 1992.

I Will Try to Send You All the Particulars of the Fight, by David S. Moore, Albany, 1995.

Landscapes of The Civil War, by Constance Sullivan, New York, 1995.

Last Stand In The Carolinas: The Battle of Bentonville, by Mark L. Bradley, Campbell, 1996.

Life In The North During The Civil War, by George Winston Smith and Charles Judah, Albuquerque, 1966.

The Life of Billy Yank, by Bell Irvin Wiley, Baton Rouge, 1943.

The Life of Johnny Reb, by Bell Irvin Wiley, Baton Rouge, 1943.

Lincoln: An Illustrated Biography, by Philip B. Cunhardt, Jr., New York, 1992.

Marching Through Georgia, by Lee Kennett, New York, 1995.

Marching Through Georgia by Henry C. Work, Boston, 1889.

The March To The Sea and Beyond, by Joseph T. Glatthaar, Baton Rouge, 1995.

Mathew Brady's Illustrated History of The Civil War, by Benson J. Lossing, LL.D., New York, 1912.

Merchant Steam Vessels of The United States, 1790-1868, by William M. Lytle and Forrest R. Holdcamper, Staten Island, 1975.

Mountain Campaigns In Georgia, by Jos. M. Brown, Buffalo, 1890.

Mr. Lincoln's Army, by Bruce Catton, Garden City, 1951.

Mr. Lincoln's Cameraman, Mathew B. Brady, by Roy Meredith, New York, 1946.

Music In The Civil War, by Stephen Currie, Cincinnati, 1992.

Official Records of The Union and Confederate Navies In The War of Rebellion, by Dudley W. Knox, Washington, D.C., 1927.

Peekskill Messenger, Peekskill, April 6, 1865.

The Personal Memoirs of Ulysses S. Grant, 2 Volumes, by Himself, New York 1885.

Peter W. Funk Diary, By Margaret E. Harrick, Poughkeepsie, 1991.

The Photographic History of The Civil War, 10 Volumes, by O.E. Hunt, New York, 1911.

Picture History of The Civil War, by Bruce Catton, New York, 1960.

Poems and Songs of The Civil War, by Lois Hill, New York, 1990.

Poughkeepsie Daily Eagle, Poughkeepsie, July 1, 1863; July 2, 1863; July 3, 1863; Poughkeepsie, July 4, 1863; July 7, 1863;. July 17, 1863;. July 20, 1863;. July 27, 1863; July 28, 1863; August 11, 1863; September 21, 1863; August 2, 1864; November 11, 1864; December 16, 1864; December 21, 1864; December 26, 1864; May 4, 1865; May 25, 1865; April 8, 1865;. April 15, 1865; May 6, 1865.

Sherman In Georgia, by Edgar L. McCormick, Edward G. McGehee and Mary Strahl, Boston, 1961.

Sherman's March Through The Carolinas, by John G. Barrett, Chapel Hill, 1956.

Singing Soldiers: A History of The Civil War in Song, by Paul Glass, New York, 1975.

Songs of The Civil War, by Irwin Silber, New York, 1960.

Stars In Their Courses, by Shelby Foote, New York, 1963.

The Story of The Great March From The Diary Of A Staff Officer, by Brevet Major George Ward Nichols, New York, 1866.

Sherman: Soldier-Realist-American, by B.H. Liddell Hart, New York, 1929.

They Were There: The Civil War In Action As Seen By It's Combat Artists, by Philip Van Doren Stern, New York, 1959.

Touched With Fire: Civil War Letters and Diary of Oliver Wendell Holmes, Jr., by Mark DeWolfe Howe, Cambridge, 1946.

Toward A Social History of The American Civil War, by Maris A. Vinovskis, New York 1990.

Upon The Tented Field, by Bernard A. Olsen, Redbank, 1993.

The Vacant Chair: The Northern Soldier Leaves Home, by Reid Mitchell, New York, 1993

Victorian America and The Civil War, by Anne C. Rose, New York, 1992.

Victory Rode The Rails, by George Edgar Turner, Lincoln, 1992.

Walt Whitman's America, by David S. Reynolds, New York, 1995.

Yankee Correspondence: Civil War Letters Between New England Soldiers and The Homefront, by Nina Silver and Mary Beth Sievens, Charlottesville, 1996.

COMPANY K ROSTER

The Dutchess County Regiment

Mustered into the U.S. service for three years, at Camp Dutchess, Poughkeepsie, N.Y., Saturday, October 11, 1862.

Captain.

Scofield, John S.–Age, 57 years. Enrolled October 7, 1862, at Poughkeepsie, to serve three years; mustered in as Captain, Co. K, October 11, 1862.*
Commissioned Captain, November 3, 1862, with rank from October 6, 1862, original.

First Lieutenants.

Corcoran, Michael.–Age, 28 years. Enrolled at Poughkeepsie, to serve three years, and mustered in as First Lieutenant, Co. K, October 11, 1862; discharged, January 29, 1863.
Commissioned First Lieutenant, November 3, 1862, with rank from October 6, 1862, original.

Steenburgh, Wade H.–January 30, 1863. See Second Lieutenants.*

Roberts, Cyrus S.–April 22, 1865.* See 1865.* See Second Lieutenants.

Second Lieutenants.

Steenburgh, Wade H.–Age, 35 years. Enrolled at Poughkeepsie, to serve three years, and mustered in as Second Lieutenant, Co. K, October 7, 1862; as First Lieutenant, January 30, 1863; discharged for disability November 7, 1864; prior service as Captain, Twentieth Militia.
Commissioned Second Lieutenant, November 3, 1862, with rank from October 6, 1862, original; First Lieutenant, February 2, 1863, with rank from January 29, 1863, vice M.J. Corcoran resigned.

Roberts, Cyrus S.–Age, 21 years. Enrolled September 5, 1862, at Poughkeepsie, to serve three years; mustered in as private, Co. A, October 10, 1862; promoted Sergeant-Major, October 11, 1862; mustered in as Second Lieutenant, Co. K, February 13, 1863; as First Lieutenant, January 1, 1865*
Commissioned Second Lieutenant, February 2, 1863, with rank from January 29, 1863, vice W. H. Steenburgh promoted; First Lieutenant, November 30, 1864, with rank from September 6, 1864, vice W. H. Steenburgh resigned; First Lieutenant and Adjutant, not mustered, April 22, 1865, with rank from March 2, 1865, vice W.S. Van Keuren promoted; Brevet Captain and Brevet Major, U.S. Volunteers.

Van Keuren, Benjamin.–Age, 25 years. Enrolled September 29, 1862, at Poughkeepsie, to serve three years; mustered in as private, Co. C, October 11, 1862; promoted Sergeant, no date; Sergeant-Major, March 31, 1865; mustered in as Second Lieutenant, Co. K. April 1, 1865.*
Commissioned Second Lieutenant, April 22, 1865, with rank from March 16, 1865, vice S. Humeston promoted.

First Sergeant.

Sylands, Enos B.–Age, 21 years. September 5, 1862, at Rhinebeck; mustered in as Sergeant, October 25, 1864.*

Sergeants.

Buckmaster, George W.–Age, 22 years. September 13, 1862, at Rhinebeck; mustered in as Corporal, October 11, 1862; promoted Sergeant, October 26, 1864; wounded at Gettysburg, Pa.*

Heeb, Jacob.–Age, 25 years. September 5, 1862, at Rhinebeck; mustered in as Corporal, October 11, 1862; promoted Sergeant prior to April, 1863.*

Lamp, Henry, Jr.–Age, 21 years. September 6, 1862, at Rhinebeck; mustered in as Corporal, Co. K, October 11, 1862; promoted Sergeant prior to April, 1863; wounded in action, July 20, 1864, at Peach Tree Creek, Ga.*

Van Wyck, Richard T.–Age, 23 years. October 4, 1862, at East Fishkill; mustered in as Corporal, Co. K, October 11, 1862; promoted Sergeant prior to April, 1864.*
Commissioned, not mustered, First Lieutenant, May 31, 1865, with rank from March 17, 1865, vice Cyrus S. Roberts promoted.

Corporals.

Burroughs, George.–Age, 20 years. September 4, 1862, at East Fishkill; mustered in as Corporal, Co. K, October 11, 1862.*

Champlin, James M.–Age, 25 years. October 4, 1862, at Fishkill; promoted Corporal prior to April 1863; returned to ranks, no date; mustered out, July 4, 1865, at hospital, Nashville, Tenn.

Conklin, James E.–Age, 32 years. September 30, 1862, at Fishkill; promoted Corporal, October 26, 1864.*

Hevenor, Benjamin J.–Age, 24 years. September 6, 1862, at Rhinebeck; mustered in as Corporal, Co. K, October 11, 1862.

Commissioned, not mustered, First Lieutenant, June 29, 1863, with rank from April 25, 1863, vice A. Johnson discharged.

Jones, Robert M.–Age, 38 years. September 26, 1862, at Fishkill; promoted Corporal prior to April, 1863; returned to ranks prior to April, 1864.*

Moore, Peter.–Age, 25 years. September 30, 1862, at Fishkill; mustered in as Corporal, Co. K, October 11, 1862.*

Montross, Jacob G.–Age, 28 years. October 8, 1862, at East Fishkill; promoted Corporal prior to April, 1863.*

Smith, William A.–Age, 29 years. September 5, 1862, at Rhinebeck; promoted Corporal, November 1, 1864.*

Taylor, George.–Age, 25 years. August 7, 1862, at New York City; private, Co. D, 145th N.Y. Volunteers; promoted Corporal prior to April, 1864; mustered out, May 24, 1865, at McDougall Hospital, Fort Schuyler, N.Y. Harbor.Z

Tuttle, Abraham.–Age, 19 years. September 30, 1862, at Fishkill; promoted Corporal prior to April, 1864.*

Musicians.

Jones, Morris H.–Age, 15 years. November 1, 1862, at Baltimore, Md., to serve three years, and mustered in as Musician; D.F.D., November 21, 1863, at hospital, Alexandria, Va.

Mosher, Americus G.–Age, 17 years. September 29, 1862, at East Fishkill; mustered in as Musician, October 11, 1862; wounded in action, May 15, 1864, at Resaca, Ga.; mustered out, June 27, 1865, at Albany, N.Y.

Privates.

Adams, Sylvester J.–Age, 37 years. August 13, 1864, at Poughkeepsie; D.F.D., May 16, 1865, at McDougall Hospital, Fort Schuyler, N.Y. Harbor.

Allen, William.–Age, 45 years. October 6, 1862, at Poughkeepsie.*

Ashton, John.–Age, 39 years. September 18, 1862, at Fishkill; mustered out, May 24, 1865, at McDougall Hospital, Fort Schuyler, N.Y. Harbor.

Barraclough, Edward.–Age, 21 years. September 1, 1864, at Poughkeepsie, to serve one year.*

Birch, Robert.–Age, 25 years. September 11, 1862, at Fishkill; deserted, October 15, 1862, at Camp Millington, Baltimore, Md.

Brierly, John.–Age, 38 years. September 5, 1862, at Fishkill; deserted, November 4, 1862, at Camp Belger, Baltimore, Md.

Browley, Edward.–Age, 25 years. October 4, 1862, at Poughkeepsie; deserted, same date, at Camp Dutchess, Poughkeepsie, N.Y.

Browley, William.–Age, 28 years. October 4, 1862, at Poughkeepsie; deserted, same date, at Camp Dutchess, Poughkeepsie, N.Y.

Buckland, Charles M.–Age, 25 years. September 6, 1862, at Rhinebeck.*

Buckley, Patrick.–Age, 24 years. October 3, 1862, at Poughkeepsie; deserted, same date, at Camp Dutchess, Poughkeepsie, N.Y.

Burns, Michael.–Age, 33 years. October 7, 1862, at Poughkeepsie; died of chronic diarrhea, September 23, 1864, at First Division Hospital, Twentieth Army Corps, Atlanta, Ga.

Burtis, Adelbert.–Age, 18 years. August 13, 1864, at Poughkeepsie, to serve one year; never joined regiment; mustered out with detachment, May 8, 1865, at Hart's Island, N.Y. Harbor.

Carson, Charles.–Age, 25 years. August 23, 1862, at Poughkeepsie; never joined regiment.

Church, William B.–Age, 18 years. August 2, 1862, at New York City; private, Co. A, 145th N.Y. Volunteers.*Z

Clark, Clement.–Age, 32 years. October 9, 1862, at Poughkeepsie.*

Clarke, George Alexander.–Age, 37 years. September 5, 1862, at Rhinebeck; transferred to Co. C, Twentieth Regiment, V.R.C., December 12, 1863; mustered out with detachment, as first Sergeant, July 10, 1865, at Frederick City, Md.

Coghill, Michael.–Age, 22 years. October 3, 1862, at Poughkeepsie; deserted, January 1, 1863, at Camp Belger, Baltimore, Md.

Crane, Patrick.–Age, 23 years. September 29, 1862, at Poughkeepsie; wounded in action, July 3, 1863, at Gettysburg, Pa.; D.F.D., caused by wounds, May 28, 1864.

Corcoran, Michael.–Age, 21 years. September 8, 1864, at Poughkeepsie; deserted and arrested, no date; no further record.

Davison, Henry.–Age, 36 years. October 3, 1862, at Poughkeepsie; deserted, same date, at Camp Dutchess, Poughkeepsie, N.Y.

Dederick, William H.–Age, 21 years. September 6, 1862, at Rhinebeck.*

Donnelly, William.–Age, 34 years. August 21, 1864, at Poughkeepsie, to serve one year; never joined regiment.

Dore, Henry.–Age, 35 years. September 30, 1862, at Fishkill; mustered in as Sergeant, October 11, 1862; returned to ranks prior to April 30, 1863; mustered out, May 31, 1865, at McDougall Hospital, N.Y. Harbor.

Dutcher, Leonard T.–Age, 18 years. September 5, 1862, at Fishkill; transferred to Co. E, Seventh Infantry, V.R.C., no date; mustered out, July 22, 1865, at Washington, D.C.

Filkins, Henry.–Age, 44 years. October 10, 1862, at Poughkeepsie; D.F.D., May 25, 1863.

Firth, James.–Age, 27 years. August 7, 1862, at New York City; Corporal, Co. D, 145th N.Y. Volunteers.Z*

Gay, John.–Age, 28 years. October 6, 1862, at Poughkeepsie, and deserted on same date.

Gerow, Lewis C.–Age, 21 years. October 7, 1862, at Poughkeepsie.*

Goldman, Morris.–Age, 27 years. October 10, 1862, at Poughkeepsie; deserted, October 16, 1862, at Camp Millington, Baltimore, Md.

Grady, John.–Age, 20 years. September 14, 1864, at Pawling, to serve one year; never joined regiment; no further record.

Griffin, Morenous W.–Age, 28 years. September 6, 1862, at Rhinebeck; deserted, February 2, 1863, at Belger Barracks, Baltimore, Md.

Griner, John.–Age, 19 years. September 8, 1862, at Rhinebeck.*

Hawks, Daniel.–Age, 44 years. September 13, 1862, at Fishkill.*

Hendrick, John.–August 2, 1864, at Claverack.X

Higgs, Andrew J.–Age, 36 years. September 30, 1862, at Fishkill; transferred to Co. F, Fifteenth Infantry, V.R.C., no date; D.F.D., June 21, 1865, at Cairo, Ill.

Horton, Gilbert A.–Age, 32 years. September 20, 1862, at Fishkill; captured, October 18, 1864; paroled, no date; absent, at Parole Camp, Annapolis, Md., at muster-out of company.

Hunt, Robert.–Age, 31 years. October 3, 1862, at Poughkeepsie, to serve three years.X

Hyde, Richard.–Age, 35 years. July 22, 1862, at New York City; private, Co. A, 145th N.Y. Volunteers; wounded in action, July 23, 1864, and died of his wounds, July 25, 1864, before Atlanta, Ga.Z

Ireland, Henry.–Age, 32 years. September 30, 1862, at Fishkill; deserted, July 22, 1863, at Harper's Ferry, Va.

Jones, Seth.–Age, 21 years. August 29, 1864, at Ghent, to serve one year; never joined regiment; mustered out, July 11, 1865, at Albany, N.Y.

Kelly, Daniel.–Age, 25 years. October 4, 1862, at Poughkeepsie, to serve three years; deserted, October 4, 1862, at Camp Dutchess, Poughkeepsie, N.Y.

Kenny, James W.–Age, 24 years. August 27, 1864, at Clermont, to serve one year; mustered in, but never joined regiment.

Kerr, James–Age, 32 years. August 6, 1864, at Pleasant Valley, to serve one year; mustered in, but never joined regiment.

Knichel, Joseph.–Age, 27 years. September 9, 1862, at Fishkill.*

LaFrance, Joseph.–Age, 19 years. August 11, 1864, at Poughkeepsie.*Z

Lawrence, Charles H.–Age, 18 years. July 30, 1862, at New York City; Musician, Co. E, 145th N.Y. Volunteers.*Z

Leathem, George.–Age, 28 years. September 29, 1862, at Fishkill.X

Lillie, Amos T.–Age, 28 years. September 6, 1862, at Rhinebeck; mustered out with detachment, June 15, 1865, at Finley Hospital, Washington, D.C.

Lockwood, Hamilton.–Age, 16 years. April 16, 1864, at Poughkeepsie; missing in action since August 9, 1864, and at muster-out of company.

Ludorf, Henry.–Age, 32 years. October 5, 1862, at Rhinebeck; deserted, October 16, 1862, at Baltimore, Md.

Lynch, James.–Age, 45 years. September 29, 1862; wounded in action, July 3, 1863, at Gettysburg, Pa.; transferred to V.R.C., April 6, 1864.

Marshall, Henry.–Age, 37 years. August 13, 1864, at Poughkeepsie.X

Marshall, John.–Age, 23 years. September 25, 1862, at Dutchess County; deserted, November 9, 1862, at Camp Millington, Baltimore, Md.

Masten, John.–Age, 45 years. January 11, 1864, at Poughkeepsie.X

Mather, William.–Age, 20 years. September 8, 1862, at Fishkill.*

Mayfield, Peter.–Age, 35 years. August 30, 1862, at New York City; private, Co. A., 145th N.Y. Volunteers.*X

McAuliffe, Patrick.–Age, 30 years. August 8, 1862, at New York City; private, Co. A, 145th N.Y. Volunteers; mustered out, July 12, 1865, at McDougall Hospital, Fort Schuyler, N.Y. Harbor.Z

McClelland, Charles–Age, 29 years. September 8, 1862, at Fishkill.*

McCue, Patrick–Age, 18 years. August 4, 1862, at New York City; private, Co. A, 145th N.Y. Volunteers; captured in action, March 19, 1865, at Goldsboro, N.C.; paroled, April 2, 1865, at Aikens Landing, Va.; mustered out with detachment, June 26, 1865, at Camp Parole, Annapolis, Md.

McGrath, Michael.–Age, 24 years. August 25, 1862, at New York City; private, Co. A. 145th N.Y. Volunteers; absent, in hospital, at Murfreesboro, Tenn., and at muster-out of company.Z

McKinsey, John.–Age, 40 years. August 27, 1864, at Poughkeepsie, and mustered in as private, Co. K, August 27, 1864.X

McQuade, Thomas.–Age, 20 years. August 17, 1864, at Hyde Park, to serve one year; never joined regiment.

Merrick, James.–Age, 29 years. August 28, 1862, at New York City; private, Co. A, 145th Volunteers.*Z

Meyers, John.–Age, 43 years. September 5, 1864, at Greenport, to serve one year; never joined regiment.

Miller, Jacob.–Age, 43 years. September 12, 1862, at Rhinebeck; transferred to V.R.C., February 6, 1864.

Mooney, Frank.–Age, 21 years. October 7, 1862, at Poughkeepsie, to serve three years, and deserted, same date, at Poughkeepsie, N.Y.

Moore, Joseph.–Age, 22 years. September 10, 1862, at Fishkill; mustered out, July 13, 1865, at Louisville, Ky.

Murphy, Thomas.–Age, 29 years. September 4, 1862, at Fishkill, and deserted, October 8, 1862.

Murphy, William.–Age, 28 years. November 6, 1862, at Baltimore, Md.; deserted, November 27, 1862, at Fort McHenry, Baltimore, Md.

Murphy, William H.–Age, 20 years. August 29, 1862, at Hyde Park.*

Murphy, Edward.–Age, 33 years. September 18, 1862, at Fishkill.*

Newhouse, Adam.–Age, 23 years. August 23, 1864, at Ancram, to serve one year; never joined regiment.

Nichols, Washington.–Age, 30 years. July 30, 1862, at New York City; private, Co. A, 145th N.Y. Volunteers; mustered out, May 18, 1864, at Cairo, Ill.

O'Brien, Lawrence.–Age, 32 years. September 16, 1862, at Rhinebeck; discharged, May

29, 1865, at Tripler Hospital, Columbus, Ohio.

Odell, Charles H.–Age, 21 years. October 3, 1862, at Fishkill.X

Oswald, Leopold.–Age, 40 years. September 5, 1862, at Rhinebeck.*

Potenburgh, Frederick.–Age, 41 years. September 6, 1862, at Rhinebeck; wounded in action, July 3, 1863, at Gettysburg, Pa.; transferred to Co. I, 12th Regiment, V.R.C., April 28, 1864; mustered out with detachment, July 28, 1865, at Washington, D.C.

Power, Walter.–Age, 23 years. September 27, 1862, at Poughkeepsie; deserted, September 29, 1862, at Camp Dutchess, Poughkeepsie, N.Y.

Prescott, William H.–Age, 25 years. January 24, 1864, at Livingston; mustered out with detachment, May 8, 1865, at Hart's Island, N.Y. Harbor.

Rapp, Jacob.–Age, 34 years. September 5, 1862, at Rhinebeck; deserted, February 7, 1863, at Camp Belger, Baltimore, Md.

Reddy, James.–Age, 21 years. September 14, 1864, at Pawling, to serve one year; never joined regiment.

Rest, Bernhart.–Age, 44 years. September 15, 1862, at Rhinebeck; deserted, March 20, 1863, at Camp Belger, Baltimore, Md.

Rikert, Henry G.–Age, 29 years. August 28, 1862, at Stanford; deserted, same date, at Camp Dutchess, Poughkeepsie, N.Y.

Robertson, Samuel.–Age, 30 years. September 29, 1862, at Fishkill.*

Rockefeller, Albert.–Age, 31 years. October 6, 1862, at Poughkeepsie, N.Y.; deserted, same date, at Camp Dutchess, Poughkeepsie, N.Y.

Schenk, Jacob.–Age, 26 years. September 5, 1862, at Rhinebeck.X

Schryver, Ezra.–Age, 28 years. August 30, 1864, at Poughkeepsie, to serve one year.*

Shaffer, Dewitt.–Age, 18 years. September 5, 1862, at Rhinebeck.

Smith, William A.–Age, 37 years. July 18, 1862, at New York City; private, Co. I, 145th N.Y. Volunteers; discharged, March 10, 1864, at Nashville, Tenn.Z

Smith William A.–Age, 29 years. September 5, 1862, at Rhinebeck; promoted Corporal, November 1, 1864.*

Snyder, Jacob C.–Age, 21 years. August 1, 1864, at Poughkeepsie, to serve one year; mustered out, to date June 8, 1865, at New York City.

Tator, Frederick.–Age, 40 years. September 6, 1862, at Rhinebeck.*

Tator, Stephen R.–Age, 23 years. September 9, 1862, at Rhinebeck.*

Ticehurst, William.–Age, 24 years. September 30, 1862, at Fishkill.*

Traver, Henry M.–Age, 43 years. September 5, 1862, at Rhinebeck.*

Turner, John W.–Age, 28 years. October 3, 1862, at Fishkill; deserted, December 6, 1862, at Camp Belger, Baltimore, Md.

Van Nosdall, James.–Age, 18 years. September 20, 1862, at Poughkeepsie; mustered in as Sergeant, October 11, 1862; deserted, July 22, 1863, at Harper's Ferry, Va.

VanVleck, George E.–Age, 28 years. September 29, 1862, at Fishkill; mustered in as Corporal, Co. K, October 11, 1862; deserted, February 1, 1863, at Camp Belger, Baltimore, Md.

Wagner, George A.–Age, 23 years. September 5, 1862, at Rhinebeck; died of chronic diarrhea and pneumonia, October 10, 1863, at Grace Church Branch Hospital, Alexandria, Va.

Warnick, Augustus.–Age, 19 years. August 18, 1864, at Poughkeepsie, to serve one year; mustered out June 10, 1865, at McDougall Hospital, N.Y. Harbor.

Way, Alonzo.–Age, 36 years. September 30, 1862, at Fishkill, to serve three years.*

Way, Cornelius.–Age, 24 years. October 2, 1862, at Fishkill.*

Way, Thomas.–Age, 21 years. October 3, 1862, at Fishkill; wounded in action, July 3, 1863, at Gettysburg, Pa.; absent since, in Satterlee Hospital, West Philadelphia, Pa., and at muster-out of company.

Weeks, Washington.–Age, 19 years. October 3, 1862, at Fishkill; wounded in action, May 25, 1864, at Dallas, Ga.*

Weeks, William H.–Age, 20 years. October 3, 1862, at Fishkill.*

Weissart, Henry.–Age, 34 years. September 5, 1862, at Rhinebeck; deserted, February 3, 1863, at Camp Belger, Baltimore, Md.

Whiting, Charles.–Age, 18 years. August 28, 1862, at New York City; private, Co. A, 145th N.Y. Volunteers.*Z

Whitworth, James.–Age, 32 years. September 8, 1862, at Fishkill, to serve three years; wounded in action, July 20, 1864, at Peach Tree Creek, Ga.*

Wilson, Archibald.–Age, 36 years. August 11, 1862, at New York City; private, Co. A, 145th N.Y. Volunteers; V.R.C., no date.

Woodin, Alfred.–Age, 24 years. August 25, 1862 at Clinton; deserted, July 29, 1863, from hospital, Philadelphia, Pa.

Wyant, Charles.–Age, 32 years. September 5, 1862, at Rhinebeck; captured, March 11, 1865, at Fayetteville, N.C.; paroled, April 2, 1865, at Aiken's Landing, Va.; mustered out June 22, 1865, at Camp Parole, Annapolis, Md.

Unassigned men who never joined regiment.

Bowen, John C.C.–Age, 22 years. January 25, 1865, at Kingston, to serve one year; mustered out with detachment, May 8, 1865, at Hart's Island, N.Y. Harbor.

Drasho, Alexis.–Age, 41 years. March 1, 1865, at New York City; unassigned, March 2, 1865; veteran; no further record.

Dark, Isaac D.–Age, 18 years. September 27, 1862, at Poughkeepsie; no further record.

Furrenden, Peter H.–Age, 41 years. January 13, 1865, at Pleasant Valley, to serve one year; unassigned; mustered out with detachment, May 8, 1865, at Hart's Island, N.Y. Harbor.

McKenzie, John.–Age, 40 years. January 16, 1865; mustered out at Hart's Island, May 23, 1865.

Riley, James F.–Age, 31 years. January 25, 1864; deserted, May 23, 1865.

Smith, William.–No record, except deserted, March 15, 1863, at Baltimore.

Wadhams, Melville.–Age, 19 years. January 25, 1865, at New York City; unassigned; mustered out with detachment, May 8, 1865, at Hart's Island, N.Y. Harbor.

KEY:

* Mustered out with regiment on June 8, 1865, near Washington, D.C.

X Transferred to the 60th New York Volunteers, June 8, 1865, to serve out term of enlistment

V.R.C. Veteran Reserve Corps

D.F.D. Discharged for disability

Z Enlisted men who transferred from the 145th NYV to the 150 NYV on January 4, 1864.

Index of Letters

45	Mar. 11, 1863	Belger Barracks	Continuation of previous letter	75
46	Mar. 10, 1863	Belger Barracks	Robt. Johnston	76
47	Mar. 16, 1863	Belger Barracks	Sarah E. Van Vechten	78
48	Mar. 19, 1863	Belger Barracks	Mother	342
49	Mar. 24, 1863	Belger Barracks	A. Van Wyck Van Vechten	79
50	Mar. 28, 1863	Belger Barracks	Mother	80
51	Mar. 31, 1863	Belger Barracks	Sarah E. Van Vechten	82
52	Apr. 4, 1863	Belger Barracks	Mother	83
53	Apr. 11, 1863	Belger Barracks	A. Van Wyck Van Vechten	343
54	Apr. 11, 1863	Belger Barracks	Robert Johnston	344
55	Apr. 13, 1863	Belger Barracks	Mother	84
56	Apr. 17, 1863	Belger Barracks	Mother	86
57	Apr. 20, 1863	Belger Barracks	Sarah E. Van Vechten	345
58	Apr. 20, 1863	Belger Barracks	Father	87
59	Apr. 25, 1863	Belger Barracks	Father	88
60	Apr. 25, 1863	Belger Barracks	A.V.W. Van Vechten	345
61	May 2, 1863	Belger Barracks	A.V.W. Van Vechten	346
62	May 8, 1863	Pine St., N.Y.	Father	346
63	May 12, 1863	Pine St., N.Y.	Robert Johnston	346
64	May 12, 1863	Pine St., N.Y.	Robert Johnston	346
65	May 13, 1863	Belger Barracks	Gen. Sprague from Col. Ketcham	347
66	May 13, 1863	Belger Barracks	Mother	89
67	May 16, 1863	Belger Barracks	Sarah E. Van Vechten	347
68	May 18, 1863	New York	Recommendation for promotion	348
69	May 20, 1863	Johnsville, N.Y.	Van Vechten from R. Johnston	348
70	May 20, 1863	Belger Barracks	Mother	89
71	May 25, 1863	Belger Barracks	Mother	90
72	May 26, 1863	Belger Barracks	Robert Johnston	349
73	May 27, 1863	Belger Barracks	Sarah E. Van Vechten	92
74	June 3, 1863	Belger Barracks	Mother	93
75	June 4, 1863	Belger Barracks	Sarah E. Van Vechten	94
76	June 10, 1863	Belger Barracks	Mother	96
77	June 13, 1863	Belger Barracks	Sarah E. Van Vechten	97
78	June 16, 1863	Belger Barracks	Mother	98
79	June 20, 1863	Belger Barracks	Mother	98
80	June 20, 1863	Belger Barracks	A.V.W. Van Vechten	349
81	June 24, 1863	Belger Barracks	Sarah E. Van Vechten	100
82	June 25, 1863	Belger Barracks	Father	102
83	July 6, 1863	On the March	Father	106
84	July 10, 1863	On the March	Mother	107
85	July 17, 1863	Harpers Ferry	Mother	109
86	July 21, 1863	Brickers Gap, Va.	Robert Johnston	110
87	July 22, 1863	Brickers Gap	Mother	112
88	July 28, 1863	Washington Jnct., Va.	Mother	113
89	July 28, 1863	Washington Jnct.	Sarah E. Van Vechten	115
90	July 29, 1863	Washington Jnct.	Mother	116
91	July 30, 1863	Washington Jnct.	A.V.W. Van Vechten	117
92	Aug. 2, 1863	Kellys Ford, Va.	Mother	350

93	Aug. 3, 1863	Kellys Ford	Mother	118
94	Aug. 12, 1863	Kelleys Ford	Sarah E. Van Vechten	120
95	Aug. 13, 1863	Kelleys Ford	Father	350
96	Aug. 17, 1863	Kelleys Ford	Father	350
97	Aug. 18, 1863	Kelleys Ford	Mother	121
98	Aug. 29, 1863	Kelleys Ford	Sarah E. Van Vechten	122
99	Aug. 31, 1863	Kelleys Ford	Mother	123
100	Sept. 5, 1863	Kelleys Ford	A.V.W.Van Wyck	351
101	Sept. 11, 1863	Kelleys Ford	Mother	124
102	Sept. 15, 1863	Kelleys Ford	Sarah E. Van Vechten	351
103	Sept. 19, 1863	Near Raccoons Ford, Va	Mother	125
104	Sept. 25, 1863	Brandy Station, Va.	Mother	126
105	Sept. 30, 1863	On train near Wheeling	Mother	159
106	Oct. 4, 1863	Stevenson, Ala.	Mother	160
107	Oct. 11, 1863	Tullahoma, Tenn.	Mother	160
108	Oct. 23, 1863	Tullahoma	Mother	352
109	Nov. 1, 1863	Normandy, Tenn.	Mother	163
110	Nov. 5, 1863	Normandy,	Mother	164
111	Nov. 11, 1863	Normandy, Tenn.	Mother	165
112	Nov. 15, 1863	Normandy	Sarah E. Van Vechten	166
113	Nov. 21, 1863	Normandy	Mother	167
114	Nov. 25, 1863	Normandy	Mother	169
115	Nov. 26, 1863	Normandy	Sarah E. Van Vechten	172
116	Dec. 5, 1863	Normandy	Robert Johnston	174
117	Dec. 14, 1863	Normandy	Mother	175
118	Dec. 25, 1863	Normandy	Mother	352
119	Jan. 1, 1864	Normandy	Sarah E. Van Vechten	177
120	Jan. 4, 1864	Normandy	Mother	178
121	Jan. 14, 1864	Normandy	Mother	179
122	Jan. 18, 1864	Normandy	Mother	179
123	Jan. 26, 1864	Normandy	Sarah E. Van Vechten	180
124	Jan. 28, 1864	Normandy	Mother	181
125	Feb. 6, 1864	Normandy	Mother	353
126	Feb. 12, 1864	Normandy	Mother	182
127	Feb. 13, 1864	Normandy	Sarah E. Van Vechten	184
128	Feb. 24, 1864	Normandy	Sarah E. Van Vechten	185
129	Feb. 26, 1864	Normandy	Father	353
130	Mar. 1, 1864	Normandy	Mother	185
131	Mar. 7, 1864	Normandy	Mother	354
132	Mar. 15, 1864	Normandy	Sarah E. Van Vechten	187
133	Mar. 18, 1864	Normandy	Father	188
134	Mar. 21, 1864	Normandy	Mother	189
135	Apr. 10, 1864	Normandy	Sarah E. Van Vechten	190
136	Apr. 21, 1864	Normandy	Mother	355
137	Apr. 25, 1864	Normandy	Mother	191
138	May 2, 1864	Between Tenn. and Ala.	Mother	193
139	May 12, 1864	Near Dalton, Ga.	Father	197
140	May 18, 1864	On the March	Mother	205

141	May 19, 1864	Near Kingston, Ga.	Mother	205
142	June 17, 1864	Near Marietta, Ga.	Mother	210
143	June 23, 1864	Near Marietta	Father	212
144	June 28, 1864	In the Field	Mother	215
145	June 28, 1864	Near Kennesaw Mt.	Van Vechten from J.G. Mason	216
146	July 8, 1864	8 miles from Atlanta	Mother	355
147	July 11, 1864	Near Atlanta, Ga.	Sarah E. Van Vechten	219
148	July 14, 1864	Near Atlanta	Mother	220
149	July 19, 1864	East of Atlanta	Mother	222
150	July 21, 1864	Within 3 mi. of Atlanta	Mother	223
151	July 27, 1864	In Front of Atlanta	Mother	225
152	July 31, 1864	Siege of Atlanta	Father	227
153	Aug. 3, 1864	Siege of Atlanta	Sarah E. Van Vechten	228
154	Aug. 6, 1864	In Field near Atlanta	Mother	229
155	Aug. 12, 1864	In the Front of Atlanta	Mother	232
156	Aug. 21, 1864	In the Front of Atlanta	Mother	234
157	Aug. 24, 1864	In the Front of Atlanta	Mother	235
158	Aug. 27, 1864	Chattahoochee River	Mother	238
159	Aug. 27, 1864	Chattahoochee Bridge	Sarah E. Van Vechten	240
160	Sept. 1, 1864	Chattahoochee R.R.	Sarah E. Van Vechten	241
161	Sept. 2, 1864	Chattahoochee R.R.	Mother	244
162	Sept. 3, 1864	Atlanta, Ga.	Mother	356
163	Sept. 6, 1864	Atlanta	Mother	246
164	Sept. 14, 1864	Atlanta	Mother	247
165	Sept. 17, 1864	Atlanta	Mother	356
166	Sept. 21, 1864	Atlanta	Mother	249
167	Sept. 29, 1864	Atlanta	Mother	251
168	Oct. 3, 1864	Atlanta	Sarah E. Van Vechten	252
169	Oct. 14, 1864	Atlanta	Mother	254
170	Oct. 18, 1864	Atlanta	Sarah E. Van Vechten	255
171	Oct. 19, 1864	Atlanta	Father	257
172	Oct. 27, 1864	Atlanta	Mother	260
173	Nov. 1, 1864	Atlanta	Mother	262
174	Nov. 6, 1864	Atlanta	Mother	264
175	Nov. 7, 1864	Atlanta	Father	265
176	Dec. 17, 1864	Near Savannah, Ga.	Mother	271
177	Dec. 27, 1864	Savannah, Ga.	Mother	274
178	Dec. 28, 1864	Savannah	Sarah E. Van Vechten	276
179	Jan. 7, 1865	Savannah	Mother	277
180	Jan. 9, 1865	Savannah	Father	278
181	Jan. 10, 1865	Savannah	Mother	306
182	Jan. 24, 1865	Near Hardeeville, S.C.	Mother	307
183	Jan. 31, 1865	Robertville, S.C.	Mother	309
184	Mar. 12, 1865	Fayetteville, N.C.	Mother	312
185	Mar. 25, 1865	Goldsboro, N.C.	Mother	314
186	Mar. 28, 1865	Goldsboro, N.C.	Mother	315
187	Mar. 31, 1865	Goldsboro, N.C.	Sarah E. Van Vechten	317
188	Apr. 3, 1865	Goldsboro	Mother	318

INDEX

Adamstown, Md., 54, 57

Adriance, Susan, 121, 317

Allatoona, Ga., 204, 287

Ambrotypes, 51, 54, 56, 60

Andrews, Susan, 220; William, 185, 220

Anthony, Allard, 60, 62, 75, 81, 83, 341; Walter, 169

Antietam, Md., 54, 55, 59, 61, 94, 108, 110

Appomattox Court-House, Va., 320

Arcaniam, Col. E., 263

Army of the Cumberland, 162, 164, 167, 168, 176, 194, 197, 261, 262

Army of the Mississippi, 262

Army morale, 28, 31, 38, 69, 76-7, 93-4

Army officers, 25, 26, 28, 33, 43, 47, 49 50, 53, 56, 63, 67, 68, 70, 74, 76, 77, 82, 116, 121, 171, 236

Army of the Ohio, 194

Army of the Potomac, 90, 107, 109, 111, 112, 113, 164, 174, 176, 188, 326

Army of the Tennessee, 194, 197, 262

Atlanta, 192, 196, 205, 206, 212, 355; siege of, 215, 219, 220, 222, 223, 225, 226, 227, 228, 229, 231, 232, 234, 235, 236, 239, 240, 241, 242, 244, 330, 355; occupation of, 244, 245, 246, 249, 254, 255, 257, 259, 263; evacuation of, 264, 266, 274, 276, 278

Atlantic Monthly, 125, 181, 344, 352

Augusta, 192, 269, 310; Augusta and Charleston R.R., 310, 313

Baker, Congressman Stephen, 57

Barnum, Gen., 332

Barnwell, S.C., 310

Bartow, Alexander, 337; Ann, 238, 240; Miss G., 219, 355

Beaufort, S.C., 309

Beauregard, Gen., P.G.T. (CSA), 308

Bedding, 22, 24, 32, 33, 34, 36, 53, 65, 108, 122, 337

Bentley, Mr., 259, 330

Blackville, S.C., 313

Blair, Postmaster General Montogomery, 197, 354

Bragg, Gen. Buxton (CSA), 91, 127, 161, 163, 174

Branchville, S.C., 309, 313

Breastworks, barricades, etc., 100, 106, 110, 205, 207, 209, 210, 211, 212, 214, 215, 224, 229, 230, 232, 238, 239, 253, 261, 262, 355

Briggs, Gen. (USA), 77, 342

Briggs, Mr., 88, 119, 188, 258, 265

Brinckerhoff, Aben, 188; Miss E., 220, 317; John, 188; T.Van Wyck, 93

Brinks, Mr., 36

Broad River, 311

Brooklyn, 22, 47, 52, 56, 185, 260, 345, 346, 347, 354

Brooklyn Daily Eagle, 189, 354

Bull Run, 61, 109, 113

Burnside, Gen. Ambrose (USA) 46, 76, 171, 174

Burroughs, George, 36, 38, 47, 65, 66, 75, 77, 100, 108, 116, 127, 159, 168, 175, 214, 327, 340, 357

Butler, Gen. Benjamin (USA), 86, 312

Cape Fear River, 313

Calhoun, G., 204

Camp Dutchess, N.Y., 22

Camp life, evils of, 24, 27, 28-9, 62, 76, 93, 340, 341-2

Camp regimen, 24-5, 26, 29-30, 32-3, 35, 37, 41, 43, 46, 47, 48, 66, 72, 89-90, 124, 338, 342, 343, 344, 347

Cassville, G., 204, 205, 207

Catawba River, S.C., 311

Cavalry, Commission applied for, 79-81, 83, 87-89, 90-94, 101, 102, 117, 342, 343, 344, 345-46, 348, 351

Cayton, L. M., 267

Cedar Run, Va., 125

Chancellorsville, Va., 101-2, 106, 116,

Chaplains, 35, 39, 73-4, 92, 121, 173, 180, 217, 243, 251, 264, 339

Charleston, S.C., 86, 121, 123, 262, 264, 270, 275, 277, 306, 313

Chattahoochee, River, Ga., 215, 218, 220, 226, 232, 238, 240, 241, 244,

Chattanooga, Tenn., 127, 159, 161, 163, 169, 174, 175, 193, 194, 196, 234, 247, 251, 253, 254, 257, 261, 262

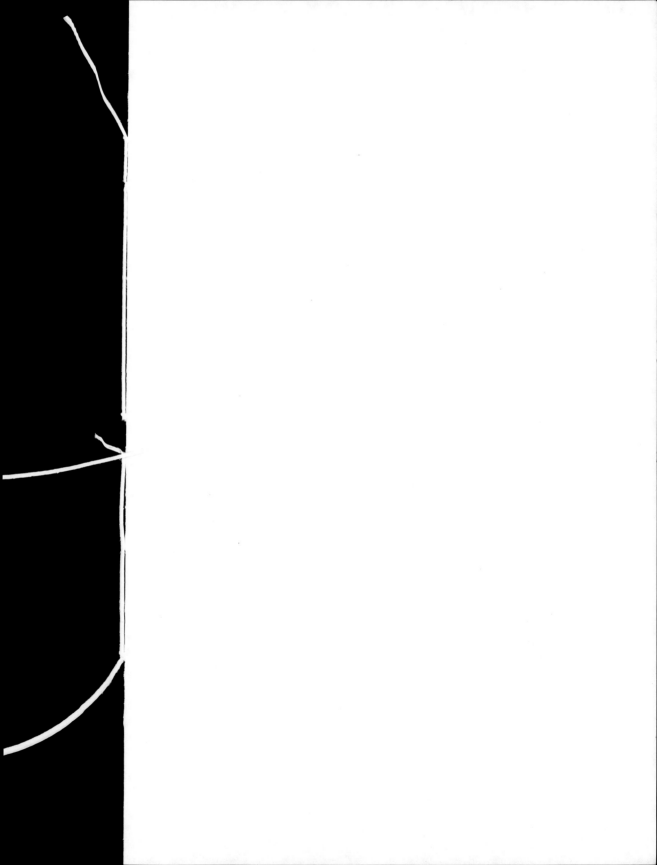